To my dear friend Vikki Ellison
Thanks for taking care of an old Broken down Fighter Pilot
All the best to a Wonderful Escort
"Tex" Hill

PREFACE

My friendship with "Tex" Hill began in the wartime skies of China more than 60 years ago. If the good Lord allows, our bond will continue for the few more years we have left in what have been two very exciting lives. Tex's grandson Reagan has written an excellent account of his grandfather's wartime exploits; the narrative moves rapidly, yet provides enough detail to give the reader a flavor of life and combat at the end of the world's longest and most hazardous supply line. The bravery, integrity, and combat skills of the story's subject carry the reader through some of the most exciting combat action in a remote but important arena of war.

As one who shared the dangers in this story, I will add a few comments on combat leadership. We were lucky to have General Chennault, who, at World War II's beginning, was undoubtedly the world's leading authority on employing fighter aviation. He gave us a warning network that told us the enemy's location before the enemy knew ours. He tutored us on the strengths and weaknesses of our aircraft, and those of our enemy, teaching us to pit our strength against their weakness. He used Chinese information sources that extended through the Japanese lines (and, often, right into Japanese encampments). Knowledge was power for our very small force, faced with a numerically superior enemy; the victory tally shows just how important.

Tex Hill was perhaps Chennault's most apt and loyal student, a fact revealed time and again in the narrative. Chennault's leadership extended through his squadron commanders to individual pilots, mechanics, and support personnel. Few in the ranks will publicly criticize their leaders; but in their hearts, they know good leaders from bad. The 75th Fighter Squadron's high scores and loyalty are ample testimony to its commander's standout leadership.

There are many qualities that define a leader, but three in particular inspire men to follow even in the face of danger. The first is integrity; no pilot wants to follow a leader he doesn't trust into great danger. The second is professional competence; no one wants to fly into battle behind a "klutz." The third is courage—courage to share the same risks faced by those who follow. Tex had these qualities in abundance: his affection and loyalty toward those who fought with him remain inspirational today.

In war, as in life, there are many "what ifs." In Chapter 18, "A Bridge From Disaster," the author relates a dramatic example. What if Tex Hill and his small force had lacked the skill to trap a Japanese army on the Salween escarpment—where they inflicted casualties so great, Japan never again conducted a major attack against China from the west? What would have happened if the AVG had not stopped their army at the river?

There was no defending Chinese army between the Salween and the vital Allied airbases in western China. If we lost those airbases, airlift from India over the "Hump" into China would cease; and China's armies would lose the military supplies from her Allies, without which they could not survive. China would fall, and Japan would use those airbases to supply her armies in Burma for another offensive—westward into India.

Indeed, if Chennault and his airmen had not stopped that tragic series of events leading to China's collapse, India would have been next—as almost happened. When Japanese forces defeated both the British Army and Stilwell's Chinese forces in Burma in early 1942, the British retreated to their stronghold at Imphal, in the mountains near the Burma-India border. Japanese forces occupying Burma remained a continuing threat to India; and in March 1944, Japan launched four divisions across the border to defeat the British Army at Imphal. India was so lightly defended that, if Imphal had fallen (and it almost did), all of India would have fallen with it.

The battle for Imphal is another story; but it is an important link in the "what ifs" following a fictional AVG failure at the Salween. Thanks to Chennault's strategic vision, and his volunteers' courage and skill, both China and India remained with us; and the rest (as they say) is history.

Major General John R. Alison,
Commander, 75th Fighter Squadron and
Deputy Commander, 1st Air Commando Group
Washington, DC
2003

With other 75th Fighter Squadron commanders at a reunion in Memphis, 1980s.
(L to R: Johnny Alison, Clyde Slocumb, Tex, Ed Goss,
Elmer Richardson, Phil Loofbourrow)

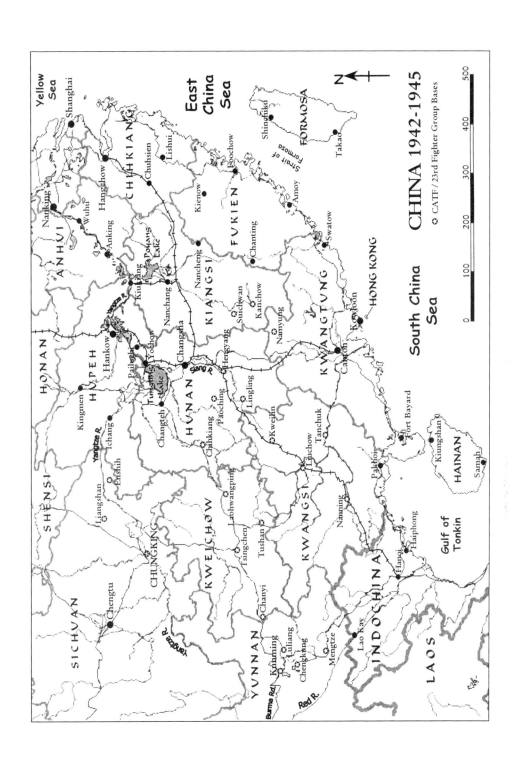

I've lived to see my children laugh and run
I've held their children's children on my knee
And told them stories of a vanished sun,
A far-off land, the way it used to be...

"During these extraordinary times, we have been reminded that our achievements in peace and war have been built on the service and sacrifice of our men and women in uniform. Your devotion to duty and your legendary courage in the air battles of World War II have earned you the respect and admiration of all Americans. I salute you for responding to the call of patriotic duty with strength and resolve. Your bravery in battle continues to be an inspiration as we face the challenges of a new era."

– *George W. Bush, Jr.,*
President of the United States,
May 17, 2002

"You took a strong stand against tyranny in behalf of the Chinese people, and your brave defense of the cause of liberty added a legendary chapter to our nation's military history. Americans dubbed your tiny force the "Flying Tigers," out of pride for your courage in battle and admiration for your success against a powerful enemy—and what an astounding success it was...Your brave exploits led the way to even greater victories in the Pacific Theater, and you can be rightly proud of the contributions of the Flying Tigers to the ultimate triumph of the Allied Forces in World War II. You have earned the lasting gratitude of the American people, and your sacrifices will never be forgotten."

– *George W. Bush, Sr.,*
President of the United States,
April 10, 1992

"...I ran into one of the real heroes of the AVG, David "Tex" Hill, an able flier who already had a number of enemy planes to his credit...Tex, whom I had always thought one of the most intelligent AVG fighting men, was in what I can only describe as an eloquent rage..."

– *Joseph W. Alsop,*
Political Journalist, I've Seen the Best of It

"Chennault...placed the eastern China operations in the hands of...Clinton ("Casey") Vincent, only twenty-nine, and he assigned to Vincent, as his deputy, Colonel David ("Tex") Hill, also twenty-nine; to these two he turned over the offensive. The young men, both accomplished combat pilots, made the forward echelon of the Fourteenth Air Force a name to conjure with. From their eastern China bases they sank over half a million tons of Japanese shipping and drove the Japanese out of the skies of China south of the Yangtze."

– *Theodore H. White,*
Life *Magazine Corresponsent,* Thunder Out of China

"When I was an aviation cadet in 1942, I read Robert L. Scott's book, God is My Co-Pilot, and Tex Hill became one of my heroes—but I never dreamed that I would later serve under him in China...He is the kind of leader you would follow anywhere. I know, because I have. This book is long overdue, and should be required reading for all flyers—in fact, for anyone that wants to read about a great American."

– *Donald Lopez,*
75th Fighter Squadron Commander and Deputy Director,
National Air and Space Museum

"Tex Hill has been an inspiration to generations of pilots. For as long as I have known Tex, he has been called "the Great Fearless Leader" by all who served under his command. When I first met Tex, I readily understood why he was so well respected. Tex, many thanks for sharing your experiences in this great book, and for all of the fine times we have shared. You will always be every aviator's 'Big Leader.'"

– Robert "Bob" Hoover,
POW, Test Pilot, and Director,
Evergreen International Aviation

"Death was our new trade. We were training to be professional killers, and one day at Tonopah, we crowded into the day room to hear an early combat veteran in the Pacific, Tex Hill, describe his dogfights against the Japanese. Man, we were in awe. Shooting down an airplane seemed an incredible feat."

– Brigadier General Charles "Chuck" Yeager,
<u>Yeager, an Autobiography</u>

"To Tex—the greatest combat commander a fighter pilot could have."

– Wiltz "Flash" Segura,
WWII Fighter Ace and Wing Commander in Vietnam

"To Tex Hill: the man that I most admire."

– Lieutenant General John P. "Jack" Flynn,
senior ranking American POW in the Vietnam War

"To my great friend Tex Hill—the greatest of the aces, and a real leader."

– Colonel Rex T. Barber,
credited with shooting down the aircraft
carrying Japanese Admiral Isoroku Yamamoto

"I, along with Steve Ritchie, Randy Cunningham and Willie Driscoll, all just back from the skies over North Vietnam, were attending the American Fighter Aces Convention in San Antonio, Texas. When I did finally meet him, I realized that Tex Hill was more than just the stories that I had heard about of his successes against a superior enemy. He was not only a fighter pilot that few could match but was also a real gentleman. Tex Hill is a great patriot and a great American..."

– Colonel Chuck DeBellevue,
Fighter Ace of the Vietnam War, 555 TFS

"My heroes as a young man were Tex Hill, Robert S. Johnson and Robert L. Scott—how could I have ever dreamed that some day I would have the honor of becoming his friend, his publisher and wearing his gift of two general's stars on my shoulders."

– Brigadier General Ed. Y. Hall,
Publisher, Honoribus Press

Tex as 23rd Fighter Group commander next to the "Bullfrog."

"TEX" HILL:
FLYING TIGER

By
David Lee "Tex" Hill,
Brigadier General, Texas Air National Guard
with
Major Reagan Schaupp, USAF

Foreword by Brigadier General Robert L. Scott, Jr., USAF (Ret.)

Cover: John Shaw

Print of cover available directly from John Shaw.
Please contact Liberty Studios at (888) 893-3786.

Library of Congress Card Number: 2003114340.

Copyright © 2003 by David Lee "Tex" Hill and Reagan Schaupp

ISBN: 1-885354-15-0

All rights reserved.
No part of this book may be reproduced without written permission from the publisher.
Published by arrangement with Universal Bookbindery.
San Antonio,, TX 78209

First Printing: July/August 2003, Honoribus Press, Spartanburg, SC.
Second Printing: June/July 2004, Universal Bookbindery, San Antonio, TX.

Universal Bookbindery, Inc.
San Antonio, Texas

DEDICATION

To my beloved wife, Mazie:
Marrying you is one thing
I have never regretted.
You are the true wings on this Tiger.

My love always,
Tex

For Dawn, my wife
and the sunrise on my heart;

And for Don Schaupp,
my father and Godly role model.

Reagan

Tex while commanding the 412th Fighter Group, Bakersfield, California, 1944.

Merry Christmas from the Hill children.
(clockwise from top left: Mazie, David, Lola, Shannon)

Tex reads to his four children
(L to R: David, Mazie, Lola, Shannon), San Antonio, 1955.

At a 23rd Fighter Group reunion with former group commanders, Fort Walton Beach, September 1991. (L to R: Robert L. Scott, Tex, Dardal, Ed Rector, Phil Loofbourrow, Bruce Holloway.)

FOREWORD

October 25th was a memorable day for us out there in China—*another* 4th of July.

Finally we were on the offensive: carrying the fight to the enemy, instead of having to sit still and wait for his attack. Oh! How wonderful it was! Two flights of our P-40s were escorting twelve of Colonel Caleb Haynes' B-25s to strike the Japanese Navy in Hong Kong Harbor. When the bombers dropped their lethal loads, we bid them farewell—and became fighters again.

Our two flights of P-40s dove toward Kai Tak airfield, and I was intuitively counting the enemy *Zeros* taking off. When my count reached eight, my throat became very dry—for that matched our own strength in P-40s, four in my flight and another four with "Tex" Hill. But as the enemy count grew to double our number, my heart was beating so loud I could hear its pounding over the roar of the engine. W*hy not accept the fact?* I thought. *It's always going to be that way out here. Just get used to it.*

At exactly that moment, I heard Tex shout with glee:

"COME ON EVERYBODY—WE OUTNUMBER THEM TODAY!"

What more need be said to introduce the life of Tex Hill?

Robert L. Scott, Jr.
Brigadier General, USAF (Ret.)

Painting of Tex's P-40 by artist Cunningham of General Dynamics, circa 1980. (Astronaut Major General Joe Engle's endorsement reads: "Tex—I dreamed of doing this since I was 7 years old. Thanks for being my role model. Good flying!")

CONTENTS

Foreword by Brigadier General Robert L. Scott, Jr., USAF (Ret.)....xiii
Introduction....xvii
1. Homecoming....21
2. Stomping Ground....27
3. Missionary Ridge....35
4. Higher Learning....43
5. Wheels and Wings....49
6. *Saratoga*....57
7. *Ranger*....63
8. The Storm Gathers....69
9. Leavetaking....75
10. Chennault....85
11. Growing Fangs....91
12. The Storm Breaks....101
13. First Blood....109
14. Into the Maelstrom....117
15. Burma Buckles....127
16. Panda Bears....137
17. Burma Collapses....145
18. A Bridge From Disaster....155
19. A Ferry Tale....163
20. "No Army Showed Up"....173
21. "You're Now Major Hill"....181
22. Farewells....191
23. The Home Front....201
24. "I Have To Meet That Girl!"....207
25. Proving Ground....215
26. The Hammer Falls....223
27. *Ichi-Go*....233
28. The Road Home....243
29. Jet Age....251
30. Mountain Home....259
31. Heart Of Africa....267
32. Oil and Ore....273
33. Losing China....283
34. Sunset....291
 "Pappy"....295
 Afterword....297
 Acknowledgements....299
 Bibliography....301
 Scrapbook....303
 Index....309

Major General Claire L. Chennault as 14th Air Force commander, 1944.

INTRODUCTION

Deep in the northern jungles of Thailand, in the gray gloom before dawn, a rice farmer awakened in his bamboo hut. Slowly he realized there was something unfamiliar about his simple environment. A new noise, one he'd never heard, brought him from the family's bed to pad out his door into the chill dimness of night nearing sunrise. He peered about, blinking sleepily. The sound seemed to come from above: a steady droning, sharp and unearthly, was moving overhead. The farmer was at once frightened and fascinated. He studied the lightening sky to pinpoint the sound, but saw nothing. Gradually the noise faded into silence, but the farmer stood a long time in the doorway, wondering what it might mean. At last, shaking his head in incomprehension, he crept back to the still-warm bed.

If the farmer could have instantly ascended to an altitude of ten thousand feet he would have seen more, but probably understood even less. There, three aircraft cruised northeast at 250 mph, holding a loose formation as they drove on a course that crossed from Burma into Thailand. They were single-engine Curtiss P-40 *Tomahawk* fighter planes, bearing the white-and-blue sun insignia of the Chinese Air Force. All three had menacing shark mouths, replete with bared teeth, painted on either side of the air intakes below the propeller spinners. Glaring eyes set above the gaping maws completed images of the fearsome maritime predator. The startling effect sometimes made even the men who knew the planes look twice.

The pilots were not Chinese at all. They were J.V. "Jack" Newkirk, Jim Howard, and David Lee "Tex" Hill of the American Volunteer Group, 2nd Squadron. On this particular morning, their mission was the first of its kind for the AVG: they were hoping to catch and strafe their enemies' aircraft on the ground, at a Japanese-controlled airfield called Raheng.

In one cockpit, Tex Hill kept his head on the proverbial swivel, watching the ground below grow more distinct with the slow rising of the sun. Unlike others in the AVG, he had not yet seen aerial combat, and he definitely did not want his first opportunity to be his last—not that the pilots expected much enemy activity at this early hour. They were counting on surprise to boost their chances of success. If they did succeed, there would be the return trip to think about. Navigation in this part of the world, whether in an aircraft or on the ground, might as well have been a mystic art. Bailing out into the jungle below, should it become necessary, was not the kind of "career broadening" any of them wanted. They had begun the mission with a fourth companion, Allen "Bert" Christman; but a short while earlier, he had been forced to turn his P-40 back to the AVG base near Rangoon, Burma with engine trouble.

The jungle thinned below them, yielding gradually to water-soaked rice paddies. Ahead of Tex and to his right, the sun began to climb above the horizon. Visibility was improving dramatically—but where was the airfield? None of the pilots had ever been there, and Tex wondered briefly just how accurate their intelligence about the place was. Maybe the Chinese had gotten something mixed up—though their information was usually very good. Taking care to stay on Jim Howard's wing, he peered at the landscape in all directions.

Tex's radio crackled to life. "Something at eleven o'clock," came Jack Newkirk's voice. "Could be it."

Tex looked. A large, lighter-colored clearing was coming into view far ahead. Newkirk gently banked fifteen degrees left, and the others followed. It could indeed be an airfield. Tex's pulse quickened inexorably. Unconsciously he let his index finger creep to the gun switch on his stick.

It was an airfield—undoubtedly the very one they sought—and all three pilots saw the aircraft at the same time. Some dozen large, twin-engine bombers were parked neatly beside the airstrip, with several smaller fighters nearby. The large red balls on the upper side of every wing seemed lit by the sunrise, leaving no doubt whose aircraft they were. Tex's wait for combat was at an end.

The Japanese would hear or see their attackers within seconds at this range, something all three Americans were thinking as Newkirk's voice came again, tense with anticipation. "String formation—let's go." The others recognized the order to line up their P-40s one behind another in preparation for a strafing run. The nose of Newkirk's aircraft dipped as he sent it into a dive. Howard followed seconds later. Tex "bent it over" in turn, hearing the pitch of his 1200-horsepower Allison engine scale angrily upward as the P-40 picked up speed. 270 mph. He knew the ground was rushing up to meet them, but it seemed to approach with agonizing slowness. Now he could see the enemy planes on the airfield perfectly clearly. Japanese ground crews milled around them.

Tex's altimeter spun counterclockwise through seven thousand feet. He constantly made precise adjustments to the trim tabs to keep the *Tomahawk's* nose true in the dive; the propeller's massive torque had a tendency to pull the aircraft to the right. Howard was out in front now, with Tex and then Newkirk strung behind him. Their engines screamed past 300 mph.

Tex just had time to see Howard level out below to begin strafing before he had to look further ahead, to focus on the bombers and prepare to line up his own shots. Switching his guns on, he glanced at the altimeter just as it passed five thousand feet. Now the Japs on the field were reacting all right, running in all directions, but it was too late. The AVG pilots had achieved their surprise.

Something made him glance at Howard again—and he sucked in a breath of surprise. In front of Tex, another aircraft was flying into the "pattern" from a different direction, and it was not a P-40. Its red balls and fixed landing gear identified it as a Nakajima Ki-27 Type 97 "Nate" (which the AVG called simply an "I-97"), among the most agile of the Imperial Japanese Army's fighters. Tex had been so intent on lining up a ground target, he had ignored the cardinal rule of combat aviation: keep looking everywhere, constantly. A vision of his commander Claire Chennault's disapproving look popped into his head as he executed a quick, slight bank back toward his wingman and poured on the coal. He forgot all about strafing, staring in tight-lipped amazement as the nimble Japanese fighter whipped around onto Howard's tail.

Tex realized what must have happened in an instant. From somewhere in the air, the "Nate" had seen the Americans approaching—then "jumped" them after they swooped down to strafe the airfield. Now flashes appeared from the enemy aircraft as it began firing on Howard. Tex forced himself to stay calm, willing his P-40 to close the distance with all his might. Howard was also firing—at the ground. As Tex rocketed through 320 mph, he watched the "Nate's" tracers move closer to Howard's ship. Howard didn't see the enemy! He was making no attempt to evade the bullets, concentrating obliviously on his own strafing run. It looked like the Jap was scoring hits on Howard's tail. *I'm too late*, Tex thought with a sickening feeling.

Now Tex was directly behind the "Nate" and, he judged, just within range. Forgetting to use the ring-and-bead gunsight, he mashed the trigger and watched as bullets sprayed toward the enemy plane. As though wielding a garden hose, Tex adjusted the control stick until his tracers were pouring right into the Japanese aircraft. Still he held down the trigger, forgetting all of Chennault's instruction about "short bursts"—and with a brilliant flash, the I-97 exploded before his eyes.

Instantly it dawned on him that he was too close to avoid the fireball ahead of him. His P-40, its speed augmented by the tremendous dive, had overtaken the enemy aircraft more quickly than he realized. There was no time to maneuver: Tex gritted his teeth and arrowed directly through the conflagration and out the other side. The first thing he noticed was Howard's P-40, still airborne and riddling a second enemy bomber on the field below.

Like many combat pilots, Tex had no time to recover from his first aerial victory. A split-second after spotting Howard, he noticed a second "Nate" charging his own P-40 from directly ahead and slightly above. The enemy was in a shallow dive as Tex pulled up. The front aspect of the I-97 matched Chennault's drawings and chalkboard lectures, but just now it was a lot more interesting—especially when flashes erupted from the Jap's machine guns.

Tex lost no time hitting his own trigger. The four .30-caliber guns in the P-40's wings opened up in concert with the slower, more devastating .50-calibers synchronized to fire through the propeller arc. But this time the roar of Tex's guns was mingled with a strange, staccato *thud-thud-thud*. It was a sound every pilot dreaded and recognized immediately: he was being hit. The two aircraft were closing at 600 mph. Suddenly the Japanese plane belched smoke and dove earthward, and Tex pulled up into a tight turn. Craning to look over his shoulder, he watched the stricken enemy fighter plunge into the jungle.

But something was wrong. Tex was shaking, but surely not *that* badly. His P-40 was vibrating and shuddering so violently that he concluded the engine was coming out of the plane. The Jap's bullets had obviously found their mark too. With a sinking feeling, Tex realized he probably did not have long to remain in the air. He turned immediately westward for Burma, hoping to put as much distance as possible between himself and the enemy before the engine gave out. Checking quickly in all directions, he noted that he was alone in the air, separated from Newkirk and Howard in the melée.

The return flight was nerve-wracking and extremely uncomfortable. Tex was sure the aircraft was rattling his brains right out of his head. His only coherent thought was that he preferred a shaking engine to one that quit over enemy territory. He sweated out the shuddering ride, expecting every minute to begin a slow dive into the jungle—but somehow, the struggling P-40 stayed doggedly in flight. At last the Burmese coast came into view, and he landed with some difficulty at Mingaladon Airfield. After taxiing and shutting down the clattering engine, he took a deep breath and removed his perspiration-soaked helmet before opening the canopy. He saw Howard and Newkirk, who had landed only minutes before, talking beside the squadron leader's plane.

"Some fun, huh, Tex!" Jack Newkirk exclaimed with a grin as Tex approached. "I got two in the air, head-on passes. Jim here didn't even know there were any Japs up there. He burned four of theirs on the ground—all bombers. How did you do?"

"All right," said Tex slowly. He looked at Howard. "Good thing I shot that Nip off your tail, though."

The normally serious Howard looked nonplused. "Nip? What are you talking about? There was nobody on my tail."

"Really? Come take a look at this," Tex replied, ambling toward Howard's P-40. He pointed out the 7.7-millimeter bullet holes in his wingman's tail where the enemy's rounds had struck. They counted eleven, and Howard sobered up even further.

"My ship was running rough as the devil all the way back," Tex continued. "I mean, I thought my eyeballs were going to shake loose. I probably picked up some lead too." He headed for the front of his own P-40, number 48, and stared at the propeller in amazement. Stuck in one of his prop blades were several rounds of the same type as those in Howard's tail—only these hadn't made it through. The extra weight of the bullets, embedded in the propeller, had thrown its rotation out of balance and caused the aircraft's teeth-rattling vibration on the return trip.

"I'll be damned," Tex said, shaking his head.

"Hey, Tex, what happened back here?" It was Newkirk, and he was standing by number 48's cockpit. The others moved to look, and Tex got another surprise. Newkirk was pointing at dozens of bullet holes all around the cockpit and wing root. There were more on the other side of the plane. The impact angle was steep, indicating the shots had been taken on an overhead pass—normally the most accurate for marksmanship. There were thirty-three holes.

"How the hell they didn't get you, I have no idea," said Newkirk with a wry smile, clapping his taller comrade on the shoulder. "Let's get over to operations."

Tex stood shaking his head for a moment, looking thoughtfully at the bullet holes. He realized the sharp thudding during his head-on pass with the second "Nate" had very nearly been the last sound he ever heard. A third, unseen enemy aircraft had made a near-perfect overhead pass on him at the same time, and Tex had been completely oblivious. It was a chilling lesson, not soon forgotten: in this business, life lasted just as long as "eyeball dexterity" held out. Tex strode toward the operations hut with the others.

It was January 3, 1942. The shock of Pearl Harbor was less than a month old. Over the jungles of Burma and China, a legend was being born.

Chapter 1

HOMECOMING

With a nickname like "Tex," it seemed obvious where David Lee Hill must have been born. But it was not in Texas, nor even in the United States. His father, Dr. Pierre Bernard Hill, was a Presbyterian minister whom the Lord called to perform the work of a missionary. In 1912 Dr. "P.B." Hill departed America with his wife Ella, sons Sam and John, and infant daughter Martha to answer that calling in the country of Korea. It was there, three years later on the other side of the world, that David Lee entered the world. He was born in the town of Kwangju on July 13, 1915.

Throughout most of history, the world has usually taken little notice of quiet Korea, but at certain times the country has seen flashes of innovation. Amid extreme, perpetual poverty and merciless living conditions, they were Koreans who managed to invent the world's first magnetic compasses, glass lenses, and even ironclad ships. But for the fifteen million Korean souls early in the twentieth century, life was still simple and severe—and had been from beyond memory. In the Korean interior, farmers plowed their fields with scrawny cows, lacking machinery to aid them. Cargo moving any distance was carried on horses; automobiles were never seen. Houses were mostly built of mud and straw, though rare dwellings of stone existed. Native porters balanced and carried loads incomprehensible to westerners on their backs. The land's inhabitants were austere in appearance from continual toil, but the landscape itself was exotically beautiful. It was into this country that Dr. P.B. Hill poured his energy, striving to bring the light of God into the gloom of Korean life.

David was the last of the Hills' four children. When he was born, Sam, the oldest, was nine; John was seven; and his sister Martha was almost three. The three older children had all been born in the United States, where Dr. Hill had pastored several churches before beginning his missionary work. When the Hills later returned to America, David was the only child too young to have memories of their life in Korea.

The Hill family's life was a reflection of the country's primitive state. During the first two years of their missionary assignment, the Hills led a simple existence in Mokpo, a coastal town of some ten or fifteen thousand people. They worked hand in hand with a dozen other missionary families to operate a mission that overlooked the town. The Hills' home was a two-story affair with a tile roof—and no electricity, telephone, or central heating. They used oil lamps for illumination. They toted drinking water from a spring five miles away—and then boiled it to prevent dysentery. The family grew their own crops, ground their own flour and meal, and shopped in town for staples such as meat, milk, and sugar. In time they moved to David's birthplace, the interior town of Kwangju, where conditions were much the same. David was too young to comprehend the grime and filth that were inevitably part of Korean life. The streets were muddy with waste, the markets were dirty, and poverty was everywhere.

At that time, the Empire of Japan controlled Korea's national administration. Japan's takeover had occurred in 1910, a few years before the Hill family arrived. The Japanese maintained military garrisons at strategic locations throughout the country, although not yet in great force. The occupying Japs were antagonistic to Koreans and foreigners alike, and the Hill family aroused a double dose of irritation in them, since they were both white and Christian.

Occasionally there were incidents. Japanese soldiers would approach the house, pound on the door, and demand to search the place for "contraband." Dr. Hill was never impressed by such displays. Folding his arms slowly, he would plant his large frame in the doorway and coolly inform the soldiers that the first man to lay a hand on him would die. Eventually the diminutive Japanese would leave—angry, but somehow knowing better than to test the tall American. As time went on, the Japs' harassment grew more malicious and aggressive. It was a theme with which David would one day become very familiar.

Pierre Bernard Hill was a man with singleness of purpose. His chief goal in life was to glorify his Maker, to be used by Him to bring the lost to repentance and a saving knowledge of Jesus Christ. In the multitude of roles he filled—father, pastor, missionary, lawman—his focus never changed, enabling him to accomplish the deeds set before him. With God as the bedrock in his life, he feared nothing; the Japanese worried him not at all.

At the same time, a Christ-like spirit of gentleness balanced Dr. Hill's inner strength. His care for his missionary charges was heartfelt and evident, and their poverty and suffering moved him to compassion time and again. When the family moved to Kwangju, Dr. Hill spent many hours at the town's hospital for lepers, disregarding the health risk to perform services for the unfortunate patients. In charge of the hospital was Dr. R. M. Wilson, who also served as the Hills' family doctor.

The strain of their life and missionary work eventually took its toll on Dr. and Mrs. Hill. In the summer of 1916, when David was just a year old, their health began to waver. Among other ailments, they suffered from toxemia in their teeth, especially Dr. Hill. The malady was an unfortunate result of eating food grown in the Korean soil. The most painful symptom was a severe, throbbing headache. Inexplicably, the children were spared the condition. Dr. Wilson explained the family's plight to Dr. Hill, along with the unfortunate news that they would not find a competent dentist in all of Korea. Wilson advised Dr. Hill to seek treatment for their teeth back in the United States. After much prayer and consideration, Dr. Hill decided it was time to put in for a furlough back to America. It was granted immediately.

The British liner *Empress of Russia* provided passage for the family across the Pacific, and in late September the Hill family stood once more on American soil—David, just fifteen months old, for the first time. They crossed the country to Virginia and stayed a few months with Ella's father, Marse John Thraves, and his family. Dr. Hill and John Thraves, a fellow pastor, were very close, and Thraves helped Dr. Hill locate a six-hundred-acre farm near the town of Chula, Virginia on which to settle. Dr. Hill bought it, and under the friendly tutelage of Ella's family, the Hills quickly learned the "ins and outs" of running a farm. As he worked in the Virginia sun, Dr. Hill believed he would return to the Far East within a few years, but he was mistaken. That fate would fall instead to his youngest son.

Some of David Hill's earliest childhood memories were of farming in Virginia. There were endless rows of crops to be tended, and no pesticides or other farming aids to simplify such labor in that era. The children performed whatever tasks they could; David spent hours walking the rows of cabbages, picking off insects by hand. His older brothers were soon able to take on more difficult chores, and the Hills settled into the industrious routine so familiar to a farming family. In the mild Virginia climate, the parents' toxemia receded, and their health improved.

Thousands of miles across the Atlantic Ocean, a generation of young men was dying *en masse* on the fields of France and the European lowlands. The First World War had reached its full fury. When the United States entered the conflict in April 1917, David was nearly two. The U.S. Army soon offered Dr. Hill a commission as a chaplain; but he had a different idea. Always a man of action and very patriotic, he turned down the offer and volunteered for the artillery instead. But when the Army learned of his medical furlough from missionary work, they returned the favor and turned *him* down for any position whatsoever. Unable to perform military service for his country, Dr. Hill instead cast about for a place to minister and further the Lord's work.

It wasn't long before the elders of the Second Presbyterian Church in Roanoke invited Dr. Hill to their town and pulpit. Their pastor was away doing YMCA work for the war effort, and they were looking for a "supply pastor." Dr. Hill had been seeking just such an opportunity for ministry, so he sold the farm and the Hills moved to Roanoke. Their stay would be short, and David was still too young to remember much about it. When the war mercifully ended and the regular pastor returned to his church, Dr. Hill had already planned the family's next move. They relocated to Louisville, Kentucky, where the First Presbyterian Church hoped to secure Dr. Hill as their regular pastor.

By the time of the Hills' move to Louisville, David was shaping up to be something of a "handful." A wide streak of curiosity ran through the Hill bloodline, and David was hardly an exception. There was the occasion when he decided to investigate some clothes from the dry cleaners. These were returned in a paper sack and promptly hung in a closet. There, safe from prying eyes, David inspected the sack and boldly began a very short career as a scientist. His maiden experiment involved the properties of matches and paper sacks, and the results were swift and inevitable. David fled the closet wide-eyed, slamming the door behind him on the blazing sack of clothes. He charged downstairs to find his mother sitting at the piano, as she often was. Oblivious to his arsonist activities, Mrs. Hill was cheerfully playing a favorite old hymn: "Brighten the Corner Where You Are." (When David shouted out the situation in the middle of the third stanza, Mrs. Hill did not seem to appreciate the irony.) When the fire was eventually extinguished, the family had to spend the night at the neighbors'. David spent somewhat longer in the "doghouse."

Dr. Hill found First Church caught up in an ongoing rivalry between the Northern and Southern Assemblies of the Presbytery, chiefly a result of economic differences. The richer Northern branch vied with the Southern for congregation members and prestige. First Church was a member of the Southern Assembly, but Warren Memorial Church, just next door, was Northern. Just before the Hills arrived, a group of contentious and quarrelsome members from First had departed to attend Warren instead. It looked as though Dr. Hill might be in for a disappointing ministry, but it turned out that the low point had passed. Under God's blessing and Dr. Hill's leadership, First Church united with another Southern Assembly congregation, and soon enjoyed unprecedented growth and success.

Dr. Hill's pastoral reputation grew with the church, and tempting offers of larger pastorates soon began to reach his ears. But he believed that his true calling was missionary work, and his thoughts inevitably returned to Korea. He grew restless to serve the Lord there again. The Presbyterian Assembly was aware of his wishes, but they were slow to approve. It might be a "waste," they reasoned, to send such a gifted pastor back to the mission field.

Dr. Hill never returned to Korea, but it was only a doctor's advice that finally resigned him to the fact. E.S. Allen, medical advisor for the Presbyterian Committee of Foreign Missions, examined Dr. Hill for a return to missionary work in the spring of 1921. Dr. Allen pronounced him fit enough, but offered this wisdom: if he went back to Korea, the toxemia would set in again, and Dr. and Mrs. Hill would soon find their health in the same straits as before. Indeed, Ella's overall health had weakened considerably during the previous missionary assignment, culminating in anemia, and Dr. Allen expressed doubts about her very survival. With some reluctance Dr. Hill agreed, and abandoned his hopes of returning to the Far East. Instead, as was his habit, he focused his efforts on the tasks at hand.

David was nearing the age to enter school when the Hill family moved once more. At a meeting of the Southern Assembly in St. Louis, two elders from the First Presbyterian Church of San Antonio, Texas approached David's father. Their pastor was leaving, and they had come on behalf of the board of elders to ask Dr. Hill if he would consider filling the position. P.B. Hill had never set foot in Texas, but the elders were so persistent that he agreed to a trip to San Antonio "to look things over." He made the journey in June, and (somewhat to his surprise) found the city and the church much to his liking. He was tempted to accept. Taking stock of things at First Church in Louisville, he saw that he would leave matters in fine shape. When Dr. Allen mentioned that the dry climate would probably help Ella's anemia, Dr. Hill was won over; he called the elders and agreed to be their pastor.

* * *

Half a world away, the sprawling nation of China was a cauldron of turmoil and confusion. The year before the Hills' departure to Korea, young revolutionary Sun Yat-Sen began a movement to overthrow the nation's dynastic rule of tyranny. By the time David was born, the Manchu Emperor had abdicated the throne. The victorious Sun assumed the mantle of China's leadership; but he was never able to bring her many independent warlords under his control. Sun's unstable rule persisted for nearly ten years.

In 1921, as the Hills moved to San Antonio, a Communist Party was founded in China. It drew little fanfare and less notice.

While Dr. Hill was trying to secure a commission in the artillery, a schoolteacher from Louisiana was filling out applications to become a U.S. Army pilot. He was rejected; an evaluating lieutenant commented that he simply "did not have the necessary qualifications to become a successful aviator." Undaunted, the young man entered and completed Officer Training School in Indianapolis, determined to do anything to fly. In 1920, several assignments later, he was finally graduated from Army Flight School at Kelly Field and received his wings. His name was Claire Lee Chennault.

Dr. P.B. Hill, Chaplain of the Texas Rangers, riding "Nellie."

*The Hill family, mid-1930s.
(L to R: Martha, John, David, Dr. P.B. Hill, Ella, Sam.
Seated in front is Ella's mother, Patty Thraves.)*

Chapter 2

STOMPING GROUND

Of all times of the year to arrive in San Antonio, the Hill family stepped off the train into a blistering afternoon in late July. Now six years old, David stood on the railway platform and squinted in the sunlight, drooping in the blazing heat and wondering what came next. One of the trustees of First Presbyterian was on hand to give the Hills a friendly welcome and escort them to the city's posh Gunter Hotel, where they would spend the night before boarding another train the next day. A nearly renovated pastor's manse in the city was not quite ready for the family to occupy, so they would be staying some 65 miles "up the road" in Kerrville for a few weeks. Kerrville was the site of the Westminster Encampment for Young People.

The town lay up in the hill country of Texas, a land of scrubby trees, savvy game, and sweltering heat. It was a region of sheep and goats, once more a different world from any David had seen. The Westminster Encampment itself was a primitive affair, dotted with wooden frame tents covered in canvas. The Hills were comfortable there, though with the lack of electricity and indoor plumbing, they were ruefully reminded of Korea. Mrs. Hill, worn out from the cross-country trip and still recovering from tenacious anemia, lay in bed for several weeks gathering her strength. While Dr. Hill immediately took on his pastoral duties in San Antonio, the Hill boys set about getting the lay of the land.

Fondness for the outdoors had been taking root in David for years, and in the Texas hill country, that affection grew into a great love that would last his entire life. There were golden afternoons spent fishing with his father in a nearby creek, David watching Dr. Hill carefully and imitating every motion as best he could. One day, confident that he "knew the ropes," David went to the creek on his own. His fishing skills were indeed formidable, and soon rewarded as he pulled in a good-sized catfish with great excitement. Practically dancing with delight, David skipped barefoot around his flopping prize to admire it from all angles. Then it happened; he planted a wayward step right on top of his catch. The catfish's sudden sting was the worst pain he could ever remember. David's hollering as he fled the scene spooked sheep and goats for some distance.

Such escapades never dampened his spirits. It wasn't long before he decided to take a ride on horseback—by himself, of course, as his father often did. Placing Dr. Hill's English saddle on the wary horse, David mounted with some difficulty (but supreme confidence). Unimpressed, the horse took off at top speed. The resulting breakneck gallop would have done any Light Brigade cavalryman proud, but goggle-eyed David could only clutch the saddle for dear life, sure in his heart that this was "the end." By maintaining the death-grip he somehow survived, until at last the winded horse stopped in the Kerrville cemetery and nonchalantly proceeded to munch grass.

Such adventures most often ended in a "whupping" from his mother, and it was the hands-down consensus of the boys that Mother's wrath was decidedly more dangerous than Daddy's. Ella Hill was a strict disciplinarian, and did not spare the rod. But her strictness was born of the great, manifest love she had for her family. Aside from minor church work when time allowed, her life was devoted to her husband and the children, raising her sons and daughter in accordance with Biblical principles, "training them up in the way they should go." This was a full-time profession: often thankless, always difficult. But surely enough, as the Author of the Bible promised, when the children grew older, they did not depart from that way.

Hunting was the activity that David came to enjoy most, then and ever after. When he was still too young to carry a gun, his brother Sam allowed him to tag along on dove hunting excursions. At fifteen, Sam was already an accomplished hunter. After he did the shooting, the job of carrying the doves fell to David. There were no bags to hold their game, so David used a looped piece of string to collect the birds, draping it over his neck. He watched Sam and learned. For the rest of David's life, he pursued the hunt with a passion, seldom returning to the hill country without taking time for it. The countryside was awash with eligible game: mostly wild turkeys, doves, and deer. John often hunted as well, and of course the boys' father excelled at it, having taught them all in the first place. The Hills were decidedly a family of hunters.

When the family had been at the Encampment for nearly a month, renovation of the pastor's manse in San Antonio was completed. Dr. Hill was already commuting frequently into the city to organize matters at First Presbyterian Church; now his family departed Kerrville by train to join him. The residence the congregation had selected for their pastor, at 1040 West Woodlawn Avenue, was spacious and upscale, in the best part of town. Mrs. Hill, finally well rested and healthy after the stay in Kerrville, set about turning the place into a home. It happened that she and the children arrived in the city only days after the San Antonio River's worst flood in over a century. The business district had been submerged under eight feet of water, and many residents had drowned. One of Dr. Hill's first tasks was to roll up his sleeves and assist in the emergency relief effort.

San Antonio was a thriving city, the largest the Hills had lived in. Catholicism was the predominant religion, and had been for over one hundred years. In 1845, the Reverend John McCullough had founded First Presbyterian Church mere blocks away from the Alamo, and it was the oldest Protestant church in the city. Such was the legacy that Dr. Hill inherited, and he lost no time laying plans to further expand the church's ministry.

In the years that followed, the Lord accomplished mighty things through the pastor. When he accepted leadership of First Presbyterian, the congregation was struggling through a "spiritual desert" and a sharp downturn in membership. Under Dr. Hill, the church grew into the largest body in the Southern Assembly. The stately old building could not hold its members; Dr. Hill eventually founded five satellite churches around the city. He had no mysterious formula for success, nor did he resort to any gimmick to get people in the church's doors. He preached the Word of God and lived according to it, never swerving from scripture or giving place to the winds of popularity. The Lord had gifted him with an ability to speak in easy, familiar tones; it seemed to listeners that they were casually conversing with a friend on a Sunday afternoon. Indeed, David always believed his father's sermons were aimed straight at him. Oddly, so did everyone else.

By 1923 the age of radio was dawning, and new stations sprang up around the nation in droves. One was WOAI in San Antonio, the first "clear channel" station in the country, able to broadcast its fifty-watt signal at tremendous range. As part of their initial programming lineup on Sundays, the producers decided to feature Dr. Hill's weekly sermon. The pastor's listening audience suddenly jumped to thousands, tuning in from as far away as Georgia and Arizona. Thirty-seven years later, long after Dr. Hill's retirement and two years after his death, WOAI made a programming change: they would no longer feature the Sunday sermon from First Presbyterian. It marked the end of perhaps the longest-running program in the history of radio.

Even at the peak of the church's expansion under Dr. Hill, the pastor's staff remained at an unlikely total of three persons. There was no assistant pastor. Mrs. Hoon was the secretary; she supervised another girl who performed typing and filing; and a man known only as "Charlie the Janitor" performed cleaning and maintenance. Dr. Hill conducted all the weddings, funerals, hospital visits, and myriad of other pastoral duties for his huge flock, and he accomplished them alone. Nevertheless, David noticed that somehow his father always seemed to have time to spend with him—and outdoors was where they both liked to spend it, especially hunting.

The house on West Woodlawn was the setting for a new series of David's adventures. Children adjust to new surroundings quickly, but moving from the primitive hill country encampment to upscale "suburbia" was enough to cause growing pains in anyone. Next door to the Hills lived Mrs. Winkenhauer, an elderly widow. She seldom crossed paths with David, and her sole companion in life was a fierce and territorial fox terrier with the bark of a canine twice his size. One unfortunate day David ran afoul of the beast, which, deciding the boy represented the incarnation of criminal intent, sank its jaws into David's hand between the thumb and forefinger, and held on for dear life. The damage faded in time, but ever afterward David maintained a healthy "respect" for dogs.

Dr. Hill had a Korean helper, Hung Nim, whose name meant "moon" in his native language. Mr. Moon, as they all called him, was a convert from Dr. Hill's missionary days, and he followed the Hills from his homeland back to America to offer his services in whatever capacity. Mr. Moon knew the art of making the intricate Korean kites, and these fascinated David immediately. The Korean's patience seemed inexhaustible as he taught David first how to build, then how to fly them. As he learned to control the soaring, diving kites, David became fascinated with the aerial maneuvers that were possible. Somewhere in his heart, a chord was struck.

After less than a year in the house on Woodlawn, the family moved again to 121 East Park, where they settled in for several more years. During this time David became fast friends with one of his schoolmates, Joseph Frost, Jr. Joe's father owned one of the larger banks in San Antonio, and father and son were both crack shots who later went on to win international marksmanship awards with their shotguns. If possible, Joe was more bent on mischief than David, and together the two discovered no end of trouble in turning over trashcans, picking fights, and finding devious ways to interfere with streetcar operations on nearby McCullough Avenue. One Halloween evening, as the boys perpetrated pranks and practical jokes to their heart's content, a pair of policemen observed the two hooligans in action and took off after them. A short footrace ensued: Joe and David fleeing down back alleys with the flashlight-wielding officers in pursuit. While taking one fateful glance backward, David barreled headlong into a telephone pole. Dazed and almost knocked out cold, he managed to stagger into a hiding place in the alley, and the police charged by without apprehending him. However, that evening's events were enough for Dr. and Mrs. Hill; the two bosom companions were separated from that time forward.

David's first year in San Antonio also saw his introduction into the world of academics. He was enrolled at the Travis Elementary School, named after legendary Texas martyr William Barrett Travis, who had lost his life at the Alamo a century and a half before. The Hill boys were widely spaced in school: as seven-year-old David entered first grade, John went into fifth, and Sam was old enough to begin seventh at the San Antonio Academy. Martha, meanwhile, attended third grade at the Westmoreland Girls' Elementary School. By 1924 the older boys had graduated from the Academy; David followed later.

At school, David's experience was that of a typical intelligent youngster: he learned quickly and enjoyed it. By the third or fourth grade he could read and write well, and understood basic mathematics. White and Hispanic boys made up almost the entire student body, and there were no problems associated with race. Indeed, there were few problems of any kind, due to the strict discipline enforced by the faculty and staff.

Good order was expected, both at Travis and later at the San Antonio Academy. Mrs. Berry, Travis' principal, would not hesitate a second to haul a misbehaving youngster into her office and instill "wall-to-wall counseling." David learned fast. His early attempts to "act up" at the Academy were summarily curtailed by the likes of Professor Culver, who would approach mischief-makers like David from behind with a textbook and administer a resounding whack on the back of the head. David would see stars. Coach Baker's method was to pull out a paddle roughly the size of a door and "whale the donuts" out of recalcitrant students. "Fear the Lord and depart from evil" was the faculty's watchword—though it wasn't usually the Lord whom David was worried about. He learned quickly to mind his "P's and Q's" just as much as when his mother was present. Lack of respect for authority was not a widespread failing in the Hill family.

The San Antonio Academy provided the finest education available to a young man in that part of the country, but paying for it was a strain on the meager finances of a pastor's family. Dr. Hill was paid a salary of $650 per month, with which he supported the family of six. Nevertheless, he routinely accepted only $600, turning down the remainder and explaining to the children with a smile, "*Jehovah Jireh*—the Lord will provide."

He was correct. Members of Dr. Hill's congregation—some of them the city's wealthiest citizens—kept a protective eye on their pastor and his family, ensuring they lacked no necessities, and often going beyond. Drs. P.I. Nixon and Dennis Duckworth saw to the medical needs of the Hills without the usual fees. After a couple of years, widow Campbell, a member of his congregation, approached Dr. Hill with an offer. The Campbell family owned a house in the small town of Hunt, Texas, near Kerrville. They wouldn't be using it during the upcoming summer; would the Hills like to spend a month or two up there? Dr. Hill gladly accepted, remembering his boys' fun in the hill country when they first arrived in Texas. The same offer would be repeated, and taken up, for several summers after that. Those were golden summers for David, when he could hunt and fish to his heart's content. Ever afterward, he considered the hill country his home.

The Campbell place was nestled in a fork of the lazy Guadalupe River, and David routinely succumbed to the age-old magnetism between boys and rivers. A knock on the door one morning, early in the family's vacation, heralded instant companionship: there stood Pete and Haskell Shoemaker, neighbor boys about David's age. The Shoemakers occasionally brought around butter and eggs to sell from their home on a nearby hill. Not a day went by without the boys plunging into the river for swims, catching the prolific green tree snakes (or, sometimes, more dangerous kinds), beating the brush to see what turned up, and generally being boys.

But the expeditions with his father were the times David enjoyed most. Before sunrise they would visit a nearby lake, just the two of them, to spend a few quiet hours fishing. Or they might visit a ranch owned by friends of the family's to take a hunting trip, when David would learn marksmanship and woodcraft from a master—his father. Other times the two would grab some bedrolls, bacon, and eggs, and range out into the austerely beautiful rimrock country in west Texas. Father and son would pass through towns with names like Rock Springs, Hondo, and Sanderson, and nightfall would find them somewhere on the scrub hills under the stars. David would watch through half-closed eyes as his father arranged a large campfire for the night—and when he would open them again in the morning, there was his Daddy, cooking bacon and eggs over the embers. It was a boy's dream, and he was content.

Occasionally, their safaris were interrupted. A man on horseback might find the pair after a diligent search, to soberly tell the pastor of a death or illness in the congregation. Dr. Hill would listen, promise to return as soon as he could, and begin packing up their gear. Often they were far from home, and the return trip would not be a short one. David watched his father carefully on such occasions, but the man never complained or betrayed the slightest irritation. Dr. Hill did not give in to the temptation to feel that he deserved time off or an occasional break from his pastoral duties. God had called him to minister, and even the allure of the hill country could not cloud his understanding of that fact. *Singleness of purpose*: it began to sink into the heart of his son.

When the Hills had spent several summers in Hunt, each one a wonderful time, Dr. Hill began to consider acquiring some property in the area. The hill country was a place he could imagine himself "settling down." In 1925, sixteen acres on the Guadalupe River became available, only a mile or so from the Campbell's. Living there would mean an 80-mile commute for the pastor to reach First Presbyterian in San Antonio; but to his mind it seemed worth the trouble. Would the family like to move up to the hill country permanently? They certainly would! Once the transaction was complete and the land secured, there remained one "small" matter to be resolved. The property was unimproved; the Hills would have to build their own home.

It was a daunting project. Sam, now nineteen, and John, seventeen, were away at school. Dr. Hill had plenty of help from neighbors and their families, but there was still more than enough work to keep ten-year-old David busy. He spent days out in the heat on a nearby mountainside, quarrying rock for walls with the Shoemaker boys and their father. When the walls went up, he shingled the roofs. He toted water from a riverside spring, then later helped install pipe that would carry it to the house. And in a burst of motivation that he could never afterward explain (or duplicate), David single-handedly built a large shed that would serve as a chicken coop and storage area. When he caught his parents' vision for their home, he went to work with a will.

The family completed the project within a year. Not by accident, the first structure to go up was the kitchen, followed by an L-shaped, single-room main building for sleeping and living areas, and finally David's shed. Flagstones joined the buildings. They called it home for good; it remained in the family for some seventy years afterward. Dr. Hill's grandchildren and great-grandchildren ran in the yards, climbed the trees, and swam the river with as much enjoyment as David.

David's fascination with the kites of Mr. Moon, his father's Korean helper, began to lead him to experiment with other aerial contraptions. He learned that he could build a superb "model airplane" using a straight stick, some aluminum, and the rubber that could be unwound from the golf balls of the time. Unfortunately, the boy's only sources of aluminum were small containers called "Merry Widows," and David wasn't supposed to know anything about the original contents. In spite of his mother's protests, David stockpiled the aluminum along with the other materials, crafting a number of the planes. Their lightness allowed them to fly for quite awhile with a makeshift propeller before running out of steam. When Army Air Corps cadets from Kelly Field came over to the house in San Antonio for dates with his sister Martha, David studied them (a couple of them, C.B. "Skip" Adair and Bill Fisher, he would meet again). Their uniforms, complete with Sam Browne belts and flyer's goggles, were fascinatingly heroic. Wouldn't it be great to really fly in an airplane? David turned over the idea in his head.

One Sunday, he decided it was time to find out. When the Hills arrived at First Presbyterian Church for worship, David pulled aside schoolmate Chester Sluder and told him what they were going to do. Chet's eyes were wide, but he agreed to the plan. As the service began and Dr. Hill welcomed the congregation, two boys might have been seen slipping surreptitiously toward the doors.

"Still got your collection money?" David asked. At a nod from Chet, the two were gone. Somehow they talked a chauffeur in the service of congregation member Mr. Weakly into giving them a ride. Their destination was Winburn Field, a small grass area on the other side of town.

It was the boys' good fortune that Dick Hair, a barnstormer by trade, was out at Winburn that morning. When David approached him and offered the boys' coins in exchange for "a spin around the field," Hair immediately understood the situation. It was just the kind of thing he would have done himself. Chuckling, he boosted them into the front seat of his TravelAir E-4000 biplane and fired up the Wright five-cylinder engine. After a short taxi, the plane roared, accelerated, and the boys were airborne.

Hair caught the gleam in David's eye as they lifted off. With a grin, the pilot zoomed to altitude and banked the old aircraft around the pattern. He wasn't about to perform acrobatics with the inexperienced boys aboard, and he didn't have to. His circuit of the field was as plain an "airplane ride" as could be, but to the boys it was unbelievably exciting. Hair brought the biplane down on the field once more, taxied, and cut the engine. David and Chet were grinning from ear to ear. He boosted them out and let them walk around the plane for a while in wonder, regaling them with descriptions of aerobatics, as they looked on wide-eyed. "You better get back to the church if you don't want to catch it," he concluded. As the boys took off toward the waiting car, Hair watched David. *That boy is going to fly*, he thought, *even if he doesn't know it yet.*

* * *

In China, Sun Yat-Sen finally consolidated his rule of the nation through the National People's Party, or Kuomintang. Sun sent the commander of his army, who was also his brother-in-law, to Russia to study military tactics. At 36 years old, this commanding general was a stockbroker by trade, but had taken up the sword to fulfill Sun's vision of a united China. Upon Sun's death, the general assumed leadership of the Kuomintang and began a successful campaign to conquer the last of the rebellious warlords. In 1927, he subdued the Communist movement and declared the formation of a new Nationalist Chinese government, moving the capital from Peiping to Nanking. His name was Generalissimo Chiang Kai-Shek.

While the Hills moved to San Antonio, new Army pilot Claire Chennault took his first assignment with the 1st Pursuit Group at Ellington Field in Texas. He rapidly gained a reputation as a daring flyer and masterful tactician, serving with the famous 94th "Hat-in-the-Ring" Pursuit Squadron before earning his own squadron command— the 18th Pursuit at Luke Field, Hawaii. These were the golden years of Chennault's military service, and he looked back on them with great fondness. Eventually he was reassigned to Maxwell Field, Alabama, where he drew upon his Louisiana school teaching experience to instruct at the Air Corps Tactical School. It was there that some of his troubles began.

Marion P. "Dick" Hair beside his TravelAir E4000 biplane at Winburn Field, San Antonio, Texas. Hair gave David his first plane ride.

San Antonio Academy class of 1928. David is 2nd row from bottom, 3rd boy from right. (Chet Sluder is on David's right; Joe Frost, Jr. is bottom row, 3rd from right.)

Chapter 3

MISSIONARY RIDGE

In the spring of 1928, David was graduated from the San Antonio Academy. He was a tall, lanky, fair-haired boy of nearly thirteen, an uneasy mix of disciplined intelligence and independent spirit. It was plain that he had excelled in school; but though he enjoyed the military structure of the Academy, his penchant for mischief and adventure was also very much in evidence. He was ready to move on, ready for the future.

The future was the McCallie School, a prestigious military institution nestled in the foothills of the Appalachian Mountains around Chattanooga, Tennessee. There the countryside was resplendent; mountains could be seen in all directions, and the school itself lay partway up Missionary Ridge, site of a significant Union victory during the Civil War. David's older brother John had preceded him to McCallie years before, describing it in glowing terms, and David was eager to go. Nevertheless it was difficult to leave his home hundreds of miles behind, in the hill country that held so many joyful hours and friendships for him.

When summer ended, David boarded the train in San Antonio and began the journey by rail across the country. With him was Bruce Martindale, a longtime friend from First Presbyterian Church and fellow newcomer to McCallie. As the locomotive steamed across the Louisiana border, rolling eastward toward New Orleans, David and Bruce had the intoxicating sense of high adventure that only boys on their own for the first time know. When the long ride ended three days later, the two were assigned to the same room at McCallie, a happy arrangement that would last for David's first two years there.

The environment of military discipline at McCallie was familiar to David from his Academy days, and he adjusted quickly to the uniforms and rules. His fellow students were mostly older, naturally, ranging from thirteen to eighteen years. "Hazing" became practically a lost art in later years, but in David's time at McCallie it was alive and well—and practiced with enthusiasm. As the grand finale of their initiation, freshmen were made to run a gauntlet of grinning upperclassmen. The older cadets wielded their Sam Browne belts with vigor as David and his classmates flew down the line, breaking all previous land speed records. It was harmless fun. Before the first semester was over, David had settled into the day-to-day academic routine and begun to soak up an outstanding education.

His easygoing, engaging personality made David generally well-liked, and his tendency to take a dare made him a definite crowd-pleaser. One winter day, he stood with a group of cadets on the steep slopes of the island in the center of the school's lake. Some of the cadets had set up a toboggan run down the hill—but they were careful not to take it all the way to the bottom; the lake had not quite frozen.

A cadet named Lawson, breathless after a downhill race and uphill climb, hailed David at the top. "It's a pretty good run," he panted. "Too bad you're not dressed for it."

"Who needs to be dressed for it? I'd do it anyway," David replied.

Lawson chuckled. "Sure, and catch it from the prof for ruining your uniform."

"Nuts to the prof. Let me see that," David drawled, reaching for the reins of the toboggan as it was oriented for another run. Then he was off down the hill at top speed, hat flying off as the sled bumped and flew toward the bottom. Unfortunately, he didn't know about "bailing out" before he reached the lake. Too late he understood his situation, realizing with a shock that he was going to take a very cold dip. The toboggan plowed crazily down the last of the slope and went straight into the lake, depositing the flailing David into waist-deep, icy water. He splashed back to shore to the hoots and cheers of his fellows, waving his hand, unable to hide a characteristic grin despite the cold.

There were only five cadets at McCallie who hailed from states west of the Mississippi, and with David's lanky gait and slow Texas drawl, he stood out like the proverbial "sore thumb." No one knew who first hung his nickname on him, but it fitted perfectly and stuck inevitably. By the end of his freshman year, David was "Tex" Hill to all but the faculty and his family. He didn't mind; he even began to introduce himself that way—and seventy years later, he would still be at it.

The years at McCallie were a time of evolution from boyhood to manhood for Tex and, as is often the case, the process was not entirely smooth. Dormitory prefects and classroom professors strictly enforced the school rules, and usually rewarded troublemaking with either a whipping or a restriction to the school grounds known as being "campused." For his pranks and dares, harmless but not tolerated, Tex found himself "campused" more often than not. It was disheartening for him to regularly miss the activities that were available outside the school—but rules were rules. Until the day Tex decided he wasn't going to follow them.

Most of his more notorious schemes involved an accomplice, and for the biggest one so far, his partner was a fellow cadet from Virginia named Hogue. Both young men were "campused" and feeling miserable one winter in Tex's sophomore year, and somehow, in the long hours of boredom, they managed to talk each other into running away from the school. "Riding away" was more appropriate, as they slipped out the front gate of McCallie and made for Chattanooga's railway station. The air was chill. They wore extra shirts against the cold, but carried no other belongings. Tex and Hogue had no idea where they were going. They just wanted some adventure, a change from the drab walls of the school.

The Great Depression had engulfed the nation the year before, but had not yet reached its full depth. Nevertheless, the scene on the railways was grim, with droves of homeless men "riding the rails" from town to town in search of employment—or at least food. The "hobos" burrowed into paper-filled boxcars seeking some protection against the cold while they slept, wearing and eating whatever they could find. Yet they shared a kind of comradeship and code of behavior; faced with common misfortune, they helped one another when they could. This understanding also extended to the railway workers, who found reason to "overlook" the unfortunate stowaways they discovered. When Tex and Hogue hopped aboard a tender, they found the hobos friendly and curious.

"Where are we headed?" Tex asked one, trying to sound confident.

"Mississippi," came the reply. That sounded OK to Tex.

The tender they rode in carried coal, and before long, everyone inside was wearing garb of the same color: black. As the train puffed toward the state line, it entered a long tunnel that burrowed through a mountain. Inside, Tex peered into the absolute pitch. He thought he could see eyeballs. Was this trip really a good idea?

The train emerged from the tunnel, and eventually came to a stop in Meridian, Mississippi. All the stowaways disembarked, and the two young men made for some nearby businesses in the town to ask for food. They had brought none with them, and they tried not to think of the tasty meals in the mess hall back at McCallie while they scrounged for whatever they could find. Bakers and restaurateurs looked long and hard at them, taken aback by their youth, usually offering stale bread or something similar. Not really satisfied, the boys returned to catch the train.

Another trip buried in the grimy coal seemed intolerable, so this time they decided to try boarding a boxcar. They soon located one and scrambled aboard. As Tex stepped into the paper that filled the car, something moved beneath it—accompanied by a string of profanity. A disgruntled hobo, on whom Tex had just trod, told the surprised runaways in colorful language to find their own spot, sit down, and leave the other decent transients alone. Tex and Hogue did just that. One unfortunate man was sitting in the boxcar's doorway, legs dangling over the side, when the locomotive lurched into motion and abruptly tightened the slack between cars. The huge boxcar door jerked closed in a blink, and the hobo had no time to get out of the way. Both of his legs were severed in an instant; two others jumped out to pull their screaming comrade off the train before it picked up speed. Tex and Hogue could only watch in horrified disbelief.

Their next stop was Hulbert, Arkansas, and once more the two runaways disembarked to search for food. They were less successful this time, and both were also beginning to feel a good deal of remorse for what they had done. By good fortune—or divine appointment—they finally knocked upon the door of a minister, who let the boys in and gave them a Spartan meal, which they wolfed down. After watching the boys and wisely discerning the situation, the minister asked if they wouldn't like to telephone their parents. Contrition welled in their hearts, and Tex morosely agreed to call his father. He had not understood until now, he thought, how good his "lot" really was.

Dr. Hill listened patiently on the phone while Tex glumly told him the story. When he was finished, there were no harsh words or scolding. The father sensed the remorse in his son's voice, and knew he had learned a valuable lesson. Dr. Hill had always shown great mercy to those with a repentant heart, following the example set by his own Redeemer. He asked to speak to the minister.

Dr. Hill could not afford to take a week to drive to Arkansas and retrieve the boys, but he soon made arrangements to wire enough money for them to buy a train ticket back to McCallie. Would the minister allow them to stay the night until the money got there? He would, and assured his fellow pastor that he would take care of everything. When Tex and Hogue finally pulled into Chattanooga, this time as paying passengers, they knew they were in for trouble from the faculty at McCallie. They were correct—"campused" for the remainder of the year. But it could have been worse.

Dr. Hill's mercy and discernment were valuable gifts for raising children, but they proved equally valuable in another capacity. In the spring of 1925, John Rogers, one of the elders in his congregation, approached him. Rogers held the rank of captain in the famous Texas Rangers, a group of some eighty hard-nosed, rugged lawmen uniquely suited for keeping the peace in a state where the West was not quite "won." Since the time of the Civil War, the Rangers had rounded up horse thieves, brought highwaymen to justice, and vigilantly patrolled the border with Mexico. They were organized into companies, but often worked alone; if there were such things as incarnations of the Texan spirit of proud independence, they were these tall, dour-handed lawmen.

Rogers asked Dr. Hill if he would be interested in taking on the duties of chaplain for the Texas Rangers. The group had never had one, and Rogers perceived a need for spiritual guidance within their ranks. If Dr. Hill was willing, he would be attached to the company of Captain Bill Sterling, headquartered near the Rio Grande in western Texas. It was difficult to imagine the six-foot-seven Sterling needing guidance of any kind, but Dr. Hill knew better. If there were some way to join the Rangers while remaining in San Antonio to pastor his church, he told Rogers, he would be willing to serve as their chaplain. Governor Dan Moody provided a special dispensation to affect this, and officially enrolled Dr. Hill as a Texas Ranger. It was a landmark event in the pastor's life.

When Tex came home from McCallie for his first summer vacation, he met some of the Rangers—and was awestruck. These tough men talked seriously with his father about criminals, raids, shooting and getting shot. They carried enormous sidearms—and some had telling scars—which lent credibility to their accounts. Besides Bill Sterling, men visited the Hill home with names like Frank Hamer, Manny Gault, and John Hughes. There was a stark difference between their stony, weather-beaten visages and Dr. Hill's warm expression, but Tex was not misled. His father shared a quiet inner strength with the lawmen; he, too, could be as tough as boot leather when necessary. The Rangers knew it, and welcomed the minister into their ranks as a brother, where he formed lifelong friendships.

When the Rangers needed Private Hill for a mission, Captain Sterling would send word, and the pastor would set off to lend support. To the shotgun that he normally carried in his truck, Dr. Hill added a handsome revolver that the Rangers had presented to him. After beating the brush and camping under the stars—Dr. Hill neither expected nor received special treatment in Ranger operations—the mission would usually conclude with the apprehension of some outlaw. Then their chaplain would return to San Antonio, setting aside his boots and brush jacket for familiar ministerial garb. He enjoyed every minute of it. Within a couple of years, he was promoted to captain and attached to Frank Hamer's headquarters unit in Austin.

Aside from watching visiting Rangers while at home during the summer, Tex had a number of jobs to occupy his time. His maternal grandmother, Miss Patty Thraves, came to live with the Hills in Hunt following the death of her husband at age eighty-six. The family decided it was time to expand the house; to the L-shaped main building, they would add a large room that squared it off. For Tex, therefore, it was back to the mountainside with the Shoemaker boys to quarry more rock for the walls, and later, the job of shingling the roof. He made a little extra money working the fields on the Mayhews' nearby farm. Also, of course, he hunted a great deal. When Mr. Shoemaker asked him to help cut sugar cane for the Shoemaker family's yearly molasses production, Tex pitched in eagerly, hoping that more spending money would be forthcoming. When the job was complete, John Shoemaker presented Tex with his wages—and the young man fought to conceal his disappointment. He was paid in molasses.

The wages were much better with the Texas State Highway Department one summer. The Department was employing troops of men to work on the road between San Antonio and Fredericksburg. Tex decided to give it a try. After signing up, he arrived at the construction site one morning, ready to pitch in. The foreman told Tex to start driving stakes, and pointed toward a couple of sledgehammers lying nearby. Tex picked up the smaller of the two.

The man chuckled down at him. "Sorry, son," he said, "you'll need the other one."

It was long, hard work, day after day, barely tolerable in the searing Texas heat. Tex hardly noticed one day when a spider bit him; he went home tired that day as usual. But late that evening, he began to have difficulty breathing. It felt as though someone was squeezing him around the chest. The spider had been a black widow.

His older brother John drove him to the Nix Hospital in San Antonio, where a doctor gave the wheezing Tex a few shots. In a short while Tex felt the effects of the poison easing, and was allowed to return home. "You had a close call there, brother," John told him with relief.

Tex spent the next few weeks recuperating at his brother Sam's home in Beeville. More highway work was underway near Rockport, and eventually Tex was able to commute from Sam's to participate.

Meanwhile, his father and mother were thinking a good deal about Tex's runaway adventure from McCallie, though it was long since forgiven. It seemed as though their son was all-too-regularly in trouble with the school authorities, and this was wearing thin with both faculty and parents. They all knew he wasn't the least bit malicious, but he was decidedly a free spirit who didn't just "behave." After careful thought, Dr. and Mrs. Hill elected not to enroll Tex at McCallie for the following year. Dr. Hill intended to spend a good deal of time with his son, perhaps taking the opportunity to pass along some wisdom. It was the right decision. As Tex hunted, worked the neighbors' fields, and spent time with his father, he had plenty of time to think about the future.

During the ensuing school year, in which he was enrolled at Main Avenue and Jefferson High Schools, Tex grew considerably more mature. For one thing, he decided that he did want to finish school; he would just have to find a way to keep his daredevil nature under control. If he didn't, he realized sooner or later it would land him in a situation from which he couldn't recover. That was sobering. He talked with his parents and told them that if they would let him go back to McCallie, he would not let them down again. Dr. Hill smiled and said he thought that could be arranged, silently thanking the Lord for the work He had done in his son's heart. That fall, Tex was back on the train to McCallie in high spirits.

Although in good physical condition, Tex was not a tremendously gifted athlete. Most organized sports at McCallie held little appeal for him. He did enjoy football somewhat, lettering in it one year on the 3rd-string squad, and also ran track. The exception to his ambivalence about sports was boxing, which he took up at the start of his senior year—the first year McCallie had the program—and became extremely skilled. This was not the mayhem of boyhood fistfights with Joe Frost Junior, he discovered, but rather a disciplined combination of footwork, control, and an eye for the opponent's weakness. Under the expert instruction of Coach Flowers, Tex quickly became the best boxer at the school, lettering and winning the Tennessee Middleweight Championship in 1934, a few months before his graduation. "Glad I didn't have to go a round with you!" a classmate wrote in Tex's yearbook.

He enjoyed such success in the boxing ring at McCallie that he began to consider making a career of the sport. His lean frame carried less weight than other boxers' did, but his long reach always trumped his opponents' by several inches, and that usually proved decisive in a match. His quick eye and reflexes didn't hurt either. He was good, but how good? One day in his senior year he decided to try the next step: a professional bout. He lined up a match with an Army soldier from Fort Oglethorp, Georgia. McCallie was not far from five different states—all of which could be seen on a clear day from the area's Lookout Mountain—and the drive to the Army post did not take long.

Neither did the boxing match. To his surprise, Tex found himself seriously outclassed, and in short order the Army man knocked him into a thirty-minute "unsolicited nap." Tex had found the limits of his skill. When he came to, he "saw the light": it would be a tough way to make a living. When he left McCallie, his boxing gloves stayed behind for good.

Graduation came at long last in the spring of 1934. Proof of Tex's adherence to the "straight and narrow" arrived: near-perfect scores on his college entrance exams. He was near the top of his class, and once more the future looked bright. As he waited for his train to pull out of the station in Chattanooga for the last time, he leaned out the window to bid a classmate farewell.

"See you, Tex. Hey, I heard you did well on your exams for college."

"I did all right," Tex replied with a smile, "but it doesn't matter. I'm not going to college." As he spoke, the train started into motion.

"No kidding?" his friend wondered, taking a few steps down the platform to keep up. "What are you going to do then?"

Tex grinned. "I'm going into the Navy!" The train pulled away.

✳ ✳ ✳

While Tex spent his year out of McCallie, China faced both an obvious and a subtle threat. The Empire of Japan opened its long campaign of Asian conquest with an invasion of the Chinese province of Manchuria. Within two months, they controlled most of it. *The following year they fortified the island of Formosa, and occupied Shanghai on the east China coast. Chiang Kai-Shek appealed to Great Britain and the United States for help, but Britain was unwilling to anger Japan. America, in the throes of the Depression, was unable.*

The subtle threat began with an announcement by the diminutive leader of the fledgling Communist Party in China. From his base in Kiangsi Province, he proclaimed the formation of a new "Chinese Soviet Republic," and swore to overthrow Chiang's rule. His name was Mao Tse-Tung.

As senior instructor of fighter tactics at Maxwell Air Force Base, Claire Chennault found himself the lone preacher of a difficult gospel. The "experts" of the day touted bomber aircraft as the last word in aerial weaponry. These "Bomber Advocates" curtly informed Chennault that fighter escort might be a historical item of interest, but the next war would obviously be decided by high-altitude, unescorted bombers, unloading bombs by the thousands onto the enemy's industrial heartland, then sailing away untouched. Chennault was disgusted. He knew better, and said so in his own definitive textbook, <u>The Role of Defensive Pursuit</u>. The text won him few friends.

There was a task that Chennault found thoroughly enjoyable, however, somewhat mitigating his frustration with the conventional airpower "wisdom" of the time. When the Navy Helldivers, the service's aerobatic team, performed a show at Maxwell one day, the base commander promptly ordered that an Army aerobatic team be formed; he was "damned if he'd let the Navy show up the Air Corps." All fingers pointed to Chennault as the man to do it; his skill was widely known. With wingmen Billy McDonald and Luke Williamson, Chennault drilled in every precision maneuver in the book—and then some. These "Three Men on the Flying Trapeze," as they called their act, toured the country with a show that onlookers watched in thrilled amazement. Some of their stunts were never duplicated. At their final performance during the Miami All-American Air Races in 1936, one man in the audience came away looking unusually thoughtful. He was Mow Pang-Tsu, commander of the Chinese Air Force.

Graduation from the McCallie School, 1934.

Portrait of Tex at Austin College, Sherman, Texas.

Chapter 4

HIGHER LEARNING

Tex was nearly seventeen. He had settled on pursuing a military career, and he was old enough to enlist in the Navy—but just barely. For recruits of his age, the Navy required letters of recommendation from community and civic leaders, as well as written permission from a young man's parents. Tex set to work collecting the necessary paperwork, and at last obtained the final letter from Mayor Quinn, who shook his hand and wished him the best of luck in his endeavors—

The final letter but one, that was. Dr. and Mrs. Hill had nothing against a Navy enlistment; in fact, Tex's father thought it an excellent move. But Dr. Hill also knew the value of a college degree, and was concerned that his son would pass up a chance to get one—a chance that might not return. He was willing to write the letter of permission for Tex, but wouldn't his son consider the benefits of college? He advised Tex that it would be well worth it down the road, pointing out that his brother had proved it.

Sam Hill, the oldest son, had graduated from Austin College a year after Tex entered McCallie. Sam's love in life was ranching, but he also felt called to follow his father's footsteps into the ministry. He decided to attend Austin Theological Seminary, completing a Bachelor of Divinity degree two years before David graduated from McCallie. Now Sam was the pastor of a small church in Beeville, Texas.

"Son," Dr. Hill told Tex, "if you've made up your mind to go into the Navy, we won't stop you. But I'll tell you one thing: your opportunities with a college degree are unlimited. You'll really be glad you have one."

Tex considered. His father had never given bad advice.

In the end Tex agreed that higher education was for him, but he felt no desire to enroll in Austin College. The appeal of the military was strong. That fall Dr. Hill put Tex on a train bound north for the town of College Station. There the young man enrolled in the Texas Agricultural and Mechanical College, a military school more often called by its shortened name: Texas A&M.

The Corps of Cadets provided enjoyable company for Tex. He was assigned to Cavalry Troop A along with two dozen of his fellows. He was long since accustomed to military schools, but with college came a greater freedom of action that suited him. He declared a major of Chemical Engineering, and found that the academic preparation at McCallie made it easy for him to cruise through his freshman year without much study. His performance in and out of the classroom was good enough to earn him a coveted stripe of rank by his sophomore year. Meanwhile there were all kinds of Corps activities for fun, and he relished the fraternal friendship of his fellow cadets in Troop A. His family was only an hour or two down the road, should he have a mind to visit on weekends. The town of College Station was right outside the door, along with neighboring Bryan.

After his first year at A&M, Tex spent a pleasant summer vacation back in the hill country with his family. In the fall, he returned to the school anticipating a happy reunion with his friends in Cavalry Troop A. The semester began well indeed, but it wasn't long before an unwelcome surprise came. The Corps was forming a new division: Chemical Warfare. It needed cadets to fill its ranks, and Chemical Engineering students naturally topped the list—including Tex. Realization that, before long, he would have to leave his companions was a bitter blow.

The remainder of the semester was markedly different from his jubilant freshman year. Faced with the prospect of being thrown in with cadets he didn't know—and surely, he thought, wouldn't enjoy as much—Tex's only goal was to remain in Cavalry Troop A however he could. He tried changing his major; it didn't wash with the faculty. Frustrated, he changed it a second time. His grades began to slip. He hadn't needed to study much for the freshman curriculum; and now, when study was really necessary, he found himself glumly unmotivated. He was losing his focus, feeling betrayed by what he perceived as an arbitrary reorganization. By the time Thanksgiving came around, Tex had allowed his grades to sink to a dangerously low point. When he went home for Christmas, they were abysmal. He had decided to drop out.

It was a sober holiday season in the house at Hunt. Tex found himself wondering how things had gone downhill so quickly, but once more he found a patient listener in his father. Dr. Hill did not condemn his son, and resolved with the Lord's help to lend David some perspective.

"You don't have to decide this minute what you're going to do, son," the pastor explained gently. "Take some time and think about it. If you want, you can come with me on a little trip I'll be making soon."

By this time, Dr. Hill's reputation within the Texas Rangers was high. The short messages and prayers he shared with them, out in the hills on duty, were sincere and straightforward. Most of the Rangers were wise enough to believe in the sovereignty of God, and Dr. Hill's life was a testimony to it. His example affected a part of the hardened lawmen that seldom showed. Time after time, the Rangers brought him captured thieves, outlaws, and other criminals, asking their chaplain whether the men could be rehabilitated. Dr. Hill's keen insight into a man's character gave him the answer in only a single conversation. Over the years, he recommended that many of the criminals be released into his personal custody, and not a single one "went bad" on him. It was uncanny, unless one understood from Whom the pastor's discernment came.

The trip Dr. Hill had mentioned to Tex was to Hampden-Sydney, Virginia, site of his own alma mater, a university that bore the same name as the town. It was a long journey, giving father and son plenty of time to talk—and to be together without talking. It was just what Tex needed. His father emphasized that he would support him in anything he did, that he knew his son could accomplish whatever he set a mind to, and that the Lord wasn't about to let either one of them down. In Virginia, Dr. Hill spent time visiting with several old friends from his college graduating class. Tex noticed their mutual respect for one another's accomplishments. Somewhere along the way, Tex made up his mind to finish college; unfortunately, he knew the door back to Texas A&M was closed to him.

On the return trip, Dr. Hill thought he knew what was passing through his son's mind. Casually, he mentioned that if Tex were interested, he was sure that his position on the board of trustees at Austin College would open the way for admission to that institution. Austin wasn't Texas A&M, nor a military school at all, but it could provide solid education and a degree. That, after all, was the "main thing." It didn't take Tex long to accept his father's offer. He enrolled that fall, and discovered with relief that most of his credits from Texas A&M would count toward a degree at Austin. Half-constructed buildings scattered about the campus were evidence that the school didn't enjoy the plentiful grant money a big university would have; but a top-notch faculty ensured the education was at least as good.

It was a new lease on academic life, and Tex would never again allow circumstances to dictate his efforts. From that time, his life would be marked by intensity toward whatever task he took on. He excelled academically. An amiable manner and quick smile were still his hallmarks; and life at Austin College, although lacking the pageantry and structure of the Corps of Cadets, was enjoyable.

Especially the football games. Austin College enrolled less than three hundred students; but, as any small-school alumnus knows, loyal fans care little about their school's size. Every school has an arch-rival—though maybe not as famous as Alabama for Auburn, or the University of Texas for Texas A&M—and Austin College was no exception. Austin's perennial "most-hated enemy" was Trinity University, located at that time in Waxahatchie, Texas. As the football schedule rolled toward the two schools' annual clash in Tex's senior year, he felt an urge to do something big—really big—to fan the flames of the rivalry. As he read the Austin newspaper one day, an article about Trinity University's "big game preparations" caught his attention.

A large bonfire on game day was a Trinity University tradition (just as it had been at Texas A&M). Students piled up an enormous quantity of wood, and just before the Austin-Trinity contest began, they fired it—to the frantic cheers of the Trinity faithful. Some years, Austin College students had made small-scale "raids" on Trinity's campus, where they might paint the Austin logo on a wall or commit some other minor act of vandalism. During the Depression, such activities had tapered off, since cars were scarce and gasoline was expensive. But Tex really wanted to make a foray this time. He thought carefully about the bonfire.

"Look at this, fellows: 'Biggest Bonfire Ever at Trinity University,'" Tex read, displaying the headline to a small group of his friends and fellow classmates. He paused, smiling mischievously. "If you'll help pay my way down there to Waxahatchie, I'll burn that thing down."

His classmates' eyes lit up. "I've got a car," said one. "It ain't much, but it'll get you there and back if you get some gas in it." He looked around the group. Little by little, with much digging, money began to emerge from pockets, until they had gathered enough to finance the expedition.

The frigid night before the big game, Tex and his fellow conspirators gathered around the rattletrap vehicle. They could see their breath in the fall cold.

"You fellows won't regret this. It'll be good, I can guarantee that," said Tex, chuckling as he climbed into the passenger seat. "Let's go."

Quentin Miller, a classmate, sat ready behind the wheel. "Don't wait up!" he hollered to the whooping group of students, as the two sped off down the road.

The drive to Waxahatchie took some time. It was the middle of the night when Tex and Miller arrived. They drove toward the plowed field next to Trinity's small stadium, turning off their lights to avoid detection. They could see the huge pile of wood, a twenty-five-foot mountain of fuel that blocked out the stars, on the south side of the field. Atop it was the *piece de résistance*, a wooden outhouse (called a "Chick Sale" after the famous comedian). Gathered around a small fire nearby, stamping and blowing on their hands to keep warm, stood a group of Trinity freshmen. Their job was to keep a watch on the gargantuan woodpile—not that the upperclassmen expected it to go anywhere. It was a traditional fraternity initiation task for the shivering "fish."

Out of earshot, Miller shut the car off and silently gave Tex an encouraging "thumbs-up." Tex got out and walked some distance across the field, approaching the freshmen from the opposite side of the bonfire with a hunter's skill. Patiently he watched them awhile, noting their activities. When the fire had warmed them somewhat, a few "fish" would occasionally walk away from the blaze to collect some more wood, adding it to the already huge, unlit main pile. When their fingers became numb, they returned to their fire.

Tex had seen enough. He returned to the car and told Miller to drive to a nearby gas station, where Tex filled a gallon-size coffee can with gasoline. Thus equipped, they returned to the field, and Tex crept back to his observation post after a last warning to Miller: "Be ready to go—and I mean *go*." When the next foray of "fish" returned to their small fire for warmth, Tex went into action. Creeping up behind the mammoth woodpile, he proceeded to slosh the gasoline over the heap. A gallon was about right, wasn't it? He seemed to be sloshing for an eternity, but actually finished in seconds. He stepped back, struck a match, leaned forward, and tossed it into the mound.

With an angry *whoosh*, the gasoline-soaked wood exploded into flames. The sudden heat made Tex throw his hand protectively across his face—but not before his eyebrows were nearly singed off. His only thought—other than *I think I just burned my face off*—was to get away. He high-tailed it across the frozen field to the car.

As he fled the scene, a shrill yell came from behind him: "Aw, hell! There goes our bonfire!"

Miller was guffawing as the sprinting Tex hurled himself into the car; the driver lost no time making good their getaway.

"Did—did you see that outhouse on top?" asked Miller, nearly choking with laughter.

"Yeah—hope there was nobody in that thing!" Tex snorted. The two cackled with mirth.

There were no more articles in the paper.

As he progressed through college, a career in the military appealed more and more to Tex. In the spring of 1938, he decided to apply for the Army Air Corps' aviation program, recalling the cadets that used to visit his home in San Antonio for dates with his sister Martha. So, home at Hunt one weekend, Tex drove to San Antonio to visit nearby Randolph Field. The evaluation for the Army's aviation program included a battery of written tests, medical exams, and interviews by Army psychiatrists. Tex waded through them all, then returned to await the results. A few weeks later they arrived: he had failed to qualify. No reason was given, and Tex never learned it.

The setback wasn't going to deter him. He thought once more of the Navy—which also had a good aviation program, according to some literature he'd read. When he talked to a recruiter and explained that he wanted to fly pursuit planes, the Navy man went over the possibilities with Tex. One of the requirements for entering Naval aviation training was to have a college degree—and Tex gratefully realized how wise his parents had been in encouraging him to complete one. The recruiting pitch sounded all right, so one morning Tex drove down to Dallas for the Navy's version of the tests. They were essentially identical to the Army's as far as Tex could tell; and once again, he played the waiting game back at Austin College. This time, however, the news was good: Tex had been accepted as a candidate for aviation training.

He would have to enlist immediately upon graduation as a seaman, second class. The Navy made no guarantee that candidates would actually become aviators; and it wanted to retain them even if they failed to complete the difficult training. This was a risk Tex was willing to take. He "signed on the dotted line." A couple of months after graduation from Austin College, he was off to Navy Flight Elimination Training, held at a place with the unlikely name of Opa Locka, Florida.

* * *

In China, the Communists fared poorly in their military campaign against the armies of Chiang Kai-Shek. At the time Tex was enrolling in Austin College, Communist forces broke out from their besieged bases in Kiangsi Province to begin the famous, year-long, 6,000-mile "Long March" north to Yenan Province. When the March was over, Chiang was able to keep them bottled up in Yenan for years; but there was an unfortunate price. Chiang had to maintain a large army in the area to contain the Communists—an army which could not fight the Japanese. Eventually, faced with the common Japanese threat, Chiang and the Communists signed an uneasy truce. Despite their military defeats, the Communists seemed to be growing in numbers. One of Mao's fanatical lieutenants spurred on the Party's recruiting efforts with great success. His name was Chou En-Lai.

Generalissimo Chiang Kai-Shek placed his young wife in charge of the Chinese Air Force. Until then, the superior numbers and aircraft of the Japanese had regularly trounced it. She sought the advice of her senior generals. Mow Pang-Tsu recalled the skill and daring of the American pilot who led the "Three Men on the Flying Trapeze" at the air show years before; thus, the name of Claire Chennault was first mentioned in the Chinese capital. American-educated Madame Chiang was thoughtful.

As Tex finished his first year at Austin College, Claire Chennault's Army career came to a frustrating end. The Air Corps Tactical School's leaders, convinced that pursuit aviation was outmoded and useless, discontinued its inclusion in the curriculum. The Army retired Chennault from his next assignment, as 20th Pursuit Group executive officer, for chronic bronchitis and deafness. He was 47 years old.

Just a few weeks before, however, he had received a letter from China. Madame Chiang Kai-Shek requested his services to perform a "confidential evaluation" of the readiness of the Chinese Air Force. Was he willing to come to China for three months? With nothing left for him in the Army, he decided he was.

Only a month into Chennault's visit to the Orient, the Japanese perpetrated the Marco Polo Bridge Incident, renewing hostilities with the Chinese on a large scale. Many considered it the true beginning of the Second World War. The date was July 7, 1937.

Chennault immediately offered his services to Chiang Kai-Shek in "whatever capacity might be needed." Chiang placed him in charge of instruction at the flight school in Hangchow. His assignment was to prepare the pitiful Chinese Air Force—which included less than one hundred obsolete planes—for combat. It was an impossible task; although there were some successful engagements using his tactics, the improving Jap fighter aircraft gradually mopped up the hapless Chinese.

In rapid succession, the Japanese invaded and captured Shanghai and Canton; then they turned their attention to the capital of Nanking. It fell in December, and the atrocities of murder, torture, and pillage perpetrated on the city—all filmed by the victorious Japanese—gained worldwide infamy. This was the "Rape of Nanking," in which some 300,000 Chinese were slaughtered, raped, or mutilated. Chiang and the government were forced to retreat and move the capital inland to Nanchang; the Japanese continued to advance.

Tex in flight gear while a member of Bombing Four (VB-4) on the U.S.S. Ranger.

Chapter 5

WHEELS AND WINGS

Tex couldn't say when his interest in motorcycles began. It might never have arisen, had it not been for an ongoing comedy between him and his father concerning "things that go." When the Hills lived in San Antonio, young David got his hands on a bicycle; and he rode it with the typical abandon of an eight-year-old with no concept of safety.

"Son, you'll kill yourself on that thing, if you don't slow down and be careful," Dr. Hill would admonish. The advice didn't sink in.

Mysteriously one night, the bike disappeared from its parking place. When David discovered the crime, he went straight to his father.

"Daddy, my bike's gone! Somebody stole it!"

Dr. Hill seemed to have a pressing interest in the wallpaper. "Is that right? Are you sure you didn't misplace it?"

"No way. I asked, and nobody knows where it is. Somebody took it, I know it," the boy pronounced with a glare.

"Well, all right," his father looked nonchalant. "I'll talk to the police and see what can be done. Meanwhile, I see you've got two perfectly good feet there. I reckon they'll get you around."

In the following days, David noticed, with dissatisfaction, that his father didn't seem to be making an enormous effort to recover his missing bicycle. Ever afterward, he harbored a suspicion that his Daddy might even have had something to do with its disappearance. Dr. Hill was right about one thing, though: his feet worked just fine.

Years later, home from McCallie on summer vacation, Tex was again interested in a means of getting around. He was old enough to drive, and somehow was able to acquire an aging Model "T." It wasn't much to look at; but for a young man his age, it came with immeasurable prestige—and fun. Driving it, Tex exercised precisely the same amount of caution he'd had on his old bicycle: none. His father's rebukes ("Drive like you've got something between those sizable ears!") had little effect.

A day came when Tex parked the car around the back of the house at 121 East Park as usual—and it was stolen as well. Dr. Hill, conveniently, was in the *front* yard at the time of the heist. Could one of the Ranger chaplain's parolees have lifted it—maybe even upon "special request," David wondered? Once again Dr. Hill's "Herculean efforts" to recover the missing machine turned up nothing. Tex suspected something fishy was going on.

Though his bicycles and cars just didn't seem to stick around for long, it didn't matter. One day between semesters at Austin College, Tex discovered what he really wanted: a motorcycle. A friend of his older brother John owned a 1200-cc. Harley-Davidson 74VL. Exerting his utmost powers of persuasion, Tex finally prevailed upon John to borrow the motorcycle; and the two of them took it to Breckenridge Park in the city for Tex's maiden ride. There, they reasoned, he would be least likely to kill anyone.

"Just take it slow, David," John cautioned, in a tone that said he didn't have the money to buy his friend a new Harley. After some basic instruction, Tex roared off into the undergrowth to "solo." In minutes, a unique bond between cycle and rider was formed amid blue smoke and fleeing woodland creatures. How had he missed out on this before, he wondered? Wind streamed past and the engine roared beneath him. It was a revelation. This, he wanted.

Shepherding the limited funds he earned from summer jobs, Tex finally saved enough by his junior year to buy a Harley 45. Like John's friend's, it was another side valve twin cycle, light and somewhat underpowered. Tex didn't mind; with great joy, he made the long-awaited purchase and proceeded to "wring it out." The bike might not have been the biggest in town, but it was his. That fall he returned to Sherman, Texas for school, while Dr. Hill waved goodbye—certain that the next time he got news of his son, it would be in the obituary column. Would the Lord please keep an eye on him?

No word of a fatality reached Dr. Hill's ears; and Tex continued to save money, already planning to buy a bigger and better bike. In his senior year of college, he got it: a 1938 Harley-Davidson 61EL, fondly dubbed the "Knucklehead." This was no light-engined pretender. It was a high-performance, state-of-the-art, chromium steel monster that whispered: *you may own me, but you cannot tame me.* The overhead valves on the 1000-cc. engine were a "first" in motorcycle design, doubling the horsepower output with a 6:1 compression ratio and rocketing the bike to a top speed of over 90 mph. It all added up to a genuine racing cycle that was destined to become a collector's machine, worth much more in later years than the $550 Tex paid in 1938. He blasted up to his home in Hunt on the new wheels, as Dr. Hill strolled amiably out the front door.

"What do you think?" asked the young man, dismounting. He was wearing the usual Tex Hill grin.

The pastor scratched his head and looked it over. "Well, son," he said, "if the Lord can keep you safe on this thing, I reckon you'd be all right riding a goosed rhino." He paused—then returned his son's smile. "She's mighty good-looking, though."

Tex was entirely happy with his new transportation, and rode it everywhere. On the trip back from Dallas, after completing the tests for Naval aviation training, he ran into some difficulty. Eyes dilated from the medical exam, Tex roared along the highway, wondering why he couldn't read anything—including ten-foot-high billboards. The blobby landscape raced indistinctly past. He finally made it back to Sherman—at least, he figured it was Sherman, since some of the blobs seemed familiar.

With college graduation behind him and his diploma safely secured, Tex spent the enjoyable summer months in Hunt with his parents, marking time until his September report date to aviation training at Opa Locka. As the August sun gave the Texas hill country its customary baking, a new and unique event approached in Dr. Hill's ministry. It was the first annual Cowboy Camp Meeting, a gathering of ranchers and their families to worship God and fellowship together. The two-hundred-eighty-acre plot of land that held the site of the Meeting was a donation to the pastor. People from far and wide pitched in to construct a large open-air tabernacle, and raise a myriad of tents in which to eat and sleep.

On the Cowboy Camp Meeting's first evening, Dr. Hill took the pulpit to preach. The hot August air reminded everyone that they were not in the sanctuary of First Presbyterian in the city. The Meeting drew hundreds of people from far across the open range to a setting where they could worship in their own element. They praised the Creator while surveying His creation, from stars to scrub trees, beyond the edges of the tent. It was a weeklong gathering. For meals, everyone lent a hand to prepare the deep-fried steaks and *frijole* pinto beans that were the hill country folks' favorites. During sermons, Tex noticed that his father's abilities had not diminished. Dr. Hill was still able to convey the teaching of scripture to people as conversationally as if only two were having a friendly talk beneath the tent. When Tex left the Hill home a few weeks later for Opa Locka, it was with the feeling that he had partaken in something unique. Sixty-five years later, the Cowboy Camp Meeting would still be a mainstay event of every hill country summer.

As a rule of thumb, they say, a happy motorcyclist can be identified by the many bugs on his teeth. Tex's spirits and his "bug count" were both high as he sped eastward on his beloved Harley, toward Florida and Naval Flight Elimination Training. It was a long, easy trip—despite frequent bug-wiping stops in Louisiana to maintain visibility—and a new adventure waited at the end. Unfortunately, the adventurer would have to do without his motorcycle; at Opa Locka, another man had recently been killed riding one, and the base commander had ordered all motorcycles to be stored off base. After some thought, Tex decided he wasn't interested in keeping the bike if he couldn't ride it. He reluctantly sold the Harley, knowing he would miss it.

Opa Locka was an old U.S. Marine Corps base, which the Navy had taken over when the Marines no longer needed it. There the Navy had set up the important initial phase of its aviation training program. The word "elimination" in "Flight Elimination Training" was no accident. The training of pilots was—and would always be—an expensive effort for the military services. That was one reason they selected relatively few applicants for it. When Tex arrived, he found that only twelve candidates, including himself, would be taking the three-week class. When he discreetly inquired about the other ninety-eight who had crowded through the tests in Dallas, he was told that only this group of a dozen had been accepted.

However, before it spent large sums of money training even twelve aviators, the Navy wanted to make sure the men possessed a few rudimentary skills. Instructors taught them for many hours in the classroom, then provided ten hours of flying instruction in a Stearman NS-1 biplane trainer. Even flying this basic aircraft required a certain amount of aptitude. Tex soaked up the classroom academics, put them into practice in the cockpit, and had no trouble soloing in the Stearman when his turn came. However, two of the twelve candidates washed out at this stage, leaving ten successful aviators-in-training.

Then Tex and his class were on their way to Naval Flight Training in Pensacola, Florida. It would be far more difficult than Opa Locka: thirteen months of detailed, demanding instruction on flying all the primary aircraft types in the Navy's inventory. For reserve officer candidates, like Tex, the school doubled as officers' training. Regular officers from Annapolis had already received four years of that, so the two groups were mostly separated for the duration. But they all had their eyes on the same prize: the gold wings of a Naval aviator, waiting at the end.

The storied town of Pensacola was a sleepy southern seaside burg of some 80,000 residents, with the Naval base right on the shore. It was the first time Tex had been near the sea for more than a day or two, and he found the wheeling gulls and hissing surf new and fascinating. The Naval base itself was stately and rambling; old redbrick buildings and colonial trimmings were much in evidence.

At flight training, Tex was enrolled in class 121-C. The school ran classes in parallel, with a new one beginning every month or so; 121-C found itself at the end of a line of some six other classes, ranging from beginners to near-graduates. A single large, brick building with several wings served as both sleeping quarters and mess hall for the cadets. The facilities were simple, yet comfortable. Tex found that the rules—written and unwritten—for cadet behavior were not very different from those during his years of military school. He fit in well. A blaring fire alarm awakened all the cadets at 0500 every morning for calisthenics on the verandah. Afterward, they thronged into the mess hall, populating long rows of tables for morning "chow." Then they scattered to the four winds for that particular day's training.

Each class began flight training in Squadron One: basic instruction on primary seaplanes. Many cadets immediately recognized the Naval Aircraft Factory N3N *Canary* trainer aircraft—nicknamed the "Yellow Peril"—by the large pontoons mounted underneath in lieu of wheels. Seaplanes could land anywhere—as long it was on the water. Tex's instructor was Lieutenant Donald Frasier, an amiable fellow, long on patience with the blunders of cadet aviators. Don shepherded Tex easily through the first fifteen hours of flight instruction, which concluded with a "check ride" in late March. Tex passed with flying colors. It was the halfway mark in Squadron One training.

After the fifteen-hour check, Frasier explained to Tex that he was going on leave to study for a promotion exam. He was confident Tex would have no trouble with the remainder of the seaplane phase.

Unfortunately, things didn't go as smoothly as Frasier predicted. Tex's instructor for the second half of primary seaplanes was a surly, impatient senior man with an air of superiority. Long since, the grumpy aviator had decided that if a student wasn't doing things his way, it was the wrong way. His attitude was completely incompatible with Tex's air of amiable independence; and a personality clash of the first order ensued. Tex learned nothing from his new instructor. When the end-of-phase check came in mid-April after thirty flying hours, Tex's deficiencies were all too apparent. He "busted it straight."

Failing a check ride in the course was called a "down," and there were meticulous procedures followed in such an instance. The first step was to give the student extra flying instruction, known as "squadron time," after which the trainee took another evaluation. If a second "bust" occurred, a board would convene to consider the merits of allowing the cadet another chance. Often they would be lenient, and allot a few additional hours of training, known as "board time." If the student turned in a third unsatisfactory performance, only intervention by the commandant of the school could save him. Such grace was rare.

Tex was allowed the additional squadron time, but a few more hours of training—even from a better instructor—proved insufficient to make up for the many wasted hours of non-learning. Sure enough, three days later, Tex "busted" his second check. As the board met to weigh his fate, word of Tex's misfortune reached the ears of Don Frasier, who was still on leave studying. Frasier immediately returned to the school and went before the board.

"I'm telling you, this guy can fly," he insisted. "I don't know what happened when he switched instructors, but if you give me three hours with him, I guarantee he'll be up to speed. I'll come in off of leave to do it."

Impressed, the board agreed. Under Frasier's expert tutelage, Tex quickly absorbed the knowledge he needed to pass the check. Sure enough, his third and last-chance ride in early May was an "up." For the rest of his time at Pensacola, he never flew another "down"; it would have been a ticket home. Don Frasier had saved Tex's career.

Tex and his classmates pressed on through the various squadrons of instruction. Squadron Two focused on primary land planes; they flew the Stearman NS-1, familiar to them from their time at Opa Locka. Squadron Three trained in the Vought SBU and O3U *Corsair* scouting aircraft. Cadets who would be going on to aircraft carrier assignments, including Tex, skipped Squadron Four; it provided instruction on "big boats," as the transport versions of the Consolidated PBY *Catalina* were called. In Squadron Five, Tex received instrument flying instruction in the treacherous North American NJ-1; fighter time, including gunnery and acrobatics, in the Boeing F4B-4; and several hours of familiarization with torpedo bombers. Naval Aviation Training was rigorous and difficult, much longer than its counterpart school in the Army Air Corps. Graduating aviators had a solid baseline of instruction in all basic airframes, aerial gunnery, the various types of bombing, and other fundamentals required for their trade.

Flight training was plenty of fun, too—and sometimes the fun took an extra-curricular turn. Tex enjoyed occasionally peeling off from the prescribed flight path to "buzz" the local shoreline trysting spots at treetop level, whereupon goggle-eyed couples emerged from their cars to stare after him. It was harmless, but rewarded his mischievousness handsomely.

As training went on at Pensacola, Tex gradually met members of the other classes. There were about ten cadets in each class, so the school held some sixty students at any one time. With his outgoing disposition that put others at ease, Tex made many friends. In his own 121-C were John Hennessey, Robert "Buster" Keeton, and Tommy Cole. Ahead of him in training were new friends "Swede" Vejtesa, Bert Christman, and Frank Lawlor. Strung out behind him in later classes were fellows with names like "Gil" Bright, Joe Rosbert, and George "Pappy" Paxton. As Tex neared graduation, another class started that included an outstanding athlete from North Carolina who took the football squad by storm. His name was Ed Rector.

Camaraderie made the year at Pensacola go by quickly. Tex had no inkling that, within two years, he would be reunited with many of his classmates. It would be seven thousand miles away, with their backs to the wall, in a fight for their lives and a nation's survival.

As the excited cadets moved inexorably closer to graduation, all became anxious to know what their subsequent assignments would be. The rigors of the program had washed out several more men in Class 121-C; and there were a number of possibilities for the six that remained. If assigned to an aircraft carrier, an aviator would fly one of the types of planes aboard: fighters, bombers, torpedo bombers, or dive-bombers. Outside the carrier arena, there were the "big boats"—transport versions of the PBY *Catalina*. Tex wanted to fly pursuit planes—fighters. So did just about every other cadet; but the number of pursuit aviator openings available to each class varied. The top graduates usually snapped up those coveted billets, and with Tex's two "downs," he was ranked number three out of six. He wasn't holding his breath.

On the cool first morning of November in 1939, Flight Training finally came to an end for class 121-C. After a commissioning ceremony that transformed Tex and his classmates from cadets into Naval officers with the rank of ensign, the school commandant pinned the long-sought, hard-earned gold wings on their dress uniforms. It was a feeling like no other. After all the years of support and sacrifice from his father and mother, at last Tex felt their investment in him was paying off. Dr. and Mrs. Hill could hand their son over to the Navy with the certainty of a job very, very well done. As Tex happily packed his bags for a short visit home, he looked for the twentieth time at the orders he'd received for his assignment. He was headed to the west coast, to fly torpedo bombers on the aircraft carrier U.S.S. *Saratoga*.

* * *

As Tex passed through the guardhouse at Pensacola for the first time, Chinese airpower was "on the ropes." Scores of Japanese Type 96 "Nell" fighters shot their opponents' outmoded planes out of the sky like ducks. A fighter and bomber group on loan to the Chinese from the Russians, and the international "Gypsy Squadron" before them, had fared little better. Under Chennault's direction, construction began on large airfields near the eastern Chinese cities of Kweilin, Lingling, Hengyang, and Liuchow. He set up the Chinese radio warning net, which immediately proved invaluable to the helpless city residents; and he began a new flying training school at Kunming. While Tex was recovering from his "bust" in training, Chennault flew his final mission over China the last of many as a combat observer in his Curtiss 75 "Hawk Special."

In October, the provisional capital of Hankow fell to the Japanese ground advance, and Chiang Kai-Shek moved again. This time it was far into the interior, to the city of Chungking. The move was an age-old Chinese wartime tactic—trading land for time— and one of the few things China had no shortage of was land. Nevertheless, by the following May, the Japanese were bombing the capital of Chungking and Chennault's flying school at Kunming every day. Chennault had no chance to get his air force program off the ground. In the skies for the first time was the Mitsubishi A6M Zero, the Japanese Navy's new mass-production fighter. At the time, it could fly circles around anything else in the world. Once they demolished the Chinese aerial defenses, the merciless Japs began strafing Chinese civilians in Chungking's city streets.

Far to the west, the governor of China's Yunnan Province completed a miracle of engineering: a 700-mile route that wound from the city of Kunming all the way to the Burma border. From that point, British engineers extended it to the town of Lashio in Burma, where a railhead linked the route to its terminus at the Burmese port of Rangoon. As the Japanese stranglehold on Chinese ports tightened, China leaned more and more heavily on this precipitous lifeline. It was dubbed the Burma Road.

A couple of "Knuckleheads"? Tex shows off on his new Harley-Davidson 61EL.

Tex's class at Naval Flight Elimination Training, Opalocka, Florida, 1938.

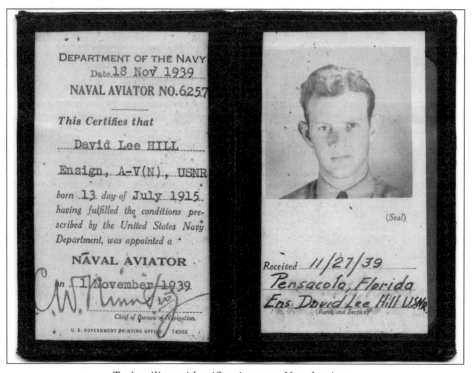

Tex's military identification as a Naval aviator.

Portrait as Naval Aviation Cadet, Pensacola, 1938.

Sketch of graduation from Naval aviation training, November 1, 1939. Logo is of Torpedo Squadron Three (VT-3).

Chapter 6

SARATOGA

Early in September 1939, as Tex neared graduation from Pensacola, the world's attention was suddenly riveted to Eastern Europe when fifty-three German divisions smashed into Poland. *Wehrmacht* Panzers mowed down archaic Polish cavalry and completed a brief sprint to Warsaw. Shortly thereafter, the Russians invaded Poland from the east. By the start of November, as Tex received his aviator wings, Poland was neatly divided between her two attackers, in accordance with their secret agreement, reached months before.

Just as the United States had not assisted China in fighting her Japanese invaders, neither did they follow Britain and France in declaring war on Hitler's Germany. American isolationism was strong, and her Great Depression still persisted. Her surrounding oceans were wide. The U.S. Navy, which made those oceans its responsibility, was divided into Atlantic and Pacific Fleets. As Tex traveled to San Diego to go aboard the *Saratoga*, his counterparts in the Atlantic were ordered to keep an eye out for German submarines—just in case.

The U.S.S. *Saratoga*, designation CV-3, was the sixth ship to bear that name—and it would not be the last. Previous incarnations of the *Sara* had seen action as long ago as the War of 1812. The current edition was a nine-hundred-foot converted battle cruiser, commissioned twelve years before. She displaced 33,000 tons, and carried a crew of over three thousand. When Tex spotted her in the San Diego harbor that December, the first thing he noticed was the array of eighty-six aircraft packed onto her enormous deck. There were Brewster *Buffaloes*, Vought SB2U *Vindicators*, and—soon to be his own aircraft—Douglas TBD-1 *Devastators*. Shortly after Tex went aboard, the carrier steamed away from North Island and motored up to her cruising speed of thirty-four knots.

The largest water-faring vessel he had been aboard before was a rowboat, so shipboard life was a completely new experience for Tex. Aboard the *Saratoga*, as on all naval vessels, space was at a premium, and all rooms were small. Tex was amazed that such a mass of humanity could eat, sleep, and work in such cramped quarters; but navies had been making a science of this over the course of many centuries. By contrast, when an aviator and his plane catapulted off the flight deck and lifted skyward, there was as much room as he wanted.

Tex was assigned to Torpedo Squadron Three (VT-3), whose operations consisted of torpedo dropping, horizontal bombing, and gunnery. The aviators of VT-3 flew the Douglas TBD-1, a vastly different aircraft from anything Tex had handled in flight training. Put into service only the year before, the *Devastator* could barely reach 200 mph or 20,000 feet altitude; but slung beneath its belly, the one-ton gyro-controlled "fish," as its torpedo was called, spelled bad news for targeted enemy ships. While Tex was looking the aircraft over closely for the first time on the *Sara's* deck, a friendly-looking ensign approached, and introduced himself as Bob Dosé.

"I guess I was at Pensacola a few classes before you," the man said, clasping Tex's hand. "Good to have you aboard."

"Yeah, thanks. This is some outfit you've got here," replied Tex, indicating the huge carrier. "What are you in?"

"Torpedo Three, same as you. Matter of fact, you're supposed to get your orientation ride from yours truly—starting now. Ready? Okay, here's the deal..." Dosé went straight into instruction, walking Tex through an inspection of the torpedo bomber. Tex was even more "all ears" than usual.

A crew of three normally operated the aircraft: an officer pilot, an enlisted Aviation Pilot (AP), and an enlisted radio operator. The TBD could carry a load of conventional bombs as easily as torpedoes. During regular bombing—called "horizontal bombing" in the Navy, to distinguish it from dive-bombing—the AP would climb down into a lowered section of the plane's belly, aim through the bomb sight, and release at the right moment. On torpedo runs, though, the pilot did everything, and performed all navigation duties regardless of the mission. The TBD was an early, rather ungainly example of a multi-role aircraft.

Dosé spent some time going over the aircraft's "specs" with Tex, then gestured to the cockpit and said the words Tex was waiting for: "Let's fly her. After you, Tex."

Once they were in the air, out of sight of the carrier, the older ensign began a series of loops and rolls to show Tex the performance range of the plane. Tex had to chuckle.

"Man, I'll tell you what—we would have washed out at Pensacola doing this kind of stuff," he said.

"Yeah, I was there, remember?" Dosé replied, grinning. "But it's a new ball game out here in the fleet. If the plane can handle it, you've got to know how to do it. You can't snap-roll or anything real fancy in this, by the way."

In the weeks that followed, Tex settled gradually into the routine of shipboard life. He fine-tuned his skills at operating the TBD, learning the airframe and its capabilities inside and out. Sailors in the Pacific Fleet were increasingly alert, as they looked westward toward expansionist Japan. Fleet aviators honed their combat skills through competition, which took place at all levels: between aviators, squadrons, air groups, and even carriers. Day after day, the air group drilled in the tactics they would use if called upon: dive-bombing, gunnery, torpedo drops, and pursuit. Everyone strove fiercely for the coveted letter "E's" that were awarded for excellence in a particular skill area. More than anything else, the E's marked the Navy's standout performers. Once earned, E's decorated the sides of aircraft and even the carriers themselves. Tex would eventually accumulate three of them—for gunnery, torpedo dropping, and horizontal bombing.

Long before he received a single "E," however, Tex had other lessons to learn. The first few dozen flights he made in Torpedo Three were called "bounce drills." For these, the runway at North Island was marked off to resemble the deck of the *Saratoga*, complete with a landing signal officer to direct aviators during final touchdown. For his first few flights, Tex rode as a passenger in the back seat, observing the tricky operation. Then he began to practice touch-and-gos, and soon landed the TBD himself. Eventually, the day came when he had to put the aircraft down on the deck of the real *Saratoga*.

Landing a plane on the deck of an aircraft carrier was (and still is), hands-down, one of the most difficult feats anyone attempts on a regular basis. It sounds easy: put the plane down on the deck; catch one of the dozen or so arresting gear (metal cables) strung across the deck with a hook protruding from beneath the plane's tail; and let the cable's tension drag the aircraft to a stop. But the carrier's motion in water made the deck gyrate constantly, and in rough seas her rolling was even more pronounced. Landing the plane without destroying it, therefore, was a feat comparable to spoon-feeding a two-year-old on a trampoline. Worse still, if the aircraft's tail hook missed all the deck cables, the only remaining "safety net" was neither safe nor a net at all: a reinforced barrier at the end of the deck. It would halt anything—in a pile of twisted metal. To call a carrier landing "a daunting task" understated the case.

When Tex descended for his first landing on the *Sara's* deck, everything went fine—until touchdown. The hook beneath his aircraft half-caught the cable-but didn't hold, causing the TBD to skid violently to the left. It was the worst possible situation: the edge of the deck rushed toward him, and he would never be able to climb the aircraft out to come around again. In a second, he realized that he was probably going over the edge. The TBD crashed along the rough side of the deck, snapping cables and demolishing pieces of the superstructure. The nose dipped, the plane dropped, and...nothing. In an eerie silence, Tex opened his eyes—and saw that his aircraft had miraculously dropped partway into one of the *Sara's* gun galleries, set several feet below the level of the deck. His TBD was hanging halfway out into open space, caught and held by metal and cable. Out the left side of his canopy, Tex had a marvelous view of the blue Pacific.

Rarely in aviation history was a more careful exit from an aircraft made than the one Tex performed. He crept gingerly back to safety, while the crew on deck gaped and ran for emergency equipment.

Following his inauspicious debut, though, Tex made ninety-nine more carrier landings without mishap.

It did not take him long to learn what all seasoned aviators in the fleet knew: the enlisted APs were the fleet's best pilots. They were carefully screened to gain their positions, with only the best making it through the selection process. Fighting Two, a squadron on the *Sara's* sister carrier *Lexington*, routinely won pursuit competitions hands-down; and that squadron was made up entirely of enlisted pilots. They were outstanding as a rule, and Tex learned much from Torpedo Three's APs. Several of them would turn up later in China, as members of the American Volunteer Group; and Tex would be only too glad to fight alongside them.

Torpedo bombing was, in a manner of speaking, an exact science. The cantankerous "fish" had a stubborn tendency to do whatever the pilot *didn't* want them to. They were often erratic, sometimes comically so. A torpedo bomber pilot had to fly right on the deck toward his target, maintaining the bomber's speed and altitude within minute tolerances. At the precise moment, he would release the "fish," which free-fell into the water and—if the stars were aligned favorably—self-activated its engine, churning toward a fiery rendezvous with the target surface vessel.

Tex had a few harrowing incidents plying this trade. Taking off from the *Sara* one morning near North Island, he proceeded to turn in his usual good performance on a torpedo run. When the moment to drop came, Tex hit the switch—and nothing happened. His skin crawled as he instantly recognized the symptoms of a "hung up" torpedo, one of the TBD's most hazardous situations. The danger lay in the unknown status of the torpedo. It might be "dead," or hanging by one clip, or armed and counting down to detonation at any second. Tex was piloting a flying bomb.

The regulations were clear about one thing: pilots absolutely did not return to the carrier with a "hung" torpedo, for obvious reasons. Tex banked toward North Island's runway in a cold sweat. Still the torpedo did not detonate. After some minutes, he began to believe his chances of escaping alive were increasing from "slim" to "lean." He radioed his situation to the tower at North Island. Controllers cleared the runway, and fire crews stood by. Tex saw them as he made his approach, fervently hoping that their morning wouldn't get any more exciting. He made his all-time softest landing—and high-tailed it off the flight line.

The morale aboard any ship depends greatly upon her captain; and the *Saratoga's* skipper was very popular with her crew. When morale is high, performance usually follows, and the *Sara's* crew conducted itself well in the ongoing fleet competitions. Tex got to know many of his shipmates well, in Torpedo Three and elsewhere among the crew of several thousand. The other squadrons in the air group aboard the *Sara* included Fighting Three, Scouting Three, and Bombing Three. Some of Tex's friends in those squadrons would surface again down the long road to China—men like Bob Neale, Charlie Mott, Percy Bartelt, Lynn Hurst, and John Overley. For the present, though, they basked in the satisfaction of knowing they were important parts of one *very* large, powerful, floating weapon system.

The U.S. Navy historically exercised its fleets within the framework of a series of "Fleet Problems." These were large-scale, live rehearsals involving many ships and aircraft. "Friendly" and "enemy" surface and air groups would maneuver for simulated strikes, invasions, or other operations that higher headquarters directed. The primary mission of the Hawaiian Detachment of the Pacific Fleet, to which the *Sara* was assigned, was in fact specifically to conduct Fleet Problems. Over time, settings for the exercises had included Hawaii, Manila, the Panama Canal, and other areas of strategic importance. During Fleet Problem XIX, held several years before Tex came aboard, the *Sara* had been the centerpiece for a particularly interesting exercise: she launched a surprise air attack on Oahu, from some 100 miles west of the island. The Japanese Navy had studied this with great interest.

Five months into Tex's tour on the *Sara*, excitement began to build among the crew. Fleet Problem XXI was coming up, to be held that year in the vicinity of Hawaii. The annual exercise was always an opportunity for the *Sara* to shine; as the Pacific Fleet's first "fast" carrier, she had set the tone for Fleet Problems for several years, much as the queen commands the chessboard. The scenario for that year's Problem involved a large "enemy" fleet approaching from the western Pacific to strike at Guam, Wake Island, and Hawaii. The Navy knew that Japan was the only nation capable of really amassing such a force; and they made no secret of the fact that they intended to rehearse exactly that scenario. Three months were allotted for the exercise. On the first of April, the *Saratoga* arrived off Hawaii, and the "games" began.

It was high competition, and Tex enjoyed every minute of it. Torpedo Three's crews carried out simulated torpedo runs against "enemy" ships with practiced deadliness, and the squadron gave a good account of itself. Best of all, after "fighting" hard during the week, the air group would put in at Oahu for the weekend. There, the weary aviators could enjoy the idyllic island paradise for forty-eight hours, before heading out to sea once more. Even news that German armies had invaded the Low Countries, which they received one month into the Problem, did not spoil their enjoyment of the warm Pacific and the beautiful Hawaiian Islands.

Fleet Problem XXI concluded near the end of June; and the *Saratoga* reluctantly cruised northeast once more, toward her familiar patrol area around San Diego and San Pedro. The exercise was supposed to have convinced the Japanese that the U.S. Navy was ready for any aggression Japan might be contemplating. The Japanese understood that objective, but were not impressed. Their ambitious doctrine assumed no nation could withstand the inexorable military might of the Imperial Japanese Navy. At the right time and place, their admirals assured each other, a decisive blow could be struck. Only one Admiral of the Empire's inner circle shook his head in disagreement with the opinion of the majority. His name was Isoroku Yamamoto.

* * *

As the Saratoga *returned to San Diego from the Fleet Problem, Japan was expanding her terror bombing campaign to include every major city in free China. Clouds of bombers unloaded millions of tons of incendiaries onto the helpless civilian population. Wooden and bamboo houses burned by the thousands like tinder. Over Chungking alone, one hundred fifty bombers were overhead every day. Tragically, much of the shrapnel inside Japanese demolition bombs came straight from American scrap iron shipments, until an embargo in September ended that supply.*

With his flying school students killed by bombs and his aircraft destroyed as fast as he could procure them, Chennault had little success mustering aerial resistance to the Japanese. Instead, he took many pictures and made copious notes on the technical specifications and capabilities of the Japanese Zero, *which was making mincemeat of anything it encountered. Chennault wanted to ensure that America, at least, would not be caught flat-footed by the nimble little fighter when the time came. He would be disappointed.*

Desperate to stop the murderous fire-bombings throughout his country, Chiang Kai-Shek ordered Chennault to return to the United States in October to plead for American assistance. Skeptical, but willing to try, Chennault made the trip to Washington, D.C.

with General Mow Pang-Tsu. Once in the capital, Chennault first delivered his painstakingly gathered material on the Zero to the War Department. After looking it over, Army Air Corps engineers acidly informed Chennault that the performance specs he had recorded were impossible—such a plane could not exist. The photographs, they deemed, were fakes. His reports went into the wastebasket.

In the basement of China Defense Supplies headquarters in Washington, D.C., Chennault spent a cold and frustrating winter formulating and lobbying a plan to get an air force for China.

Tex's Douglas TBD-1 Devastator, *on the runway at Naval Air Station North Island. Note the "E" on the fuselage for excellence.*

Navy Torpedo Squadron Three (VT-3) aboard the Saratoga. *Tex is top row, 3rd from left.*

Chapter 7

RANGER

In the late fall of 1939, the U.S. Navy had something of a revelation regarding horizontal bombing. The conventional method called for each aircraft's bombardier to individually perform accuracy calculations, aim, and release. If six planes made a bombing run, six bombardiers were calculating furiously—and there were six chances for a miss. The new theory was that if a single bomber took the lead, equipped with a state-of-the-art bombsight, the trailing bombers—echeloned in a "V" behind it—could drop in turn on a visual cue. If it worked, the Navy could remove heavy and expensive bombsight equipment from all but the lead TBD. The catch, of course, was that the lead bombardier had to be right on target; otherwise, everyone would miss.

The Navy was determined to test the concept, and selected six TBD crews from the *Saratoga* to do it. Tex was one of the pilots. The group was to transfer to the East Coast and go aboard the U.S.S. *Ranger*. From there, they would fly lead aircraft in bombing sorties, cueing their wingmen to drop successfully. As usual, Tex was excited about the prospect of something new; he shook the hands of his comrades in Torpedo Three and wished them luck. Within eighteen months, many of the men he left behind would be fighting and dying in the Pacific skies near an island called Midway.

The *Ranger*, designation CV-4, was the first vessel ever "laid down" in an American shipyard as an aircraft carrier. Earlier carriers had all been converted from other ship types, like battle cruisers. The *Ranger* was smaller than the *Sara*, displacing less than half the tonnage; but she carried nearly as many airplanes and crew. Her primary mission was Neutrality Patrol operations, which brought Tex much closer to the European war than on the *Saratoga*. The *Ranger's* mode of operation was to link up with a merchant convoy out of Bermuda and escort it all the way to the Azores, sailing ahead of the commercial ships in a pattern of expanding curves, scouting for belligerent vessels—especially German submarines.

Tex and his companions from the *Sara* ran into problems before they ever saw the *Ranger*. The TBDs they were supposed to pick up at Norfolk and land aboard her were not exactly ready for combat. They had been sitting outdoors without any maintenance for a long while, neglected, and grass was literally growing from dirt in the cockpits. The aviators looked at one another in disgust, wondering what they were supposed to do.

What they did was go aboard the *Ranger* as ordered, even without the TBDs. The Navy never tried the new horizontal-bombing concept for which Tex was transferred; war overtook the United States before there was time to attempt it. Tex and company found the *Ranger* just completing her overhaul at Norfolk's shipyard, preparing to depart for Guantanamo Bay, Cuba—known as "Gitmo" to the sailors—to begin another Neutrality Patrol. There was no going back to the Pacific Fleet. But Tex's spirits lifted immediately when he checked into the barracks on New Year's Eve: there was Ed Rector, an old schoolmate from Pensacola. The two hit it off immediately, and their friendship would be a warm and permanent one.

Handsome and athletic, Edward Rector was a young North Carolina gentleman who typified the sons of the Old South. He was soft-spoken and generous, with a passion for reading and a quick wit. A standout on the gridiron, Rector had turned down a college football scholarship to join the Navy; but he still gave an outstanding account of himself in a number of sports at Pensacola. He was fiercely competitive, and just as fiercely loyal. Rector would open and close the chapter of American air combat in China in the Second World War. He would score the Flying Tigers' first aerial victory over Kunming; and, more than three years later, he would record the last in a long list of 23rd Fighter Group air-to-air kills. From the time of their meeting aboard the *Ranger*, Tex and Rector were nearly inseparable.

Rounding out the trio of Pensacola alumni was Allen "Bert" Christman, a quiet and introspective Coloradan. Christman was a talented artist with a knack for capturing real-world likenesses in cartoons. His skills had caught the attention of Milton Caniff, creator of the famous strip *Terry and the Pirates*. Caniff had hired Christman as a part-time art assistant. Meanwhile, Christman had his own strip—titled *"Scorchy" Smith*—that appeared in a number of newspapers during his tour on the *Ranger*. Christman also kept a sketchbook diary called *Logan's Log*, in which he drew an event or scene from each day's activities. When he wasn't drawing, Christman could usually be found with Ed Rector and Tex.

All three of them were assigned to Bombing Squadron Four (VB-4). As the *Ranger* steamed toward Cuba, Rector explained that Tex would have to "check out" in the SB2U *Vindicator*.

"Damn the torpedoes," Ed quipped with a smile. "You're in dive bombing country now, Tex."

The SB2U was a very different aircraft from the TBD, designed for an entirely separate mission. In horizontal bombing, a bombardier achieved accuracy with meticulous calculation and careful manipulation of the bombsight. Dive-bombing, as the name implied, called for a more aggressive approach: the pilot "bent it over" into a seventy-degree plunge straight toward his target, nearly ramming the ordnance home before peeling away. Although it involved precision, dive-bombing was much more forgiving than torpedo operations; and Tex liked it a good deal better. Unlike the clumsy TBD, the SB2U was an agile aircraft with considerably more speed, ceiling, and range, and its pilot could quickly maneuver into position for a dive-bombing run. Perhaps, Tex reflected, finding the TBDs at Norfolk filled with grass hadn't been so unfortunate.

After Tex checked out in the SB2U at Guantanamo, the *Ranger* conducted minor exercises in the Caribbean before beginning her convoy escort duties. During these drills, Tex was assigned his first mission with the squadron. He took his place as "Junior Birdman," last in a formation of dive-bombers, with anticipation. On the target run, eager to make a good impression, Tex peeled off and delivered his bomb accurately—only to look around and discover that his flight was nowhere in sight. While he'd been concentrating on the target, they had left the area without him.

He was only lost for a minute; his navigation skills soon led him back to the *Ranger*. But his troubles were just beginning. Bombing Four's squadron leader, Lieutenant Commander "Pinky" Hopkins, was waiting for him, a sour expression on his face. Hopkins was considered a less-than-outstanding aviator—a rarity for his position, since Navy squadron commanders usually set the piloting standard for their men to follow. Hopkins knew he was merely an average pilot, and carried something of a chip on his shoulder as a result.

"Well, Ensign Hill, I'm not sure what that performance was called!" Hopkins blustered angrily. "You want to tell me what happened up there?"

"Sir, I guess I got disoriented on my target run, and lost the other guys. It won't happen again."

"Damn right it won't, because you're with me from now on. I don't know what kind of 'flying' they do on the *Saratoga*; but here in the Atlantic Fleet, we stay with our element leaders. It's a pretty basic concept. Think you can manage it?" asked Hopkins sarcastically.

"I believe I can, sir," Tex replied, keeping his voice calm despite his rising temper at his commander's words.

"Outstanding!" Hopkins snapped. "You can start by flying on my wing from now on. Stay on it—or there'll be hell to pay!"

Hopkins stomped off. Tex fumed. He tried to think of a way to make the squadron commander regret his tirade, without overstepping the bounds of propriety or professionalism.

He began with his formation flying with Hopkins. If the skipper wanted it tight, he would get it tight! Tex "glued" himself to Hopkins' plane, nearly sticking his wing into the man's ear during flight. When Hopkins would ease away, nervous, Tex would sidle right back up close again. The ongoing antics were comic. The commander eventually became so jittery with Tex's aircraft constantly looming outside his cockpit, he moved the ensign back to his old flight. Meanwhile, Tex also concentrated on honing his skills, wanting to show Hopkins up; and he began to acquire "E's" for excellence in several areas. He knew that "Pinky" Hopkins had never been able to earn an "E." In spite of Tex's vengeful motives, he was doing an excellent job in the squadron.

Within a couple of months, Hopkins' tour ended anyway; and his replacement was an entirely different breed of cat. Commander Bill Harris, an accomplished flyer, came aboard. He immediately established a level of rapport with his men that few skippers can manage. The configuration of the air group was changing as well. VB-4 had just been split into two Scouting squadrons, VS-41 and VS-42. Tex, Ed Rector, and Bert Christman learned with satisfaction that they would remain together, under Harris, in Scouting Forty-One.

The United States was not at war with Germany in the spring of 1940, and U.S. Navy convoy escort missions proved to be politically tricky undertakings. Adolf Hitler, deeming that the time was not ripe, had ordered his *Kriegsmarine* officers not to attack United States vessels. But the U.S. did not know about the order, and the Navy maintained the Atlantic Fleet on a wartime footing during Neutrality Patrol operations. If they sighted Axis vessels, the Americans reported them—to the British Royal Navy, who would prosecute the enemy. American-German relations were icy and worsening, and the *Ranger's* skipper was not foolish. He kept twelve SB2U *Vindicators* on deck alert, armed and ready to launch at any time.

At length, the *Ranger* steamed out of Bermuda with her convoy, commencing reconnaissance for German U-boats. She completed several escort missions to the Azores and back, sweeping out in widening curves ahead of the convoys, while Tex and the aviators of Scouting Forty-One searched the dark Atlantic waters for activity. Tex began to feel at home in the SB2U, and "rolled up" some five hundred hours in the aircraft hunting for submarines. The familiar spirit of competition that typified Navy units was alive and well on the *Ranger*; each day, the crew drilled in their missions to stay sharp and earn bragging rights over the next aviator, squadron, or carrier.

A British task force was at sea nearby as well, prepared to conduct an attack if enemies should be sighted. The ships of the Royal Navy, in fact, were the primary convoy escorts; the U.S. Navy simply augmented British forces, the better to locate the enemy. The *Ranger* worked closely with the Royal Navy carrier HMS *Eagle* and the heavy cruiser *Diomedes*. A light cruiser and five destroyers rounded out the British task force. The arrangement was simple: if the *Ranger* sighted something, she would radio the British "in the clear," forgoing coded communications to save precious time.

The Americans did have sightings. Flying a patrol one day, Tex spotted two German submarines and a submarine tender on the surface. His flight immediately called these out in the clear. Both the *Ranger* and the British task force heard it. As the Royal Navy closed in, the *Ranger* continued on a search curve that took her away from the enemy vessels, and Tex did not see the ensuing attack. But when the *Ranger* made her return sweep, Tex saw the results. As the cruiser *Diomedes* steamed away, debris littered the ocean, and large oil slicks were evident. The British had made short work of the tender, and dropped depth charges to destroy the fleeing submarines. For the Americans, still technically neutral, it was an eye-opening experience.

On a later escort, Tex and his patrol flight spotted the Spanish registry vessel *San Adolfo*. Spain was Germany's ally, and the Allies knew Spanish ships were providing fuel from Spanish Guinea to German submarines, enabling the U-Boats to operate in the Caribbean Sea. Once again, the *Ranger* notified the British; but Tex and his shipmates had to wait until their return from the Azores to learn the fate of the *San Adolfo*. When they steamed into the harbor in Bermuda, there she was—impounded. The British task force had captured her.

Every sailor on the *Ranger*, Tex included, agreed that the most enjoyable part of Neutrality Patrol was the shore leave they spent on the British colony of Bermuda. Although the island was on a wartime footing and stayed blacked out at night, there were still plenty of opportunities to enjoy its people and sights. At the conclusion of one patrol, when the *Ranger* had dropped anchor in the harbor of Grassy Bay, Tex and shipmate Pete Wright went eagerly ashore with passes in their pockets. An hour's train ride into the capital of Hamilton found them sipping refreshments in the *Ace of Spades* and chatting with the bartender. Wright began to "move in" on a pretty, dark-haired French *mademoiselle* he had spotted.

"There's a dance tonight, fellows, over at a hotel around the other side of the bay," the bartender informed them. "You guys ought to go."

"Yeah...what kind of a dance is that?" Tex asked languidly. He eyed Wright, considering whether to try and "cut him out of the pattern" with the French girl.

The bartender leaned over conspiratorially, putting his elbows on the bar. "A dance hosted by the four hundred young ladies who censor the mail that goes in and out of the island," he replied, smiling.

Hours later, Tex stepped out the door of the *Ace of Spades* with the French girl on his arm. He signaled to one of the native horse-and-buggy drivers waiting nearby, who was smartly dressed and sported a top hat. The pair climbed aboard the buggy, talking and laughing, and proceeded happily along the waterfront to the *clop-clop* of horses' hooves. It was a fine night, and romance was in the air.

After a mile or so, Tex realized that the effects of consuming so much refreshment were moving to their inevitable conclusion: the "call of nature" was becoming rather loud. He signaled the buggy driver to stop, disembarked, and walked unsteadily toward the hip-high stone wall at the edge of the raised harbor road. He peered about in the darkness for some foliage that might serve his purpose. *There!* He spotted some likely-looking bushes, and confidently vaulted over the barrier to take care of business.

Never in Tex's life was he more surprised than when he went over the wall. What he had seen on the other side were not bushes, but the topmost leaves of trees. Too shocked even to yell, the flailing Tex commenced a painful thirty-foot descent to the sand below, crashing through snapping twigs and branches. In seconds, it was over. He lay in a stunned heap, staring up at the stars, feeling as though he'd been beaten half to death. He thought of sitting up, but groaned at the prospect and lay still. No part of him felt damaged beyond repair. He thought he could hear the distant *clop-clop* of hooves fading into the night...and in another minute, he was unconscious.

It was very dark when he came to, and he had no idea what time it was. After scrambling about to get his bearings, he made his way painfully back to the harbor road, and headed directly for the dock. Fortunately, the *Ranger's* captain's gig was moored there, preparing to depart—the last boat returning to the carrier that night. Feeling considerably worse for the wear, Tex went aboard just in time.

The following morning, Rector and Christman had plenty of laughs at Tex's expense.

When the *Ranger's* quota of escort missions across the Atlantic was fulfilled, she set her course back to Norfolk for maintenance. Standing on the deck with his friends in the warm Caribbean spring, Tex looked forward to setting foot on American soil once more. The three of them had no idea that their shore time in Norfolk would include a meeting that would change their lives.

* * *

While Tex sailed for Guantanamo Bay as Bombing Four's newest member, Claire Chennault and Harvard-educated T.V. Soong—former governor of the Central Bank of China—presented their plan for a Chinese air force to the Presidential Liaison Committee. The plan called for 500 pursuit planes, 150 trainers, and 10 transports to form the backbone of the force. Chennault was denied all of it; however, through the efforts of men like Joe Alsop, Lauchlin Currie, and Tommy "the Cork" Corcoran, President Roosevelt was convinced that some measure was necessary to keep China from falling to Japan. China no longer had an air force; and if Japanese terror bombings were not stopped soon, Chinese resistance would collapse. Two days before Christmas, 1940, Roosevelt signed a secret executive order authorizing one hundred planes and three hundred men to go to China and oppose the Japanese.

The military's top "brass" was furious, for they knew where the men and equipment would have to come from. At one juncture, Chennault stood toe-to-toe with General Henry "Hap" Arnold, Chief of the Army Air Corps, and requested one hundred Army pilots with five hundred hours of pursuit experience.

"If I gave you that many men with that kind of flying time," Arnold growled, "it would fold up my entire pursuit section!"

"General," snapped Chennault, "if you can't spare a hundred men with that kind of experience, you haven't got a pursuit section to begin with!"

Such forthrightness did not often endear Chennault to his superiors. The Presidential order stood, but it was obvious that Chennault and his recruiting staff would have difficulty prying their air force from the grasp of the Army and Navy.

In China, by the end of the year, the Zero had racked up an amazing 111 Chinese aircraft destroyed in the air and on the ground—with no losses. The Chinese simply had nothing capable enough to fight it. 1940 ended bitterly, with the Japanese controlling two-thirds of China's land area and bombing the remainder into rubble. If drastic help did not arrive soon, it would be too late.

Tex and "Swede" Vejtesa in Pensacola during Naval Flight Flight Training, 1939. (Vejtesa was one of the Navy's finest aviators.)

Chapter 8

THE STORM GATHERS

The flight of three SB2Us touched down neatly; but not on the battleship-gray deck of an aircraft carrier. Instead, they were returning to the runway at Norfolk after an early morning flight. Tex Hill, Ed Rector, and Bert Christman, together as usual, climbed from their cockpits and into a temperate Virginia morning.

"What do you think, Tex?" Ed queried him, as they headed for the operations building. "Landing on the ground just isn't the same. Too easy, wouldn't you say?"

"Well," Tex replied, "at least it's a landing. It sure beats the alternative."

They walked through the door into the squadron operations office to see Gus Widhelm, Scouting Forty-One's operations officer, talking to a man they didn't recognize. Widhelm turned toward the new arrivals.

"Hey, here's some guys that'll go with you," he said to his companion, who wore the silver oak leaves of a Navy commander. "Fellows, meet Commander Irvine." Widhelm gave their names to the senior man.

Tex shook Irvine's hand. "Good to meet you," he said, then looked at Widhelm, puzzled. "Go where?"

Irvine answered by diving into a subject he had obviously discussed many times. Unbeknownst to the three aviators, he was a recruiter for Claire Chennault. President Roosevelt's secret executive order authorized military pilots and ground crew members to resign their commissions and serve in the new American Volunteer Group. This prompted Chennault to send a team of picked recruiters to every major Army Air Corps base and Naval Air Station in the country. They were talking it up with the pilots and ground crews, trying to generate interest in going to China, in protecting her thin supply lifeline and opposing the Japanese. Irvine was doing just that, and the subject was difficult to approach gently.

"Boys, I'll tell you why I'm here," he said crisply. "On behalf of the President, we're looking for pilots who are interested in going to Burma—interested in joining an American Volunteer Group, to keep the only remaining supply line into China open."

There was a brief silence as the men digested this.

"Where in the hell is Burma?" asked Tex.

Ed Rector chuckled. "You can do better than that, Tex. It's Kipling country, the Far East. Have you missed out on my talented recital of *The Road to Mandalay*?"

Tex was suddenly interested, thinking of his Korean birthplace, which he could not remember. Ever since his father had told him stories of that remote oriental country, he had harbored a desire to return and see that part of the world. The Navy, he knew, provided one of the most likely ways to get there. Recently, he had even submitted a request for transfer to the U.S.S. *Houston*, a heavy cruiser on patrol in the western Pacific. Tex wondered what was really going on here. Commander Irvine unrolled a large map on the counter.

"You're correct, Mr. Rector," Irvine said, pointing to the map. "Gentlemen, this is Burma here, between China and India. With the Japanese blockade of China, there are only two ways for the Chinese to get supplies. One is by flying them across the Himalayas."

He indicated the world's highest mountain range on the map.

"Sounds like a difficult prospect," commented Rector.

"To say the least, yes. The other route is by land, up the Burma Road."

His finger moved to a large city on the coast. "This is Rangoon, where our lend-lease supplies are offloaded. Then they move north by train to Toungoo, passing these towns..."

Irvine began to point out places with exotic-sounding names like Magwe, Heho, Myitkyina, and Mandalay.

"From Toungoo, here, everything is loaded onto trucks and driven the whole seven hundred miles..." he traced a long line across the border from Burma into China, "to Kunming. We're looking for pilots to patrol the air over the Burma Road, and keep it open to traffic."

Christman frowned. "Keep it open? Do the Japanese go after those supplies? That's a long way from Japan."

"They haven't attacked the route itself yet, but the distance isn't a problem. They're already bombing Kunming almost every day. There are airbases throughout Indochina, here; and if the Japs were to take over that country, they could use those bases to start hitting Rangoon with bombers—as soon as they feel ready to declare war on the British. We think," he added, in a lower voice, looking carefully at the men, "that time may not be far away."

The friends exchanged looks. This fit with the intelligence they had seen. For some time, the Navy had been observing signs of growing Japanese maritime strength, and they believed that open war with Japan was only a matter of time.

Irvine continued, "You'd be flying fighters there, so ideally, we're looking for pilots with fighter time. But the AVG needs to get moving, so we're accepting volunteers from other types of aircraft now."

Tex reflected that the only fighter experience he had was flying the F4B4s in training at Pensacola.

"All right," said Tex, "how is this deal supposed to happen? I mean, we're not at war with Japan yet or anything."

Irvine looked him in the eye. "No," he said, "and the United States will remain neutral for the present. This is a secret arrangement, and must be kept confidential. Volunteers will have to resign their commissions and operate as employees of CAMCO—that's the Central Aircraft Manufacturing Company. The Chinese government would pay your salaries through that agency. It's a civilian outfit, and their charter is to maintain and test-fly the planes. At least, that's what the contract will say," he said slowly, with a significant look. "What you'll really do, if necessary, is keep the Japs away from that road."

Everyone was silent for a moment.

"Mercenaries," said Ed Rector with a wry smile. He looked at Tex. "Sounds rather exciting, doesn't it?"

Several other men walked into the room, and Commander Irvine deftly began rolling up the map. "I'd like to know if you're interested, so I can begin making the necessary contractual arrangements with CAMCO. Either way, I'll need you to keep our conversation to yourselves, for security reasons. We can't recruit regular officers," he continued, and then paused again. "Married men aren't eligible either, I'm afraid...with the risk involved."

"Well, I'm interested," said Tex, while Rector and Christman nodded agreement. "I don't know what the skipper's reaction would be, though."

"I understand, but it's going to happen anyway," Irvine replied. "Volunteers will be released from the service; that direction comes from the top. I'll be in touch with you again soon."

Tex assumed he would go aboard the *Ranger* again before long to resume Neutrality Patrol, but things turned out somewhat differently. By late spring, German U-boats were taking a heavy toll on Allied merchant shipping in the Atlantic; and the United States decided to strengthen the fleet's presence there. The carrier *Yorktown*, among other vessels, transited the Panama Canal from the Pacific and arrived in Bermuda. For the *Yorktown's* first Atlantic cruise, Tex's air group from the *Ranger* was to go aboard her.

The procedure for unit rotations in the Navy was unlike the other services. Now steaming in the Caribbean, Tex's entire air group picked up and went aboard their sister carrier without so much as a twitch, making the transition on the open sea. Since an air group functioned as a self-contained unit, it was much more effective to move the whole group than to pick out squadrons or pilots. By keeping the group together, their procedures and familiarity could remain intact; *esprit de corps* and morale were high; and mission performance was good. Tex's own crew chief, in fact, had been in the air group for seventeen years, repeatedly refusing any promotion that would move him out of it. It was a smart way for a unit to operate; the results proved it. At the conclusion of the patrol, they would relocate back to the *Ranger*.

As the *Yorktown* sailed east toward the Azores, the aviators who had talked to Irvine discussed among themselves the prospect of going to Burma. It was generally agreed that the U.S. would go to war with Japan sooner or later; and joining the AVG might offer a chance to "get in on the ground floor." With all volunteers and some good leadership, they reasoned, even a mercenary group could turn out to be a mighty hot combat unit.

But there were skeptics, too. With hostilities imminent, the Navy was not releasing men from active duty service for any reason whatsoever, predicting that it would need them all. Not knowing about the executive order, the men found it hard to believe that the Navy would simply let them go. As the patrol wore on, many of them discounted the possibility that there could be anything to Commander Irvine's "pitch," and forgot about the matter.

Tex and his friends hoped it was true. Tales of the mysterious Far East stirred Tex's thoughts, and Ed Rector described the wonders of the Orient he'd read about in the works of Rudyard Kipling. Bert Christman figured the adventure could mean a whole new chapter in his sketch diary, *Logan's Log*. In the end, the three of them resolved that, if the deal turned out to be legitimate, they would all go.

A month later, when the patrol ended and the *Yorktown* steamed into Norfolk, the three aviators found Commander Irvine waiting for them. He was as good as his word. At a meeting in one of the city's hotels, he presented contracts to the men from the *Ranger* who had professed an interest in the AVG. The prospective volunteers looked the documents over. The pay was considerably higher than an ensign's salary, even with flight pay. AVG squadron leaders would receive $750 per month, flight leaders $650, and wingmen $600.

"If you're serious about this," said Irvine to the men, "you need to know a couple of other things. First, because the U.S. is not at war, you can understand the sensitive position our government would be in if you were discovered to be in China fighting the Japanese. If that does happen, our national leadership will deny any knowledge of your group's existence or activities."

There was a sobering silence in the room, but everyone understood the sense of this.

"The other item concerns the pay," Irvine continued, and several heads lifted from reading the documents. "The Chinese government has agreed to award a bonus of five hundred dollars for every Japanese plane shot down or destroyed on the ground. That's not in the contract, as you can see; but I've been reliably assured that this is the case."

This last bit of news did not harm Irvine's cause at all, but Tex and several others were less interested in their pay than the adventure and the prospect of combat. As naval aviators, most of them were already making plenty of money for their needs.

"Still," said Rector, "it can't hurt, can it?" No one disagreed.

Eight men from the *Ranger* signed CAMCO contracts that day. Along with Tex, Rector, and Christman, there were ensigns John Armstrong, Noel Bacon, and John Petach from Fighting Four; and Gil Bright and Pete Wright from Scouting Forty-Two. When the men had signed, Irvine collected the documents, and explained that their discharge orders would be coming through shortly. They would gather in San Francisco to set sail for the Far East. As the meeting ended, the commander shook each of their hands.

"Welcome to the American Volunteer Group," he said. "We're sure glad to have you."

The aviators were excited about their forthcoming adventure, but their squadron commanders were not. Bill Harris would be losing three experienced pilots in positions of leadership—in effect, gutting his squadron of its key personnel. Because the AVG recruiters only revealed the true nature of their mission to prospective volunteers, Harris had no idea what it was even about. When he heard that three of his dive-bombing mainstays were to be discharged, he flew to Washington D.C. immediately. Who in the hell had ordered this? In his demands for an explanation, Harris found himself in good company; Rear Admiral Arthur H. Cook, commander of aircraft in the Atlantic Fleet, was also looking into the matter and trying to stop it. The Department of the Navy told both of them that it was a secret, and that their AVG recruits would have to be released. The orders came straight from the top. Harris resigned himself to the situation and returned to Norfolk, calling Tex and the other volunteers into his office.

"Fellows, I hate to lose you, especially when I don't even know what's going on. But whatever it is, it's bigger than me. All I can say is, I hope you're leaving for a damn good reason."

Tex and the others looked somewhat sheepish, wishing they could tell their skipper the truth. After a long pause, Harris continued, "If you've got to go, I'm afraid there's only one thing I can do in this situation." He glared at them...then cracked a sudden smile. "We're going to have to celebrate."

This was typical of Harris' camaraderie with his men, and the party that followed was a memorable one. The men of Scouting Forty-One said good-bye to their comrades, wishing them well wherever they fared. The air group on the *Ranger* held several records in the fleet, and she was considered its most battle-ready carrier. In addition, the Navy was in a period of expansion, and experienced officers were being spread thinly across many new units. Tex and the others would be missed.

It wasn't long before the discharge paperwork came through for the eight pilots. At the time, they believed that when the year-long CAMCO contract was fulfilled, they would rejoin the Navy without any loss of rank, giving up only a year of time in service, as the contract specified. But the momentous events of the following year would make such concerns irrelevant for Tex. He packed his bags and prepared to board the train going west.

* * *

As the ranks of the AVG pilots and ground crew began to fill out, Claire Chennault turned his attention to the aircraft. On behalf of China, he was able to make an arrangement with aircraft manufacturer Curtiss-Wright to secure one hundred P-40B Tomahawk *fighters. The planes had been originally slated to go to the British, who considered them obsolete by that time.*

It was at this juncture that the AVG nearly died stillborn, as CAMCO executive William Pawley entered the picture. Although he had nothing to do with the sale of the P-40s to China, Pawley insisted on his usual generous commission for it—$400,000 in this case. When Curtiss-Wright refused, Pawley threatened to obtain an injunction that would halt the sale altogether, tying up the matter in court indefinitely. Knowing that the AVG's mission depended upon timeliness, a frustrated Secretary of the Treasury Henry Morgenthau finally allowed Pawley to be paid $250,000, and the operation proceeded. Ever after, Pawley claimed to have had a hand in "forming the AVG." The truth was, he came far nearer to squashing it.

On June 5, a Japanese bombing raid on Chungking turned into a massacre, as helpless residents packed themselves into a 7500-foot tunnel beneath the city for protection. After the "all-clear" was given and they began to file out, the alarm sounded suddenly for a second raid. Guards shut the tunnel gates; and in the ensuing panic, some 4,000 Chinese were trampled to death.

That same week, the first AVG volunteers began to assemble in San Francisco. Chennault received word from Washington that the President had authorized a second AVG, consisting of bomber aircraft and crews, to follow in November; and a third, early in 1942. But the course of events would change all that, and the other groups would never make it to China.

Tex's TBD after his first landing attempt on the Saratoga— *at rest in Number Four Gun Gallery.*

Chapter 9

LEAVETAKING

A taxicab stopped in front of a hotel in downtown San Francisco, and Tex Hill got out of it. Although it was late July, he had to peer through afternoon fog to check the name of the place. *There can't be two of 'em*, he thought, and went inside. The Bellview Hotel was the spot designated for AVG recruits to gather before sailing for Burma. Two contingents of them had assembled and departed already: a group of forty ground crew had left on the U.S.S. *President Pierce* in early June, and a mix of 123 pilots and ground crew had sailed aboard the Dutch registry *Jaegersfontein* on July 10th.

The AVG's mission was supposed to be secret; and to prevent Japan from learning of it, the government had issued false passports to the volunteers. Many raised an eyebrow as they noted their supposed profession: "farmer," "student," "trader," or even "vaudeville entertainer." When they were issued the documents, Rector elbowed a chuckling Tex.

"What, may I ask, is so funny?" Rector wanted to know.

"Well, it says I'm a rancher," Tex said, grinning, "from Texas."

But Japanese intelligence was good, and the false passports fooled them not a bit. There had been much embarrassment when the *President Pierce* prepared to depart in June; for just then, Radio Tokyo announced that they knew all about the mission of the "American bandits" going to fight for China. The Japs smugly made a promise to the world: their Imperial Navy would see to it that the AVG ships only reached one destination—the bottom of the Pacific. Nevertheless, both the *President Pierce* and the *Jaegersfontein* had arrived at Rangoon intact, after taking long, circuitous routes south to Australia and then dodging through the Indonesian islands. Tex and his friends looked forward to an interesting trip.

Before long, Rector and Christman joined Tex at the Bellview, and the three companions waited in the lobby for a scheduled meeting with another member of Chennault's staff. During the obligatory liquid refreshment, other volunteers began to trickle in, and Tex was soon making friends left and right. In the brief time they had to compare notes and wonder aloud what their future held, the three friends learned that the others' fighter aircraft experience ranged from substantial to none, and the men had been recruited from a wide array of aviation backgrounds.

At length, Chennault's man summoned the volunteers upstairs for a short administrative briefing. Afterward, the AVG members were left with a couple of days to "burn" in San Francisco before they set sail. That was plenty of time to sample the nightlife in the Golden Gate City—an eye-opening experience for some of them, to say the least. The men that came from small towns, like Tex, or sheltered lives, felt as if their "gyro had tumbled" at a few of the bars and nightclubs; and their more worldly-wise companions found much amusement at their expense.

In the last days of July, Tex and his twenty-four companions went aboard the *Bloemfontein*, another Dutch registry vessel of the Java Pacific Line, which would carry them on the long voyage. After boarding, Tex explored briefly to get a look at her, and concluded that they were in for a very pleasant voyage. The *Bloemfontein* was a comfortable passenger liner that featured relatively large quarters, an elegant dining room, a bar and lounge complete with piano, and even a swimming pool astern on the second deck. The only cause for concern, in the minds of some volunteers, involved the passenger list. Besides the AVG, there were some thirty missionaries aboard, en route to various Far Eastern destinations. Tex, of course, felt completely at home with that development.

The *Bloemfontein* weighed anchor at midday and began a stately cruise out of the harbor. The Golden Gate Bridge and Alcatraz were the last sights etched in Tex's mind as he watched his country's shore recede into the haze. Some of his new friends would never see it again; but no one thought of that. As the open waters of the Pacific welcomed them, everyone pondered loved ones behind—or the lands ahead.

All of the former Navy men, including Tex, emerged on the second day refreshed, following a good night's sleep in quarters much roomier than those aboard an aircraft carrier; and they ventured out to see about breakfast. They were surprised, and somewhat amused, to learn that not all of their companions had fared as well. Those from the Army were violently seasick to a man, having spent a miserable night retching in their rooms. Few now had the fortitude to stagger onto the deck, and those that did spent their time draped over the rail. The sympathetic ex-sailors assured their comrades that it would "most likely" pass within a few days. The ex-soldiers' fears that they would surely perish were chased by fears that they wouldn't—that they might have to endure their green-faced condition, without respite, all the way to Burma. When they finally did find their sea legs, there was great relief all around.

It was going to be a long haul, and everyone had plenty of time to get acquainted. Back at the Bellview, Tex had already met Robert T. Smith and Paul J. Greene, a couple of former Army pilots nicknamed "R.T." and "P.J." respectively. The volunteers ranged in age from youngsters like Rector, with scarcely eighteen months of service time, to venerable radio operator Alex "Mickey" Mihalko, a crusty salt of forty-two years. Most areas of the U.S. were represented, from Matt Kuykendall's San Saba, Texas to Robert "Duke" Hedman's South Dakota—and everywhere between.

Chennault's representative had promised the men that the food and service aboard the ship would be good; and he was right. The Javanese cabin boys were eager to serve, and the dining room produced excellent fare at mealtimes. The men whiled away the long voyage in various ways. There were always takers for games of acey-deucey, poker, craps, backgammon, or bingo. Badminton, quoits, and shuffleboard were available on deck, as was the swimming pool. The ship's library was well-stocked.

More importantly, though, the bar was well-stocked. The volunteers gathered in the lounge in the evenings to drink whiskey and listen to "Duke" Hedman play "rinky-tink" tunes on the piano. The missionaries frowned disapprovingly upon the AVG's boisterous imbibing; and a comic contest ensued. The missionaries retaliated by singing and playing early-morning hymns on the same piano with great gusto, bringing the bleary-eyed volunteers stumbling out of their rooms. In return, the young men produced popular swing records, and played them on the lounge phonograph at top volume. The missionaries could see that here, indeed, was a fertile field for their work; but by the end of the voyage, they had to admit little success.

One morning, just three days out of San Francisco, the ship's daily newspaper proclaimed that Japan had invaded French Indochina. To some of the volunteers, the sun-gilt waters of the Pacific began to seem deceptive. They were steaming toward a war that seemed determined to meet them halfway, and they had no escort or protection.

The following day, the *Bloemfontein* made port in Honolulu, Hawaii, and the men had a chance to go ashore for the night. The next afternoon she was underway again, but now the Pacific conflict began to make itself felt upon the passengers. International relations between the Dutch and Japanese were hostile, though they were not yet at war; and ships of the Java Pacific Line preferred to keep their distance from known Japanese naval patrol areas, to avoid any miniature submarines or surface ships. As the *Bloemfontein* left Honolulu behind, she still lacked the protection of any surface warships; the U.S. heavy cruisers *Northampton* and *Salt Lake City*, which had provided escort for the earlier shiploads of AVG volunteers, were conspicuously absent. Alone on the water, the *Bloemfontein* steamed toward the Coral Sea.

Within four days, her Dutch captain took a second protective measure. He announced to the crew that they were changing course, and would not be sailing almost due west for Manila as planned. He declined to disclose their new destination, but admitted that the trip would lengthen by about a week as a result. Furthermore, a nightly blackout would be in effect on the ship, to lessen the chances of detection by the Japanese. It was sobering news. As the ship turned to a southwesterly course, Tex studied the stars and exercised a little celestial navigation. By his estimate, they were heading for Australia.

After several days' headway on the new course, the AVG men began to talk up a momentous event that was fast approaching. The *Bloemfontein* would be crossing the equator; and by Navy tradition, a first-time crossing was cause for celebration and ceremony in any sailor's career. "Legend" held that King Neptune himself, monarch of the watery depths, would "come aboard" to sanctify seafaring neophytes with certain oceanic rites. Although he was from the Navy, Tex had never crossed the equator, so he was numbered with the uninitiated. Mihalko and the other "hard-shells," already longtime veterans of the King Neptune ceremonies, planned appropriate festivities. On the day of the crossing, activities commenced in spades.

It was a grand afternoon-long party, more than enough to make the missionaries frown in righteous indignation. Tex and his fellow "pollywogs" were seized and held down while members of Neptune's "court" slathered them with a foul-smelling paste of dubious origin. The pollywogs were then forced to drink an equally nauseating liquid brew of some sort. Next, a battle royal ensued as King Neptune—dressed in "finery," but bearing a suspicious resemblance to Mihalko—ordered the unwilling initiates to be cast into the pool. Throughout the proceedings, strong drink flowed freely; and it was a tired, but happy, bunch that finally turned in late that evening on the blacked-out *Bloemfontein*.

The ship picked its way carefully through the Solomon Islands. On the tenth of August, thirteen days at sea from Hawaii, Tex discovered he was correct about their destination. The *Bloemfontein* sighted the eastern Australian coastline, and pulled into Brisbane. It was a welcome stop, even for the seafarers in the group, and Tex went ashore eagerly with his friends to stretch his legs. However, they were surprised and sobered by the city's atmosphere. Australia was at war with Japan, and Brisbane's residents maintained a healthy respect for the Japanese Navy. Stores were closed, and most residents stayed indoors; the few alert-looking people they met were all business.

The AVG men did receive a welcome from the American ambassador, however—a friendly fellow who gave the men a quick run-down on what was going on.

"Boys," he said with a rueful smile, "you wouldn't believe the headaches I've got."

He went on to explain that Australian troops, known as "diggers," were off to war; and the ratio of women to men in the country just then was about five to one.

"A couple of American cruisers came through here, and we couldn't keep the sailors on them. These women just swarm over them—the men figure they've died and gone to heaven. I've never seen more cases of jumping ship in my life. We've been rounding up deserters for weeks!"

It was an amusing "problem," and some of the AVG might have regretted that their stay would only be overnight.

The following day, the *Bloemfontein* weighed anchor again, hugging the Australian coastline as she sailed northwest through the Coral Sea and the Torres Straits. On the eight-day run to Luzon, the principal island in the Philippines, the ship skirted New Guinea to the south, and then threaded through the Dutch East Indies along the Molucca passage. At night on the Banda Sea, phosphorescent microorganisms rose to the surface and turned the ocean into a serene mirror of fire. The men of the AVG didn't know it, but within a year, the lands and waters they passed would all be crushed in the noontide power of the Rising Sun.

On the last day, they steamed past Mindoro and into Manila Bay, passing the tiny rock of Corregidor, which bristled with gun emplacements. To port loomed a dark peninsula, whose name would soon fall bitterly from American lips: Bataan.

Manila, a thriving city of half a million, housed the largest American Naval base west of Hawaii. Although it was much closer to Japan than Brisbane, the Philippines' capital displayed a sharp contrast to the quiet of the Australian port. Swarms of dark-skinned native taxi drivers thronged to the docks, loudly offering their services to travelers. The AVG men could see immediately that rumors of war did nothing to curb the lively activity in the streets. Tex spent a few days exploring with Rector and Christman, fascinated by his first glimpse of the Pacific island nation and its people.

The U.S. Navy based in Manila harbored no illusions about Japanese power, nor about their growing hostility. As the *Bloemfontein* prepared to sail several days later, Naval intelligence officers quietly advised her captain that a southwesterly course through the South China Sea toward Malaya, the most direct route to Rangoon, would put them in great danger of encountering the Japanese. The captain needed little persuasion to plot a safer—though much longer—course due south between Borneo and the Celebes Islands. The ship navigated the Makassar Straits between these two, then turned west toward Java. After four days, she dropped anchor at Batavia, and the group went ashore again.

Batavia was the capital of the Dutch East Indies, as well as the hub of operations for the Java Pacific Line; and the *Bloemfontein*'s crew returned to it with relief. The seafaring Dutch had transformed the one-time village into a major port. Everywhere Tex looked on the shoreline, there were Europeans and natives loading, unloading, resting, swearing, and sweating. In the city interior, crisscrossing, sedate canals were as common—and commonly used—as the sometimes-paved roads. The natives were similar in appearance to the Filipinos, and plied their simple existence with obvious content. Tex, Rector, and Christman decided to spend the few days they had ashore by taking a trip to Bandung, the summer capital of the island; and they had a wonderful time. All too soon it was time to set sail once again; but when the hour arrived to depart, the AVG's head count came up two short.

Estill Durbin and James Dyson had "jumped ship." They were neither the first nor the last AVG recruits to do so; and most of the fellows thought they could guess the reason. An AVG contract provided the only legal way to leave military service as war drew near to the United States, and there were some who took advantage of the offer to do just that. When these men disappeared on the voyage, they knew there would be no court-martial waiting for them—for they were no longer military deserters. Instead, they had merely defaulted on a contract, suffering no more harm than forgoing payment for their trouble. The volunteers who "stayed the course" were not impressed. They didn't think much of their temporary comrades, and such "disappearing acts" did nothing to make them doubt their own decisions.

The *Bloemfontein*'s departure from Batavia was delayed slightly while a cargo of coffee beans was loaded on board—she was a merchant ship, after all. Tex and his companions watched the operation from the rail, fascinated. The diminutive Javanese workers, with supreme balancing skill, hoisted enormous bags of coffee beans onto their backs, trotted nimbly up the gangplank, and dropped them into the hold.

"Those damn bags have got to weigh about twice what the natives do," commented one volunteer.

Earl "Hook" Wagner, an AVG man from Georgia, was still feeling the pleasant effects of a few "farewell to Java" toasts he had indulged in earlier. He frowned, peering hard at the sacks of coffee.

"They ain't that heavy," he muttered.

Suddenly Wagner was off down the passenger ramp, puffing along the dock to where the line of native dockhands was loading like clockwork. Wagner was large and solidly built. He tapped the foreman's shoulder and used gestures to indicate that he wanted to help. The small Javanese shook his head and looked uncomfortable, but "Hook" would not be deterred. Finally, the foreman shrugged, and ordered a couple of workers to load a sack onto Wagner's back.

When the workers let go of the sack of coffee beans, "Hook" Wagner hit the deck, with the sack on top of him. He struggled to his knees, red-faced, straining to stand until he nearly popped a vein. When Wagner looked well on his way to an embolism, the Javanese workers pulled the coffee beans off of him, and he slumped over. The hoots and laughs from his comrades at the side rail of the *Bloemfontein* had him up again in a moment, though, angrily demanding to be given another chance. This time "Hook" stayed upright with the sack of beans; but actually taking a step with it on his back proved beyond his utmost powers. He finally dropped it with a crash and stomped back up the ship's ramp, defeated. Behind him, a Javanese dockworker, about a third of Wagner's size and weight, nonchalantly hoisted the bag and resumed loading.

From Batavia, it was only a few days' travel to Singapore, the vast island trade bastion of the British Empire near the southern tip of the Malay Peninsula. Approaching the city in a deluge of rain, the *Bloemfontein* was met by a pilot ship, sent to guide them on an intricate path through the defensive minefields that were laid in the water. Huge shoreline gun emplacements frowned over the harbor entrance, and inside thronged more vessels than the men could count. When the *Bloemfontein* weighed anchor alongside warships of the Royal Navy, it was the end of the line for her. Passage on to Rangoon would have to be arranged on a different vessel. In the meantime, the men would have a number of days to spend in the city, and they disembarked with excitement. A causeway ran from the island city to the tip of Malaya. As he stepped onto land, Tex did not realize that he was nearly within a stone's throw of the Asian mainland for the first time since his family's missionary days.

The Chinese Consul General was aware of the AVG's arrival, and, with the usual gracious hospitality of his people, requested permission to express his gratitude for their mission: he invited them to dinner. Not knowing quite what to expect, Tex and his companions gathered in a Chinese restaurant at the predetermined hour, filling up several tables. The food began to arrive, and the men lost count of the number of courses as they feasted on a multitude of delicious dishes. Tex couldn't pronounce them, and he found the chopsticks unwieldy; but the food "spoke" for itself, and everyone enjoyed that first evening in the city.

Many of the men were quartered in the famous Raffles Hotel, named for the founder of the British colony a century and a quarter before. As they began to explore the city, the AVG discovered an interesting mix of Britain and the Orient. Chinese coolies towed passengers atop rickshaws in all directions. Pith-helmeted shopkeepers maintained a "stiff upper lip" as they conducted business. Indian merchants promised unheard-of bargains on silver, ivory, and jewelry. Prices were low, for those willing to haggle a bit. Some of the men picked up more souvenirs than others.

All too soon, it was over. Word got around within the group that passage for them had been arranged on the *Penang Trader*, a Chinese registry vessel. As the men went aboard her, some noticed that the captain and the crew's three officers were Norwegian. The remaining crew was a motley gaggle of Orientals, which could admirably have stood in for any pirate crew from an R.L. Stevenson novel. The AVG men also noted sourly that the *Trader* was no *Bloemfontein*; it was much smaller, and lacked most of the comfortable amenities to which they had become accustomed. There was no swimming pool or piano lounge. The dining room was small enough to require eating in shifts. Dirt and corrosion festooned the ship, and Tex reflected that the Navy would never have tolerated such poor upkeep of its vessels. Fortunately, the voyage was only supposed to last five days.

Five days it was, but they passed slowly. The coastal freighter sailed through the Strait of Malacca and up the west side of the Malay Peninsula under blackout. The very first night provided Tex and the others with an unpleasant surprise. When the lights went out at dusk, their cramped cabins were immediately filled with a concerto of *scritching* and *scratching*. Tex sprang out of bed in seconds and bolted to the deck.

"What the hell is that noise?" he asked a passing Norwegian crewmember.

"That?" the man replied, with a heavy accent. "Ah, probably the cockroaches—heh! But do not worry," he continued with a gap-toothed smile, "there are probably only a few thousand in your room—and they only get about this big." He held up a thumb and finger three inches apart.

That was enough for the wide-eyed Tex. He put together a makeshift bed in the moonlight, right on the deck. As he was trying to get comfortable, other volunteers emerged with the same story.

"You too?" one asked Tex.

"Yeah. Man, I got out of the way while I still could."

The other man grunted in agreement, and they were soon asleep in the fresh night air.

Uncomfortable as the AVG men were, there was another group aboard that was worse off. Tex discovered this one night when he awakened to see several Oriental crewmembers huddled around a deck hatch that opened onto the steerage section below. They were talking in low voices. Tex thought he would get up and take a look. Conversation died as he approached, and he had no trouble seeing over the shorter crewmembers. Below, in the pale light of steerage, dozens of dark faces returned his gaze with misery. A smell of unwashed humanity, mingled with opium, wafted out the hatch. Shaken, Tex turned away and went back to his bed on the open deck.

On the fifth day from Singapore, the *Penang Trader* sighted land, and by mid-morning she was approaching the coastal city of Rangoon. At long last, the volunteers were nearing their journey's end. The city of four hundred thousand souls adjoined the wide Irrawaddy River delta; and docks and warehouses dotted the shoreline for some distance upstream. It was mid-September, and the Asian sun beat down upon the glistening Gulf of Martaban. Fifty-three days had passed since Tex had watched San Francisco's Golden Gate Bridge recede into the horizon. He was glad the trip was coming to a close, a sentiment shared by all twenty-three AVG men as they lined the rail to watch the approaching shoreline.

Rangoon: it was an exotic name, conjuring up images of elephants, teakwood, temples, and bamboo. The city itself did not disappoint; Kipling had described it masterfully. The sun glinted off the golden spire of the legendary Shwe Dagon Pagoda that dominated the skyline, the most famous Buddhist shrine in the region. As the *Trader* sidled toward the docks, dozens of "lighters" shot out from the shore and sped toward her. Resembling small rafts, they were piled with chopped fruit, nuts, and other goods, and were piloted by Burmese eager to sell their wares. The natives' cries were a foreign-tongued cacophony to the Americans, who looked on with interest. At that hour, the docks were full with a horde of vessels; and the captain announced that, unless the men fancied a long wait, they should seek passage to shore on a passenger lighter. Tex now noticed that some of the little rafts beside them were empty; and, sure enough, their pilots gesticulated wildly to indicate they would carry passengers—for a small fee.

"Just think of it as a taxi," Ed Rector was telling Tex, who peered at a lighter suspiciously. "I'm sure this gentleman has been plying his trade for years. Why, he probably hasn't dropped more than a few dozen passengers in the drink."

After a very short ride, Tex was safely on the docks, and Rector was paying the smiling Burmese. Two men were waiting for them on shore—and Tex, surprised, recognized one of them. It took him a minute to place the gentleman, but then he had it: he was C.B. "Skip" Adair, one of the Army aviation cadets who had visited the Hill home at 121 East Park Avenue for dates with Tex's sister Martha. Tex remembered with amusement how big and important Adair had seemed at the time, with his sharply creased cadet uniform, Sam Browne belt, helmet, and goggles. Tex walked up and introduced himself; and the two chatted like old friends until the whole group was ashore.

"How is your sister, anyway?" asked Adair casually.

"Married to a Raymond Armstrong," replied Tex, watching Adair's wistful look with further amusement.

Adair had been in China for some years with Claire Chennault. He had trained Chinese pilots at the old school in Hangchow, until the Japanese had obliterated it with bombs—long since. During the AVG recruiting drive, Adair had heavily canvassed Army bases back in the States. Standing beside him now on the Rangoon docks was the Curtiss-Wright representative to China, William Pawley.

"Welcome to Burma, gentlemen," Adair declared, smiling, when everyone had gathered. "This is Bill Pawley, president of the Central Aircraft Manufacturing Company. We're headed to the Strand Hotel, so if you'll follow us, we'll see about getting a bite to eat and your first month's pay." This last part met with murmurs of approval from the volunteers, many of whose cash reserves were running low from "living large" at their many ports of call.

As they traveled further into the city interior, Tex was fascinated by the completely new world around him. The heat was stifling and oppressive, even on the coast. Black-eyed women smoked long, fat cheroots as they whisked by in colorful skirts. Wearing the same garments, the men smiled a welcome through lips stained blood-red from the mildly narcotic *betel* nuts they chewed constantly. Tall, turbaned Indian *sikhs* stalked the storefronts, loudly beckoning the men to gaze on the wonders inside. The newcomers gaped through shop windows at works of jade, ivory, ruby, and the occasional tiger or leopard skin. Sandaled, brown children with jet-black hair darted everywhere; and tantalizing smells wafted from the carts of street food vendors. Horses and bulls clattered by, pulling passengers on the *gharries* that served for taxis.

Once at the Strand Hotel, Tex and the others sipped a potent beverage or two and dined, while Adair filled them in on their schedule. They were to leave Rangoon that very afternoon, traveling north by rail to the AVG's base in the interior of Burma.

Rector was talking excitedly. "It's simply marvelous, Tex—just like the books. It will take some getting used to."

"I'll tell you one thing: I'm already used to the temperature," Tex replied, looking out into the sweltering noon and thinking of summer heat in the Texas hill country.

The pair watched Adair, who was talking to several of the men.

"It's all training at the base for now," he was explaining. "You'll get settled in and meet the others. And you'll get to meet Colonel Chennault," he added, with a smile.

Rector turned to Tex and spoke in a low voice. "How much have you heard about this Colonel Chennault?"

"Not much," Tex replied. "Sure hope he knows how to run this outfit."

* * *

Six ships carrying AVG men eventually completed the long voyage to Rangoon, with the last group arriving in mid-November. The lead element of ground crew members on the President Pierce *had set up a training base for the AVG at Toungoo, Burma. The P-40 aircraft were removed in pieces from their crates on the docks at Rangoon, and then hauled to the nearby British airfield of Mingaladon. There, CAMCO mechanics painstakingly assembled them, and the AVG flew them to Toungoo one by one. By the time Tex landed in Rangoon, less than half of the P-40s had been assembled and delivered.*

Two days before the Penang Trader *left Singapore, the AVG sustained its first fatality. As they tangled in a mock dogfight during training, John "Army" Armstrong and "Gil" Bright—both recruits from the Ranger, like Tex—spiraled upward together, each trying to gain an altitude advantage over the other. At the top of their converging "high scissors" maneuver, neither would yield; and the two P-40s collided. Bright bailed out. Armstrong was killed instantly.*

The S.S. Bloemfontein, *which provided Tex and other volunteers passage to Burma.*

Chapter 10

CHENNAULT

Rangoon's railway station wasn't much to look at; and the locomotive that eventually came wheezing up from the south merited a similar description. As it ground to an emphysemic halt, Tex could just make out fading letters stenciled on the side of its boiler: *Mandalay Express*.

"Mandalay! Tremendous!" exclaimed Ed Rector, as the AVG men loaded their bags. Others looked askance at him, raising eyebrows. Once their meager luggage was stowed, "Skip" Adair piled on board with the AVG in tow; and the train lurched painfully into motion once more.

There were several rail lines leading north from Rangoon, and the *Express* threaded its way out of the city on one of them. The railroad's bed had been built up some meters in height above the surrounding landscape, to keep it dry in flood season. As they moved into the countryside, the exotic panorama continued; beautiful rice paddies, teak plantations, and vivid jungle rolled past. Burmese workers tilled and felled, ignoring the chugging locomotive. Large, menacing-looking insects droned through the passenger car. Tex looked at Rector, who was examining one of the paper *rupees* they had just been paid in.

"Whose picture is on that, Ed?" he asked.

"I have no idea. You'd probably have to ask the natives."

"Yeah, I'll sure do that. Excuse me a minute, I'm gonna make a quick run to the head."

Rector grinned enigmatically. "Well...have fun."

"What are you talking about?"

"You'll see, Tex."

Upon opening the door to the train's "water closet," Tex had to stop and study the arrangement for a minute. At the back of the tiny compartment was a raised platform—really just a piece of wood with a hole cut into it. Forward of that were two smaller wooden pieces, which might have been foot rests. The whole thing looked like a shoeshine stand; and when Tex doubtfully ventured up to peer into the hole, he saw the iron railway track whizzing past beneath. He had to chuckle.

The train made its way shakily along the track, its top speed something less than thirty miles per hour, as dusk fell over the country. There were a number of brief stops in villages along the way. The insects began to get more aggressive, and there was much swinging and swatting as the trip wore on.

One of the men piped up grumpily. "What's the name of this place we're headed to? Kung fu?"

"Toungoo, my friend," said Rector. "It's a good hundred and seventy miles up country. Mr. Adair assures us that we will arrive at nine-thirty sharp."

Darkness was falling, and everyone was ready for the trip to end. At length they saw the flickering lights of oil lamps ahead, and the locomotive's rhythm slowed. Many hours had elapsed; they were pulling into Toungoo at last. With a final lurch, the train "gave up the ghost," and the men disembarked with sighs of relief. It was 9:30 p.m.

Waiting for them on the platform, cheering and whooping a welcome, stood many volunteers that had preceded Tex's group. On an unseen cue, a three-piece Burmese band mightily struck up a blaring, disjointed tune that might have been *The Stars and Stripes Forever*. The newcomers had to laugh; and in another moment, they were shaking hands and being welcomed all around.

The previous group of pilots had been at Toungoo for a month; and, as everyone left the railway station, "war stories" began to emerge about the conditions awaiting them at nearby Kyedaw Airfield. After tossing the luggage into a large truck, all the men crowded into a miscellaneous collection of station wagons, and bumped off down the road on the last eight-mile leg of their journey. When they finally arrived at Kyedaw, the newcomers were bone-weary; but the old hands insisted that they meet the other pilots. As he followed the crowd, Tex was dimly aware of thatched-roof buildings around him in the darkness. They entered what was apparently a primitive mess hall.

A chorus of welcome went up as the new group came through the door. Gathered in the building were some 150 AVG members, waiting up late to welcome their comrades. Drink was flowing freely. Tex shook off his weariness temporarily, as he was welcomed by smiling friends new and old. In the crowd he spotted Gil Bright, Pete Wright, John Petach, and Noel Bacon, all fellow volunteers from the *Ranger*. There were many Pensacola classmates as well: "Bus" Keeton, Jim Howard, Bob Layher, Joe Rosbert, Frank Lawlor, "Pappy" Paxton, and others. Someone was tapping him on the shoulder; turning around, he saw Charlie Mott, Bob Neale, Percy Bartelt, and Lynn "Tex" Hurst, all former shipmates on the *Saratoga*.

"Hey Tex, who let you into this outfit?" Neale joked, as the two shook hands.

It was a happy reunion; and at the moment, the adventure looked to be a grand time. The only shadow on the evening came when his friends told him about the fate of John Armstrong, killed only a week earlier in the practice dogfight with Gil Bright. Tex shook his head, unable to really believe it. When the bar closed and the men called it a night, Tex followed them in a tired stumble to the barracks, where he climbed into a primitive bunk draped with mosquito netting, and was soon asleep.

Late the following morning, sunlight awakened Tex from a long slumber. Slowly, he got up to take stock of his surroundings. The bed he had been lying on, now visible, turned out to be a simple wooden-frame affair, with a straw mattress covering a mesh of rope. He had to un-tuck the mosquito netting from beneath the mattress to exit. Judging from the legions of mosquitoes he'd noticed, Tex estimated that, without the netting, there wouldn't be anything left of him but bones. The mosquitoes were enormous, and showed more than a passing interest in the AVG.

The barracks was long and narrow, with a high pointed roof, and held two rows of beds lining either side of a central walkway. A few light bulbs hung from chains attached to the rafters overhead. Burmese youngsters were busily making up the men's beds and gathering laundry. Tex ambled out to the washroom, which was simple enough; the latrines were in separate outhouses that didn't even rate a door. Studying the showers, he discovered that they were fed from a large tank of rainwater atop a short tower outside the building. When a chain was pulled, gravity brought the water down through bamboo pipes, at the same temperature as when nature provided it. Water from the same tank fed the sinks. After a quick shower, Tex went back to the barracks to dress. Then he emerged to have a look around the place.

Kyedaw airfield was a piece of work. In addition to the barracks and pilot's mess, there were an operations building, dispensary, runway, and hangars to round out the small base. Kyedaw belonged to the British, but they had allowed the AVG to use it for training during the summer months. The British were making no great sacrifice in doing so; they routinely abandoned the field during this season anyway, considering the stifling midday heat unbearable for man or beast. Indeed, the AVG trained and worked in the mornings or late afternoons to avoid a baking when the sun was high. In the trees nearby, droves of monkeys watched the daily proceedings with great interest.

The insects didn't seem to mind the heat in the least. They came in a flying and crawling menagerie, their shapes and sizes right from an entomologist's dream. In the mess hall, the Americans quickly covered their plates of food with second plates as they carried them to the table; then they removed these and wolfed down their meal before the insects could descend upon it to "share." It was a race the men won only occasionally.

Fred Hodges, one of the pilots, had come to exactly the wrong place out of the entire world: he suffered a pathological dread of insects. When his companions learned of it, they routinely captured the largest and most horrifying varieties to slip beneath Hodges' mosquito netting at night. Shrieking, "Fearless Freddie" would nearly tear a hole in the netting making a panic-stricken exit. He was living his worst nightmare; yet he stuck with the group.

Nepalese *ghurka* guards protected the facilities at Kyedaw with grim tenacity, especially the airplanes in their hangars. It was the first time Tex had seen these exotic troops. The *ghurkas* carried rifles, but their weapon of choice was the huge, curved knife—almost a machete—that always hung at their sides. By tradition, they would not draw this weapon and re-sheath it without drawing blood; so, they would often nick themselves before putting it away. Before a *ghurka* unit went into combat, they held a ceremony in which gradually larger animals were beheaded, one by one, with the fearsome blades. They started small, and worked their way up to a bull. If the head was not removed cleanly with one stroke, it meant bad luck for the company. Few intruders were ever seen around the facilities at Kyedaw.

Meals at the base were nutritious, but not particularly appetizing. Potatoes and rice were main staples; meat, when available, was usually from water buffalo. Vegetables were in short supply, since those grown in Burma were sure to cause dysentery in westerners. By far, the most common spice was curry, and the men learned to get used to it. Mercifully, curry could hide the flavor of water buffalo meat. There were eggs for breakfast, but the Indians had only a vague idea of how to cook them to American tastes.

The oppressive humidity made the thermometer-popping temperatures even worse to bear. Kyedaw, in the Irrawaddy River valley, was a soupy sauna that called to mind a Turkish bath with every breath. The smell of rotting jungle vegetation permeated the air. The place was also home to an unnamed, fast-growing mold that appeared overnight on boots, belts, buttons, beds, and even the cockpits of the P-40s themselves, turning all these the same "interesting" shade of green. The men grimaced at first, as they painstakingly scraped the stuff from their clothing; after awhile, many didn't bother. To top it all off, the AVG's three doctors had plenty of business between cases of malaria, dysentery, and dengue fever.

The primitive conditions were the last straw for some of the men. Weeks before Tex's arrival, Chennault had flown down from Kunming to greet the first wave of volunteers. Five of the pilots immediately handed him resignations. These men hadn't jumped ship during the voyage; but after taking one look around Kyedaw, they thought of comfortable airline jobs available back in the States, and opted to "punch out." They had joined the AVG to leave the military; and now that they were out, even Chennault couldn't keep them around. Fifteen pilots eventually quit, leaving the AVG with eighty-five.

Tex noted ruefully that Burma's heat put even his Texas hill country to shame. It wasn't going to be easy to live with. But that first morning, his mind was occupied with bigger things—like what lay ahead. In the mess hall he saw Rector and Christman, and they sat down enthusiastically to a breakfast of eggs.

"I guess the Old Man saw fit to let us sleep in this morning," Rector observed, around a mouthful.

"The 'Old Man?'" echoed Tex.

"That's what everyone calls Colonel Chennault. Not to his face, of course; then it's 'Colonel.' No disrespect intended, from what I can tell."

"You got that right," said Tex. "Seems like that guy has earned everybody's respect, I can tell that."

"We're supposed to go over to his office and meet him this morning," Rector continued. "Then we can head out to the flight line and see the sights." It sounded like a good suggestion, so they cleaned up quickly and left.

Rector had already identified the small building that served as Chennault's office, and the trio entered somewhat hesitantly. Inside, Tex's eyes fell on a man he had never met, but whom he knew immediately must be the leader of the AVG.

Claire Lee Chennault was an inch or two shy of six feet, solidly built and athletic, and might have had his picture in the dictionary next to the word *command*. His square jaw and firm handshake told Tex that the man had no patience for nonsense; but a quick smile and friendly flash in his coal-black Cajun eyes said that he heartily welcomed the volunteers. Chennault's face was deeply creased, especially around the eyes. He was handsome, in a ruggedly independent sort of way. When he spoke, even amiably, the quiet was immediate.

He grasped each man's hand in turn, welcoming him. "We're glad to have you here," he said simply. They knew he meant it.

Chennault was a unique man in a unique situation. Ostracism by his peers and superiors in the Army Air Corps had not changed his convictions about airpower one iota. When circumstances landed him as leader of the AVG, he welcomed the opportunity. Almost no one had ever been given the autonomy to train a group of combat pilots in his own particular tactics, but that was exactly the chance Chennault had with the AVG. If it lacked the most modern planes or veteran fighter pilots, he did not care. It was his group. Few other men, if any, could have held together the maverick AVG at all, let alone have accomplished anything noteworthy with them. But it never occurred to the confident Chennault that the group would do anything but succeed.

He had been a natural leader from boyhood, one of the greatest the United States ever produced. His courage was unquestioned; the men saw it firsthand. He never asked them to do anything that was outside his own experience. He had "been there." Chennault was silent about his own tally of aerial victories, but not about the tactics he'd employed to earn it. He needed no hare-brained ideas, for proven strategy was at his fingertips. The man's confidence was tangible and contagious. He had little use for military rules and paperwork, and less for anyone who didn't want to fight the Japanese. His sense of personal discipline served to keep his men in line better than any list of rules would have done.

Chennault was also a consummate competitor, a characteristic of almost any fighter pilot. Watching him throw his supreme effort into even a softball game, the men caught themselves believing that the World Series was at stake. Chennault had three approaches to any contest: win, win, and win. He possessed exceptional athleticism and dexterity, necessary to have led the "Three Men on the Flying Trapeze," his old aerobatic team. Tex watched in amazement on one occasion as Chennault idly signed his name with both hands, simultaneously, upside-down and backwards. He was a crack shot. Tex would later learn that Chennault was a native Texan, and shared Tex's love for hunting.

Sadly, it wasn't difficult to decipher the reason the Army Air Corps had shunned one of its brightest stars. When there was a difference of opinion, and Chennault knew he was right, he simply would not back down. There was not a compromising bone in his body in such cases. He spoke the truth, or his personal conviction, in straight language, not sparing a single word for tact. With Generalissimo Chiang Kai-Shek, this rare characteristic immediately earned him the highest respect and a reputation for truthfulness. With the Army brass and the hidebound War Department, it earned him a ticket to nowhere. They got tired of being told they were using their bombers and fighters inefficiently. Friend or foe, everyone knew they would get nothing but frankness from Chennault.

As the three friends departed Chennault's office, Ed Rector nudged Tex and indicated the building.

"What do you think?" he asked quietly.

Tex shook his head, impressed. "Seems to me like that's a guy who knows what the hell he's doing." Ed nodded in agreement.

As they approached the airstrip, Tex saw that it was a short one, paved with asphalt. Its four-thousand-foot length would make landings a little more challenging, but it would have to do. What captured the attention of all three of them, however, were the runway's occupants. Lined up neatly in the parking area were a number of sleek, sharp-nosed P-40B *Tomahawks*.

"Nice lines," said Rector. Tex had to agree.

The P-40's narrow nose began with a pointed propeller spinner. This was mounted ahead of an in-line, liquid-cooled engine, rather than the more traditional radial air-cooled kind. The exhaust pipes extended just outside the metal surface on either side. The nose tapered back into a slim fuselage. The wings, riveted on for durability, featured the classic Curtiss-Wright straight leading edge, with rounded tips and a trailing edge that angled back from wingtip to body. The cockpit was set much farther back than on a radial-engine craft, causing pilots who had flown the latter to have problems with visibility, until they got used to it. The P-40's firepower was much in evidence, in the form of four .30-caliber machine guns—two mounted on each wing—and two heavier .50-caliber guns on top of the fuselage just behind the prop, synchronized to fire through it. It was a good-looking airplane; and gazing at it, Tex and his friends felt an itch in their trigger fingers.

As the three stood admiring, they heard an unmistakable noise: a plane was approaching the field at full throttle. Christman pointed, and they saw the P-40 coming directly toward them, a hundred feet or so off the ground. Its engine crescendoed angrily as it shot not-quite-overhead. The pilot waved to the three on the ground, who turned to watch it climb in the distance.

There was a long pause, and then Rector turned to Tex, grinning from ear to ear.

"Life," he said slowly, emphasizing each word, "is good."

Tex smiled and clapped him on the shoulder, nodding agreement.

Tex visits a Chinese monument to the AVG in Rangoon, Burma, spring 1944. The site includes Bert Christman's grave.

Chapter 11

GROWING FANGS

Tex was back in school again. The class sat in neat rows of chairs, while the professor wielded chalk and a large pointer. The blackboard bore the marks of heavy use, and his fellow students took sporadic notes on paper. For a second his memory pulled him back to McCallie; and in spite of himself, he looked out the single window for a glance at the majestic Appalachians.

Instead of the mountains of Tennessee, the view was of a soggy airstrip at Kyedaw, with several P-40s sitting forlornly in the parking area. Jungle lurked in the background, and monsoon rains cast a damp shroud over the scene. The illusion was shattered. Instead of cadets, his fellow volunteers flanked him in rapt attention to the front of the room. It was not "Prof" Culver at the chalkboard imparting knowledge, but Colonel Chennault, clad in mismatched sports shirt and khaki shorts; and the subject matter was such that no one had trouble paying attention. Indeed, their lives might depend upon learning it.

It was during their first days at Kyedaw that Chennault drew heaviest upon his skills of instruction, providing his men with the basic, crucial knowledge that he himself had taken great pains to learn. His aerial tactics program began in the classroom, with five hours of familiarization with the P-40B. If the AVG was to be an effective weapon in Chennault's hands, the aircraft itself would first have to be an effective weapon in the hands of his men. That meant knowing the *Tomahawk* inside and out. Chennault had the teacher's knack of making his every sentence seem critical; the men listened attentively as he went over the P-40's dimensions, construction, armament, flight controls, performance ranges, strengths, and weaknesses. Waves of muggy heat rose from the ground, and the teakwood classroom felt like an oven as the morning wore on.

"Our friends the British consider these P-40s obsolete, and I've learned that the same opinion is growing in the Air Corps," Chennault was saying, as he faced the men.

They glanced sidelong at each other; some of them had, indeed, heard less-than-glowing reports on the plane.

"It is more difficult to fly than some other aircraft. But it's no 'killer,'" Chennault went on. "Also, it's all we've got. There won't be any more planes, even if money were suddenly found to pay for them. These P-40s can't be replaced. They're invaluable, and you have got to treat them as such."

Tex paid even closer attention when Chennault began to describe the performance capabilities of their potential enemies. It quickly became apparent that the Japanese aircraft they might be facing had some advantages over their P-40s.

"The Japs have good planes," Chennault declared, as if reading Tex's thoughts, "but your P-40s are much better than is generally realized. The key to success will be to match the strong points of the P-40 against the weak points of the enemy aircraft.

"Take the Nakajima I-97 as an example. As you can see from the sheets I've handed out, it has a higher ceiling, faster climb rate, and much greater maneuverability than the P-40." There was a general shuffling of papers.

"What the hell are our advantages, sir?" came a shaky voice from the rear.

The men laughed, some nervously; and Chennault held up a hand. "There are several, and you should be confident in them. The P-40 is faster in level flight and in a dive. It has significantly greater firepower than the 'Nate.' And your aircraft, though much heavier, is a good deal tougher—more sturdily constructed. Remember the armor plating I've mentioned, behind your cockpit? The Japs don't have any."

"That figures," another volunteer piped in. "Their piss-poor pilots don't care if they live or die."

"That is the usual notion I find in the United States," Chennault remonstrated, "but you'd best get one thing straight right now. That kind of thinking is dead wrong. Forget everything you've heard about the Japanese pilot. He is not cowardly, he is not suicidal, and he is not a poor shot. He is much less interested in dying for Emperor Hirohito than in making *you* do so.

"The Japs are very disciplined flyers, and their training is good. You will quickly learn that they hold formation as well as anyone you've seen. They bomb accurately, they shoot accurately, and they know how to handle their planes. I know, because I've tangled with them. These are not the Japanese pilots you read about in the Western press."

Chennault paused and looked around the room. The men were getting the message, and a few looked somewhat uncomfortable. It was time to let the other shoe drop.

"Now," he said, "I'm going to tell you how to beat them. They may be good; but they're not invincible, not by a long shot. The most significant weakness of their pilots is that they do not adapt well to a new situation. If you let them carry out their mission as planned, it will go off like clockwork. But their regimented discipline in the air is their Achilles' heel. Throw a wrench into the works—mess up their plan—and they won't know what to do.

"Here is that wrench. The way to attack their formations is by getting above them," Chennault said, as he began sketching on the blackboard. "Dive into the formation at high speed, pick your target, fire at it, then continue on through, breaking away in a dive until you're clear of the formation. Once you're well away from the fight, climb back up above them and do the same thing.

"Above all," he said, turning to the men with his eyes glinting keenly, "above *all*, *never* turn with their fighters. The P-40 cannot do it; they'll be right behind you in one turn, maybe two. Don't even think about it! If you do, we'll be picking up pieces of you all over the jungle. They *will* shoot you down, gentlemen. Make no mistake."

Silence filled the room, except for someone swatting a mosquito.

"Sir," asked one man, "what if we miss a target on our first pass? It seems like a waste to have to dive out and come back on top again."

Chennault looked at him steadily, but not unkindly. "Getting shot down would be a much greater waste," he said. "Your gunnery has to be accurate. The P-40's wing guns are boresighted to cross at three hundred yards. Fire short bursts, and make every bullet count. *Don't* miss."

It wasn't long before Tex began to go over every inch of the P-40 using the pilot's manual he had been issued. As he inspected the engine one morning with a more senior volunteer, Tex shook his head at the unfamiliar design.

"I'm just not used to these liquid-cooled deals," he said to the other man. Pointing at the coolant lines, he continued, "What happens if you get hit in one of these? Doesn't your Prestone bleed off pretty fast—and then your engine quit?"

His companion looked hard at him in silence. "Yep," he said, after a meaningful pause. "Try not to get hit there."

Day followed sweltering day in the classroom, where the men soaked up Chennault's knowledge of aerial combat like sponges. Along with the others, Tex quickly gained an appreciation for the Old Man's experience and insight into enemy tactics. Tex realized that Chennault's genius did not lie in figuring out complex theories no one else had thought of. Rather, it was the same mix Tex had learned in boxing at McCallie years before: discipline in the fight, application of proven tactics, and an eye for the opponent's weakness.

"Here is the problem with dogfighting the Japanese," Chennault would say to his students, who were reluctantly trying to understand why their old pursuit tactics would not work. "You won't be able to out-maneuver them to get on their tail. They'll turn tight, and you'll try to turn with them. To get the shortest possible turn radius, you'll 'reef it in' and bleed off your airspeed."

The men were nodding. They had all done it.

Chennault continued, "By the time you realize you *still* can't turn inside that Jap—and believe me, the P-40 cannot do it—it's too late. You'll throttle up to full power; but you're already slow, and the Jap is not. He'll be on your tail in a second, and you can't accelerate fast enough—even in a dive—to get away from him. Your vacation in Burma," he said, pausing significantly and tapping the chalkboard, "is at an end."

Dive in, fire accurately, break away, and climb. "Dive-squirt-pass-run." These were the mantras that Chennault ingrained into his men, drilling them in the concept until they knew it in their sleep. He made a doctrinal departure from the conventional three-ship element tactics the Army and Navy taught, advocating a two-ship formation instead. As the leader made a firing pass, his wingman would follow to protect him from enemy planes that might get on his tail. It was the first time Americans had used the two-ship tactic; but its impending success in the Far East would secure its place as the standard in later years.

Along with classroom lectures, the training program soon began to include flying time. Tex spent many hours studying the P-40 manual before declaring he was ready to solo. When the time came, he sat in the cockpit of the number 48 plane and stared at its long, pointed nose. It blocked the forward visibility he was accustomed to in Navy aircraft; and as he taxied down the runway, he found himself weaving back and forth more than usual to get glimpses of what lay in front of him. The coast was clear, of course. He would just have to get used to it.

With a deep breath, Tex opened the throttle. The buzz of the engine jumped to a roar, and he was pressed back into the seat as the scenery slid past with increasing velocity. He reached takeoff speed and pulled up, feeling the bumpy runway change to smooth air beneath him. The gear retracted, the plane climbed, and Tex felt himself relax. He was in his element once more.

Soloing was not meant to be a high-performance "wringing out" of the aircraft; but right away, as he performed some basic maneuvers, Tex noticed some exhilarating differences between the P-40 and the Navy planes he'd flown. The first was speed. Neither the TBD nor the SB2U had provided Tex with the available top speed of the *Tomahawk*: 340 knots, courtesy of the Allison power plant. The second difference was maneuverability. Despite Chennault's cautions that the P-40 could not turn with Japanese fighters, Tex found that it certainly could have flown rings around the old U.S. Navy bombers. Naturally so; for the P-40 was a fighter plane, designed without concern for any other mission. Tex brought it around and approached the field for the most difficult part of any solo flight: the landing.

It was here that a third difference in performance became all too apparent. In the classroom, Tex had learned that a pilot must maintain a much higher landing speed for the P-40 than for other types of aircraft; it would feel, Chennault told him, like he was bringing it in too "hot." If he lost his nerve and throttled back, however, the plane would stall out before touching down, which could have disastrous results. In spite of a few sweaty moments, he managed to bring it down safely, and climbed from the cockpit to the hoots and cheers of several squadron mates. His solo in the P-40 was a success: number 48 was his.

Other first-timers were not so lucky. The transition from other aircraft to the P-40 was challenging; and the greater the differences between aircraft, the more difficult was the switch. The Navy "big boat" pilots had the worst time. The huge pontoons on their old aircraft had elevated the pilot quite high above the water, even after landing. Coming down in the P-40, it felt to them like touchdown was imminent when they reached about the same height. They would throttle back, stall the P-40 many feet in the air, and "crack up" the aircraft when it slammed down on the runway. Many of the former Army pilots had only flown heavy bombers, and encountered similar problems with landing. Still others, like Tex, had only to become accustomed to the higher landing speeds and minor differences between the P-40 and other single-engine planes. In the months of training at Toungoo, plenty of the precious fighters were damaged or ruined in landing accidents, as the pilots struggled to become proficient with their new aircraft.

Other difficulties contributed to the problematic training. The monsoon season was not quite over when Tex arrived; and some days, it rained an inch or two for many weeks afterward. Often, the treacherous weather turned an ordinary-seeming flight into a dangerous undertaking. Then, too, only a fraction of the aircraft had been assembled and ferried back from Rangoon; at first, there were thirty-seven pilots sharing only thirteen planes, making flying time scarce until more arrived.

Less than a week after Tex's arrival, Maax Hammer, a shipmate from the *Bloemfontein*, was practicing acrobatic maneuvers near Kyedaw. Suddenly his P-40 stalled while in an inverted attitude, and the controls immediately went slack. Unable to bail out, and lacking the altitude to "kick it" into a normal spin and recover, Hammer crashed to his death. It was a shock to the group. Hammer had been well-liked, and, in Tex's estimation, likely to be one of their best pilots. Following Armstrong's dogfighting death, this accident served as a second grim reminder that there were no guarantees.

In some cases the P-40 itself, usually very reliable, betrayed the pilot. Dogfighting with Erik Shilling, Frank Schiel discovered a nasty tendency of the aircraft to go into a spin—once again, while inverted. Fortunately, Schiel's eight thousand feet of altitude allowed him time to bail out unhurt; but the plane was a total loss. Another time, Pete Atkinson, testing an aircraft newly flown in from Rangoon, had the propeller governor fail, sending his prop into a state of "over-rev." Freed from restraint, the engine screamed as it plunged Atkinson into a 600-mph power dive from ten thousand feet straight into the ground, his aircraft disintegrating around him before it struck only a few yards from the Kyedaw barracks. The horrible shrieking noise emptied the barracks in seconds, and the shaken men poked morosely through the wreckage. It was the third AVG death in scarcely six weeks.

Despite the hellish climate and the accidents, the men gradually honed their combat skills with mock dogfights and target practice. They became, with a few exceptions, very good pilots. (Chennault was quick to remind them, though, that the "dogfights" were solely to familiarize them with the performance characteristics of the aircraft; if they ever tried to mix it up like that with the Japs, it would all be over.) Later in training, the syllabus included formation flying and mock "attack runs" against British bomber formations that would obligingly cruise up from Rangoon so the AVG could practice on them. Tex won some dogfights and lost others, generally finding that his skills ranked fairly high among the pilots. There were others whose touch on the controls was better; but Tex's marksmanship was top-notch. He also noticed that the former Navy pilots tended to perform better than those from the Army Air Corps, and he came to appreciate the difficulty of the thirteen-month training program at Pensacola. Aerial gunnery was one area in which the Naval volunteers especially stood out, though all were improving their skill with practice. Tex spent many hours boresighting his guns on the firing range with the others; years of hunting had taught him the value of well-sighted weapons long before he joined the Navy.

Within a month or so, the last P-40 was finally assembled and delivered from Rangoon to Kyedaw Field. There had been a total of ninety-nine aircraft assembled—one having been unhappily dropped into the harbor as its crate was offloaded. By that time, Chennault had divided the AVG into three squadrons, each consisting of thirty-three planes and some twenty-six pilots: the 1st, 2nd, and 3rd Pursuit Squadrons. Tex found himself assigned to the 2nd Squadron, along with Ed Rector, Bert Christman, and most of the AVG who had been in the Navy. Their leader was Jack Newkirk, a diplomatic and well-liked man from Scarsdale, New York. Newkirk had an air of sophistication that fit right in, as it happened, with the British. There were better pilots; but Tex considered "Scarsdale Jack" a fine squadron leader.

Every squadron must have an insignia and a nickname; and the men of the 2nd promptly conferred together to determine what theirs would be. It was quiet Bert Christman who came up with the "Panda Bears," after one of the area's native animals; and it stuck. Christman immediately began decorating the fuselage of each 2nd Squadron aircraft with a small, personalized panda bear.

With his artistic skill, the bears bore a striking resemblance to their pilots. Jack Newkirk's bear gave a rakish grin, wearing a monocle and top hat, leaning jauntily on a cane, and clenching a cigarette in a holder with its teeth. Gil Bright's bear trailed a parachute (Bright himself had been forced to bail out a number of times). John Petach's panda, complete with handlebar moustache, whizzed past on a bicycle. Frank Swartz's pontificated and gestured from atop a treestump. Pete Wright's bear had a prominent posterior—which was immediately identifiable, much to Wright's chagrin. Robert "Moose" Moss, a native of Doerun, Georgia, had a pudgy mascot that slumbered in a chair with its feet up on a checkerboard, a hat over its eyes and an empty jug of moonshine dangling from one finger.

"Wow," remarked Ed Rector, inspecting Christman's work alongside Tex, "that's Moose, all right."

Tex's own panda sported a brace of six-shooters in a holster, ten-gallon hat, and cowboy boots, with a cactus nearby and a longhorn skull lying on the ground. Christman's charicatures were a big hit with the pilots; they eagerly waited their turn to have their own airplanes done.

The other two squadrons had formed their identities as well. 1st Squadron aircraft sported an apple with a snake coiled around it, and a woman chasing a uniformed AVG member in the foreground. They were the "Adam and Eves," their insignia a pun on the world's historical "first pursuit." The original idea had called for a red apple; but it looked too much like the rising sun insignia of their enemies, so designer Charlie Bond changed it to green. The 3rd Squadron had adopted the moniker "Hell's Angels," and their planes featured shapely, red, winged female "angels" in varying poses.

Recreation for the men during training at Kyedaw was usually limited by rain, heat, or work schedule. In clearer weather, many would turn out for softball games; and these turned to high competition—with Chennault right in the middle of it, usually pitching. The town of Toungoo was seven miles away, and Chennault purposely declared the AVG's few automobiles "off limits" for trips there. He wanted them to ride their bicycles to town instead—virtually everyone had bought one—to stay in shape. Tex did just that. He found Toungoo unkempt and mostly uninteresting; but he did visit several jewelry shops, and, on one occasion, bought a beautiful star sapphire. Many of the other men bought gemstones too, which were priced incredibly low. The largest jade mine in the world was only a short distance from the town.

In bad weather, Tex and the others stayed indoors and dealt hands of poker or Red Dog in the barracks or the bar, with friends and drinks for company. A few movies were shown on an archaic projector in the mess hall after dinner, but the machine often broke. There simply wasn't much to do. Sometimes they would hold meetings to discuss combat tactics, but these were neither organized nor consistent. The occasional rainy doldrums were a strain on morale; during those times, only the mosquitoes, scorpions, and *kraits*—tiny snakes whose bite would kill a man in seconds—seemed to be fully motivated. More pilots and ground crewmembers handed in their resignations to Chennault during this dismal period; but most stuck with him.

There were occasional episodes that bordered on the comic. One night, Tex and "Moose" Moss were on their way to Toungoo, hoping to find something to break the monotony at one of the town's bars or clubs. When a sudden commotion arose ahead of them in the dark, the pair stepped quickly into the brush alongside the road. A few seconds later, a rickshaw, going at top speed, shot from around the bend ahead; but there was something unusual about it. Perched atop the contraption in the passenger's spot was the native Burmese driver, grinning from ear to ear. Pulling the rickshaw—Tex did a double take—was an AVG man, obviously heavily "sauced," scowling and going like mad. Moss started to say something, but Tex put a cautioning hand on his arm. When the rickshaw disappeared down the path and the noise faded, the two looked at each other.

"Who was that guy?" asked Tex, who hadn't recognized the American.

"Oh, that's 'Pappy' Boyington. He's one of the new pilots, a Marine," replied Moss with a smile.

Tex chuckled, clasping Moss's shoulder. "Man, I know we're a little short of planes to practice in, but..."

They both laughed and continued toward Toungoo. Tex never found out the story behind the strange sight.

Tex had to admire Chennault's approach to unit discipline. There were plenty in the AVG who, having recently "escaped" the military, wanted no part of the rules and regimen the services had imposed on them. Others, though, liked military structure and discipline; they wished the Old Man would enforce more rules. Chennault decided a democratic approach was best. He let the men gather and determine among themselves the hours of operation for the bar, time for "lights out," and other issues that affected everyone. Chennault wisely concluded that rules the men made themselves would be much more effective—and better enforced.

In one area, though, he did insist upon complete discipline to the letter of his instructions, and that was in the air. There was simply too much at stake to tolerate sloppiness or insubordination in that arena. When the AVG later faced combat, the pilots quickly understood how right Chennault had been on that score.

The ranks of the AVG gradually filled out, with two more shiploads arriving in October, and the final two in November. These brought the personnel strength of the group to its height—somewhat less than three hundred. Along with everybody else, Tex was glad to welcome the new men. He took his turn shepherding them through aircraft inspections and passing on valuable lessons learned in the months at Toungoo. As he took stock of the fully formed AVG, Tex concluded it must have been as motley a group as had ever been assembled for combat. There were troublemakers, patriots, veterans, youngsters, brawlers, misfits, and some that were a little of each.

"How many men do you think we'd need to give the Japs a licking?" Rector wondered aloud one day to Tex, as they walked off the runway after a particularly "hairy" training flight.

"One," Tex replied, jabbing a finger at the corrugated metal headquarters building. "He's sitting at that desk in there."

The training accidents continued. Edwin Conant, a late arrival and former "big boat" pilot, cracked up three P-40s in four days early in November, on his way to an eventual total of five. He simply could not get the hang of landing them, and the price was excruciating. Conant had previously washed out of pilot training in the States; then he re-entered—and graduated—under an assumed name. Later in the war, he would find his "niche" in rotary-wing aircraft, eventually becoming one of the most decorated helicopter pilots in the U.S. Army. One of Conant's washouts occurred on November 3rd, a day when four other accidents in the group added up to five planes knocked out.

Chennault nearly tore his hair out.

Four days later, Tex's squadron mate Tom Jones became lost en route to Lashio, and "bellied in" to "scratch" another P-40. Late arrival Jim Cross had his engine throw a connecting rod on his solo flight; and after Cross "hit the silk," only the wings could be saved from the resulting wreckage. A few days into December, Chennault grimly took stock of his aircraft strength: sixty-two P-40s remained in commission, and seventeen more could be repaired. The remaining twenty-one, over one-fifth of their entire force, had been destroyed in the four months of training at Kyedaw. Was it worth it? He knew his pilots were getting good, but the bill was terribly steep. Nevertheless, the meaning of "giving up" was unknown to him.

Even the hardships and mishaps of training at Toungoo paled beside the single greatest problem confronting Chennault and the AVG: lack of supplies and spare parts. The P-40s had been intended to come with spare parts, but the ship carrying those had been sunk on the voyage to China. Once assembled, the planes were complete—but lacked even a single spare bolt or rivet to replace anything that broke. And during training—to say nothing of combat—plenty of things broke.

Within weeks, there were critical shortages of almost every part. The crew chiefs stuffed tail wheel tires with rope or straw when they blew out, often after only a couple of landings on the rough runway. No one bothered to check their magnetos before a flight—if they had, no one would have flown. There were no extra spark plugs; pilots poured the coal to the engine on takeoff, hoping the carbon on their plugs would burn off in time to get off the ground. Solenoid switches to charge the guns were guarded like treasure. Not long after their first battle, the AVG would have to modify their tactics and fly split-altitude formations: those that still had oxygen bottles flew high, while those that did not were limited to less than fifteen thousand feet. Electric switches, batteries, radio tubes, carburetors—the list of unavailable but necessary equipment was endless. The Old Man had people scrounging the length of Asia to beg, borrow, or steal these wherever they could. In later combat, perfectly serviceable planes that lacked some "trivial" piece of equipment in order to fly would be forced to sit idle. It was maddening.

It was because of this potentially crippling situation that the AVG ground crews outshone everyone. Throughout the long year of training and combat, they raised efficiency and improvisation in aircraft maintenance to an art form. Rarely in history—perhaps never—has a group of maintainers and armorers worked such miracles with so few resources. They began with no tools to fit any of the hundreds of parts in the P-40. They had to make their own A-frames by hand to perform engine work. They had no equipment to move heavy pieces around, no instructions, and no safety regulations—yet they changed engine after engine *overnight*, a procedure that took three days with a "normal" crew. In sweltering heat they re-armed and refueled the planes time after time with blazing speed, always finishing quickly enough to allow the pilots time to gain precious altitude to meet the enemy. And in spite of all the limitations, there was never—even once—an instance of mechanical failure of anything the ground crews repaired in a P-40. Their success was beyond outstanding; it was mind-boggling. Decades later, Tex would still insist that the real heroes of the AVG had been men like Harry Fox, John Carter, Don Rodewald, J.J. Harrington, John Overley, and Carl Quick. There were many, many more.

On a mid-November evening in Toungoo, several of the men saw a picture in a magazine. It portrayed a plane painted with shark's teeth on the engine cowling. They thought it was a great idea—and ideal for the shape of their P-40s. Within days, the *Tomahawks* sported the gaping maws as well. The shape of the prop spinners and air intakes lent themselves perfectly to the shark-mouth design; and a glaring eye provided the finishing touch. When his crew chief finished the painting job on his plane, Tex stepped back in satisfaction to examine it. The "face" of a shark seemed to bring the aircraft to menacing, ferocious life.

In a sense, the men had grown "fangs" as well. Their bodies were honed by the merciless climate; their skills were sharpened by a wise instructor. November was giving grudging way to December, and the monsoons had been over for a month. The AVG was ready for combat, and awaited only a word from their leader to move operations at a moment's notice.

* * *

The international situation steadily deteriorated in the fall of 1941. A week after Maax Hammer's death in a P-40, Germany broke her pact with the Soviet Union in Poland and threw millions of men and tanks across the line into Russia. That summer's U.S. oil embargo on Japan made it imperative for the latter to secure new petroleum supplies—which Burma happened to carry, in enormous oil fields in the heart of the country. In October, Chennault began to receive intelligence reports of a buildup of Japanese forces along the border between Indochina and Thailand. The Japs were more than tripling their air forces based in that region as well, and Chennault had no doubt that they intended to move on Rangoon before long. The British read these reports with a characteristic lack of alarm, unwilling to believe that the Japanese could present a serious threat.

In late October, the AVG began to conduct reconnaissance flights over the potential Japanese bases in Thailand, less than sixty miles from Toungoo, watching for anything that might indicate enemy activity. Chennault's warning net did not extend into Burma, and he calculated that the Japanese could easily wipe out the fledgling AVG with a surprise raid on Kyedaw Field.

A message came from T.V. Soong in Washington, relaying snide War Department comments that Chennault's group could not be ready before February, and in any case would not last two weeks in combat.

"We'll be ready in two weeks," the Old Man shot back, "and we'll last as long as we're needed."

The first week of December ticked away quietly.

Barracks at Kyedaw Airfield, Toungoo, fall 1941.

*2nd Squadron Panda Bears at Kunming, late 1941.
(L to R: unknown, Pete Wright, Freeman Ricketts, Jack Newkirk, unknown, Tex, Hank Geselbracht, Gil Bright.)*

The last P-40, #99, is assembled at Mingaladon Airfield, Rangoon, fall 1941.

Chapter 12

THE STORM BREAKS

It was time for breakfast and then another early training flight for Tex, who was starting to wonder what the Old Man was thinking. When would Chennault move the group to engage the Japanese, and where would they go? The weather had cooled somewhat, improving the climate considerably; but Toungoo's scene was wearing thin on everyone. With the monsoons over with, it could only be a matter of time before the Japanese renewed their perennial firebombing campaign against China's cities. Chennault had issued orders to be ready to move to Kunming; but "being ready" did not look like "going." He wanted to squeeze every bit of training time out of their stay in Toungoo, raising as many pilots as possible to a level he considered combat-ready. There were still some of them who, in his judgment, were not fully trained.

It was the eighth of December, Burma dateline. Tex and several of his squadron mates were just getting ready to leave the mess hall when one of the radio operators came trotting in.

"Hey, guys," he said, his voice carrying an undertone of intensity, "the Japs just hit Pearl Harbor."

A skeptical silence followed the announcement. One pilot chuckled. "Man, I wish they *would* hit it," he said. "If we don't mix with them pretty soon, I'm going to go crazy."

Tex had to smile, too. "Well, I sure hope they got Fleet Problem Twenty-One solved this time," he joked.

"I'm not kidding. It's all over the radio. Come hear for yourself," the radioman said, beckoning them toward the hangar.

It was true, of course. Approaching stealthily from the west before the Sunday sunrise, some three hundred fifty Japanese aircraft had launched from six carriers of the *Nagumo* Task Force on a mission that would change the face of the war. They achieved complete surprise, had their way in the skies over Oahu, and returned the way they came.

Theirs was one of the most successful operational victories in history. Meeting practically no resistance, "Val" dive-bombers and "Kate" torpedo bombers unloaded exploding destruction into the sleeping U.S. Pacific Fleet. American sailors drowned by the hundreds as battleship after crippled battleship went to the bottom: *Oklahoma, West Virginia, Arizona, Nevada, California*. Japanese torpedoes ripped into many vessels that did not sink, but sustained horrible casualties: *Helena, Pennsylvania, Tennessee, Raleigh, Honolulu, Maryland*. Idyllic Pearl Harbor became a stricken seascape of burning ships, crumbling superstructures, and men slipping beneath the waves to their death.

On land, things were almost as bad. The air above Wheeler and Hickham Fields was alive with Japanese *Zeros*, making their American combat debut in deadly style. The relentless Japs riddled scores of U.S. fighters and bombers "on alert" with merciless fire and bombing. A few American planes managed to get into the air, and some even scored aerial victories; but most were promptly shot down. The enemy knew his work, and performed it well.

When it was over, the shocking facts began to reach an outraged American nation. The Japanese had killed nearly three thousand servicemen, mostly Navy sailors, in the space of a few hours. Five battleships, three heavy cruisers, three destroyers, and a number of other vessels had been sunk; and many more ships were crippled. Finally, the Japs had destroyed some three hundred U.S. aircraft—nearly as many as they had brought with them to do the job. The enemy's losses were inconsequential. The only bright spot in the disaster was the fact that the U.S. Navy's aircraft carriers were all absent from Pearl that day, for various reasons. The *Enterprise*, the nearest one at two hundred miles, had sent eleven fighter aircraft to their swift destruction during the battle. It was, as President Roosevelt bitterly proclaimed over the radio, "A day that will live in infamy..."

Halfway around the world, Tex's training flight was canceled. When the truth of the situation dawned on them, the men of the AVG reacted in various ways. Many set their jaws and muttered darkly about what they would do to the next Jap they saw. A few began to reflect that jobs with the airlines were suddenly looking mighty attractive. Tex himself was "plenty hot," but not really surprised; he, and others, had known for some time that war with the Japanese was rolling inevitably closer. In his mind, the disaster at Pearl Harbor crystallized the mission the AVG had to accomplish. He and his friends were no longer mercenary pilots; they were citizens of a country at war. It changed everything.

Chennault immediately called a meeting of the group and passed along information that was coming in. Although Pearl Harbor was the most devastating Japanese strike, it was far from the only one. The list of the Empire's other targets that day was long: Wake Island, Guam, Luzon, Malaya, Hong Kong, and Singapore. Japanese troops were pouring into nearby Thailand as well, meeting no resistance. The Pacific was suddenly alive with sound and fury; the buildup of the preceding months had boiled over. The Old Man's biggest fear was that surely now, the Japanese would send a raiding force to eliminate the AVG; their proximity to Thailand would make such a bomber strike a mere "hop." Even if the Americans received warning early enough to get airborne and fight, enemy aircraft now within striking range of Toungoo outnumbered the AVG's threescore operational P-40s by more than ten to one.

Under Chennault's direction, Tex and his comrades took several immediate precautions. They set up an alert rotation, beginning regular patrol flights above the field.

Starting that night, they blacked out Kyedaw—and prominently lit an auxiliary field, some forty miles to the north. The threat of a Japanese attack with paratroopers was high; so, many of the volunteers bought sidearms wherever they could find them. Chennault had an air raid siren installed. He himself spent many hours atop a nearby observation tower with Tom Gentry, his surgeon, peering through binoculars to detect specks in the sky, and listening for engine noise. Everyone was jittery. They knew they had to move soon, or be bombed into extinction.

Unexpectedly, the question of where to move the AVG from Toungoo instantly became the subject of debate. The British insisted that the AVG be relocated to Rangoon, to augment their few dozen Royal Air Force planes in defending the city against the blow they now knew was coming. But Generalissimo Chiang Kai-Shek, whose AVG it was, had always intended to move them to Kunming, to provide aerial defense against the inevitable Japanese terror bombings. However, Chiang wanted to help the British if he could; and after some hasty negotiations, they reached a compromise. The 1st and 2nd Squadrons would cross into China when needed and set up at Kunming, while the 3rd Squadron would proceed to Rangoon and fight alongside the RAF. Meanwhile, Chennault learned with frustration that the men and planes for his promised bomber group—the "Second AVG"—had dissolved into the American military's frantic mobilization effort.

The morning after the Pearl Harbor attack, the volunteers found that their new air raid siren worked—no less than six times. But they were all false alarms; no Japanese planes ever came near the field. It was obvious everyone's nerves were on edge.

Long before dawn on the 10th of December, Tex and Ed Rector sat in the alert shack with a couple of other pilots. It was their turn for night alert duty, and they were playing a few hands of Red Dog, trying to stay awake. When the phone rang suddenly, everyone dropped their cards, sat bolt upright, and riveted their attention on the pilot who picked it up.

"Yeah?...All right. Yeah. Got it." He hung up, and the look on his face said it all. "Heavy engine noise heard heading this way. Let's go."

He hardly got the sentence out before the air raid siren split the night silence outside. Tex and his three companions raced to their planes, started the engines, and taxied for takeoff. They sped off the runway in quick succession, and Tex could feel adrenaline sharpening his thoughts and reflexes. It was critically important to get to altitude and find the raiders before they could make an accurate bombing run.

They reached eighteen thousand feet in minutes, all four pilots searching in every direction through the darkness. The P-40 was equipped with no night-fighting equipment whatsoever; so the pilots had to depend upon their radios for cues and direction from the ground. None came.

"Looks like another false one," Rector eventually remarked into his microphone. The flight leader concurred; and after circling for over an hour, they received instructions to bring the planes down.

Tex was the last to land, right after Ed Rector. As he descended toward the field in darkness, he watched his wingman's lights. Rector turned about at the end of the runway, and began taxiing back along its side. Kyedaw's strip was short and narrow, lit sparingly and only while the planes were landing. Tex realized he would have to take great care to put down safely and avoid colliding with Rector.

He tried to divide his attention between his instruments, the runway, and Rector's taxiing aircraft, but it was difficult. Lowering the gear, he decided he could clear the other plane all right. As he gently descended the last few feet to touchdown, however, Tex noticed that he was landing somewhat long; when his wheels made contact, a good deal of the runway was already behind him. Should he "open it up" and come around again? No—he believed could squeeze the landing in. Flaps, throttle back, brakes. He zipped by Rector's plane. Tex's P-40 was slowing; but too late, he knew that he had made the wrong decision. He wasn't stopping fast enough! It was going to be close. The end of the runway mushroomed in his vision.

With a jolt, Tex's number 48 left the apron and bounced over a few yards of broken ground on its way into the jungle. Fortunately, he only had a little speed left; and, after some snapping and crashing through the undergrowth, his aircraft came to a halt several yards into the trees. Somewhat shaken and supremely embarrassed, Tex climbed out of his plane as bobbing flashlights heralded the arrival of a wide-eyed ground crew.

"Gee, Tex," one asked, "are you OK?"

"Yeah," replied Tex, clearing his throat and smiling ruefully, trying to make light of the situation. "Ah...I tried something like that in the Navy once. Just wanted to see if it still worked."

Chennault was frustrated, and Tex didn't make excuses as he concluded his report.

"It was one hundred percent pilot error, Colonel," he said. "You have my word I'll make it up to you."

The Old Man looked at him sternly, but then smiled. "I believe you will, Tex," he said.

The Japanese raiding force had missed Toungoo altogether that night, mistakenly unloading their bombs on an empty auxiliary field to the south. Later that day came the news that Thailand had "surrendered" to the Japanese; the government had really been a puppet structure of Japan's. That meant the only land barrier between Japanese forces and Burma was gone.

When Tex's friends Rector and Christman returned from escorting Erik Shilling on a reconnaissance flight over Bangkok, Chennault cringed at their photographs. They showed enemy planes literally packed together at Don Maung Airdrome—perfect targets!—but the AVG had no bombers to hit them with. It was heartbreaking, for they all knew where those planes were going next.

Events picked up speed after that, and every day found the men waiting for the next bit of news over the radio. Guam fell the day after Tex's landing accident. Japanese bombers sank the HMS *Prince of Wales* and *Repulse*, which the British were rushing to augment their defense of the Malayan coast. Tex sensed the rising nervousness and eagerness within the AVG as the 3rd Squadron bid them goodbye on December 12th; the Hell's Angels droned off for Rangoon and an uncertain fate. Though Tex's face seldom betrayed great emotion, he felt like a coiled spring. In a practice dogfight that afternoon with Robert "Buster" Keeton, he let off some steam by pressing home his attacks with extra intensity.

"Jeez, Tex," a sweating Keeton expostulated, as they climbed out of their planes afterward, "you whipped the hell out of me."

It wasn't until the 18th of December, eleven days after the attack on Pearl Harbor, that the news Chennault was waiting for finally arrived. Word came from Kunming that the Japanese had resumed their bombing of the city that very morning, and the Americans could not get there too soon. Chennault immediately ordered the 1st and 2nd Squadrons to relocate to Kunming that afternoon. He intended to have the group in place and on combat alert by dawn the next day—a feat that would have been impossible in the traditional administration-heavy military structure. In a short time, Tex was airborne once more; and the sky seemed full of P-40s as dozens of pilots from the 2nd formed up for the flight.

After refueling at the temple city of Lashio, the AVG continued across the border into China. Tex watched the exotic highlands unfold beneath him. Yunnan Province was replete with picturesque mountains and wide, level plains. Beautiful Lake Tien Chih rolled toward him from the horizon; and on its northern shore was the ancient walled city of Kunming itself. The Panda Bears pilots covered the approach of the Adam and Eves before taking their own turn to land. As he descended with his flight, Tex noted that the "runway" at Kunming was only a grass strip. At least it was much larger than the one at Toungoo. Still, their P-40s would have to take off and land into the wind to be safe.

Opening his canopy after landing, Tex sucked in a surprised breath of cold air. The group had just traveled from the sea-level Irrawaddy valley to the six-thousand-foot Yunnan highlands; and the temperature had taken a definite dive. One of the first orders of business would be to get some warm winter clothes. As the pilots gathered next to the runway, Tex looked around, taking stock of their surroundings.

"Looks like the place is under construction," he commented to Ed Rector, pointing to a busy group of hundreds of Chinese "coolies."

They were preparing to pave the wide main strip, crushing rocks into gravel by hand to lay a two-foot foundation for a topping of asphalt. Though the men didn't know it then, Chennault intended for the runway to accommodate long-range bombers in the future. The coolies' breath rose in the chill air, and Tex had to admire their purposeful efforts.

"They don't look exactly bundled up," said Rector doubtfully.

The support buildings surrounding the airstrip were new, and the pilots nodded with approval at the revetments that would afford their aircraft some protection from enemy bombs. The two hostels that the men would occupy were separate, some distance from the field; and when they arrived after a short drive, their jaws dropped.

Hostel Number One, home of the 2nd Squadron, represented a quantum improvement over the rickety teakwood barracks of Kyedaw. The old stone building, formerly part of an agricultural college, featured clean rooms that would each hold two men; large beds, with the requisite mosquito netting; and hot baths. There were room-boys to look after bedding and clothes; and every day, they put a brazier of glowing charcoal in each room to warm it in the evening. (Tex nearly asphyxiated on carbon monoxide the first night with the charcoal in his room, having neglected to remove the rice paper from his window for ventilation.) The outstanding mess hall had—oh joy!—delicious food, and the cooks knew how to "fix American." Movies were shown in the hostel in the evenings (on a projector that didn't break), and the men could set up a large recreation area outside for softball. Rounding out the amenities were *two* well-stocked bars. Tex and his comrades felt like a team of Robinson Crusoes come home to England. After dropping off their belongings at the hostel and donning some extra clothing, Tex and some of the others decided to venture into the city, which had seemed so interesting from the air, to have a look before dark.

Kunming had been the chief city of the region for millennia; and as he explored it, Tex thought he could almost feel the age of the place seeping through the worn road-slabs into his feet. Four immense, towering wooden gates provided the only openings in a huge stone wall that ringed the city. That ancient barrier had thwarted centuries of invaders. Outside the western gate, the Burma Road ended its seven-hundred-mile course from Lashio. Amid the crowds of curious Chinese, the Americans glimpsed wilder, eastern faces; toughly dressed traders sought provisions for excursions to Tibet, or other distant destinations. Carts, rickshaws, and a few bicycles darted in and out of side alleys. Tex and his friends stared as if they had entered a new world—for a new world it was; they beheld a way of life that had gone virtually unchanged for four thousand years.

The sun was sinking, and a strange mix of bitterness and celebration permeated the city. The effects of the morning's bombing remained, all too apparent: piles of rubble and twisted bodies lay in stark contrast to the exotic surroundings. Maimed and bandaged men and women gazed mournfully from doorways. It was the first time Tex and the others had seen the devastation of the Japanese bombings close at hand; and it only stiffened their resolve. But in spite of the day's tragedy, the residents were overjoyed to see the AVG, of whom they had heard some report, and on whom they pinned their hopes for a respite. Smiling, gap-toothed shopkeepers gave friendly waves, and children ran up to the tall Americans to give a thumbs-up and an enthusiastic *"Ding hao!"* More than ever, the volunteers wanted to get into the air and give the Japs someone their own size to pick on.

As they headed back toward the hostel and dinner, Tex found himself wondering how the Hell's Angels were faring at Rangoon.

"Say, Ed," he asked, "what does that mean—'ding hao'? Any idea?"

"It means 'good job,' I believe," his friend replied.

"Good job? Well, we haven't done anything yet."

"Tomorrow's another day, though, Tex."

* * *

Following the surprise attack on Pearl Harbor, the Allied situation in China was grim indeed. In the slow war of the previous four years and more, Japan had tightened her grasp on key seaports and industries, her control spreading slowly across most of China's populated area. The Empire kept pressure up on the remaining populace in the form of fire-bombings; and now, Japanese Army pilots prepared to carry out the missions with the usual lack of opposition. Intelligence reports that the remainder of the AVG would soon be moving to Kunming did not worry them at all.

Elsewhere, Japanese regulars fought their way with unbelievable speed down the Malay Peninsula toward the "invincible" bastion of Singapore. Wake Island fell within days. The enemy turned a baleful eye on British-held Burma, amassing hundreds of aircraft in preparation to wipe the British and New Zealanders out of the skies over Rangoon. Japan's pilots thought the few dozen British planes and their small band of American allies did not really pose even a worthy threat.

Half a world away, a college student and his date emerged from a movie theater near the University of Alabama. They chatted pleasantly about the matinee they had just seen—Sergeant York. Hailing a taxi, Sam Dixon held the door for the striking coed at his side. When they were inside the cab, the driver glanced back at them.

"So, have you heard the news?" asked the driver excitedly.

"What news is that?" replied the distracted young man.

"The Japs just attacked Pearl Harbor."

"Where's Pearl Harbor?" the two passengers wondered aloud in unison.

"Beats me."

There was silence in the car for a long moment. The young lady noticed the keen look in her beau's eye.

"What does that mean, Sam?" she asked tentatively.

"It means," he said, looking at her, "that I'm going to war."

She gazed out the window on the drive back to the Phi Delta Theta House, lost in thought. Her name was Mazie Sale.

Tex next to P-40 #48 at Kyedaw (Toungoo), fall 1941.

Tex, Ed Rector, and Bert Christman at the Raffles Hotel, Singapore, September 1941.

Panda Bears J.V. "Jack" Newkirk and Tom Jones at Kunming, December 1941.

Chapter 13

FIRST BLOOD

The Panda Bears had no time to relax and become gradually accustomed to their new surroundings in Kunming. The enemy had struck the city, and Chennault knew he would return soon. The AVG's leader had arrived, along with his staff, aboard several transports of the China National Aviation Corporation (CNAC); and he arranged alert schedules for the pilots as soon as they landed. With luck, Chennault thought, the Japanese would have no idea the AVG was even in the country yet, so swiftly had they relocated; but it was difficult to determine what intelligence the enemy had on the group. In any event, Tex and company would have one major advantage they had not enjoyed at Kyedaw: the Chinese radio warning net.

This invention of Chennault's was in the same vein as most of his ideas and tactics: simple, but extremely effective. The Chinese had nothing like radar to warn of incoming enemy aircraft; and Chennault was unlikely to get his hands on one of the primitive radar sets the British and Americans were beginning to operate. Instead, his idea was to use the huge population of China itself as a massive detection system. Even the most unschooled peasant villager could unfailingly recognize airplane engine noise—from bitter experience.

When villagers in outlying areas saw or heard an aircraft, a Chinese radio operator stationed there picked up a continuous-wave transmitter—which had been installed in the village just for the purpose—and reported the details to one of several "hub" radio stations, which Chennault had carefully placed. At these hubs, an American radioman, assisted by Chinese translators and helpers, would consolidate the information and transmit it back to Kunming. Listening operators at Kunming copied down the coded messages: *See three above station BC-5...Noise of many at station D-9...Heavy engine noise near X-3*, and the like. By pegging these locations on a wall map in the operations room at Kunming, the enemy's trail could quickly be plotted, and their intent determined.

The Japs knew about the warning net, and often executed purposeful feints to confound it; but they rarely fooled Chennault.

When the incoming enemy aircraft got close enough, the *jing bao* system kicked in. On a pole in the middle of the airfield, large balls constructed of bamboo were raised one by one to indicate the dwindling time remaining before the Japs' arrival. By the time three balls were on the pole—if there had been sufficient warning—the only remaining signs of the P-40s were dust clouds on the runway.

Weather reports were a "snap" using the warning net; there was no guesswork to it. If someone wanted to know what the weather was like at their destination, they could simply call the radio station in the area. A brief look out the window at a remote site was all it took to observe the atmospheric conditions. It was simple and effective—classic Chennault.

The morning after their arrival in Kunming, the AVG waited tensely for the Japanese to return—and were mildly surprised when all was quiet. AVG pilots made reconnaissance flights over outlying friendly airfields still under construction, and reported them unusable; but nothing more exciting occurred. Tex went to bed, after checking the duty roster to note that he was scheduled for morning alert again the next day.

On the morrow, Tex and several other vigilant Panda Bears watched the sun climb toward ten o'clock outside the small alert building.

"I'm going to take a coffee break, fellows," sighed Tex, and he made for a nearby building.

In the few minutes he was absent, it happened: a ball ran up the *jing bao* pole, and an air raid was on. A standby pilot sprinted for Tex's aircraft along with the others. When he emerged with coffee, Tex could only watch helplessly from the ground as the already airborne P-40s climbed to altitude. Cursing his luck, he made a quick count: eight members of the 2nd Squadron and sixteen pilots from the 1st were going up for the interception. Tex would have to watch.

In the air, radio exchanges were terse as the pilots listened to reports from the operations building, which came from the warning net. Ten bombers had been sighted. Jack Newkirk and Jim Howard led two four-ship flights of Panda Bears on a swift ascent eastward. Newkirk's flight sped off in the reported direction of the enemy planes, climbing to fifteen thousand feet, while Howard's four remained poised over Kunming. Sandy Sandell's sixteen Adam and Eves patrolled west of the city along the probable exit route of the enemy, waiting for a signal from the ground. With his pieces thus in place, Chennault waited for the trap to spring.

From a solid overcast to the south, there suddenly emerged the ten large, ominous shapes everyone was expecting—Japanese Ki-21 "Sally" bombers. Newkirk's flight spotted the Japs just as they saw his P-40s; and after a startled moment of hesitation on both sides, the Japanese reacted first. They turned tail, dove for speed, and jettisoned their bombs over the mountainsides below. The pursuing Panda Bears tried a few shots, but were far out of range. With the enemy fleeing into the clouds and his own radio cutting out, Newkirk announced that they were heading back to base. But only two of his P-40s rendezvoused with him; the third pilot charged on, in hot pursuit of the bombers, with a wide-open throttle and death in his eyes. It was Ed Rector.

On the ground, Chennault sensed what was going on despite the radio problems, and played the card he held up his sleeve. He ordered Sandell's flight of sixteen south, toward Iliang, to cut off the bombers' escape. It was the perfect move: Sandell's P-40s spotted the "Sallys" almost immediately. As the Adam and Eves picked out their targets against the overcast below them, they were surprised to see a lone P-40 roaring after the enemy bombers—and closing. His engine "firewalled," Ed Rector finally caught up with the Japanese just as the 1st Squadron pounced from above.

If it wasn't the disciplined, tactically sound engagement the Old Man had hoped for, at least it was effective. Despite the wild, 90-degree deflection shots attempted, lack of teamwork, and lessons forgotten in the heat of a first battle, the AVG pumped enough lead into the twin-engined aircraft to send three of them, with their seven-man crews, into oblivion. Ed Rector, his fuel gauge nearing empty, pressed home an attack from above on the leftmost bomber's rear quarter, ignoring the tail gunner who was returning fire. Rector only avoided slamming into the larger aircraft at the last possible second, shoving his stick forward and darting beneath it. When he looked back, the "Sally" was exhaling a sheet of flame all along its length, and immediately nosed over into a terminal trajectory.

The battle ranged out for many miles. After the P-40s turned for home, six more of the damaged bombers gave up the ghost. The stricken Japanese aircraft belched smoke and struggled to stay airborne, but one by one, they staggered out of formation and plunged to earth. One lone bomber survived to bring the news to the Japanese: the AVG was in China. The raid had cost them nine aircraft and 63 airmen. No Japanese plane would come near Kunming again for more than a year.

While the battle raged, scores of the AVG waited on the ground for their comrades to return; and one by one, the pilots landed—the 1st Squadron performing victory rolls. Finally, only one man was unaccounted for. Then, word arrived that Ed Rector had been forced to put down on an auxiliary field to the east. He had run completely out of gas, but only after getting what he was after: sending a Japanese bomber down in flames.

Tex was intensely disappointed to have missed the aerial contest, but steeled himself to patience. There would surely be plenty of chances to earn his keep. Meanwhile, he rejoiced with his friends at their terrific debut; and there was much slapping of backs and motioning with hands as they talked up the action with jumbled excitement.

"The Japs know we're here now—they'll be back!"

"Let 'em come back—and tell them to bring enough for everybody."

"Next time you make a pass, Jack, I recommend turning on your gun switches."

"Very funny," replied the crestfallen leader of the Panda Bears, who had indeed left his guns switched off accidentally.

"I was lined up on my third Jap, and my guns jammed—"

"Your guns didn't jam, Wolf. Take a look—you're out of ammo!"

Even Chennault couldn't suppress a smile at the success of the AVG's first encounter. He called for a debriefing immediately, intending to use the opportunity to instruct the men while the combat was fresh on their minds.

After a careful review of the battle in detail, he made his concise assessment: "Next time, get them all."

The bar was open later than usual that night, with plenty of customers.

After the AVG's first fight, Chennault's stock rose considerably among the men. What they realized, even if they didn't say so, was that everything had gone exactly as he'd said it would. The Japs' tenaciously held formations, the Ki-21's vulnerable approaches, the P-40's combat performance—all of it was just as the Old Man had taught them. Tex reflected that the AVG might just be able to turn the tables on Japan in China's skies.

The next few days passed without incident. It seemed the Japanese were uncertain about what to do with the AVG at Kunming; so instead, they focused their attention on the other end of China's only supply route. On December 23rd, an aerial force seven times that of the Kunming raid darkened the sky over Rangoon, where the 3rd Squadron had been dispatched to aid the British. On this occasion, Japan's bombers brought escorting fighters with them—Japanese pilots who had cut their teeth on the demolition of the Chinese Air Force for four years.

Mingaladon Airfield, some distance north of the city, served as the base of operations for both the British and the AVG's 3rd Squadron. Unlike Chennault's radio warning system, the British "alert system" around Rangoon was comprised of observers on foot, who carried mirrors to "flash" alerts back to the base. It was unreliable at best; and in cloudy weather, it was useless. The British also had a prototype radar set, which detected reasonably well in certain directions, but poorly in others.

Without any warning of their own, the Hell's Angels had to rely upon the British for their cue to scramble. The RAF pilots generally regarded the AVG as a less-than-respectable outfit; and half the time, they didn't bother to inform them that an air raid was even underway.

So it was this time: the AVG pilots sitting alert only knew what was going on when one of them glanced out the window and hollered, as he saw British aircraft taxiing down the runway. By the time the 3rd Squadron got fourteen P-40s airborne, the bombing raid was already well underway. Nevertheless, the Hell's Angels managed to shoot down six bombers and four fighters, including a couple of I-97 "Nates" and Ki-43 "Oscars." The British did not fare as well; their outmatched Brewster *Buffaloes* traded kills about equally with the Japanese.

The first AVG victories over Rangoon came with a high price: pilots Neil Martin and Henry Gilbert were shot down in flames, the first two of the group to die in combat. P.J. Greene was shot up and forced to bail out, but survived; and Matt Kuykendall got a shallow, bloody wound when a bullet punctured his cockpit and grazed his scalp, on the way to burying itself in the instrument panel.

On the ground at Mingaladon, the AVG's borrowed operations building took a direct hit from an enemy bomb, whose blast wounded a couple of ground crewmen. But that was nothing compared to the devastation wrought on the city of Rangoon. In spite of their losses, the Jap "Sally" bombers had pressed on to their target, releasing tons of bombs over the city. Structures disintegrated; enormous fires raged across whole blocks; and the ensuing explosions and shrapnel killed three thousand residents. The Hell's Angels had given better than they got in the air; but by sheer weight of numbers, the Japanese had forced their way through to hammer Rangoon. There had been no way to stop them.

While Tex and his comrades at Kunming read telegrams reporting on the battle, the situation in Rangoon began to worsen. Fearing that the raid was the beginning of the end for their city, many Burmese and Indian residents packed up their belongings, or closed up shop, and fled. That included many of the cooks and support personnel who had serviced the men at Mingaladon Airfield. Nothing the British authorities did could stem the evacuation. Far down the peninsula to the southeast, British Army troops were holding the line against the advancing Japanese for the present; but the natives had little faith in the defense. The mass exodus from Rangoon left the AVG in the unenviable position of doing their own laundry and making meals out of bread, beer, and anything else that could be foraged.

More bad news followed soon. Three AVG pilots had been sent to Toungoo, to ferry a trio of new Curtiss CW-21 *Demon* fighter planes back to Kunming. The CW-21s had been manufactured at the CAMCO plant, which had recently been moved to Loiwing from its longtime location near Rangoon. Fresh off the assembly line, these lightweight fighters were supposed to have performance specifications that outmatched even the vaunted *Zero*, including a record-breaking 5,000-feet-per-minute rate of climb. On the pilots' return trip, after refueling at Lashio, they became lost on the final leg into Kunming. No airfield was anywhere in sight; and after casting about in several directions, the CW-21s ran out of fuel. Erik Shilling and Ken Merritt, two of Tex's squadron mates, managed successful wheels-up crash landings. The third man, Lacy Mangleburg, tried a wheels-down landing in a stream, changed his mind after dipping his propeller, and slammed into a hillside after a futile attempt to gain altitude. The CW-21's ammunition exploded, killing him instantly.

Christmas at Kunming dawned cold and gray. Under the circumstances, Tex found it difficult to salvage much holiday spirit. Not a Christmas tree was to be found (though jungle flora was very much in evidence); and the only "presents" they were likely to receive would fall from the bomb bays of the Japanese. In fact, Radio Tokyo had broadcast that the 3rd Squadron at Rangoon—sweltering in 115-degree heat—should expect as much. It turned out the Japs weren't kidding.

Eighty bombers roared toward the city, with some four dozen I-97s alongside. They were bent on wiping out the upstart AVG once and for all. The huge force was echeloned into several waves, intended to give the defenders no rest as they were pounded off the map. But this time, the 3rd Squadron did have advance warning from the British; so they managed to get their planes to altitude with a little time to spare. Still, the odds were gruesome, with the dozen P-40s outnumbered by ten to one.

The ensuing battle turned out to be the Hell's Angels' finest hour. It ranged far out over the Gulf of Martaban, whose blue waters swallowed numerous Japanese casualties that would never be verified. Instead of dealing the blow they intended, the Japs became the victims of a beating they would never forget. The P-40s tore into the enemy fighters and bombers alike, diving and firing with deadly accuracy as Chennault had taught them, breaking up persistent formations, and turning the shocked Japanese into dying streaks of fire.

At the heart of the battle flew R.P. "Duke" Hedman. Ripping off bursts in quick succession, he burned no less than five Japanese aircraft out of the sky before his ammunition gave out. In a matter of minutes, he went from untried pilot to the AVG's first ace. As the Japanese sped for home, they were forced to turn repeatedly to engage the doggedly pursuing P-40s. Many enemy fighter pilots ran out of gas and dropped into the jungle.

When the long day was over, the weary Hell's Angels went wild with excitement: they had lost none of their own—and felled thirteen fighters and fifteen heavy bombers, in a resounding twenty-eight-to-nothing licking.

Weeks later, several Army Air Corps personnel arrived from the States to "research the gunnery tactics Duke Hedman had employed" in the wildly successful engagement. The Army airmen began to question Hedman, prepared take copious notes. The AVG man looked thoughtful; then he began to gesture with his hands.

"Well," he began authoritatively, as the Army flyers leaned forward in anticipation, "you move up to about fifty feet behind 'em...hold down the trigger until they drop...and then move in to the next one. When you're out of ammo, go on in and land."

There was a pause. The researchers nodded uncertainly, looking somewhat bewildered. They eventually left, shaking their heads.

At chilly Kunming, Tex was enjoying a celebration of another sort. Generalissimo and Madame Chiang Kai-Shek honored the men of the AVG with a personal visit, throwing them a party at one of the AVG's own hostels. It was a new experience for the Americans; the food was delicious, and the pageantry that accompanied such occasions in China was impressive. It was also Tex's first opportunity to meet the ruling couple of China.

The Generalissimo was trim and austere in appearance, with a pleasant smile and modestly adorned military uniform. Although he spoke little English, he was the soul of courtesy, making no secret of his gratitude and praise for the AVG. His features revealed intelligence and discernment, giving an impression of quiet command. Tex thought it curious that the man who had single-handedly managed to bring tumultuous China under unified leadership should project such an air of benevolence.

The striking Madame Chiang was just as courteous as her husband, impressing the Americans in quite a different way. Her petite figure was wrapped in an exquisite robe of the most intricate workmanship. She was completely enchanting, greeting each of the men in English better than most of theirs, the product of a Wellesley education. She gushed over their accomplishments thus far; and afterward, Tex and the others found themselves more impressed with the Madame than even the Generalissimo.

Only one incident marred the evening. Chennault had asked the AVG not to drink until after the party, since their hosts, as a rule, did not partake of alcohol. Some grumbled at this; but Madame Chiang's charm quickly dissipated any hard feelings. During the meal, Tex noticed two empty seats at the banquet table, but didn't know whose they were. After dinner, Chennault asked Tex if he would escort the ruling couple for a brief tour of the hostel. Honored, Tex agreed.

When the small entourage entered one of the lounges on the lower floor, there was an awkward pause. There were Greg "Pappy" Boyington and Percy Bartelt, at the bar; and they had obviously been ignoring the no-drinks-till-afterward instructions with gusto. Chennault tried to introduce the pair to the Chiangs anyway; but they were too drunk even to stand. The Old Man flushed with anger, but held his temper to avoid losing face. Chiang Kai-Shek was far too polite to mention the matter, which proved a relatively small embarrassment in an otherwise superb evening. It was Boyington's first and only meeting with the ruler of China.

The early successes of the AVG had not escaped the notice of the American press—quite the reverse. There were a few reporters in Kunming. Many more were in Rangoon;

it was common to see journalists and fighter pilots mingling at the "Silver Grill," a favorite local establishment of the British and Americans alike. The reporters talked up the pilots' exploits with them, and stories of the AVG began to appear in major U.S. newspapers and magazines. It was a dark time of the war for the United States and her allies; at the time, they were losing ground on every front around the world. Even on the day of the Christmas victory over Rangoon, the Japanese wrested control of Hong Kong from the British. The AVG's accomplishments made for rare good news that encouraged folks back home. Sometimes the stories were even exaggerated, much to the amusement of the volunteers themselves.

One American-based Chinese newspaper described the group in glowing terms, dubbing them the "Flying Tigers." The name stuck. Within a week, stories were proliferating nationwide about the aerial deeds of the Flying Tigers; and the AVG was perfectly happy with the title. The American readership ate it up, too, eager to learn about action in one area of the world where they were winning. Decades later, the nickname would still bring instant recognition.

In Rangoon, the 3rd Squadron was less interested in a great nickname than in their dwindling supply of combat-worthy aircraft. Several had been destroyed or shot up in the two enemy raids on the city; the Hell's Angels were down to only eleven flyable planes. On the 27th of December, Chennault decided to send the 2nd Squadron, Tex's Panda Bears, down to Rangoon to relieve the 3rd. Before the switch could take place, though, the Japanese returned to Rangoon for another raid. Fortunately, they brought only a small force; and the weary Angels managed to down another two enemy planes. They were plenty ready for a break from combat when their fresh comrades arrived on December 30th.

In Burma once more, Tex surveyed deserted Rangoon and wondered if the vanished residents knew something the AVG did not. 1941 was drawing to a close, and the city wore a look of impending doom.

* * *

One day before the massive aerial contests began above Rangoon, a top-level meeting among the Allied nations took place in Chungking. Generalissimo Chiang offered the British six Chinese divisions, along with his precious and irreplaceable motorized artillery, to aid in the defense of Burma. Field Marshal Sir Archibald Wavell hastily declined, believing that if ever the Chinese entered Burma, they might not be rooted out, even after the war; it could, he thought, make post-war restoration of the colonial boundaries difficult. Four months later, the remnants of the British Army would be fleeing north to India in tatters.

As the two-week AVG lifespan predicted by the War Department drew to a close, CAMCO executive Bill Pawley dealt a treacherous card. With his Loiwing aircraft factory beginning to turn out new—and profitable—CW-21 fighters, Pawley forbid his workers to perform "useless" repair work on the outdated P-40s of the Flying Tigers. By thus breaking his written agreement, Pawley nearly finished off the group for the second time. AVG mechanics, along with some Chinese CAMCO workers who would not abandon them, were left "holding the bag" as best they could.

In the opening days of 1942, Japanese forces swept into Manila. Douglas MacArthur's attempted counterattack on the enemy's landing points failed, and the Filipino-American forces withdrew to dig in on the peninsula of Bataan. Starving and riddled by disease, they would beat back tremendously superior Japanese forces for over three months before a final, reluctant surrender.

Confined to bed by his annual attack of chronic bronchitis, Chennault's weathered face broke into a grin as he read a Christmas Day telegram from 3rd Squadron Leader Arvid "Ole" Olson: "Like shooting ducks—would put entire Jap force out of commission with group here."

P-40 #48 after Tex "lengthened the runway" at Kyedaw following an attempted night intercept of Japanese bombers, December 10, 1941.

Tex next to P-40 #48 at Kyedaw (Toungoo), fall 1941. Note that shark's teeth have not yet been painted on the P-40s.

Chapter 14

INTO THE MAELSTROM

At any other time, Tex would have called the view through the microscope fascinating, an incredible window into another world. Under the circumstances, however, he felt only a sinking feeling as he watched a menagerie of microorganisms float in and out of the instrument's illuminated circle. He was looking at a sample of water he had brought from his quarters near Mingaladon Airfield to the British hospital in Rangoon.

"Is all this stuff supposed to be in there?" he asked doubtfully, looking up at the British doctor who stood nearby with folded arms, watching Tex.

"Afraid not, old chap—not in your drinking water. This sample confirms what I suspected from your symptoms: you have a case of bacillary dysentery."

Tex cursed. "Well, I mean, is it something I can get rid of? This stuff is pretty bad news, I can tell you."

"Fortunately, yes. I have the proper medication here somewhere, which, if taken faithfully," he said, rummaging through a cabinet as he spoke, "should have you back in the pink in no time. Ah—here we are," he concluded, producing a container of pills and offering it to Tex. "Two a day until they're gone. Be thankful that you don't have amebic dysentery, my good man."

Tex gratefully accepted the pills and headed back to the airfield. He had suspected trouble was coming when he noticed his Indian *bara*, who took care of the men in Tex's quarters, straining their drinking water through cheesecloth. Tex had instructed the man to boil it before making it available, but the bara had apparently thought that was too much trouble. Realizing he had been drinking the unboiled water for a couple of days, Tex wasn't surprised when the symptoms of dysentery hit him: cramping, nausea, dehydration, and weakness. With the medicine from the hospital, he hoped to be rid of the condition quickly.

The Panda Bears had been in Rangoon for a week, and Tex had settled into something like a routine. Since the 2nd Squadron's arrival, the Japanese had not yet returned to the city in any force. The AVG figured the Japs were licking their wounds from the aerial battles during Christmas week, probably gathering their strength for another "decisive blow" that might come any time.

The city of Rangoon was a cowed shadow of its former splendor. Destruction from the two big raids was evident everywhere; charred buildings and blasted rubble dominated the landscape. Gone were most of the Indian shopkeepers and the native Burmese in their colorful attire. Smoke curled up from fires that had burned for over a week. Buddhist monks in yellow robes, some sympathetic to the Japanese and hiding long knives beneath their clothing, peered silently at the Americans. Burmese attacks against small groups of Britons had long since become commonplace. Upon their departure, the Hell's Angels had advised Tex and his companions to arm themselves when traveling through the city.

Some areas had suffered relatively little damage, however; and a few establishments were even open for business when the Panda Bears arrived. The Silver Grill was one of these. Tex himself had taken the train from Toungoo into Rangoon once to visit the Grill, back during training; but he hadn't been overly impressed with the crowded cabaret. This time, he preferred to spend his time at a place around the corner, owned by a Greek named Minos. The proprietor was a cheerful fellow, who could get a customer anything they wanted—black market activity was rampant—but he expected the customer to pay the corresponding price without complaint. He served tasty rice dishes that Tex learned to scoop up with his hand and push into his mouth using his thumb (Minos offered no utensils). There was a dance floor of sorts in the place as well; and Minos had three beautiful daughters, who enjoyed associating with his American patrons. Two daughters were eventually married to men of the AVG.

The Panda Bears were initially quartered in an old, rickety barracks beside the field at Mingaladon; but the arrangement was short-lived. In the middle of their first night, they were awakened in their cots by the sound they most feared: exploding bombs. After an initial scare, they learned this was common. Instead of large raids, enemy bombers regularly came over the city and airfield alone, or in pairs, during the night. They droned overhead at high altitude and dropped a few bombs, not expecting to hit anything, but hoping to disrupt the pilots' rest. It was an effective tactic, since neither the AVG nor the British had planes with any night-fighting capability whatsoever. Both groups tried repeatedly to get airborne and find the bombers in the darkness, but without success. The Japs continued their nocturnal "nuisance raids" unmolested.

Desperate for a good night's sleep, Tex and some of his companions quickly vacated the barracks at the airfield and moved out to the surrounding area, in search of a decent bed. In the end, they stayed in a variety of places. A group of Britons that worked for the Burma Oil Company took in a number of the men, sharing their comfortable dwellings with them, and "wining and dining" the pilots on company fare. Ed Rector was among those who received such hospitality. Others, like Tex, had to be content with "roughing it" a long way from the field in *bashas*—bamboo huts with palm-leaf roofs—along with the ground crews.

Each evening, the pilots and crew chiefs saw to it that the precious P-40s were flown from Mingaladon out into the surrounding auxiliary fields and camouflaged. Then the pilots flew them back for combat alert the next morning. Such dispersal ensured that a lucky enemy bomb couldn't damage them. Tex made many flights to shuttle the P-40s back and forth; and, of course, by sleeping in the *bashas*, he wasn't kept awake at night by air raids and exploding bombs.

In the first days of January, Chennault's intelligence reports indicated Japanese aircraft were gathering thickly at bases in Thailand, within easy striking distance of Rangoon. Since the Japs apparently weren't ready to continue the fight over the city immediately, the Old Man decided that the AVG would go on the offensive. It was on January 3rd that he sent Tex, Newkirk, Howard, and Christman to strafe Raheng, a small outlying field across the border. Tex's first taste of combat was bittersweet: he shot down two enemy fighters, but was nearly shot down himself. It was the beginning of a series of effective AVG raids on the enemy's Thailand bases, proving that the Flying Tigers did not require "home field advantage" to be effective.

The day after Tex's mission over Raheng, angry enemy fighter pilots retaliated. They came straight to Mingaladon to punish the Tigers, not bothering to bring any bombers along. Thirty fighters descended upon the airfield. Only six P-40s of the 2nd Squadron were able to intercept them. In a rare defeat for the Flying Tigers, the Japs shot three P-40s out of the sky; only Ken Merritt managed to destroy a Japanese aircraft. Fortunately, all three downed AVG pilots survived. One of these was Bert Christman, who narrowly escaped being strafed to death in his parachute after he bailed out.

Not on alert that day, Tex watched the battle from the ground. At one point during the action, fellow Texan George "Pappy" Paxton came careening toward the runway in his P-40; opinion was divided upon whether he was crashing or trying to land. The plane wobbled and sputtered, its hydraulics shot up and its landing gear dangling loosely, as Paxton tried to put it down. Forgetting to turn off the gun switch on his control stick, he hauled back on it to avoid crashing on the runway—and released a spray of bullets that ricocheted in all directions. Ground crews dove for cover as the hapless Paxton screeched to a halt, sparks and ammunition flying. When he stopped, the men rushed to pull him out of the cockpit. They could see that enemy bullets had shattered the armor plate behind his seat, and the resulting shrapnel had torn into his back like a shotgun blast. The wounds were messy, but fortunately, mostly superficial. As he was extricated from his smoking plane, "Pappy" shook his fist at the sky and gave a final shout.

"I still say those little bastards can't shoot!"

Then he promptly fainted dead away.

The Japanese kept up their night solo raids; and it wasn't long before some of the exhausted AVG, still housed at the airfield, simply slept through them—bombs exploding nearby and all. Eventually, the Burma Oil Company employees in Rangoon moved into their underground bomb shelters—well-stocked with refreshment and comforts—and took their Flying Tiger "boarders" with them. Tex was impressed when he visited these; but he continued to make do in the primitive quarters near an auxiliary field dubbed "Johnny Walker" (all of them were named after favorite drinks).

The wee hours of the morning on January 8th found Tex, Ed Rector, and Ken Merritt speeding through the darkness toward Mingaladon in one of the group's cars. The Japanese had come over as usual; but this time, Panda Bears Jim Howard, Gil Bright, and Pete Wright had decided to try an interception. Tex and the others listened for any gunfire, but there was none; the paltry moonlight still wasn't enough for the pilots to locate the enemy. When the trio arrived, Rector parked the car near the end of the runway and off to one side, switching off the engine.

"Looks like they're coming in. I need to stretch the old legs a bit if I'm going to stay awake," Rector said. He and Tex got out of the car.

"Merritt must be asleep. Yeah, he is," Tex pronounced, peering into the back seat. The two friends walked a short distance away to watch the first P-40 descend toward the runway in the humid air.

In the plane's cockpit, Pete Wright was mildly frustrated by their latest unsuccessful attempt to catch the wily Japanese bombers. On final approach, he activated the mechanism to lower his landing gear—and was hit right in the eyes with a spray of hydraulic fluid from a line that suddenly burst.

Blind and cursing, he fumbled for his goggles. The spray continued as he donned them, covering his gauges and instruments. Wright knew he had to put the plane down before the fluid ran out completely. Wiping his goggles constantly, he thought he could just make out the runway. As the fluid covered the inside of his windshield, he braced himself for what he hoped would be a survivable touchdown.

"What's wrong with him?" asked Tex with alarm, seeing Wright's P-40 wobble as it approached. "He couldn't have gotten hit by anything, could he?"

"He's off center—he's over the center line—oh hell!" shouted Rector.

Rector and Tex watched in horror as the P-40 drunkenly drifted right, hovered, and then, with a metallic screech, crashed directly into the car they had left less than a minute before. Tex found himself sprinting back toward the demolished vehicle as the plane skewed sideways, sliding to a halt. He knew that Merritt had to be dead.

It was tough enough to lose a friend in combat; but losing Merritt that way was nearly intolerable—especially for Pete Wright, who had unknowingly plowed right into him. With no lights on the car, and the blinding emergency in the cockpit, there was no possible way Wright could have seen anything; but he spent many sleepless nights re-living the incident anyway. It shook Tex and Rector up as well, more than they cared to admit. They had escaped death by less than a minute—and not for the last time.

Later that day, Tex noticed that a return strafing mission was scheduled to Raheng in Thailand, where he had scored his two aerial victories. Charlie Mott, the Panda Bears' operations officer, was to lead it. Hailing from Alabama, Mott was a mechanical genius with a superlative touch on aircraft controls. During the aircraft assembly at Rangoon, Mott had designed an optical gunsight to replace the standard P-40 ring-and-bead sight. Mott's design implemented a British-made device to project a beam of light onto the windscreen from below. The beam illuminated a 30mm-wide target reticule Mott had made, about the size of an enemy bomber's wing at a specific range. The setup provided greatly increased accuracy—though, in the end, only a few P-40s could be outfitted with it.

With the 2nd Squadron's leaders Jack Newkirk and Jim Howard *hors de combat* that day, Mott was in charge, and he was wasting no time.

"Hey, Charlie," drawled Tex, striding into the operations tent, "Why don't you put me on this mission?"

It was mid-morning, and Mott's group of four was preparing to take off.

"Why, Tex?" Mott wondered, frowning.

"Well, I've been there before," he replied, "so I kind of know the area."

"I know it, but I'm going to take this one. Seems like you want to hog all these missions. Let's give these other guys a chance," Mott said, chuckling and gesturing at Percy Bartelt, Gil Bright, and "Moose" Moss, who were donning their flight gear.

Tex wished he could go, but offered no further argument; and the four P-40s took off. Hours later, only three of them returned, bringing unhappy news: Charlie Mott had been shot down by ground fire around the target. He had been forced to bail out in enemy territory. Mott had given a good account of himself, burning three enemy planes on the ground before being hit; and the group as a whole had accounted for eight. But the loss of their leader was heavy. Tex winced as he remembered how close he himself had come to being shot down in the same area.

Shortly afterward, the AVG learned through Chinese intelligence that the Japs had captured Mott. He spent the rest of the war in the prison camp on the infamous Kwai River, constructing a railroad from Thailand to Burma—a brutal Japanese forced-labor project that eventually cost the lives of some 165,000 prisoners. Mott, however, survived. Upon his release, he rejoined the Navy and enjoyed an outstanding career. He did resolve, however, never to argue with Tex again.

When not in combat, there was plenty of time with little to do at Mingaladon; and Tex enjoyed occasionally wandering down to the docks at Rangoon to see what he could see—armed with his .45-caliber pistol. The gun had been a gift from one of his uncles, who had used it in the Great War and passed it on to Tex when he learned of his nephew's coming voyage to China. Most of the AVG men carried a sidearm, and a few of them had even acquired heavier weapons.

At the docks, there was still a great deal of activity going on; the American lend-lease supplies being unloaded there remained critical for China. Tex greeted and spoke with the dock crews in his easygoing way, telling them what he knew about the goings-on on elsewhere in Burma. Sailors on the ships at anchor often reciprocated with news from the west, and occasionally invited him aboard for conversation or a meal. The food was usually a good deal better than the fare available at Mingaladon.

One happy evening, a newfound friend invited Tex aboard a liberty ship, the *Shik Shinny*.

"We're having steak tonight," the crewman announced, smiling. "What do you say?"

"Man, that sounds great," said Tex, trying to keep from drooling on the deck.

Preparation took some time, and Tex spent it in the friendly company of the ship's crew. Dusk had faded to darkness before all was ready. Finally, Tex sat down with anticipation as the piping-hot sirloin was placed before him.

Just then, a siren went off in the city. It was an air raid alert; and Tex knew the alert pilots at Mingaladon would be scrambling—or, with luck, already in the air. Instinctively, he stood up and started to run for the gangplank; but when he realized the situation, he stopped. There was no way he could reach the airfield in time to affect the outcome of the battle; and, by golly, he wanted to eat that sizzling steak, even if it meant sitting through a bombardment.

As it turned out, it *did* mean sitting through a bombardment. The Japanese objective that night was the very dock area where the *Shik Shinny* was anchored. Fortunately, this time—as on most occasions—the enemy's bombs were inaccurate, most falling harmlessly into the bay. A few found marks on land some distance away. Wolfing down the delicious steak, Tex decided that if his "number was up" this time, at least he would go out happy.

A few days later, Tex flew P-40 number 48 back to the old training base at Toungoo to re-boresight his guns. Upon returning to Mingaladon, he found that eight members of the 1st Squadron, led by Tex's former shipmate Bob Neale, were joining them. Some of these Adam and Eves were veterans of the first air battle over Kunming; and from their faces, Tex could see they wanted another crack at the enemy. They were a welcome addition at Mingaladon. The 2nd Squadron had lost several aircraft in taxiing accidents on the crater-pocked runway and other mishaps, and was down to ten flyable P-40s. Five Panda Bears were in the British hospital with illness or shrapnel wounds.

"Not much going on right now up at Kunming," said Neale, explaining their arrival, "so the Old Man sent us down here to see if we could get gainfully employed."

"We'll start you at $500 a plane," someone quipped, prompting general laughter. Neale and his men settled in quickly; the Flying Tigers expected a fight any day.

But for the next ten days, they did not see or hear a single enemy plane near Rangoon in daylight. Various minor actions did occur elsewhere in the region, and everyone began to get edgy. In China, three Japanese bombers attempted a raid on the auxiliary AVG airfield of Mengtze; but they quickly jettisoned their bombs and ran when four Hell's Angels raced to intercept them from Kunming. Four days later, the Japs tried the same trick again, but ran out of luck: a four-ship of 3rd Squadron P-40s caught and plastered them, downing all three Japanese bombers. Jim Howard led a flight of four back into Thailand, where they ripped up a bomber on the runway and strafed an enemy barracks. Newkirk took six more P-40s to escort British *Blenheim* bombers over the front near Tavoy; they lost "Moose" Moss's plane in a dogfight when seven Japanese fighters "jumped" them suddenly. When a reconnaissance flight over Hanoi revealed over a dozen enemy bombers parked on the airfield, eighteen antiquated Russian-built Chinese SB-3 bombers from Chanyi planned a mission to hit them. On January 22nd, "Sandy" Sandell took off with ten P-40s to escort the SB-3s; but the rickety bombers got lost when they failed to calculate for wind, and the mission was aborted.

These operations broke the monotony, but the men considered them "small fry." They were getting intelligence reports that the Japs were moving some three hundred planes—two-fifths of them fighters—to within striking range of Rangoon. Something bigger had to be coming.

Exactly one month after the first Japanese raid on Rangoon, something bigger arrived. Around mid-morning, while his aircraft underwent maintenance, Tex sat in the alert tent beside the runway at Mingaladon, flipping through a magazine. Outside, he could hear RAF *Hurricane* fighters, newly ferried from India, landing one by one. Almost all the other AVG pilots were away on a mission. Tex was supposed to be enjoying a day off, but didn't have anything particular in mind to do. When the telephone rang and a British officer told him in clipped tones that an enemy raid was incoming, Tex dropped the magazine and ran for the door—almost barreling into an AVG ground crewman who charged in, out of breath.

"Hey, Tex—we've only got two planes ready. Yours is still opened up. They caught us right in the middle of maintenance," the engineer said with a grimace.

"Well, I'll take one of them. Where's Lawlor?"

Tex was out the door, followed by the crewman. Frank Lawlor, Tex knew, was the only other pilot likely to be around.

"I just passed him. He knows," the man replied, puffing along behind.

Tex was running for the pair of P-40s, and saw Lawlor already clambering up the side of one and getting in. The only other aircraft that looked ready to go was Jim

Howard's number 57. Tex swung up into the cockpit in haste. Howard's leather helmet was sitting on the stick. Tex donned it; it was several sizes too large.

"Minor details," he grunted, starting the engine and taxiing after Lawlor.

A small dust cloud had formed where the *Hurricanes* had landed, and Tex could see the RAF ground crews swarming around the new fighters, making a frenzied effort to refuel them quickly. *They're gonna be too late.*

He switched on the command set and raised his squadron mate. "What have we got, Frank?"

"Many bandits southeast—that's all we know," came the reply over the headset.

Frank Lawlor, an ex-Navy man from California, was cool and efficient in combat, regarded as an excellent shot. If they had to take on heavy odds, Tex could think of worse pilots to have flying with him.

In a short while, they had climbed to twelve thousand feet, just below a small bank of clouds, keeping a tight formation and eyes peeled for the enemy. They did not have long to wait.

"One o'clock low, Frank." said Tex, starting his dive.

"Got 'em."

All twenty-three of them—Tex counted twice—were "Nate" fighters. It seemed to Tex that the entire extended family of the ones he had shot down over Raheng must have come for revenge. The thought flashed in his mind that he had never seen this many enemy planes in the air at one time; but he went right to work. Both men knew that if the Japs got through to Mingaladon, they would tear up the helpless *Hurricanes* like vultures.

Side by side, the two P-40s arrowed into the top of the enemy formation, striving to break it up. The effect was like kicking an anthill. "Nates" scattered in all directions. Tex lost sight of Lawlor as he deftly snapped bursts of fire at several enemy fighters in his line of flight. He seemed to hit one; but then his attention was instinctively riveted to one particular I-97, whose pilot did not appear to see him. Tex's first burst missed, but his second chewed into the "Nate's" tail and fuselage. The panicking enemy pilot banked sharply; but Tex's third stream of bullets was already on the way. They peppered the cockpit, sending the little fighter into a final spin as the P-40 screamed out through the bottom of the Japanese swarm.

Tex "checked six," reminding himself that the gaggle of enemy fighters chasing him could not catch the P-40 in a dive. Lawlor was nowhere in sight, but Tex had no time to look for him. He pulled away and climbed to altitude once more. The pursuing "Nates" had broken off, as he knew they would, and were trying to rejoin the main formation. A second pass would be much more difficult, Tex judged, since they knew he was coming; the Japs could concentrate their firepower on just one or two P-40s with deadly results. The fight was moving steadily closer to Mingaladon.

On the ground, AVG crewmen were setting a world record for closing up engine covers and making final adjustments to three more flyable P-40s. Jack Newkirk, Bert Christman, and Fred Hodges had returned from their mission, and waited impatiently for a chance to get airborne again before it was too late. Across the field, the *Hurricane* pilots hadn't even left their cockpits, and were shouting for their ground crews to hurry with the refueling. They still had extra gas tanks attached from the ferry trip, and their guns were not even boresighted; but they were going up anyway. Everyone could hear engine noise from the aerial battle, and kept one eye on the sky.

Frank Lawlor had decided to make the most of their two P-40s; so while Tex had made his first diving pass, Lawlor fired a brief burst and zoomed back upward, straight into the protection of the cloudbank. He maintained altitude for a few seconds, turning; then he dipped out into the clear to take another snap burst at the nearest enemy fighter. It worked beautifully. Repeating the maneuver several times, he caught several of the enemy completely unawares. The Japs couldn't draw a bead on Lawlor before he popped back up into the clouds. The ensuing spectacle resembled a bizarre game of aerial "whack-a-mole." Within minutes, Lawlor had shot three oblivious "Nates" out of the formation to crash in the rice paddies below.

Finally regaining enough altitude, Tex came around for a second pass. As he dove toward them, he imagined that every enemy pilot was staring straight at him. Just before he came within firing range, he executed a "split-S," hoping to make himself a more difficult target. After a half-roll, he hauled back on the stick, plummeting toward the Japanese at a suddenly different angle. Howard's helmet slipped briefly down over his eyes, and Tex shoved it back. When he did, he spotted a second "Nate" that had banked away and seemed not to notice him. Expecting bullets to arrive any moment, Tex lined up quickly and fired a medium-length burst toward the other plane as it crossed his gunsights, moving away from him. The P-40's tracers reached for the "Nate," tearing a wing off and causing it to skid horribly to the right before flipping over and fluttering earthward.

The bullets he expected came; but Tex's maneuvering had almost done the trick. As he dove for daylight once more, 7.7mm bullets slammed into the underside of his right wing, jolting it upward and sending the P-40 into a slight bank. Then Tex was clear, once more pulling away from a handful of trailing fighters.

The two Flying Tigers had held the line for ten minutes; and it was enough. Instead of making a beeline for Mingaladon, the enemy fighters had elected to dogfight with two maddeningly elusive opponents. Now the odds were about to even. The three just-readied P-40s rose from the runway.

The Japanese were wavering, having lost five of their number already. In another minute, Frank Lawlor had scratched a sixth—his fourth of the battle—and Bill Bartling roared into the fray to account for a seventh. It was enough for the Japs, and they fled. Tex brought his P-40 down to land as the concluding salvoes were echoing in the air above. He was nearly out of ammunition.

As he taxied to a stop, he saw a stone-faced Jim Howard glaring at him with folded arms. Tex removed Howard's oversized helmet, slid back the canopy, and stepped onto the wing.

"Hope you took good care of her," Howard snapped, with steel in his voice. He was looking number 57 over with a suspicious eye.

"Well Jim," Tex gave an amiable grin, "I think she held up all right, considering the odds."

"What do you mean, 'held up all right?'" Howard wanted to know. Then he scowled, spotting the battle damage under the wing. The son of missionary parents himself, Howard was not given to epithets—but his look spoke volumes.

"This is just great! Now she'll have to be patched up. There must be a dozen bullet holes here," Howard growled as he counted. "Yep. Eleven."

Tex had taken a few steps toward the hangar, but stopped. "How many did you say?"

"Eleven," Howard said angrily, crossing his arms, "*and* you got my helmet all sweaty."

"Eleven holes," said Tex slowly, "is how many *you* had last time we were on a mission together. Remember that one?"

Howard's face fell; he recalled how Tex had probably saved his life over Raheng three weeks earlier, by knocking a Jap fighter off his tail.

"Yeah, Tex," he said more gently, "I remember."

Tex grinned and put his hand on his friend's shoulder.

"Only eleven! The boys will have those patched up in no time."

While the two talked, the bulk of the 2nd Squadron had landed from their mission. It had been uneventful; but when they heard of the action that had occurred right over Mingaladon, they became excited. Most of the group, including Tex, figured there was a good chance of a "follow-up" wave of enemy aircraft. The faithful ground crews were already refueling and re-arming every available P-40. The pilots took a few minutes to grab sandwiches and cold tea. Newkirk ordered a patrol up as soon as four planes became available.

Instead of a patrol, there was a mass scramble as the air raid signal sounded again. Sure enough, exactly one hundred minutes after the first wave, the Japs' second echelon approached the airfield. Their strategy had been to engage and "tie up" the Allies with the first group of fighters, and then catch them helpless on the ground, refueling, with a follow-on force of bombers. What the Japanese never counted on was the efficiency of the AVG ground crews, who had miraculously readied the P-40s for takeoff in time to gain altitude before the bombers arrived. It would become a dismally familiar theme for the Japanese.

Naturally, Jim Howard insisted on taking his own plane up to meet the bombers; so Tex was relegated to observing the battle from the ground. Jack Newkirk led ten of the AVG aloft as the reports came in: thirty-one Army Type 98 bombers were converging on Mingaladon, intending to hammer it into extinction; and almost as many fighters escorted them. Ed Rector and Bert Christman were airborne this time, and Tex wished fervently for a plane so he could join them.

It was simply not Japan's day. The surprised bomber pilots jettisoned their loads when they saw ten P-40s diving at them from fifteen thousand feet; but, thus lightened, they still lacked the speed to get away cleanly. Bombs splashed into the landscape below as the AVG and RAF riddled their victims, attacking back and forth across the "V" formation. The Japanese fighters, flying behind the bombers as usual, eventually caught up to the battle, but fared poorly. The Tigers shot down five bombers and four "Nates" in the swirling melee.

But there were Allied losses, too. An RAF pilot perished in a fireball with his *Hurricane* after trying to turn with a maneuverable "Nate." Jack Newkirk, caught in a morass of enemy fighters after flaming one of the bombers, shot one of the nimble aircraft down; but he paid for it, as others hammered his plane with cannon shells. Newkirk managed to bring the P-40 down onto the airfield below with a sputtering engine and his flaps torn away. He overshot the runway's end and nosed over, fortunately emerging unhurt. Bill Bartling also had to crash-land after shooting down three bombers, totaling his aircraft, but escaping without injury. The worst blow came as Ed Rector and Bert Christman turned in tandem from their attacks on the bombers to intercept the flock of oncoming fighters.

Just behind Rector as they plowed into the "Nates," Christman sustained several hits in the P-40's vulnerable liquid cooling lines. Spewing Prestone coolant at full power, his engine sputtered and overheated almost immediately. Christman realized he couldn't "ride it down." Sliding the canopy open, he stood amid the howling airstream, then tumbled out of the plane, ready to open his chute. It was Christman's fourth bailout, so he knew what to do—but this time was different. A Japanese fighter pilot saw him, swooped, and opened up a merciless spray of bullets as the young man dropped through the air.

The fire found its mark many times. Christman was gone long before his body hit the ground.

* * *

As the Panda Bears arrived in Rangoon, Japanese ground forces far to the east, in China, drove westward from long-established positions. They were attempting to engage Chiang Kai-Shek's armies and prevent him from sending support to the Allied defense of Burma. In the line of the Japanese advance lay the strategic city of Changsha, successfully defended three times already by Hsueh Yo, a standout Chinese Army general. Against vastly superior weaponry, Hsueh stubbornly held his ground; then, impossibly, executed an encircling counterattack that caught the enemy completely by surprise. By the 5th of January, the Japanese had been thrown back a fourth time; nearly fifty-seven thousand Jap soldiers would not rise again from the fields around Changsha. It was the first great land victory of the war for the Allies—anywhere in the world.

Five days later, aboard a CNAC transport, Chennault returned to Kunming from a conference in Chungking. During the flight, the eager Army Air Corps colonel piloting the plane wanted to know everything about the air battles in Burma. He was desperately seeking a way to get into combat, to be transferred across the "Hump"—the huge chain of Himalayas between India and China—and operate with the AVG. He itched to get his hands on the controls of a P-40. His name was Robert L. Scott.

In mid-January, Japanese General Shojiro Iida sent his 15th Army slipping through the jungle across the Thailand border into the southern tip of Burma, driving toward British-held Moulmein. It was the opening move in what would become a gargantuan ground contest for control of the country.

Tex at Kunming, late 1941. Note Chinese Air Force headgear.

Chapter 15

BURMA BUCKLES

Air from an oxygen bottle, no matter how pure, has an unmistakable taste to it. Combined with the rubber mask that allows a pilot to breathe at higher altitudes, the taste comes across as something between medicine and carbon monoxide. Tex never enjoyed using the apparatus, but he had long since become used to the flavor. There was no getting around it anyway since, without the ability to fly above fifteen thousand feet, it would often have been impossible to effectively engage Japanese airplanes. Enemy fighters and bombers both varied their altitude significantly, depending on what they were trying to accomplish—and what resistance they expected. Even with its pilot on oxygen, though, the P-40 turned in a drunken performance above twenty-five thousand feet, stalling and "falling out" at just over twenty-seven thousand.

At the moment, Tex was airborne at eighteen thousand feet, breathing from the bottle and peering at the landscape below. Bob Neale, leading their two-plane patrol, flew ahead and to Tex's left. Far below their planes, the dark-green jungle looked solid, until it met the shining azure flatness of the Gulf of Martaban away to the right. Behind them lay Rangoon and their AVG companions, at Mingaladon Airfield; ahead, the exotic peninsula curved gracefully south for many miles.

Tex gazed morosely at the jungle. Somewhere beneath that dark canopy lay Bert Christman's body, half-buried in a rice paddy, full of Japanese 20mm cannon slugs. Somewhere below, also, moved a small party of Flying Tigers, led by "Pappy" Paxton, seeking to find and return Christman for burial among his friends. It was a loss Tex didn't want to think about right now.

The next moment he had something else to think about, as Neale's voice broke in. "Tex! Bandits, dead ahead low. You see them?"

Sure enough, seven twin-engine enemy bombers cruised directly toward them, some four thousand feet below. Tex cleared his throat and tried to sound upbeat.

"Yeah, I see them. Ready to break up this little Sunday drive?"

The two of them pushed it over and applied full military power; but the bombers continued to drone straight ahead. It was impossible to tell whether the Japanese crews had seen the P-40s, since they always held their formations with dogged tenacity, even in retreat. Tex pondered what a "break" it was to catch these bombers alone, without the protection of...

Then Tex saw them: a single vee-shaped flight of tiny, dark specks, far behind the bombers, keeping a formation just as disciplined.

"Bob, there's more—"

"I got 'em. We have some help, too," Neale replied.

Tex looked around quickly and spotted a pair of stubby fighters far below, climbing toward the enemy bombers from another direction. The pair could only be RAF Brewster *Buffaloes*—outmatched by almost any Japanese fighter, but flown with courage and skill by their devoted pilots.

Tex and Neale's diving attack on the bombers was potentially risky, since the twin-engine Ki-21 "Sallys" all had top-mounted machine-gun turrets. The Tigers would have to count on their speed to protect them, until they could get beneath the bombers and attack their vulnerable lower rear quarters. The *Buffaloes* were well aware of their own advantageous position; and they were also closer than the P-40s. Tex saw muzzle flashes winking from the guns of the RAF fighters, leaving characteristic puffs of smoke in a neat line. After several long bursts, one of the "Sallys" spouted flame from an engine, rolling slowly out of formation to its destruction. The *Buffaloes* broke away and right, to line up for another pass.

Now the droning bombers were within range of Tex's own guns, so he snapped a few bursts at the lumbering rightmost aircraft. Tracers from several bombers' top turrets reached hungrily toward Tex in return—some gut-wrenchingly close—but passed above or below him. The Japanese gunners weren't leading the P-40s enough, not accounting for their speed. Tex had an instant to see his target flash by, a wisp of white smoke coming from the engine he had hit; and then he was breaking hard to the left, to get away and come back around.

There was a sudden muffled *crump*. Looking quickly over his shoulder, Tex glimpsed Neale's target burning, in two pieces, as it began a fatal spin. That was two down.

It was time to check on the Jap fighters. Good—they were still well behind. Why on earth the Japanese consistently put their fighter cover a fair distance behind their bombers, Tex never figured out. It allowed exactly the kind of thing that was happening now.

Behind the formation now, both AVG pilots hauled their P-40s around in a tight turn. Tex felt the force of several G's press him into his seat. At this altitude, he no longer needed the oxygen; but in the heat of battle, he had completely forgotten to remove the mask. Looking directly out the top of his canopy in the turn, he noticed that the bombers had jettisoned some ordnance, and were making shallow dives to gain speed. However, they still maintained the usual well-regimented formation, continuing on a beeline for the target they wanted: Mingaladon.

Tex glanced down as he leveled out, noting that the bombs were going to hit harmlessly in the jungle; and there weren't as many as he had expected, either. Apparently the Japanese were saving some ordnance to get the job done—*if they live long enough*, he added mentally.

Mingaladon was coming into view when Tex charged in from the rear once more. This time, he and Bob Neale were in a high-low tandem, intended to catch the bombers in a crossfire. The British were also converging again, from the other side of the formation.

Slightly higher than the left-hand "Sally," Tex opened up with all his guns. With satisfaction, he watched debris tear out of the Ki-21's left engine. He moved his fire over to the turret gunner just before breaking left and away, but couldn't see the result. Neale was hitting the same bomber from below, breaking right and diving after his pass. Now sweating beneath his sheepskin-lined flight jacket, Tex finally realized his mask was still on; he tugged it free.

The Japanese fighters had caught up at last, and Tex could imagine the epithets they would be spitting as they waited for the Tigers' next pass. But as he looked back, his heart leaped: there were four more P-40s, driving into the fighter formation from the south. Pulling his own aircraft around, he watched the enemy fighters peel off onto their fresh opponents; and in a few seconds, all were engaged in a swirling dogfight some distance from the bombers.

Tex wasn't going to look a gift horse in the mouth. Checking in all directions, he saw that Neale, an RAF *Buffalo*, and he himself were still positioned to attack the bombers while the fighters were occupied. As Tex roared toward the remaining five "Bettys," the RAF pilot scored another victory, flaming his second of the day.

Suddenly the lead bomber exploded, momentarily startling Tex as he was lining up his sights on the right-hand plane. As far as he could tell, none of the Allied pilots had fired a single shot at the plane; he could only guess that a bomb had detonated while still aboard. Now the "Sallys" were unloading their ordnance over Mingaladon Airfield, hoping the results would be worth the beating they were taking. When their bombing run was complete, they immediately began turning back the way they had come; but Tex remained focused on the right-hand aircraft. Finally, he came within range.

His guns roared once more, and he watched the tracer impacts "walk" their way from the wing roots out to the engine, and then along the fuselage. Debris flew everywhere. At the last moment, Tex broke off his burst and banked hard to the right—just as the bomber exploded.

A split-second later, he felt and heard a deafening impact, as something violently jarred his P-40 further to the right. Sure that he had been fatally damaged somehow, Tex quickly examined what he could see of his fighter. There it was: flying shrapnel from the stricken bomber had punched a wide hole through his left wing. It was an ugly wound, and looked as if it might easily have blown the wing off completely. But it had not; and once righted, the rugged P-40 flew tolerably well. Nevertheless, it was high time to get her down.

He could not do it immediately, however; for at that moment, his keen eyes noticed something his comrades were missing. A lone Japanese fighter was speeding into the conflict, hoping to avenge the bombers by "getting the drop" on an unsuspecting Allied pilot. Praying that his right wing would hold up, Tex made a final hard left-hand turn, bringing him in line for a shot on the little fighter from the rear.

By good fortune, the Jap was concentrating on his intended victim, and didn't notice his attacker. Tex poured a salvo directly into the aircraft's cockpit. Flames licked from the shattered radial engine; and Tex guessed that the pilot was dead long before the enemy plane spun in.

Tex was directly above the runway. As he descended, he noticed with relief that the Japs' bombs had impacted harmlessly southwest of the field. The aerial dogfight now raged some distance to the southeast, where Bob Neale was methodically working over the two remaining "Sallys" with the *Buffalo* pilot. By the time Tex landed, his two comrades had split the pair of bombers between them. Once on the ground, Tex's adrenaline-knotted muscles gradually uncoiled. Divine providence had brought him down alive from another close call.

That afternoon, the Flying Tigers buried Bert Christman with honors in a small military cemetery near the airfield. Tex and Ed Rector led the pallbearers, struggling to contain their sorrow as they lowered his body into the grave. Chaplain Paul Frillman gave a short, subdued eulogy for the young man from Colorado; many of the RAF pilots had also gathered to pay their respects. Though they might disapprove of what they called the AVG's "lack of discipline," these Britons found no fault with their courage.

Tex remembered Christman as he had been on the *Ranger*, in the inseparable trio of friends. He had not spoken with Ed Rector's eloquence; nor could he deliver a one-liner like Tex. But his quiet friendship had lent stability to those two. With his artist's soul, he had immortalized his squadron mates, in the panda pears they bore on their aircraft into battle. To say that he would merely "be missed" failed to do justice to Bert Christman's loss.

It never crossed Tex's mind that he had become a fighter ace in the battle that day, downing his fifth and six enemy planes. The Flying Tigers had more than enough to occupy them, carrying on their aerial war; the most important enemy kill was always the next one.

The Japanese had not finished for the day. Early that afternoon, they sent another two dozen fighters to strafe the field at Mingaladon. Expecting just such a tactic, the AVG— including Tex—patrolled at twenty thousand feet; but they didn't see their enemies until it was too late to engage them. The Japs made a single pass on the airfield, far below the vigilant P-40s, and departed. Their strafing was poor, though, causing little damage.

The two days of hard fighting were the opening rounds in a massive six-day Japanese effort to wipe out the Allies at Mingaladon. Most days, the Tiger pilots were in the air more than once, defending their base; and the ground crew worked like mad to keep them airborne. The day after Bert Christman was buried, reinforcements arrived at Mingaladon, in the form of eleven more 1st Squadron P-40s, led by Missouri native Robert "Sandy" Sandell. These Adam and Eves were especially welcome, since the Panda Bears were down to only a dozen planes; ten had been knocked out of commission by enemy fire, and a few others had been destroyed.

The day after Sandell's arrival, Japanese fighters returned to Mingaladon and picked a dogfight in which they enjoyed twenty-to-seven odds. The Japs shot down and killed Louis "Cokey" Hoffman, the oldest AVG pilot at forty-three; they paid for Hoffman with three of their own.

The enemy had gradually discarded the idea of sending bombers over during daylight—especially after the fiasco a few days before, in which they had lost an entire formation. They continued to plague the AVG with solo night bombings, leaving daylight attacks to their horde of fighter planes. But each time, the would-be enemy strafers limped back to their bases with heavy losses. Forty I-97s came in low and fast on the 28th, but sixteen Tigers were ready for them. The AVG destroyed ten of the "Nates" without losing a single plane—though one suicidal enemy pilot attempted to smash into "Sandy" Sandell's aircraft after the 1st Squadron's leader had been forced down, damaging the P-40's tail. By that time, the Panda Bears were forced to share their dwindling flyable aircraft among a number of pilots; so Tex had to be content to watch his comrades' victory from the runway.

The next day was different, as another wave of thirty-plus "Nates" tried yet again to deliver a "final blow" to Mingaladon. It was Tex's turn in the air, and the Flying Tigers decimated another ten I-97s without a loss. Tex's seventh victory came, as they usually did, by sending a stream of bullets into the rear quarter of an oblivious enemy. Black smoke gushed from the aircraft as it dove for the last time. The date, January 29th, marked the end of the Japs' attempts to squash the AVG in Rangoon by repeated assaults. They had thrown everything they had into the effort, and failed.

However, the Flying Tigers were hardly unscathed from their successful defense. They had suffered almost as many planes shot up or totaled as they now had left to fight with. Both pilots and ground crews were exhausted, only pausing from the fever pitch of constant combat or alert to grab a few hours' sleep—while the enemy did his best to rain bombs on their heads. Food was running out; Tex's crew chief, Carl Quick, had long since taken on the job of buying and preparing meals from one of the city's markets (it was an alternative to the British fare, which most of the AVG loathed). Now, Quick resorted to scrounging from the neighborhood for whatever he could find. The streets were increasingly dangerous, as the remaining residents realized law enforcement was evaporating. Worst of all, during the peak fighting, were the losses of Christman and Hoffman.

The next two weeks were free of the intense aerial combat of the previous six days, but they were nevertheless eventful—unfortunately. Panda Bear Tom Cole was killed by small arms fire while conducting a strafing pass on enemy trucks south of Moulmein; Ed Rector watched helplessly from his top cover position as Cole's P-40 plowed into the ground. (Tex had warned others that such missions were very dangerous, since enemy soldiers were nearly impossible to identify in the thick terrain.) The Japs stepped up their nocturnal bombings over the city of Rangoon, killing many residents; but during daylight, the AVG denied them that opportunity—nor could the Japs disrupt the offloading of lend-lease supplies on the docks. Finally, The RAF attempted to reinforce their paltry aerial strength at Mingaladon by sending eighteen fighters from Calcutta. In a heartbreaking misfortune, all of them—including five state-of-the-art *Spitfires*—crashed to their destruction in China, far off course and out of gas.

Japan's air force felt it could exercise patience in destroying the infuriating AVG—with good reason. They believed their ground forces, now pouring into the southern tip of Burma, would defeat the British Army and make the issue a moot one. After being forced to retreat from Tavoy, stoic British defenders at Moulmein simply stood and watched as the Japanese executed a basic encircling maneuver that cut off the defenders. When the enemy drew the noose tight with unexpected ferocity, the British were forced to retreat with loss once more, yielding control of the important Moulmein airfield. The Panda Bears shook their heads in disbelief as they read intelligence reports from the front.

The British had called on the AVG a number of times to escort their bombers over the battlefront. On those missions, the P-40s would often dive to strafe targets that ran the gamut from foot soldiers to elephants carrying heavy artillery pieces. The Tigers already knew the Japs were disciplined and skilled in the air; if they fought the same way on the ground, the Americans decided, the British were in for an unpleasant surprise.

Unwilling to take on the AVG at Mingaladon any longer, the enemy changed tactics. One day they flew north to hit Toungoo, the AVG's old training base. By now it was empty, except for a few P-40s requiring repair. Robert "Buster" Keeton, a Panda Bear pilot supervising this work, got aloft in one and brought a Japanese bomber down in flames. But the Japs noted carefully that Keeton seemed to have no warning of their attack; and they decided to concentrate their efforts there. The next day, they hammered the field mercilessly with five waves of bombers, demolishing the hangar and operations shack, and riddling three P-40s and a handful of RAF *Blenheim* bombers that were undergoing repairs. Vengeful P-40s from Mingaladon raced to intercept the enemy, but arrived too late.

The 1st Squadron suffered a tragic loss on February 7th, when "Sandy" Sandell, testing his repaired P-40 (a Japanese pilot had rammed into it during the last big raid, destroying its tail) spun in to his death. The repaired tail end had collapsed. After a sober funeral ceremony that was becoming all too familiar, Bob Neale quietly assumed command of the Adam and Eves.

The remainder of the 1st had already relocated from Kunming to Rangoon, and Tex's battle-weary 2nd Squadron was due for a rest. Bed-ridden with bronchitis, Chennault issued the order for the Panda Bears to transfer all their remaining combat equipment to the 1st Squadron and return to Kunming. As Tex packed up his gear at Mingaladon for the last time and prepared to board a train for Lashio, he wondered if the city would hold out. Also, rumors were circulating that one of the squadrons would soon send a group of pilots to the Gold Coast of Africa to pick up brand-new P-40Es, fresh from the Curtiss-Wright assembly line in Buffalo. It sounded like an interesting trip, and Tex hoped the Old Man would pick the Panda Bears for the job.

The rail trip to Lashio was a relaxing ride after the weeks of combat intensity. The train climbed out of the smoky humidity of Rangoon onto the Burmese highlands, where the sun-drenched countryside seemed oblivious to the rumor of war away to the south. Refugees were dotted along the way, moving northward as well. At Lashio, Tex and several other 2nd Squadron pilots boarded the group's twin-engine Beechcraft transport plane and flew back to the walled city of Kunming.

Once there, he and his friends rested in style. It is impossible to understand the satisfaction from a good meal or hot shower unless these have been denied for some time; and the men reveled as they enjoyed such comforts again. Tex and Ed Rector found their room in Hostel number One just as they had left it, and happily set up house again. Disappointing news came just four days later, though: the 3rd Squadron, not the Panda Bears, was going on the ferry trip to Africa to pick up the new aircraft.

Undaunted, Tex spent his time working on a different project instead. With Japanese forces advancing on the ground, it had become painfully apparent that the most glaring gap in the AVG's combat capability was a lack of bombers. Chinese and British ground troops badly needed close air support; but the promised "bomber AVG" from the States had been sidetracked long ago. Chennault had managed to acquire several varieties of bombs: French, Chinese, and the 570-lb. Russian demolition weapons. But he had no planes to drop them.

Tex intended to change that. Like the rest of the former Navy dive-bomber pilots—Ed Rector, Frank Lawlor, Tom Jones, and others—he knew that delivering a bomb was no problem for a fighter plane. All they needed were mounting racks to carry the bombs beneath the aircraft; some means to hang them onto the racks; and a mechanism to release them. The P-40B had none of these; but Tex wagered that the mechanical wizardry of the ground crews, coupled with the know-how of the dive-bomber pilots, could overcome that. While Tex tinkered with experimental bomb racks, armorers Don "Rode" Rodewald, Chuck Baisden, Keith Christensen, and Louis Hoffman took on the excruciatingly dangerous job of deciphering the fuse timings on each of the various bombs. There was no telling whether a particular foreign bomb was set for instant or delayed detonation—until someone opened it up and looked. Needless to say, after successfully completing the risky task, the stock of the armorers rose even higher in the eyes of the group.

After much pounding, bending of bamboo, welding of metal, and a few unsuccessful attempts, Tex strode confidently into Chennault's office with good news.

"Colonel, we've got the bomb problem licked. Are you ready for a little demonstration?"

Chennault stood immediately, nodding, and they headed out to the field.

The Old Man knew what dive-bombing was, of course, but was completely unfamiliar with the details—a rarity for Chennault. The Army Air Corps, perceiving no use for the tactic, had never produced planes or trained pilots to perform that particular mission. So Chennault watched with interest as a four-ship of ex-Navy men—including Tex—climbed to altitude. They carried "dummy" bombs, sized exactly like the real things, slung beneath their P-40Bs. Other curious Tigers emerged from nearby buildings to watch.

A large circle had been marked on the ground, from which the observers kept a safe distance. The aircraft moved into an in-line formation and began their dive-bombing runs. Unlike the Navy's SB2U, which was designed for that mission, the P-40 could not dive-bomb at an angle steeper than about sixty degrees—or else the released bomb would fly straight through the propeller! One by one, the pilots dropped their "bombs" toward the target. When it was over, the spectators crowded around to survey the results. All four had hit inside the circle. Chennault was impressed; when Tex landed and approached him, he could almost "see" the wheels turning in the Old Man's mind.

"Well, sir, that's about the size of it," drawled Tex, gesturing to the target area.

The Old Man nodded, lost in thought. "That's great. I imagine it could come in handy sometime."

This was an enormous understatement, but neither man knew it just then.

Back in Rangoon, the Adam and Eves were becoming familiar with the grueling pattern of constant alert and combat—just as Tex's squadron had, weeks earlier. When Singapore fell to Japan in mid-March—labeled by Winston Churchill "the worst disaster in British military history"—it would free up hundreds of additional enemy planes to move into the Indochina bases. The Japanese air armada returned with a vengeance; and they began to hit Rangoon hard, to "soften it up" for their advancing ground armies.

The 1st Squadron had been flying missions to the front, southeast of the city, escorting British bombers; but now they had to regroup in haste, in the face of the renewed

Japanese air raids. The Tigers' first warning came while they were *en route* escorting RAF bombers; they almost passed forty Japanese fighters and a dozen enemy bombers that were headed toward Mingaladon to bomb it. Tearing into the formation, the Adam and Eves knocked out half a dozen fighters. Four days later, two raids of similar size kept the Tigers fighting almost all day over their airfield; and the following afternoon, the enemy relentlessly sent in yet another attacking force.

Each time, the Japs flew into a "meat grinder," with the AVG shooting the "stuffing" out of both fighters and bombers; but inevitable attrition finally left the Adam and Eves with only six planes that could get off the ground. In those two days alone, Bob Neale's boys scratched forty-three enemy airplanes without a single combat loss. But the P-40s took heavy damage, and the supply of Japanese aircraft seemed inexhaustible.

By this time, Rangoon was ripe for destruction. At night the men could hear artillery fire from the front, moving closer each time. As British authorities evacuated the city, they emptied the prisons and asylums, releasing lepers, madmen, and criminals onto the streets. Huge sections of Rangoon burned night and day, set alight by Japanese bombs; drunken vandals promptly looted just-closed shops. Roving bands of Burmese sought to kill the British (and Americans) on sight; and only heavily armed parties could traverse the city without being accosted.

The docks, still crammed with thousands of tons of irreplaceable lend-lease materiel, had to be abandoned. Workers fired the supplies or bulldozed equipment into the water. There was no choice; if not destroyed, it would all soon be in Japanese hands.

Knowing that they too would have to evacuate soon, Neale coordinated with Chennault to move north to Magwe—but only when it became absolutely necessary to leave. Neale's men began a considerable salvage effort at the docks, loading three trucks with what they considered the most critical goods and equipment (two of them were dedicated entirely to alcoholic beverages). Sweating like the vanished Burmese dockworkers, they spent hour after hour reclaiming anything they thought they could use, adding it to the convoy, which was preparing to move up the road to Magwe. The men nabbed several jeeps, and even a Buick, as they picked over the selection of deserted vehicles. It was the last chance to redeem anything from the clogged, doomed supply lifeline into China.

Many miles up the road to the north, fleeing British residents of Rangoon were learning a hard lesson: worldly riches meant nothing in the midst of the evacuation. Many had loaded their cars to the ground with valuables—only to learn, past the town of Bhamo, that there was no road to India navigable by car. In the end, they handed the keys over to someone else—occasionally the AVG, if a convoy was passing through—and continued on foot, bidding their accumulated possessions farewell for good.

For Rangoon, the end came in the middle of the night of February 27th. Someone shook Bob Neale awake and told him that the RAF had completely gone, leaving the base and taking with them the prototype radar set that had provided the AVG with their only warning of impending attack. Not wanting to leave a thing for the Japs, the British had also destroyed the supplies of oxygen and battery recharging depots.

It was the last straw; Neale ordered the Adam and Eves to evacuate immediately. Neale and Robert H. "Snuffy" Smith stayed an extra day to search for recently missing pilot Ed Leibolt; but within thirty-six hours, the Adam and Eves departed Mingaladon

Airfield for the last time. The remaining P-40s flew low, covering the exodus of the convoy, which was led by chaplain Paul Frillman. The vehicles wound their way slowly up the road to the north.

Seven days later, Japanese troops marched into the city, and found it lifeless. China's final land-based link to the outside world was severed.

* * *

The advance of the Japanese army from the southern tip of Burma to Rangoon was nothing short of astounding—to everyone except the Japanese. Moving with incredible speed through terrain that the British never even attempted to traverse, they threw the Allies back from front after front. After Moulmein, they made short work of the defenses at Martaban and Thatan, then swarmed up to the Belin River. There the British, awakened at last to the danger their diminutive enemies posed, offered furious resistance from prepared defenses on the northern bank. But the stand came too late; riding their momentum, Japanese ground troops forced a crossing in a matter of hours. The AVG strafed Jap infantry and escorted RAF Blenheim *bombers during the entire retreat; but they could only watch as the battlefront withdrew past Kyaikto and Bassein, finally grinding to a halt at the wide, muddy Sittang River.*

Here the Japanese had their only serious check, almost within sight of the sprawl of dying Rangoon. Determined not to let the Japs cross the river, British troops destroyed the only bridge at Mokpalin (marooning their own 17th Indian Division on the eastern shore, where it was mauled by the enemy). Nevertheless, it was some days before the Japanese were able to gather their strength for a push to cross the Sittang. When they did, fierce fighting ensued, and the enemy sustained heavy losses; but the Japs' continual pounding of the defenders with their mobile artillery on the western bank proved decisive. On February 27th, the first Japanese troops inexorably gained the far shore; and the Allies knew that Rangoon was lost.

At that point, the British began frantically evacuating Magwe, Prome, Mandalay, and the other large towns in Burma. Once the Japanese gained the western bank of the Sittang, they resumed their infiltration-and-envelopment tactics through the "impassable" jungle. Enemy troops swung north to cut the road from Rangoon to Toungoo—the city's last lifeline—and finally swept into her deserted streets on the 8th of March.

As the AVG demolished scores of Japanese aircraft in the final days of the aerial battle over Rangoon, the world watched in amazement. British Prime Minister Winston Churchill declared of the Tigers' feats: "The victories they have won in the air over the paddy fields of Burma may well prove comparable in character, if not in scope, with those won over the orchards and hop fields of Kent in the Battle of Britain."

Three days before the fall of Rangoon, Chiang Kai-Shek's new American Chief of Staff arrived in Chungking. Among the new general's six other concurrent duties was that of commander of U.S. forces in the China-Burma-India Theater. The Generalissimo immediately tasked him with salvaging the defense of Burma, and the wiry infantryman proceeded to take stock of the situation. His name was Lieutenant General Joseph W. Stilwell.

Refugees flood the Burma Road during the nation's fall to the Japanese, early 1942.

Frame from camera footage: Tex straps in for takeoff to lead the crucial mission to the Salween River Gorge, May 1942.

Chapter 16

PANDA BEARS

Two hundred miles up the meandering Irrawaddy River from Rangoon lay the town of Magwe, selected as the regrouping point for the part of the AVG in Burma. North of the town, when blowing dust did not obscure it, could be seen the southern edge of the great oil fields of Yenangyaung, which the Japanese had eyed greedily for some time. The unfinished airbase a short distance from the town had also become the primary point of British air evacuation from Burma.

When Tex and a handful of Panda Bears had returned to Kunming weeks earlier, others of his squadron had relocated to Magwe instead, to prepare the base. The British had tardily relented and allowed Chiang Kai-Shek's armies to enter Burma; and now a detachment of Chinese soldiers set up a protective perimeter around Magwe's airfield. A continuous stream of refugees moved north on the highway that ran through the town, or poled their way up the nearby Irrawaddy on rafts. Around the clock, RAF transports and bombers carried British citizens to the safety of India.

The Flying Tigers knew they were no safer at Magwe than they had been at Rangoon; a British bomber or two circling to the southeast could not provide enough warning of any air attack. Nevertheless, the advance team set up operations; and by the time Rangoon fell, elements of all three AVG squadrons were operating out of the base. Drifting dust continuously fouled the P-40s' engines, making them dangerously prone to quit outright; and the evacuation's air traffic made it difficult to "squeeze" in and out of the field. Less than ten P-40s were on hand at any one time; with luck, they might get off the ground without stalling.

Within a week, even with their problems, the 3rd Squadron had conducted several missions from Magwe. They strafed a railway bridge on the Sittang and hit enemy forces around Kyaikto and the Irrawaddy to the south. On March 19th, Hell's Angels Bill Reed and Ken Jernstedt (an ex-Marine) flew one of the AVG's greatest missions. Staging out of Toungoo on a pre-dawn take-off, they flew a reconnaissance patrol south to enemy-occupied Rangoon, then turned east across the bay, toward Moulmein. As they approached the city, they came suddenly upon an auxiliary airfield they hadn't known existed—and it contained some two dozen enemy fighters, lined up wingtip-to-wingtip.

A truckload of unarmed Japanese mechanics watched helplessly from a hundred yards' distance as the two Tigers swooped down to attack. They released 30-lb. fragmentation bombs they were carrying in their planes' flare chutes—a first-time test of this technique, which was an unqualified success. Between the frag-bombs and their guns, Reed and Jernstedt shredded fifteen of the helpless fighters in six unopposed passes above the airfield. Leaving the despairing enemy mechanics, they sped eastward to the main airfield. There, they destroyed three bombers and a couple of transport planes to add insult to injury. Finally, they returned to Toungoo, having netted the Flying Tigers' largest-ever total of individual single-mission kills.

The morrow was a banner day for the British, when they bombed Mingaladon—until recently their own airfield—and managed to demolish another sixteen enemy fighters. They lost some *Blenheims* to the defending *Zeros*, but their own fighter escort also knocked a dozen Japs out of the sky, bringing the day's score to twenty-eight. These back-to-back roaring successes were more than the angered Japanese could stand; and they bent their malice upon Magwe without waiting another day.

Lack of a warning network proved to be their base's undoing, as the men had known it would. By the time the opening wave of enemy bombers and fighters arrived above the field the following morning, the pilots had no time to get airborne before bombs were falling. What followed was twenty-five hours of continuous pounding, as the infuriated Japanese threw two hundred sixty-six aircraft at Magwe in wave after wave. Eleven British *Blenheims* were the first to crumple. When Flying Tigers Frank Swartz and John Fauth raced onto the crater-studded runway to retrieve an RAF airman hit by shrapnel, vengeful Jap fighters fatally cut them down with 7.7mm bullets. Even when three Hell's Angels returning from a recon mission shot down a Jap bomber, the enemy hardly noticed. Half a dozen P-40s and eight *Hurricanes* were lambasted on the next wave, and bomb explosions demolished the hangars. The men watched helplessly from protective "slit trenches" as their base and aircraft were turned to scrap around them. When the last wave droned away at mid-morning the *following* day, only three P-40s had any chance of being repaired; everything else was simply gone. The survivors wearily loaded up all the trucks that were still intact and set off northeast up the road for Loiwing, nearly three hundred miles distant, on the border of China. Magwe was lost.

In China, however, the next day brought something new to the mountain plateau of ancient Kunming. Tex had been making familiarization flights in the group's just-restored Ryan monoplane, seeking to make himself more useful as the 2nd Squadron spent its China rotation conducting defensive patrols. Coming down from a flight in the Ryan, he saw George McMillan and a few others standing around four unfamiliar P-40s. He recognized them as the new "E" models, and realized that some of the pilots had just returned from their ferry trip to Africa to retrieve them. Stepping from his plane with excitement, Tex walked over.

"Hey, Tex, how's everything?" McMillan greeted him.

"Great. Man, are these a sight for sore eyes! We can sure use them."

"You can say that again," agreed McMillan. "We had a hell of a time getting them back across the desert, and nobody on the way knew a damn thing about maintaining them, but...here they are."

Tex admired the aircraft. They were familiar in shape, but had several differences that would come in quite handy. One difference was the armament. The "B" model's four underpowered .30-caliber wing guns had been replaced with six deadly .50-calibers, whose worth the Tigers already knew, on the "E." The .50-cal nose guns had been removed, but the huge increase in wing firepower was well worth it. The men were practically drooling.

Then Tex almost cried out for joy when he saw the bomb racks on the new model's underbelly.

"These are great—absolutely great!" he crowed.

"Sure, I guess so," McMillan said, cocking an eyebrow at Tex. "Most folks are happier with the guns, but—"

"You have no idea," Tex said with a grin, remembering his days of toil crafting crude, handmade bomb racks for the worn-out P-40Bs. All of the new models would be able to dive-bomb right off the bat. Four P-40Es had arrived so far, and eight more would join them the next day.

That evening, after a "welcome home" dinner for the pilots returning from Africa, Tex walked into Hostel Number One, ready to turn in. Walking down the hall, he passed the room of the Panda Bears' squadron leader, Jack Newkirk. Newkirk was writing at a small desk.

"What's going on, Jack? Are you about ready to hit it?" Tex asked, noticing a look of unusual concentration on his friend's face.

"I guess I am. This mission tomorrow has got me...kind of thinking," Newkirk replied.

Tex remembered; word had come down of a strafing mission into Thailand the following day. Newkirk was taking four 2nd Squadron pilots, along with six of Bob Neale's Adam and Eves, to hit Chiengmai and Lampung, two of the enemy's most active bases. All the men knew there were heavy anti-aircraft emplacements set up around the two airfields. It would be no milk run.

"Thinking what?" asked Tex, glancing down at the desk. A half-written letter lay on it. The normally "devil-may-care" Newkirk looked long and hard at Tex before he spoke.

"Tex, I think it might be the last one for me."

Tex didn't have to ask what he meant. Many pilots wondered if their next combat would be their last; but a premonition that would prompt Newkirk to write a letter must be a strong one. There was a long pause.

"If you feel that way," Tex replied, choosing his words carefully, "let me tell you, I'd be happy to take this one. Why don't you let me do that?"

Newkirk shook his head. "No, Tex, I appreciate it, but I can't do that. I still feel like hell about forgetting to turn my gun switches on in that first fight. I guess I still haven't lived that down. I wouldn't mind you going instead, but the guys might think I'm...kind of chicken or something, you know. I've got to do it."

He glanced down at the letter, then back at Tex.

"Well, if you're sure—" Tex began.

"I'm sure. Thanks. Goodnight." Newkirk was done talking about it, and Tex wasn't going to press him. The light in his leader's room stayed on for a long time after Tex went to bed.

The next day, the pilots for the mission took off to stage out of Namsang, a mountain village in Burma eighty miles from the Thailand border. There, they stayed overnight; then took off before dawn the next day on a course due southeast.

Not dreaming the AVG could reach them, the Japanese were readying another group of forty fighters at Chiengmai for an "overkill" smash at Magwe. Neale's and Newkirk's Tigers completely surprised them, burning and riddling three-quarters of the gasoline-filled enemy aircraft on the runway, as frantic Japanese ground crews fled for cover. But sure enough, the Tigers found themselves facing down a virtual hail of anti-aircraft fire; the Japs had loaded the place with gun batteries. Jubilant with victory in spite of the danger, the pilots roared off down the road to nearby Lampang, as flames from their destroyed targets cast a glow against the sky behind them. At Lampang, the AVG had another "field day," raking their fire along convoys on the road and pumping streams of lead into railway buildings, barracks, and any other targets that looked like they could be "improved" with perforation.

Then it happened: As "Buster" Keeton pulled up from a strafing pass on some armored vehicles, a sudden flash made him look to his right. He watched in fascination as a fireball impacted in a clearing some distance away, spreading a swath of flame over a full hundred yards within seconds. But his amazement turned to horror as he realized that, with its speed, the conflagration could only have been an aircraft. It was Newkirk.

Sitting in his room back at Kunming, Tex felt a sudden chill when the Hostel telephone rang.

"Ed, I know what that is," he said quietly to his roommate.

"What's that, Tex?" Rector wondered.

"The phone. It's Newkirk."

Ed Rector stopped what he was doing and looked hard at Tex, then left the room to answer the phone. When he returned, the look on his face told the story.

"The Old Man wants to see you in his office," Rector half-mumbled.

In the headquarters building, the Old Man motioned Tex into his room.

"I guess you heard about Jack," he began, without preamble.

Tex nodded. He noticed the grim set of Chennault's jaw. The man had seen too many tragedies like this one.

"I'm going to get right to the point, Tex. He gave me a letter before he left on the mission yesterday. Among other things, he wanted me to put you in charge of the 2nd Squadron in the event of his death. I've considered it, and I agree with his choice. If you'll take it, the job is yours."

Tex was taken aback. He was still trying to grasp that Newkirk was gone. There were others more senior than Tex in the squadron, including Vice Squadron Leader Jim Howard, who normally would have moved into Newkirk's position. As he looked at the Old Man, Tex seemed to read the thoughts behind his eyes: *Take it, Tex. The men respect you, and so do I. You can lead them well. Step up to the plate.*

"Yes sir, I'll do that," Tex said slowly.

"All right. We'll talk more later," the Old Man said, nodding approval. Tex returned to the hostel.

In fact, Tex's leadership had begun long before that day in 1942; and it had not proceeded from a title. Tex led others in the most straightforward way possible: by example. He never directed his men to perform a task he had not done; and he preferred to be in the thick of things, demonstrating exactly what he meant for others to accomplish. Tex preferred to take the most difficult missions himself; and when he gave instructions, his men knew that he meant *follow* and not simply *do*. When the time came to send them into danger, they knew he had been there, and would be there again. The greatest leaders have always done exactly the same. Tex soon moved Ed Rector up to serve as his vice squadron leader.

Newkirk's sacrifice at Chiengmai had not been in vain; nor had the shootdown and capture—on the same mission—of William "Black Mac" McGarry, who spent the remainder of the war in a Bangkok jail. The terrific strike mission forced the Japanese to withdraw their entire air regiment for repair and replacements. That, in turn, allowed the British to resume their evacuation operation at Magwe, which enemy raids had cut short. A telegram arrived in Chennault's office from RAF Air Marshal D.F. Stevenson: "Many thanks for the breathing spell furnished us by your magnificent attack at Chiengmai."

Five days after the loss of Magwe as an AVG base of operations, the bedraggled convoy carrying the remnants of the 3rd Squadron staggered into Loiwing. Nestled among the mountains on the Burma-China border, the village was in an extremely remote region. Native residents spun thread and wove cloth on primitive looms, pursuing the same craft their ancestors had practiced for a hundred generations. The "airfield" was a single-strip affair, with large ditches on either side to drain monsoon rainwater; the buildings and facilities were crude, but serviceable. A short distance from the field was the CAMCO aircraft factory, where Bill Pawley's workers were trying to turn out the nimble CW-21 *Demons* at the rate of several per month.

The day after their ground crewmen arrived at Loiwing, Hell's Angels leader "Ole" Olson, who hailed from Los Angeles, flew in with eight P-40s from Kunming. Several of these were the new "E" models, and they were a welcome sight for everyone. They immediately set up aerial patrols, which proved wise; the very next day, Chuck Older shot down a Japanese reconnaissance plane over the field. It was the first time that any of the Tigers had been able to get a good shot at the annoying high-altitude observers, despite many attempts. The men knew the enemy watched them; an attack could not be far away.

By the end of March, the AVG had gathered a dozen P-40s at the base—more than they had seen in working order together for months. The Japanese began to reach closer. They bombed Lashio, the rail terminus of the Burma Road, only fifty miles to the south, while the 3rd Squadron tried unsuccessfully to intercept them. Before the first week in April was gone, eight RAF *Hurricanes* and a couple of *Blenheim* bombers joined the AVG at Loiwing—just in time for the Japanese to show up.

The enemy sent twenty fighters to test the strength of the new base, and found it plenty tough; only ten made it home. The heavier firepower of the new P-40Es, which was getting high marks from the pilots, brought down two of the Japs. The AVG suffered one P-40 riddled on the ground, and one shot up badly in the aerial battle; but on the whole, the men felt they had cause for celebration.

Festivities of a different kind were underway in Kunming, where the governor of Yunnan province had recently announced his intention to throw a party in honor of the AVG. Governor Lung Yun, nicknamed the "One-Eyed Dragon," was one of China's singular "personalities." He was the last of the independent provincial warlords, unconquered by Chiang Kai-Shek. Lung maintained a vast private army, and heretofore had declared allegiance to neither side in the war with Japan. Before the AVG's arrival in China the year before, Chennault and Chiang had been unsure whether they could operate safely out of Kunming; after all, the city was the capital of Yunnan Province, in the heart of Lung's domain. Eventually they decided to trust Governor Lung—and it was a fortunate decision. If the AVG had not had the base in Kunming, they would have had nowhere to withdraw when Burma later fell.

The party commenced in one of the governor's four houses within the walled city; and it was an unqualified "smash." The pageantry, hospitality, and entertainment of the Chinese people were in full swing. If the rice wine tasted horrible, at least it was around 160 "proof." The AVG watched the skits and listened to the speeches with delight (and passed drink after drink out the windows to grateful Chinese guards). There are times and places in which the most unlikely groups may become fast friends. It happened that night, for the people of Yunnan and the Flying Tigers.

When the P-40Es had arrived at Kunming, Tex had tested their dive-bombing capabilities—and found them quite satisfactory. A few days after Governor Lung's party, Tex led half a dozen Panda Bears into a small auxiliary airfield near Mengtze. From there, the 2nd Squadron's new commander intended to conduct another strafing raid, hitting a couple of airfields in Indochina. Two of the flight, including Ed Rector, had to turn back with mechanical trouble; but the remaining P-40s pressed on, struck their targets with modest success, and returned to Kunming. Later that day, they moved west to join their comrades in the mountains at Loiwing, where the AVG was concentrating its strength. To the south, the ground battle went poorly for the Allies; Burma was slipping away. The Tigers wondered what might happen if it fell.

* * *

As the successes of the AVG mounted, the U.S. Army Air Corps began to realize that, sooner or later, they would need an air force in the China-Burma-India Theater. As they considered who its leader should be, Chennault's name surfaced; and immediately, jealousy among the Air Corps brass reared its ugly head. Although the Old Man was the obvious choice to take command, "Hap" Arnold passed him up in favor of Colonel Clayton Bissell, perhaps remembering Chennault's brazenness during recruiting for the AVG. But Chennault would be useful, Arnold knew; so the Old Man was inducted into the Army and given the rank of colonel as well. However, Chennault's promotion to brigadier general was "held up" until the end of April—exactly one day after Bissell's— to ensure that Chennault "knew who was in charge."

Bissell originally came to China to oversee the completion of the Doolittle Raid on Tokyo. Chennault had met him years before at the Air Corps Tactical School; there, Bissell had advocated such pursuit tactics as lowering a ball-and-chain from a midair position above an enemy bomber, in order to catch it in the propeller and bring it down.

Now, the Old Man found Bissell no more savvy on airpower than he had been before—far more concerned with spit-and-polish discipline and proper paperwork than with combat success. Their personalities clashed immediately; and it was the start of a bitter relationship. At a conference in Chungking at the end of March, one of Bissell's key agenda items was to recommend the forcible induction of the entire AVG into the Army Air Corps. If this were not done, Bissell claimed, "paperwork problems" would prevent the Army from providing any further supplies (which were scant enough) to the AVG. The threat was transparent to Chennault. Generalissimo Chiang Kai-Shek agreed to consider the proposal only when Stilwell promised to replace the AVG with a complete Army Air Corps fighter group, and to retain Chennault as the senior air commander in China throughout the war. Bissell promised both, but later would break both promises.

The day after Bill Reed and Ken Jernstedt made their landmark raid on Moulmein, the troop ship U.S.S. Brazil set sail from Charleston, South Carolina for the Far East. It carried several members of a newly-formed Army Air Corps unit: the 23rd Fighter Group.

L to R: John Alison, Tex, "Ajax" Baumler, and "Mack" Mitchell at Kunming, July 1942. Note original 23rd Fighter Group logo (Disney tiger with "Uncle Sam" hat tearing through Chinese Sun) on the side of the P-40.

P-40s of the 75th Fighter Squadron in flight.

Generalissimo and Madame Chiang Kai-Shek with Chennault at Kunming, 1942.

The personalized Panda Bear on Tex's P-40 number 48, rendered by Bert Christman.

Chapter 17

BURMA COLLAPSES

At Loiwing, the Flying Tigers' mission changed. Japanese armies were advancing rapidly northward from Rangoon, and the Allies were throwing everything they had into the defense of northern Burma. Chiang Kai-Shek requested that Chennault provide as much air support to the desperate Chinese armies as he could; so the Old Man was doing just that. AVG fighters would take off in the morning, speed to the front, and interdict targets of opportunity—normally Japanese reserves moving north—by strafing and dropping fragmentation bombs. The new P-40Es were beginning to get into the act, carrying heavier ordnance, much to the pilots' satisfaction.

It was also at Loiwing that some of the AVG felt their morale begin to sag in earnest. The Generalissimo had also requested that the Flying Tigers send sorties directly over the front lines at low altitude, to provide encouragement for his troops. The Tigers were aghast. Offhand, none of them could think of a faster way to be "jumped" by an enemy fighter or shot down by small arms fire from the ground. None of them wanted to do it.

Recently, too, Chennault had been re-commissioned into the Army as a Colonel, and had discussed frankly with his men the possible induction of the Flying Tigers into the Army Air Corps. The men were plenty patriotic; but none wanted to be forced into the Army, and all would have appreciated a rotation Stateside for some rest and relaxation. Many of them had been serving as combat pilots a full four months before Pearl Harbor galvanized their countrymen into action, and they badly needed a break.

A further strain came within a week of Tex's arrival: Chennault scheduled a return mission to Chiengmai, a dangerous escort of slow-flying British bombers. When the Old Man outlined the mission's objectives, there were no volunteers; Jack Newkirk's fiery death and "Black Mac" McGarry's capture were still fresh in their minds.

After a sullen pause, Tex stood up.

"We'll take that mission," he stated simply.

Straightaway Ed Rector was at his side, along with Frank Schiel, Duke Hedman, and R.J. "Catfish" Raine; all of them said they would go with their leader.

The mission never went off. Tex and the other Tigers flew south to stage out of an auxiliary airfield as planned; but the bombers they were to escort never showed up for the rendezvous. The Tigers returned to Loiwing the following day—only to find the thorny issue of low-level strafing missions not yet resolved.

The pilots called a meeting to talk things out. Chennault had just told them that they would have to fly missions when he assigned them—that the group was "not a democracy." Some of the men were beginning to confuse the strafing missions with Chiang Kai-Shek's requests for low-level overflights of the front lines to help Chinese morale. Mostly, though, bitterness from the long months of fighting, without help or adequate supplies from the United States, had simply taken its toll on the group; and some of the Tigers thought they had nearly had enough. At the pilots' meeting, "Ole" Olson passed around a petition stating that the group wouldn't fly any more "morale missions" over the front lines.

When someone handed Tex the paper, he looked at it, then stood up.

"I'm not going to sign this damn thing," his clear voice rang out.

The alert shack quieted immediately. There was a long pause; all eyes were on him. Tex's expression was stern.

"Look, I don't like these missions any more than y'all do. Hell, I know they're dangerous. But this thing at Chiengmai wasn't going to be any 'morale mission.' There were legitimate targets down there. There were Japs on the road we were going to strafe. How many of you fellows really think the Old Man would send us down there to get killed on some useless deal?"

Dead silence prevailed. A few feet shuffled uncomfortably. Many looked at the floor.

"Y'all need to remember something," Tex continued, a reproving frown on his face. "We came over here as mercenaries—there are no bones about that. We all know it. But our country is at war now, and if you're part of the country, then you're at war too—uniform or not. These missions are the orders we've got, and the Old Man is giving 'em. I think we ought to follow them. I'm going to fly where I'm told, when I'm told. I'd say," he concluded, pointing toward the headquarters building, "with that guy, we're in pretty good hands."

Tex sat back down. The meeting dissolved around him. He had given them something to think about; and his words carried all the more weight since he had volunteered to lead the disputed mission two days before. There was some discussion; heads were nodding gravely as the pilots left for their quarters by twos and threes. Someone took the petition and handed it to Chennault anyway, but the Old Man tore it up and threw it away. It was the last time anything of the sort occurred within the AVG.

A few days later, "Pappy" Boyington disappeared for good. He had told one or two of the men that he was "fed up" and would leave; and now, he did just that. Chennault, who had recently promoted "Pappy" to Vice Squadron Leader, was incensed. But he said only one thing about the matter: that if the AVG were a military outfit, Boyington would be shot as a deserter.

In spite of his anger at Boyington's departure, Chennault was not blind to the problems that "Pappy" had caused within the group. Like most of the men, Boyington enjoyed a drink; unlike most of them, however, he didn't seem to know when to stop drinking. Time after time, he had disregarded his name on the nightly mission schedule, showing up the following morning too drunk to fly. On these occasions, someone always had to go up in Boyington's place, risking death. To Bob Neale and the other Adam and Eves taking that risk, it was unforgivable. And on one occasion, "Pappy" was responsible for wrecking seven P-40s when he failed to pay attention to a flight briefing, afterward leading his men far into the countryside, where they ran out of gas and crashed.

Boyington wasn't all bad. When he was in a condition to fly, he flew with skill; and his comrades never questioned his courage. Many considered him the toughest man in the AVG. However, his penchant for drunkenness and fighting outweighed his contributions.

For whatever reason, he bore a grudge against Chennault and Chiang Kai-Shek forever after his departure. The Flying Tigers were indignant when Boyington later claimed to have shot down six airplanes with the group; those "victories," coupled with his later ones as a U.S. Marine pilot, would have made him the leading ace of the USMC. Unfortunately for Boyington, AVG records showed clearly that his aerial victories with the group came to only two. That meant that Joe Foss was (and is) the rightful owner of the title "leading Marine ace." The Tigers could only shake their heads in later years as Boyington persisted in slandering Chennault and the Generalissimo—whom he had met only once, and that time dead drunk in the Hostel Number One bar—in many appearances on television. But the rest of the AVG decided it would be better not to begin a controversy that the media would surely play up to the hilt; and in the end, they let Boyington's statements lie.

Tex had not been long at Loiwing before he was scheduled for his first mission over the front: a reconnaissance in force. Out on the runway as the sun rose, Tex and his squadron mates were wiping heavy dew off their windshields, when...Tex heard engine noise. He looked up. Eight Japanese fighters were just peeling off into a strafing pattern on the airfield.

There was time for a single shout to warn his comrades, and then they were all scattering for the slit trenches. Inexplicably, Olson's 3rd Squadron was not overhead for their assigned air alert; and Loiwing had no other chance for warning. The lucky Japs had picked exactly the right time for an attack.

Tex saw Pete Wright dive into a trench ahead of him, and Tex followed immediately. The trenches were dug deeply enough to afford protection from bullets and bomb shrapnel—deeply enough for Tex to make a considerable impact as he landed directly on top of the unfortunate Wright, who emitted a sound like a deflating balloon. When they recovered their bearings, Tex whipped out his .45-caliber pistol and peered out, taking stock of the aerial situation.

The Japanese were enjoying a rare opportunity to riddle AVG planes on the ground unopposed, and they were making the most of it. They made low, fast passes; and Tex thought they might actually be close enough for him to hit with a shot from his pistol, if he could pull enough lead on them. Amid the strafing, he heard the staccato fire of a tripod-mounted Bren gun from a nearby trench; one of the crew chiefs had exactly the same idea in mind. On the next pass, Tex emptied his .45 trying to hit one of the little aircraft—without success. The crew chief in the other trench nearly paid for the tactic with his life; when a Japanese pilot noticed him firing the Bren gun, the enemy executed a wing-over and raked the trench with a volley of 7.7mm bullets. As the hapless crewman took to his heels, an enemy bullet blew the stock off the Bren gun.

When the Japanese planes had expended their ammunition and departed, the AVG emerged to survey the damage. Surprisingly, the raiders had done a poor job; only three of the P-40s had been shot up beyond repair. It was the last time the Tigers were ever caught unawares on the ground.

Despite the attack, Tex and his squadron mates took off on their planned mission. While they were gone, more Japanese returned to Loiwing to administer what they thought would be the *coup de grace*. Twenty-seven bombers droned toward the base, and seven P-40s got into the air when they learned of the Japs' approach. The two groups never met each other, however, for a solid overcast moved quickly into the area at mid-morning. The enemy bombers were forced to turn back without finding the field; and the P-40s, eager for vengeance, could not locate the bombers either.

Almost four hours later, the Japanese pushed their luck too far with another strafing attempt, this time sending only nine fighters. But the AVG had six P-40s of their own up in time, and inflicted terminal "lead poisoning" on four of the Japs before the others turned away. Chennault himself had arrived at Loiwing after the bomber raid, and watched the action from the field below with satisfaction.

Meanwhile, Tex and his flight refueled at Lashio and sped south toward the front. When they arrived over Toungoo, recently captured by the enemy, the pilots carefully observed the field for enemy activity. Several anti-aircraft gun batteries were in place, though not active; and a number of runways had been mysteriously repaired, enough to permit operations. The Japs could use the field any time they wished. Tex headed back to Loiwing to bring the Old Man the news.

It was the first of many reconnaissance flights over the front for Tex, whose sharp eyes and knowledge of the area made him ideal for the job. Each day for many days afterward, he would select two or three wingmen, wend his way south to the battle lines around Toungoo, Pyinmana, and Yedasho, and carefully note the positions of any forces he saw. Then he would return to Loiwing, passing the information directly on to Chennault and intelligence staffers at Stilwell's headquarters. Those men already knew where their Chinese allies' troops were; so they overlaid Tex's sightings onto their maps to determine the location of Japanese forces.

Tex, of course, was free to hit anything he felt was worthwhile (which meant anything he could identify as Japanese). On the 12th of April, while patrolling with two other Tigers between Pyinmana and Yedasho, Tex suddenly heard wingman John Croft call out seven bombers he had seen, below and to the south. Turning the flight in that direction, Tex saw nothing; overcast obscured the area. But as they went over familiar Toungoo, Tex's attention was abruptly riveted to the main runway. A bomber was just accelerating for takeoff.

Unsure what anti-aircraft fire might be waiting below, Tex directed Croft and Pete Wright to stay at altitude. Then he roared down for a strafing run. The bomber's crew never knew what hit them as Tex blazed away, ripping pieces of metal from the plane, and finally igniting the fuel tank. He tried to look around quickly as he zoomed away from the field "on the deck," but was still unsure whether anti-aircraft defenses were in the vicinity. Checking to the rear, however, he glimpsed a welcome sight: a second Jap bomber was in the pattern to land. Tex could imagine the looks on their faces as they observed the remains of their smoldering counterpart.

He brought his P-40 around for a second pass, intending to hit the other bomber while it was still in the air. His attack began well; the "E" model's six .50-caliber wing guns poured a stream of withering fire into the slow-flying bomber. Flames leaped from both engines. It bounced onto the runway, careening and skidding. With some surprise, Tex saw the pilot of the plane jump out of the cockpit and onto the bomber's wing.

Tex didn't hesitate a second; reflex took over. He steepened up his dive and banked sharply left, putting a spray of firepower right through the fleeing Jap. The man fell, permanently prevented from flying another bombing mission.

Unfortunately, the maneuver completely exposed the P-40's underbelly to a 40mm anti-aircraft gun the Japanese had hidden in the old Toungoo dispensary, on the right side of the runway. The gun opened fire. An explosive anti-aircraft shell blasted into Tex's right wing, knocking it upwards and nearly tearing it off. Tex fought to stabilize the slewing P-40. When he looked at the wing, he felt the hair on the back of his neck rise; he could see trees moving past through a gaping two-foot hole halfway between the root and wingtip. How the outer half of the wing remained attached, he had no idea.

Tex tried to keep his voice calm as he called to Croft and Wright, but there was no answer. After checking the area to ensure they weren't trying the same stunt he had, he set a course for Loiwing, and started praying. The wing held together on the return flight (perhaps with divine help). When the ground crew saw his aircraft touch down at Loiwing, their jaws dropped. Wright and Croft, who had returned after an overcast had closed in from the south, did double-takes too.

Most of his reconnaissance flights—perhaps fortunately—were not quite as exciting; but as the Japanese accelerated northward, there were plenty of opportunities to hit ground targets. On April 25th, Tex led half a dozen P-40Es, covered by five of the older P-40Bs, down the road from Loiwing to Loilem, along which Japanese armored columns had been moving rapidly. There were plenty of them still on the road, and Tex led the string of Flying Tigers as they released clusters of fragmentation bombs directly above a column. Carnage ensued as the bombs shredded vehicles, equipment, and troops who dove for cover in the underbrush beside the road. When the frag bombs were gone, the P-40s wheeled around and strafed down the line to "mop up" anything intact. Truck after truck, loaded with gasoline, went up like a torch as Tex raked eight of them with gunfire before turning away. His jubilant companions pitched right in, causing massive destruction for several miles along the length of the highway.

Then the "top cover" of P-40Bs spotted what looked like a Japanese observation plane in the distance; and with great zeal, they proceeded to chase the fleeing aircraft across the countryside. Tex was low on ammunition, but joined in anyway. The enemy plane was fast and maneuverable, and it took the combined efforts of Tex and three others to finally force its pilot into a box canyon. Risking a collision, all four P-40s shot right into the canyon behind it.

A wild chase followed. The AVG got occasional bursts into the enemy plane; its rear gunner returned fire. Finally, in a desperate full-speed tear right on the deck, the Jap caught a tree with his wingtip, flipping into a lightning-fast spin that ended by his plowing into the ground. The P-40s pulled out of the canyon exultantly; later, they agreed to split the hard-won victory credit four ways.

South of Lashio, some fifty miles down the road, Chinese ground forces were on their last legs, struggling to hold the line against the Japanese. The latter's overwhelming superiority of armament, including numerous tanks and armored vehicles, allowed them to run roughshod over the defense—but the AVG made sure they paid for it. For days on end the men flew multiple missions, screaming down the Burma Road to frag-bomb and strafe columns of Japanese motorized forces. But it seemed that for every Jap soldier they eliminated, two or three were right behind. It was a battle that could not be decided with aircraft alone; the AVG had already learned that lesson at Rangoon.

April 29th was the birthday of Hirohito, Emperor of Japan. Chennault rightly guessed that on the day before, the enemy would attempt a significant attack on the AVG base at Loiwing. They wanted good news to bring to their supreme leader on such a special occasion. Anticipating a strike, the Old Man outlined a plan he hoped would spoil the festivities. A flight of fifteen P-40s—essentially, everything that could get into the air—would take off from Loiwing and patrol south past Lashio in an attempt to intercept the predicted bombers. After that, they were to land at Mongshih, an auxiliary airfield farther northeast in China, rather than returning to Loiwing. That way, if the bombers got through to Loiwing, they would not catch the P-40s landing from the mission.

At mid-morning Tex took off, leading the flight of five 2nd Squadron P-40s that would act as top cover, and held position at fifteen thousand feet. Chennault would have liked to put all the aircraft at that altitude, but there were only five bottles of oxygen available. The other ten fighters, flown by Olson's 3rd Squadron, stacked themselves from ten to twelve thousand feet. Thus arrayed, the formation cruised toward Lashio and the enemy front lines.

It was forty-five minutes into the flight, which was starting to look like a quiet one, when Tex's keen eyes picked out what he had been watching for. Some twenty miles south of the village of Hsipaw, he spotted dozens of Japanese planes, in rigid formation, flying purposefully north on a direct course for Loiwing.

Tex was amazed. *Talk about good instincts*, he thought. *The Old Man would have been burned at the stake a century and a half ago.*

"I've got about thirty fighters here," Tex drawled into the mike, relaying the information to Rector and the others.

He also notified the Hells Angels below that, in his estimation, the enemy formation's altitude was somewhere between the two AVG flights. Just then, the radio crackled with a message from Loiwing; a separate group of Japanese fighters were strafing the Burma Road at Lashio, now a refugee-packed bottleneck. "Ole" Olson quickly peeled off a handful of his flight and sent them winging back northward to try and catch the strafers. Then the race was on, Tex's pilots pouring the coal to their Allison engines to intercept the Japanese.

As the distance closed, Tex realized he had made a mistake. The specks grew slowly into the mottled-green shapes of twin-engine bombers; there were twenty-seven of them, in three neat "V" formations. Tex knew what that meant, and in another second he spotted them: almost two dozen escorting enemy fighters, above and well behind the bombers.

The fighters had seen the Flying Tigers too, and were already firewalling their own engines to catch up before the P-40s could pounce on the ponderous bombers. Tex did some quick calculation; his flight wouldn't have time for even one pass on the bombers before the fighters were on top of them. He broke slightly left and raised his plane's shark-mouthed nose to put it straight into the fighter formation; and the rest of the boys did the same. If they had to take care of the escorts first, it was fine with them—and they never passed up a head-on engagement.

As the groups came together, the five Tigers mentally selected their targets. The trick was to pick out an enemy who was concentrating on someone else, thereby hopefully getting a shot at him unawares. With his wingman covering him, Tex zeroed in on his intended victim, who had turned away from the head-on approach, and didn't see the P-40. Tex snapped a short burst from a rear quartering position, but it went wide. Another burst—wide also. Now the enemy fighter knew he was being targeted, and slid rapidly left in preparation for some violent maneuver. This exposed his cockpit for a second; Tex had time for two more short bursts before his opponent would "wrap up" the nimble fighter right before his eyes. But Tex needed no more time; his fourth stream of tracers slammed directly into the canopy of the Japanese aircraft. A plume of smoke burst from the engine as the pilot slumped over the controls, and the plane began a graceful, shallow dive that lasted for miles before ending abruptly on a hillside below.

The engagement had become a freewheeling melee, a swirling mass of aircraft whose pilots were locked in white-knuckled efforts to get on their opponent's tails and kill them. The Japanese aircraft were much more maneuverable; they had the luxury of being able to turn out of the line of fire as soon as they knew they were being followed. On the other hand, time after time, the P-40s had to dive away to prevent the tables from being turned on them. But the Tigers had become expert at making fast passes to hit an unwary opponent, then diving out of danger when a Japanese fighter was getting the drop on them.

Tex's second victory of the day came with his victim's full awareness of what was going on. It was a rare head-on pass, the enemy pilot apparently knowing no better than to try it. The Jap had an altitude advantage, and the two planes were already fairly close as they careened toward each other through the middle of the dogfight. Tex watched his first stream of tracers fly low, then realized he was closing too fast: in another couple of seconds, he would pass right under the enemy plane.

Hauling back violently on the stick, Tex pulled his fire right through the oncoming Jap, holding it on target for the split-second needed to inflict fatal damage. His limbs felt like lead briefly as they took on the G-induced weight. The enemy's last shots passed under the P-40. Tex turned his climb into a wing-over, craning his neck around to catch a glimpse of the burning enemy plane, whose wing he had just taken off.

Sixteen of the enemy fighters fell to the guns of the AVG in the battle; but as the remainder fled, the Tigers realized that the bombers were nowhere in sight. The Japs had paid a high price—including another half-dozen of their own shot down to the north over Lashio—but the AVG had no way to stop a raid on Loiwing now. Tex's flight sped back northeast, on the lookout for the wily bombers. When they arrived over Loiwing, their fears were realized: the enemy had bombed the base and gotten away clean. Tex continued on to Mongshih and landed as ordered; and within a few hours, Chinese workers had restored Loiwing's packed-earth airstrip sufficiently to allow the P-40s to return.

The Emperor's birthday dawned chilly and overcast, and rainstorms hung about

Loiwing for many miles on all sides. In spite of the AVG's success against the Japanese in the air, it was the same old story on the ground: the Chinese had been forced to retreat. Japanese troops captured Lashio that day, forcing the Tigers to move again. Chinese General P.T. Mow sent sixty-five trucks down the Burma Road from Kunming to help the AVG evacuate. The plan was to fall back to Paoshan, a small airfield just east of the Salween River, one hundred miles into China. As the faithful ground crew and pilots with planes to fly drove out of sight down the muddy road eastward, Tex took stock of the situation at Loiwing.

He was left in charge of a handful of Panda Bear pilots and about the same number of flyable P-40s. Most of the field was soupy with rain, and pockmarked with Japanese bombs from the raid two days before. Only a single north-south strip remained usable. With the weather "socked in" overhead, and a mere five-hundred-foot ceiling, Tex wondered whether they would be flying or driving when they evacuated ahead of the advancing Japs.

Reports from the front said that advance parties of the enemy had reached a great curve in the Burma Road near the village of Nahmpakka. Tex and the others, who had no defenses except their sidearms, knew of small jungle trail—a shortcut—that ran from Nahmpakka straight to a point farther along the Burma Road, only a few miles from Loiwing. Infantry could use the trail to bypass many miles of looping roadway. Did the Japanese know about it? The Tigers weren't sure; but Tex decided he had to assume that they did. He calculated the time it would take the Japanese to march up the trail, watching the glowering overcast above. In addition to the P-40s that could be flown, twenty-two more sat in hangars in various states of repair, short of critical parts that were never forthcoming. Tex desperately needed to get the operational aircraft out of Loiwing; but the weather simply would not cooperate.

In the final hour of remaining time, just as Tex was considering giving the order for the pilots to board the few remaining trucks, the ceiling lifted to eight hundred feet. The men threw everything they could into the baggage compartments of the flyable P-40s, glancing continuously over their shoulders, expecting to see Japanese troops moving up the road at any moment. As a final task, they set fire to the twenty-two precious P-40s under repair; the Japanese would find only burned-out hulks when they arrived. Then it was into the air, squeezing into the narrow corridor between the "soup" and the ground, speeding northeast to Paoshan.

When the Japanese rolled into Loiwing right on the heels of the AVG, only the demolished CAMCO aircraft factory and twenty-two smoldering P-40 airframes remained of the Flying Tigers' operation.

※ ※ ※

From the deck of the aircraft carrier Hornet, *slipping quietly westward through the wide Pacific toward Japan, sixteen North American B-25* Mitchell *bombers of the U.S. Army lifted off to execute a mission of incredible daring. Crossing the shores of Japan in darkness, they unloaded tons of bombs over Tokyo, watching as explosions flashed in the gloom below. Then, instead of returning to the* Hornet, *they continued westward toward the Asian mainland.*

The plan, conceived by Jimmy Doolittle, was for the B-25s to press on into China, land at airfields Chennault had prepared, and place themselves under his command. There were only two problems: no one had told Chennault anything about the raid; and no one—not even Doolittle—could have imagined the effect it would have on the Japanese.

The bombers penetrated deep into China's Chihkiang province, completely lost in the darkness, before their fuel gave out. One by one, they began to descend for crash landings. If the Old Man had known, his radio warning net would have been alerted, and the Mitchells *could have been safely guided to lighted airfields. As it was, not a single bomber survived, and many of the crewmen were killed. It was a stunning loss, following such a bold strike.*

When they realized what had occurred, the Chinese banded together, led by missionary John Birch, to lead the raiders by secret routes westward to safety. This, at least, was skillfully accomplished; only eight of the "Doolittle Raiders" who survived their crashes failed to escape capture by the enemy.

But when the furious Japanese learned what had happened, they sent an expeditionary force a hundred thousand strong rampaging into East China along the Raiders' escape route, to punish the Chinese for aiding them. Whole villages were razed or bombed from the air along a wide swath. A quarter-million Chinese soldiers and civilians died without mercy in the brutal campaign. The Western Allies later remembered little about the price paid for the bombs that fell on Tokyo; the Chinese could not forget, but they never complained.

In Burma, things were going from bad to worse, as Stilwell watched his plans for defense and counterattack turn to ashes around him. The enemy thrust northward in surges along the river valleys of the Irrawaddy, Sittang, and Salween. The Japanese 55th Division captured Toungoo on the 19th of March in heavy fighting, throwing back the Chinese 200th Division with great loss. After a brief pause, the 55th continued to advance up the road to Mandalay, capturing Pyinmana. On the western route of advance, the Japs' 33rd Division tore through Prome and Magwe, and by the 17th of April they had halted on the southern border of the great Yenangyaung oil flats.

It was at this critical juncture that Stilwell unaccountably made a great error. As the Japanese 33rd enveloped Yenangyaung, they surrounded two British brigades and a tank battalion. From the center line of his defense, where the Chinese 5th Army was holding the enemy precariously at bay, Stilwell pulled the only Chinese armored division—the 38th, the bulwark of the defenders—out of its defensive position, to drive west and relieve the British. The 38th Division accomplished that mission after days of bitter fighting, recapturing Yenangyaung; but disaster struck along the now-weakened line to the east. Without the support of the 38th, the 5th and 6th Army's defense began to crumble; and Japanese troops raced through widening gaps to take their enemies from behind. The Chinese retreat turned into a rout; and before a new front could be established, the campaign was essentially over. The victorious Japanese 18th and 56th Divisions smothered their disorganized opponents as they drove to Mandalay and Lashio.

Burma was lost.

Tex in the classroom doorway, Kyedaw (Toungoo), fall 1941.

Tex in traditional Burmese sarong, Toungoo, Burma, 1941.

Tex in a makeshift "chow line" at Mingaladon. Carl Quick (far left), Tex's crew chief, is the designated "chef."

Chapter 18

A BRIDGE FROM DISASTER

Traffic along the seven-hundred-mile Burma Road had swelled into a flood. Throughout the countryside, the natives had obliviously carried on their daily routines during the invasion, right up to the point where the invading Japanese scattered them. Then the Burmese grabbed their few belongings and took to the winding highway, hoping to reach China or India before the enemy caught them. The result was a torrent of humanity that crowded along the road on foot, in oxen-drawn carts, or (rarely) riding on trucks. All were despondently wending their way out of the country, while Japanese troops raced along behind and through them.

Paoshan sat directly upon that road. From the airfield, the Flying Tigers could watch the masses filing past in numb resignation. It was a pitiful sight. The AVG itself was safe for the moment from Japanese ground troops, since the huge gulf of the Salween River gorge lay in the enemy's path, spanned by only a single bridge. However, the Tigers still had only limited means to receive warning of an airborne attack; Chennault's meticulously arranged radio warning network was most effective farther east, at Kunming. Tex and the other Panda Bears had flown on from Paoshan to Kunming, after their narrow escape from shattered Loiwing; now, Paoshan was in the hands of Bob Neale and the 1st Squadron.

When the enemy rolled into Loiwing just after the evacuation of Tex and company, the Japanese 56th Division, known as the "Red Dragons," considered its position. The Japs knew from aerial reconnaissance reports that little remained of the Chinese 66th Division, which they had been mopping up along their advance for days. They had learned a more important fact, too, with delight: there were only a few scattered Chinese forces between their position and Kunming itself—a prize which, if captured, would shake hated China to its core. Better still, initial assessments of Chinese army strength between Kunming and Chungking, the nation's wartime capital, were all very encouraging. It seemed clear that the 56th was destined to heap glory upon itself...

The Red Dragons wasted no time, but called upon their air forces to punish the American flying bandits at Paoshan, across the Salween. The Japanese had learned, to their great loss, that the Americans could be devastatingly effective strafing troops on the ground and dropping fragmentation bombs on vehicles. The 56th already bore the effects from weeks of such attacks; and they intended to remove the cause permanently.

Fifty-one bombers of the Imperial Army attacked Paoshan on the 4th of May; and once again, the Adam and Eves had no warning. But when they spotted the refugees crowding the road through the city below, the Japanese bomber crews bypassed the airfield and ruthlessly unloaded on the Chinese. Hemmed onto their winding route by rock walls and rugged terrain on either side, the refugees had no escape as enemy bombs plastered them. Explosions ripped through the people, and the packed choke points in Paoshan became a sea of horror as tens of thousands were blown apart.

Charlie Bond and Bob Little risked a similar death as they charged for their planes, unwilling to let the Japanese pound Paoshan unopposed. Somehow they managed to get airborne before the worst of the bombing, climbing to altitude in time to chase the Japs as they sailed homeward. Bond caught them, and shot down two of the bombers to exact some payment for the merciless raid. When the Japanese dove to gain speed, Bond was forced to return to Paoshan or run out of gas. As he came in low over the airfield, he made two encouraging "slow-rolls," to signal his victories.

The men watching on the ground were not encouraged, however; for they saw something Charlie Bond didn't. From high above him, three enemy fighters were diving on Bond, lining him up in their sights. Bond mistook the frantic pointing and hollering of his comrades on the ground for celebration—until it was too late. Before he could maneuver, the Japs' tracers found him. The P-40 convulsed, hammered from three directions. Flames shot from the fuselage tank and roared into the cockpit, licking greedily at the man's face; only his helmet and a hasty covering with his scarf saved Bond's features from being burned beyond recognition. In excruciating pain, his body on fire, he somehow bailed out and parachuted into a Chinese cemetery. The trio of Japanese fighters continued to make pass after pass at the airfield.

The town of Paoshan was awash with the dead and dying. Hell's Angels pilot Ben Foshee, moving through the town aboard a truck in the convoy from Loiwing, lost his leg when shrapnel tore through it. He bled to death before Doc Richards could reach him from the airfield through the press of bodies. Uncounted thousands shared the same fate; and most of the town had become a raging inferno that burned many others alive. Babies cried for mothers who lay lifeless in the mud; the wounded cast about miserably for something to stop the bleeding from their faces and bodies.

Chennault guessed that the enemy would return the next day to build upon their "success." Once again, he was correct. Just before noon, the Old Man sent Tex and six other Panda Bears from Kunming to intercept the anticipated follow-up raid. Tex had engine trouble with his P-40E before takeoff; and by the time he made it into the air, the others were out of sight. Nevertheless, he pressed on, climbing to twenty-one thousand feet and breathing oxygen. Within an hour, he found himself over rugged terrain just south of Paoshan.

Tex was not the only "visitor" to the area. Below him at about fifteen thousand feet, he spotted a flight of seven Japanese fighters, milling around with no apparent direction in mind. Quickly calling out the information to nearby radio station BC-5, Tex bent it over and shot toward them. Would he be able to surprise them, and get a pass in before they could react?

He would; the Jap fighter he picked out didn't see him until Tex was already firing. Bullets from the P-40E's six .50-caliber guns ripped into the little aircraft as it turned, belatedly, to face its attacker; and after three seconds of punishment, the Jap snapped over into a spin, never to recover. It was Tex's tenth aerial victory, but that was the last thing on his mind at the moment.

Continuing his dive straight through the surprised group of Japanese, he glimpsed a second explosion away to his right. Another enemy fighter had blown up, and Tex realized immediately that the rest of the Panda Bears must have been lending help from somewhere close by. Thus encouraged, he reached altitude once more, and pulled around for a second pass.

Once again he picked out a target, one of four enemy fighters that were heading toward him. As Tex fired, his intended target broke into a turn. Tex banked as well, holding his burst, trying to keep the Jap in his gunsight; but the P-40's tracers fell gradually further behind the more maneuverable Japanese aircraft. The attack was a clean miss. The other three were quickly dropping into position behind the P-40, and Tex knew he would have to dive out again before they made their own pass at him.

When he finally reached eighteen thousand feet once more and turned for a third attack pass, the enemy planes were gone. Tex could see nothing in the sky. The battle had brought him nearer to Paoshan, though, so he circled the airfield for some ten minutes, watching for further enemy activity. There was none. Eventually, Tex turned east and headed back to Kunming. When he landed, he learned that a follow-up wave of bombers had turned tail and run when they saw the P-40s "chewing up" their fighter escort; with Tex's victory, the AVG had accounted for another eight planes.

While Japan's air force concentrated on Paoshan, her 56th Division was fast approaching up the Burma Road. They crossed the border into China, and stormed through the villages of Mongshih and Wanting without a fight. The same day that Tex shot down the fighter south of Paoshan, advance vehicles of the 56th reached the edge of the plateau west of the Salween River, and enemy troops looked down into the gorge.

Below them was an incredible scene. Across their path, the lazy Salween stretched out of sight to the north and south. Over thousands of years, the river had worn its bed ever deeper into the plateau. Now, it flowed slowly along a channel at the bottom of a huge rocky chasm, which was several miles wide at the eye-level of the Japanese troops. The river itself was draped in mist fully a mile below them, and the Burma Road descended that distance along a tortuous thirty-five mile path, with dozens of loops and switchbacks. At the bottom, a suspension bridge spanned the river, a tiny line of steel; and from the far bank, the highway wound its way in a similar manner up the other side, to the edge of the Paoshan plateau. The panorama was breathtaking, and the Japanese paused to take it in before beginning the long trek downward.

Only one thing spoiled the view in the eyes of the 56th's soldiers. Several spans of the suspension bridge had become piles of rubble in the current below. Retreating Chinese troops had demolished parts of the structure in anticipation of their enemies' advance. They did this in spite of the fact that it left large numbers of their own forces stranded on the western side (of which Chiang Kai-Shek was fully aware; nevertheless, he saw no option but to destroy the bridge). The Japanese would attend to the cut-off Chinese soldiers in good time; just now, their only objective was to cross the river with all speed. Kunming and victory awaited them on the far side.

At Paoshan, some miles east of the gorge, the Flying Tigers were pulling out. Events of the last two days had proved that the warning net was ineffective around the airfield, and they collected their equipment to retreat for the fourth time in two months. This time, they were going all the way back to Kunming, two hundred miles up the road to the east. The AVG was returning to the nearest thing it had to a "home base," after a seven-hundred-mile fighting retreat. The Japanese, they knew, shared the same goal of reaching the city.

As the Tigers gathered in Kunming, Chennault sent an urgent telegram to the Chiangs in Chungking. In it, he reported the Japs' arrival at the Salween, and flatly stated that they could be driving their vehicles into Kunming in a few days if determined opposition was not rallied immediately. The Old Man also requested permission to strafe the enemy columns of vehicles, though he knew that with the press of Chinese refugees and troops still on the west side of the gorge, some Chinese casualties would be inevitable. He thought it best that China's leaders make such a decision.

Chiang Kai-Shek sent back word to Chennault: destroy the enemy. The potential sacrifice of Chinese lives was deemed acceptable, under the circumstances. So while the tattered remains of the Chinese 66th Division tried to regroup on the eastern slope of the gorge, Chennault summoned Tex into his office.

"Tex, remember when you gave me a lesson on dive-bombing?" asked Chennault, with the hint of a smile.

"Sure, I remember," Tex replied.

"Well, it's time for the real thing. We need to hit the Japs at the Salween River with everything we've got. I want to lead off with some dive-bombers, to try and break up the road, so they can't get out of there," the Old Man explained. He paused, as Tex nodded in understanding.

"I want you to pick three other pilots, and take off at ten hundred," Chennault continued. "I'm putting Olson and three 3rd Squadron planes up as top cover. You can refuel at Yunnanyi."

"We'll be ready," said Tex.

He broke the news to Ed Rector, who, as usual, thought the plan was "simply marvelous." Frank Lawlor and Tom Jones were the other two that Tex selected to go; both were as eager as Rector.

"Tex, the only thing is, I haven't done any dive-bombing since I left the fleet," said Jones, who had been bedridden with illness for months until recently recovering.

"Tom, it's a cliff wall a mile high," Tex replied with a grin. "You can't possibly miss."

With the morning came miserable weather; a thick overcast and light rain blanketed the field at Kunming. But they all knew the situation was critical enough that the mission must go ahead. At mid-morning, the eight planes took off, their propellers kicking spray off the sodden runway. They arrowed westward. In Tex's flight, each of the four P-40Es were loaded with clusters of 35-lb. fragmentation bombs under each wing; and along their centerline racks hung hulking 570-lb. Russian demolition bombs. Olson's four P-40Bs, including R.T. Smith, Erik Shilling, and Tom Haywood, climbed above the Panda Bears and went on the lookout through the wet weather for enemy planes.

It was fully two hundred miles from Kunming to the Salween gorge, and towering thunderheads lay in their path. Drenching rain came and went as they put down at Yunnanyi to refuel. Tex's P-40 felt heavy and sluggish from the extra weight of ordnance slung underneath it. They took off again. It was rough flying, difficult to stay in formation, as sheets of rain washed over them and glowering cumulonimbus clouds pressed from above. At last, as they drew near the point Tex figured the gorge should be, he thought he spotted a break in the weather ahead. All eight P-40s sailed through a gap in the clouds—and into sunlight, as the weather front ended, and the landscape opened up before them.

On a combat mission, it is rare to be captivated by the scenery; but this time, the pilots couldn't help it. Squinting in the sudden glare, they surveyed the purple-crowned mountains and the winding, storybook valley that cut its way through them. Sunlight painted the hillsides with rich colors, glittering blue off the tiny ribbon of the Salween below.

As they descended, details became clearer. The huge column of trucks and armored vehicles of Japan's 56th Division trailed up from the river's edge, all the way along the length of the looping highway to the top of the gorge, and well out onto the plateau beyond. Never had Tex seen so many Japanese soldiers at once; before, he had always had to pick them out in the jungle underbrush in small groups, or catch a small convoy on a road. Here, there were hundreds of tanks and trucks, and thousands of troops, all waiting for their engineers to complete a pontoon bridge across the river below.

After scanning the sky for fighters and seeing none—which surprised him—Tex continued descending. Sure enough, Japanese engineers swarmed over the shoreline like ants, readying crosspieces of a sturdy pontoon bridge that would hold up under the weight of their equipment. Some of the bridge was already in place. Tex checked left and right to make sure his flight was in position, and Ed Rector gave him a thumbs-up. They all knew what to do; without further hesitation, they slid neatly into a single line and went to work.

Tex opened up the throttle all the way as he sent the P-40 into a sixty-degree dive. He knew the Japanese troops would be shooting all kinds of small arms fire at him as soon as he came into range; so, to make himself a more difficult target, he needed all the speed he could get. Meanwhile, he lined the P-40 up to target the top of the gorge, exactly where the road dived to begin the thirty-mile switchback down to the river. Gunfire began to flash below him as the troops opened up. It seemed as though the entire force had stopped what they were doing to watch the Flying Tigers in amazement. At precisely the correct moment, Tex released his demolition bomb.

The results were better than anyone had hoped. As he pulled into a hard right turn to watch, he saw the big Russian weapon slam into the cliffside, exactly where he had aimed it. Even at the distance he was, he heard the resulting *whump*. A cloud of dusty particles blossomed out into space. Through it, Tex glimpsed great slabs of rock peeling off the cliff surface and crashing onto the curves of road below—and then, one after another, his comrades lambasted the same area in turn.

Whump. Boulders crashed down on the helpless line of men below, burying them amid screams and crumpled vehicles. *Whump*. Troops several turns down the road searched frantically for cover as rocks from baseball- to Buick-size caromed off the hillside, knocking them senselessly to their deaths. *Whump*. A cloud of dust filled the air at the top of the gorge, and spinning trucks launched themselves into emptiness to explode on the broken cliffside hundreds of feet below. Tex felt a flush of exultation as he watched the effects, roaring out over the river.

It was just the beginning. As the dust settled, the troops on the face of the slope realized with horror that the attack had cut off their only escape. The demolition bombs had transformed the road above them into a yawning wasteland of rock, impassable without hours of excavation. There was no cover, either, for at every turn, the long road down featured only a wall on one side and a sheer drop on the other. As Tex and the others wheeled around and came back toward the Japanese, utter panic ensued.

Tex flew straight toward the last switchback at the bottom of the gorge, observing the Japanese engineers clustered thickly at the river's edge. He let go a brief burst of .50-caliber machine-gun fire to send the troops scrambling for cover, then buzzed low along the road and dropped his fragmentation bombs. Bodies and pieces of equipment flew everywhere as the frag-bombs went off with dozens of flashes, and deadly shrapnel sprayed in all directions. The Japs' own ammunition stores detonated in secondary explosions; punctured gas tanks exploded into infernos that coated bystanders in flaming fuel and burned vehicles to skeletons. Screams echoed into the misty gulf as the engineers' ranks were shredded.

Tex wheeled around toward the Chinese on the other side of the river. Soldiers of the bedraggled 66th Division were beside themselves—firing their rifles into the air, shouting encouragement, and dancing for joy along the shoreline as their enemies reaped a fatal whirlwind. Rector and the others unloaded their frags with deadly precision as well, peeling off in different directions as the heart of the Red Dragon division was turned into a mass of corpses and twisted metal.

The AVG still was not finished. They made pass after pass, back and forth along the road's switchbacks, sending streams of machine-gun bullets into anything that survived. When their guns were empty, they summoned the 3rd Squadron top cover, who had been watching the proceedings with great interest. Olson's boys zoomed down and poured their ammunition into the fray until it, too, was gone.

The strike was a success unequaled by any mission the AVG had yet flown. As Tex and the others finally veered off for home, they saw the Red Dragon survivors trying to clear the rock at the top of the gorge. They were retreating back to Burma.

Four more Tigers returned to the gorge that day, hitting the same hapless troops again—and then ranging down the road westward, where the remainder of the gargantuan column of the 56th was taking to its heels. This time the P-40s carried incendiaries; they dropped these with devastating effect, turning the trail of vehicles into a conflagration. Studying photos of the damage, Chennault guessed that some of Tex's frag-bombs had exploded under a certain overhang of rock near the bottom of the gorge, which had likely sheltered the Red Dragons' field headquarters. If so, the remaining troops were probably leaderless. For the next three days, Chennault sent flight after flight across the Salween and over the road back toward Mongshih, pounding the enemy wherever he could be found.

Within a week, no Japanese unit as large as a battalion remained within a hundred miles of the Salween gorge. The snaking river descent looked like a graveyard for Japan's military vehicles and equipment. The Japanese never tried to cross the river again.

* * *

Few historians would later understand the importance of the Japanese retreat back down the Burma Road to the southwest. During the course of the Second World War, the Allied nations won a handful of key victories on which the course of history hinged: the Americans at Midway, the British at El Alamein, the Russians at Stalingrad. The Salween Gorge attack was indisputably just such a victory for the Allies. There was no effective resistance between the 56th Division and Kunming, and little from there to Chungking. China's fate depended upon stopping the drive of the Red Dragons, for the great nation was already hard-pressed to the point of exhaustion. They would doubtless have been forced to surrender upon the loss of either of these cities. China's capitulation, in turn, would have freed Japan to throw millions of soldiers westward into revolt-ripe India, just as the Germans were driving upon Cairo. It certainly would have changed the face of that campaign, probably allowing a link-up of the two Axis nations across India. What would have happened then, with the advent of the atomic bomb still three years away, can only be guessed.

One day before the Red Dragons reached the Salween Gorge, one of Tex's old carriers, the *Yorktown*, was engulfed in the Battle of the Coral Sea. It was the first maritime engagement in which the opposing naval forces were never within sight of each other; aircraft were the only weapons used. When it ended four days later, the Americans had lost the *Lexington*, sunk the *Shoho*, and prevented a Japanese invasion of Port Moresby.

A thousand miles northwest, the Japanese finally overran the fortress of Corregidor to complete their conquest of the Philippines, two months after the evacuating General Douglas MacArthur had vowed: "I shall return."

Upon the rout of his forces in Burma, Stilwell set out on foot to traverse the hundreds of miles of jungle, rivers, and mountains that lay between him and India. The retreat lasted weeks; and through it all, the general's personal courage and toughness were incredible for a sixty-year-old man, as he led the one hundred fourteen souls in his band to eventual safety. However, Chiang Kai-Shek shook his head in disbelief when he learned that his Chief of Staff, whom he desperately needed in Chungking to take command of the Chinese rout in Burma, had removed himself from any position where he could lead while trekking his way out on foot. Stilwell refused a transport plane that arrived to lift him out, flown by Robert Scott and Caleb Haynes, and further declined to give a single report to the Generalissimo during his exodus. "I doubt he knows the meaning of discipline," Chiang wrote angrily in his personal correspondence. A Chinese commander who had committed such errors in judgment would have been summarily shot. From that point forward, Chiang lost confidence in Stilwell; and even the general's contemporaries joked about the "best three-star company commander in the U.S. Army."

Alert tent at Kweilin, July 1942.

Tex with Line Chief Harry Fox at Hengyang, July 1942.

Chapter 19

A FERRY TALE

"Tex, I don't know what the hell's going on," the Old Man was saying, as they stood outside his headquarters building in the warm May afternoon. "I've got to get some of those P-43s back here. We've had two trips go to India to get them—and you've seen the results."

"Two got back the first time..." Tex reflected, scratching his head in thought.

"And one the second," Chennault finished. "Not exactly what you'd call a success. I want you and Duke Hedman to take the next group. There are ten Chinese pilots that just got here, ready to go. I'm fed up with doing without those aircraft, so I'm giving you *carte blanche* to do whatever you need to. Get those planes back here."

"We'll give it our best shot," Tex replied.

The group had to wait for a CNAC transport to take them to India, and it was several days before one was scheduled to make the trip. The morning it arrived, Tex headed out to the runway, carrying his bag for the journey. He spotted Duke Hedman already standing among a group of ten Chinese.

"Hey, Duke, everything all set?" Tex asked as he approached.

"I think so. The CNAC fellows say we can load up anytime we're ready."

"Great," Tex replied, turning to the Chinese. "Are y'all ready to go?"

They all grinned at him. Tex grinned back. The grinning continued until Hedman tapped him on the shoulder.

"They don't speak a lick of English, Tex," said Hedman with a smile. He pointed at one of the Chinese. "That guy's the interpreter."

Once this was established, they were ready to depart, and the transport lifted off the asphalt runway with all twelve men aboard. It was a long way to Karachi, the city near the mouth of the Indus River in western India, where the planes had been dropped off. After many stops, they finally reached the city on the third week of May, and checked into a hotel. Once in Karachi, the Chinese pilots went in another direction, seeming to know where they were going, so Tex didn't stop them. The two Americans had no idea where their Chinese companions stayed.

Tex and Hedman found the hotel extremely pleasant, especially after eight months of living in Burma and China. Karachi was a typical British colonial city, clean and well-regulated, with the airfield a short distance from the town. When Tex and Hedman showed up at the airfield the next morning, there were the Chinese, ready to get to work—and grinning. The whole group got a look at their new airplanes.

The Republic P-43 *Lancer* was an interim link in the chain of technological advancement in fighter aircraft. It was the first fighter built in the United States that featured a supercharger; and it could manage well at altitudes far higher than the P-40 (hence Chennault's attraction). Its ceiling was listed at over thirty-six thousand feet, but Tex would later soar to forty-four thousand in one without any problem. The P-43 also had tremendous range—and even edged out the P-40 in airspeed, topping out around 353 mph. One drawback, however, was the paltry armament: only two .50-caliber and two .30-caliber guns. It would prove useful primarily as a reconnaissance plane (and a showcase for the well-built Pratt-and-Whitney engine).

Tex and the others ogled the P-43s like "goats looking at a new gate." Republic had been willing to let these planes go to the Chinese government, since they were already beginning work on a much better model, the soon-to-be-famous P-47 *Thunderbolt*. There were no manuals to study; so Tex and Hedman proceeded to learn all they could about the planes by trial and error.

During the first half of the war, aircraft designs were, for the most part, similar and not overly complex. Thus, Tex was able to take a familiarization flight within a day or so; and he liked the way the P-43 handled on his "checkout." It was really too bad about the guns, but in equipment-starved China, the AVG was in no position to be picky. Shortly afterward, Hedman checked out; and then it was the turn of the Chinese pilots. Tex and Hedman wondered about their flying abilities, since the Chinese lacked the quality of training available to U.S. pilots.

They had cause for concern. The two Tigers' stomachs lurched as the Chinese pilots repeatedly brushed with death during the straightforward checkout flights. Even "once around the pattern" for them was a spectacle—and their landings usually had Tex cringing in anticipation of ground-loops or outright crashes. Nevertheless, somehow all ten managed to bring them up and put them down without loss of life or aircraft, for which Tex silently breathed a prayer of thanks. When the phase was complete, the pilots gathered around excitedly—all grinning, inevitably.

"I think I know why we only got three of these things back to China so far," Hedman stage-whispered to Tex, forcing a smile at the Chinese.

Tex's face wore the same expression. "Well, at least it ain't boring," he quipped.

The evenings in Karachi were very enjoyable. In his easygoing way, Tex made friends with some British RAF pilots; and they invited both AVG men to join them at a "Jim Khana" club, one of a popular chain of night spots that had excellent food, drinks, and company.

There came a day in mid-May when the troop ship U.S.S. *Brazil* arrived at the docks of Karachi. The *Brazil* carried elements of the 23rd Fighter Group, as well as a contingent of 16th Fighter Squadron pilots who had been flying P-40s off the *Ranger*—Tex's old carrier—for the first time. Of more immediate importance, the *Brazil* carried some fifty nurses who had been at sea for over a month. When the ship's gangplank lowered, the exodus looked like a jailbreak. There was not a safe male in the area. Evenings at the Jim Kana club went from "enjoyable" to "great."

Operationally, Tex was unhappy about only one thing: he didn't have access to the interpreter when the P-43s were airborne. After takeoff, there could be no communication among the group. Tex and Hedman decided they would mitigate this with disciplined formation flying; everyone was to maintain visual contact with the leader on their long trip back. The Americans spent a few more days further familiarizing themselves and their partners with the aircraft, watching the unflappable Chinese make every possible kind of landing and still walk away from it. Working through an interpreter was difficult, and Tex had to make very sure a particular pilot understood his instructions before he took off down the runway.

When they decided everyone was as proficient as they were going to get, Tex and Hedman began a week of formation flying, teaching the Chinese to stay with a wingman and fly safely in a group. There were some hairy moments; but overall, the Chinese proved to be apt learners, and near the end of May, the two Tigers figured it was "now or never."

They were sorry to leave their Briton friends and the nurses at the Jim Kana club, but it was time to depart if they were going to keep to their schedule. On the morning of the 28th, all twelve planes took off eastward for Jodphur in fair weather. The first leg of their flight was uneventful, except for a brief pass over the Taj Mahal. As they refueled in Jodphur, wind whipped through Tex's hair, and he squinted northeast, toward the Sind Desert.

"What's that?" he asked the British ground crewman refueling the P-43, pointing at a dark mass out across the desert that seemed to be coming closer. "Rain?"

The Briton shook his head and raised his voice above the wind. "Nope. That's a sandstorm, mate!"

Tex decided to chance it, and took off with the rest of the group when all had been refueled. He knew that there were two options to deal with the sandstorm: climb out above it at around five thousand feet, or stay on the deck and hope the driving grit didn't damage the engine. Tex opted for the latter, since he had no navigational aids, making it almost certain that they would become lost once they got above the swirling sand. On the deck, they could at least follow the railroad to Delhi.

Flying through the weather phenomenon was strange. Visibility was zero, and the usual noise of flight was changed to a constant soft *hisssss* as sand particles swept over the aircraft. Fortunately, the Chinese pilots had learned well to stick close to the two Flying Tigers, and Tex could still see the "iron compass" below. Two hours later, he approached Delhi with everyone still in tow.

With strong crosswinds still gusting across the runway at Delhi, it was more difficult than usual for Tex and Duke Hedman to land safely; for the Chinese, it was a life-threatening proposition. Tex was reminded of the "flying professor" acts at air shows in the States as he watched the other P-43s swerve crazily onto the runway, bounce along the ground, tilt to within an ace of flipping, and finally—by some miracle—come to rest without sustaining major structural damage.

When the last one was down, Tex grabbed the wide-eyed Hedman and started for the hangars. "Let's go—before they come over and start grinning," he said.

Hedman acquiesced, shaking his head. "Man, if I didn't have an ulcer before..."

When the weather cleared later in the day, Tex and Hedman went out to look over the planes. The storm had produced a "sandblasted" effect on the engine cowlings, and grit was deeply embedded in them; but no other damage was done. In spite of their odd appearance, they were more or less in working order.

The group spent almost a week in Delhi, which was pleasantly similar to Karachi. The city was orderly and well kept, and the two AVG men stayed at the luxurious Cecil Hotel. Also in town happened to be Harvey Greenlaw, Chennault's executive officer, and his wife Olga. These two came out to the Cecil and "shot the bull" with Tex and Hedman on the hotel's veranda beside the swimming pool, in front of Ionic pillars that lent a classical Greek feel to the place. Tex was also able to visit Fred Hodges, his fellow Panda Bear who had such dread of insects, and his British wife of two months, Helen.

Delhi had been selected as the location for the headquarters of the newly-established Tenth Air Force, with Major General Lewis H. Brereton commanding. When the headquarters "established" itself, it did so in style; it was located at the swank New Delhi Hotel, a short distance from the Cecil. Rooms, offices, dining facilities, and supplies were all plush to the point of opulence, and many "ladies" frequented the place who seemed to have little or no official business there. By August, life on "Per Diem Hill" had become the subject of scrutiny by the Inspector General, who eventually relieved then-commander Major General Earl Naiden, and forced the Tenth to tone things down somewhat. In the meantime, far from carrying a grudge about the disparity in luxuries, Tex and Hedman decided to enjoy the amenities as much as possible while they had the chance.

As the first week in June passed, all the P-43s were eventually repaired from the sandstorm's effects; and it was time for the group to travel once more. On June 5th, the twelve pilots took off from Delhi for Allahabad; and after spending a night there, they continued on to Calcutta. By then they had nearly crossed the breadth of India, a trip of some fourteen hundred miles. On the following day they winged their way toward the village of Dinjan, in upper Assam province. There, they were close to the border of Burma; the Hump loomed before them, with China and Kunming beyond.

The weather, which knew nothing of schedules, suddenly refused to cooperate. When the P-43s touched down in Dinjan, it was raining heavily; and it became apparent that the monsoons so familiar to the Far East had settled in over the area. A friendly British plantation owner invited the Tigers and their Chinese comrades to stay on his tea plantation, a short distance from the village, until the weather cleared. They accepted gratefully.

The plantation held Tex's interest in spite of the miserable weather. Rows of tea trees stretched for acres, ending at the edge of the trackless jungle that grew directly up against the Briton's fields. As Tex watched the rain-soaked skies darken at night, he heard the howls of jackals in the distance. The men turned in on cots in the owner's main hall, and Tex wondered what it would be like to work the earth for a living in such a place.

The monsoon rains remained for six days, though, and Tex and Duke Hedman finally began to wonder if they would be looking at tea trees for the rest of their lives. At last, word came in that Kunming was clear; and the twelve pilots rode quickly to the airport to take advantage of the break. Before they climbed into their cockpits, Tex gathered everyone around him and briefed them through the interpreter.

"Whatever you do, stay with us," he admonished. "Don't go up into the overcast. There's a big hole in the weather north of here, and we'll make for that. Once we hit it, we can climb up on top of the storm and rendezvous. Then we'll head for Kunming, where we know it's clear." He had the interpreter ask each man if they understood. There were grins all around, and then it was time to go.

Unfortunately, one of the pilots must not have gotten the message. As the group was forming up beneath the dark cloud ceiling, he pulled up into the gray opacity and vanished from sight. There was nothing to be done, so Tex began to lead the group eastward. Less than a minute later, a lone P-43 came spinning out from the overcast and crashed below. The pilot had lost his orientation in the opaque cloudbank above, and been unable to recover.

It was the only plane they would lose. By the time they reached Lake Tali, the clouds were behind them. It was clear flying across the Hump, with magnificent scenery to boot. Tex admired the huge Himalayas that challenged the sky, stretching out of sight to the north. They were not called the "Roof of the World" for nothing.

When he touched down at last on the familiar runway at Kunming, Tex watched in satisfaction as the nine remaining Chinese pilots made decent landings. He had returned with eleven of the twelve planes the Old Man wanted. It had been a very long trip.

Just then, a man he didn't know walked up to his P-43. The man didn't introduce himself, but politely asked for a suitcase Tex had brought. Tex had almost forgotten that just before the group departed Delhi, Fred Hodges had approached Tex, carrying the suitcase.

"Tex, would you mind taking this back to Kunming for me?" Hodges had asked.

"No, I don't mind. What do I do with it when we get back?"

"Oh, don't worry. There'll be a guy there to take it off your hands," Hodges had replied.

That had been all, and Tex had thought no more about it as he had loaded his aircraft. The suitcase had been unusually heavy.

Now the man by Tex's plane explained that Hodges had told him who to look for— "tall fellow with big ears." Tex handed over the suitcase, watching curiously as the man departed without another word. Much later, he had a chance to ask Hodges what had been in the suitcase. One half was filled with gold, which accounted for the weight; and the other half held bottles of sulfanilamide pills.

Profiteering was a practice not unknown within the AVG. It started with the evacuation from Burma; the men found, to their surprise, that certain items they had brought on convoys up the Burma Road were many times more valuable in China than they had been in Burma. Bicycles, Parker Pens, and Longine watches could be sold at tremendous profits. Cigarettes and whiskey went by the carton or bottle for $100. Sulfanilamide pills, like the ones Hodges had given Tex, were considered a "miracle drug" in China. Each pill could be bought in India for about five cents—then sold in China for seventy-five. Most of the men were happy to sell the items they happened to have, and leave it at that. But others took advantage of their access to "air transport" to make a little more profit. A few—a very few—became so caught up in the practice that they lost interest in the mission.

During Tex's ferry trip to India, the AVG had found their services somewhat less needed along the Burma Road. A small Japanese contingent had returned to the Salween gorge, but their purpose was ostensibly to dig in on the western plateau and prevent the

Chinese from counterattacking across it. The two armies began a standoff across the river that would last nearly two years.

Events further east in China, however, were capturing Chennault's attention more and more. Throughout the vast interior, the Old Man had spent years preparing airbases and facilities from which to carry on the air war against the enemy—especially against Japan's crucial shipping lifelines. The most important of his prepared bases were Kweilin, Lingling, and Hengyang, spaced fairly evenly along a two-hundred-mile stretch of the Canton-Hankow railroad; for they afforded good access to the coast. There were many smaller fields, well placed across the countryside in various states of construction, from which Chennault had intended to stage his aircraft to extend their range.

Almost a week after Tex and the ferry group departed for Karachi, Japanese bombers droned over unoccupied Kweilin and bombed it. Kweilin was the centerpiece of Chennault's array of East China bases, and he learned of the raid with concern. The bombers had struck poorly and done little damage; but when they returned six days later and tried again, Chennault decided at last that it was time to move the AVG to East China. The Burma Road was lost in any case, and the AVG was whittling away the six weeks remaining on their contracts mostly by frag-bombing and strafing targets of opportunity in northeastern Burma. Before arrangements for relocation could be completed, however, an unfortunate event occurred that struck a blow to the morale of all the Flying Tigers.

Newly promoted Brigadier General Clayton Bissell, Stilwell's Air Officer, was justifiably concerned about what would happen when the AVG contracts ran out in July. Back in March, Bissell and Stilwell had promised Chiang Kai-Shek a replacement fighter group if the AVG would agree to be inducted into the Army Air Corps. But there were two problems. First, Bissell wasn't going to have any "replacement fighter group" available anytime soon, and he knew it. Second, Chennault had told Bissell, after talking to the Flying Tigers, that almost none of them were interested in induction. What they really wanted was a rest from the fever pitch of combat.

Bissell confidently requested that Chennault allow him to speak to the men himself. The Old Man didn't think it would help the situation, and for his part, he thought the boys deserved a furlough to the States; but Bissell was insistent. Thus it was that while Tex and Duke Hedman were still practicing formation flying in the new P-43s in Karachi, most of the AVG gathered in the auditorium at Yunnanyi University to hear what the general had to say.

From the outset, Bissell's speech was an unmitigated disaster. He began by downplaying the AVG's accomplishments as negligible—adding that the Western press had fabricated and enhanced their stories to "make them look good." He continued by intimating that the Flying Tigers were a bunch of screw-ups who would have been kicked out of U.S. military service eventually, had they not signed up for the AVG. At that point in the speech, fully two-thirds of the shocked and antagonized audience got up and left the auditorium. Sitting off to one side, Chennault's features were set in stone.

Bissell concluded by remarking that if any of the men refused induction into the Army, Bissell would see to it that a military draft board was "waiting at the bottom of the gangplank" when their return ship dropped anchor in the United States. They would all, he insisted, be forcibly drafted back into the Army as Privates. With that, his speech was finished—and so were the chances of persuading most of the Flying Tigers to remain in China.

Within days of its departure for the eastern airfields, the AVG witnessed another debacle. The 11th Bombardment Squadron, equipped with medium B-25 *Mitchells* like those on the Doolittle Raid, were ordered into China to attach themselves to Chennault's command. Five of the bombers formed the first flight of new arrivals; but none of the crews had flown over the Hump into China before. That would make the navigation tricky at best; but General Bissell compounded the problem by ordering that they bomb the airfield at Lashio en route. This, he reasoned, would make the flight "productive," as well as shortening it considerably (by going straight across Japanese-infested Burma).

The hapless B-25s never made it to their target. As they winged across Burma without escort, a flight of enemy fighters spotted them and dove on the easy prey. One bomber went down in flames; a second smashed into a mountainside when it flew into a cloudbank for concealment. The other three managed to escape, but one of them became lost and "bellied in" miles to the north of Kunming. Of the two that touched down intact, one had a radio operator shot dead in the aerial battle. The co-pilot of the other had to land the B-25, since its pilot had taken a 12.7mm round through his head. It was a horrific arrival in China, but the men's courage held up: they very next day, they sent one of their bombers right back to Lashio, and scored direct hits on the airfield.

Early in June, the AVG completed its preparations to move to the eastern airfields. From Kunming, several transports carrying Chennault's headquarters personnel and equipment lifted off and flew northeast toward Peishiyi, an airfield only twenty miles from Chungking. Peishiyi, near China's wartime capital, would serve as the group's new headquarters, while the three squadrons would spread out to Kweilin, Lingling, and Hengyang. By now, almost two dozen of the newer P-40Es had been retrieved from the Gold Coast of Africa, and they were a badly needed boost to the AVG's combat power.

Following Chennault's departure to Peishiyi, the AVG "staged" a large exodus of P-40s from Kunming in the direction of Chungking. They hoped that Japanese informers would leak the news that the city was undefended, and that when the enemy attempted a raid, he would be in for a surprise. The Japs didn't take the bait, however; and after waiting three more days, the 1st and 2nd Squadrons relocated to Peishiyi in earnest.

Upon arrival, they attempted the opposite trick: after setting up a field full of dummy aircraft and keeping a small flight in the air over the city continuously, they slipped quietly out to the east, leaving the impression that the group was still in Chungking. The Panda Bears set up shop at Hengyang, while the Adam and Eves flew to Lingling. The 3rd Squadron was to remain for a time back at Kunming.

The Japanese had no idea the AVG was anywhere near eastern China, so quickly had they made the jump of hundreds of miles. Nevertheless, the enemy picked the one primary airbase to bomb that the AVG did not occupy at that moment: Kweilin. Once again they did a poor job, causing only superficial damage; so they returned the next day to try again. Chennault himself flew in that day to inspect the base, finding it suitable for operations. The following afternoon, after a third consecutive morning bombing by the Japs, the 1st Squadron slipped into Kweilin with eleven P-40s. If the enemy showed up again, the Adam and Eves would be ready.

The Japanese did return the following morning, the day before Tex returned from

India. At long last, the Flying Tigers enjoyed the full benefit of Chennault's radio warning net; eight P-40s were already high in the air as five enemy bombers approached the field. Behind the bombers were eleven I-97 "Nates," along with five fighters of a type the AVG had not seen before. The Japanese pilots were completely surprised by the Flying Tigers' attack, believing the AVG was still hundreds of miles northwest, near the capital. One-sided chaos followed as the Adam and Eves burned all but one of the bombers out of the sky, along with two "Nates." The unfamiliar fighters, which had two engines and carried .50-caliber guns in the nose and turret, proved more dangerous opponents. They shot down both Charlie Bond and Allen Wright—but lost two of their own as well. Both Tigers made safe crash landings.

The strange enemy planes turned out to be Kawasaki Ki-45 *Toryu* or "Dragon Slayers," nicknamed "Nicks." The fast and maneuverable aircraft were patterned after the German Messerschmitt Me-110, and had been in service in other areas of the Pacific for nine months. The AVG learned all this when one of the "Nick" pilots was captured after the engagement, having unhappily survived his crash landing and been taken prisoner by the Chinese.

Tex touched down at Peishiyi a few days later and sought out Chennault, to report on the ferry mission to India. The Old Man thanked him for returning with nearly all the P-43s, but his mood was more grave than usual. When Tex had finished his report, he sensed that Chennault had more to say.

"Tex, I'm sure you've heard about the boys' meeting with General Bissell by now," he said slowly.

"Yes sir, I did. They told me back at Kunming," replied Tex.

Chennault shook his head and looked at the desktop. "Hell, I think the boys are all planning to go home in two weeks. Bissell poisoned them. They all deserve a rest, but I'm going to be left holding the bag here with a handful of green Army pilots that are going to get themselves killed."

The Old Man paused, but he never strayed far from the point. "Tex, I haven't talked to you yet about your plans," he said, looking directly at the young man, "but if you leave, I don't know what I'm going to do."

"General," Tex replied without hesitation, "I'll stay around as long as you need me."

The Old Man displayed his obvious relief with a rare smile.

"That's what I hoped to hear," he said earnestly, shaking Tex's hand. Then the smile passed, and he was all business again. "I think we can get by if some of the boys would just stay on for another two weeks—extend their contracts—to get the Army pilots up to speed on how we operate over here."

Tex nodded his understanding.

Chennault continued, "I wonder if you'd be willing to talk to some of them, to see if they wouldn't stay. I know they'd listen to you."

"Sure, I'll do that," Tex agreed.

With the meeting over, he strolled out into the sunlit afternoon in time to see squadron mate John Petach heading toward him.

"Hello, Tex—welcome back," Petach said with a smile, setting down his travel bag, which was packed to the hilt, to shake hands.

"Thanks. You look about ready to pull chocks, there, John."

"Sure, isn't everybody? I was just going to say goodbye to the Old Man."

"Right. Listen, he's mighty concerned right now about losing all the guys with experience at one time," said Tex, going on to explain the group's predicament. "Any chance you'd be willing to stay on for two weeks?"

Petach pursed his lips and looked thoughtfully at the bag, then back to Tex with a smile. "Sure, Tex, I'll stay. I guess two weeks won't make much difference. I don't think "Red" will mind, either."

Emma Jane "Red" Petach, one of the AVG's two pretty nurses, had married John back in January, and the two were already expecting a baby later in the year. Tex clapped his old shipmate from the *Ranger* on the shoulder.

"Man, I know he'll appreciate it."

When Tex finally made the flight out to Hengyang to join his squadron, he found Ed Rector and the rest of the Panda Bears in high spirits as usual, glad to have their leader back. After shaking hands all round, Tex made the pitch asking them to stay the extra two weeks.

Ed chuckled, shook his head, and cursed. "Well, I was quite prepared to go home," he said. "It would have to be you asking this, Tex. I suppose you're staying?"

Tex nodded in reply.

"Well then, count me in."

Most of the men also agreed. Tex flew briefly to the other bases to check with the other Tigers as well. In the end, twenty-six pilots and fifty-seven ground crew, mostly Panda Bears, agreed to extend their contracts through the 18th of July. It was exactly the break Chennault needed to prevent his new Army pilots from getting chewed up by the Japanese, who were awaiting July 4th—the date of AVG contract expiration—with carnivorous anticipation.

* * *

As Tex arrived in Karachi, India, the final footnote was written in the Burma disaster. Twelve thousand fleeing British troops hemorrhaged into India in the wake of their defeat. More than that number had already died or deserted, and thousands of the survivors expired within weeks of their escape—from dysentery, malnutrition, and exhaustion. As Stilwell stood in front of press microphones and decried his defeat, he insisted: "I think we ought to find out what caused it, go back, and retake it." It was an admirable goal, but one he would pursue with catastrophic narrow-mindedness for many months to come.

AVG casualties continued. Tom Jones, a stalwart of the Salween gorge action, crashed to his death during dive-bombing practice ten days afterward. In another week, Bob Little was dead, pieces of his P-40 scattering into the Salween River as the bomb he was aiming at Jap artillery positions on the west bank detonated while still on his wing.

While Tex was preparing to depart from Delhi, a decisive naval battle far out in the Pacific scaled upward in intensity. Hordes of carrier-borne aircraft pounded each other and their opponents' ships, trying desperately to remove those enemy giants from the watery chessboard. When it was over, the jubilant Americans had eliminated four Japanese aircraft carriers, along with their elite planes and pilots. The price was the lost Yorktown; she had survived the fury of the Coral Sea only to sacrifice herself there, near a small island called Midway.

Tex greets Generalissimo Chiang Kai-Shek, arriving at Hengyang to give the brand-new 23rd Fighter Group a "pep talk."

Tex in a shop in Calcutta, India during the trip to ferry P-43s back to China, May 1942.

Chapter 20

"NO ARMY SHOWED UP"

Tex cocked a skeptical eyebrow at the khaki Army uniform. Then he looked at R.T. Smith, who was holding it out to him.

"You don't have one that's...thinner, do you?" asked Tex warily.

R.T. gave a hearty laugh. "Tex, I'm telling you, this is what you want. Like new, hardly used. I got it right before I saw you at the Bellview back in San Francisco. I'm not getting any thinner! It's been awhile since I was as skinny as you."

The big man paused, peering at the lanky Texan with a frown.

"Hell, I was *never* as skinny as you," he muttered. "Think of it as a comfortable fit!"

He held up the khaki short-sleeved shirt and trousers once more. R.T. Smith's Army Air Corps uniform was the only one in the group long enough to conceivably fit Tex; but it came with plenty of extra "girth," into which Tex thought he could slip about three of himself. There was really no alternative, however; and he would have to pay the full price that Smith was holding out for. Tex had to have a uniform, since he planned to be inducted into the Army Air Corps as a Major.

"Well, I'll have to take it," Tex concluded. "But if they'll let me fly in it, I can skip the parachute."

"Very funny," Smith quipped back, smiling as Tex counted out the agreed price in Chinese currency. "Just think of this as my way of getting back at you for my nickname."

"How's that?" asked Tex, folding up the uniform and picking up his hat.

"Oh, you remember...that time the guys asked what the 'T' stood for?"

"Oh, yeah. I said 'Tadpole,'" said Tex, grinning, as he headed out the door. "Well, whatever it really stands for, 'Tadpole' has got to be a lot more interesting."

Speechless, Smith watched him depart.

"By golly, he's right," he mumbled.

Only four pilots besides Tex had agreed to accept induction into the Air Corps and stay in China indefinitely: Gil Bright, Charlie Sawyer, Frank Schiel, and his old friend Ed Rector. Twenty-two ground personnel had also opted for induction. By doing so, they would provide a small but vital core of experienced leadership, upon which Chennault would lean heavily once the two-week volunteers departed. The inductees would shoulder the responsibility of veterans who "knew the ropes"—and would have to teach them to scores of new Army personnel, fast.

Some time before, Chennault's hope of having the USAAC in place to take over the China air operation lock, stock, and barrel from the Flying Tigers had crumbled. It had become apparent that only a tiny fraction of Stilwell's promised "replacement fighter group" would be anywhere in China by July 4th—and that included no airplanes whatsoever.

Personnel had been trickling in by small groups. In early May, a handful of Air Corps men had attached themselves to the AVG. Then, on June 7th, seven second lieutenants had arrived from Panama. It soon emerged that those particular pilots were all extremely well trained; it was a blessing not to have to spend many hours instructing them in the fundamentals. When three of them—Lee Minor, Dean Carter, and Leonard Butsch—showed up at Hengyang, Tex was gratified to learn that they were nearly combat-ready. In the middle of June, nineteen men of the 51st Fighter Group in Karachi were flown over the Hump to be distributed among the three AVG squadrons; and three days later, eight more Air Corps pilots showed up in Kunming. But with less than two weeks to go in the AVG's contract, barely fifty Army troops were anywhere around to take over.

On June 27th, nine USAAC P-40s of the 51st Fighter Group's 16th Fighter Squadron droned into Kunming. They were not supposed to set up camp and remain in China; rather, Chennault had invited them over from India to be attached to him for "training experience"—a welcome change of scene for the pilots from the humdrum operations of Tenth Air Force. But once they were in China, the Old man sent them on to Lingling, and never returned them. None complained; these men, too, proved to be capable combat pilots that did not require much additional training. One of them was John Alison.

Alison was a unique individual. His appearance could have fooled anyone: he rose to a mere height of five feet, five inches, and wore the innocent expression of a choirboy. He was upbeat and eager to please; one almost expected to see him whistling his way along a newspaper route, rather than climbing into the cockpit of a shark-nosed P-40.

Once in the air, though, the illusion was shattered. John Alison had the greatest pure flying skill of any pilot in the theater—a touch on the controls that knew no equal. His talents were matched only by his eagerness for combat; anyone who met him for longer than sixty seconds knew that Alison would be a potent weapon against the Japanese. When he first touched down at Lingling with the contingent from the 16th, Tex happened to be out on the runway.

Alison jogged up smartly with a musette bag and stopped in front of Tex, who regarded him with interest.

"What are you guys doing here?" drawled Tex.

"We came to fight!" barked Alison.

Tex chuckled. "Man, you came to the right place." It was the beginning of a lifelong friendship.

As Army fighter pilots and ground crew moved into the theater (all too slowly), the 11th Bombardment Squadron was rebounding from its own tragic entrance. B-25 reinforcements drifted by ones and twos into Kunming, until, by the middle of June, there were seven of the *Mitchells* parked on the airfield. Big Colonel Caleb Haynes was their leader; and he itched to "drop bombs and kill something."

A few days later, he almost got his chance when three Hell's Angels escorted Haynes' bombers westward over the Salween and into Burma. They intended to hit Lungling City, but became lost in a miserable rainstorm and couldn't find it; so eventually, they returned to Kunming. The next time they were more successful, and the time after that too.

After several of these "warm-up" raids, Haynes sent the B-25s out to Kweilin in East China. They promptly began conducting bombing raids to Hankow and Canton, while the AVG flew as escort. Eventually, the 11th moved into Hengyang with the Panda Bears.

Hengyang was a sizable town near the junction of two major railroads. Its airbase lay north of the city, in the red clay of the Siang River valley. It was nearly as hot as Burma in the summertime, but not as lifeless; the river was constantly filled with sampans, trafficking in coal and other resources. A former girls' school served as a rudimentary hostel for the Americans; that structure and one alert shack made up the facilities. The pilots had to be content with the short nine-hundred-meter runway. In addition, a number of bamboo "dummy" P-40s had been set up to make the field seem occupied by a larger force than it was. To the east were low hills, and northward the river and railroad followed a hundred-mile winding course to the town of Changsha, on the shore of Tungting Lake.

Sitting alert at Hengyang was a sweltering prospect in the summer. After a breakfast of eggs, toast, and coffee, the pilots whose names appeared on the schedule would head down to the flight line at daybreak; dawn was a common hour for the Japanese to come calling. As the sun climbed, alert pilots would fill up the time dealing hands of poker or Red Dog. The Chinese brought them tea and coffee at mid-morning, along with sandwiches; lunch at midday; and tea again in the afternoon. When the long summer daylight failed, the pilots piled into trucks and drove back to the hostel for dinner. It was not particularly exciting, unless "company" showed up, or there was an offensive mission to be flown.

Once at Hengyang, Tex had time to learn more about the nation's strategic situation. The battlefield of eastern China was staggering in its vastness; the sheer area to be covered made it impossible for the Japanese to control every quarter. Instead, they had confined their efforts to the capture and occupation of important cities and lines of communications, leaving the outlying villages and countryside alone unless there was a military objective to be gained. More than one million Japanese soldiers in East China occupied an enormous array of cities, railroads, and rivers. From this sprawling captured industrial base flowed back food, oil, and resources to the Japanese home islands, over numerous sea routes.

It was this flow, Chennault knew, that represented a critical vulnerability of Japan. All along a thousand-mile swath of Chinese coastline lay cities whose docks and harbors were jammed with Japanese war materiel coming into the country—and the "fat of the land" leaving it, moving through the South and East China seas on its way to Japan.

175

From Nanking and Shanghai in the north to Canton, Hong Kong, and Hainan Island in the south, a myriad of enemy targets were simply "begging" to be plastered. The Americans would have work aplenty.

The third week in June, after getting a look around Hengyang, Tex led the way into unknown territory on his first combat mission in East China. With a flight of P-40s, he made an early-morning foray northward along the railroad, toward Changsha and beautiful Tungting Lake. From there, they ranged northeast up the Yangtze River, looking for targets on the water. Not surprisingly, they found a Japanese gunboat escorting three transport vessels downstream toward Hankow; so the P-40s proceeded downward to give them "the works." Tex and the others made two discoveries in the attack: that Japanese soldiers on the boats were no friendlier than those in a truck convoy; and that the six .50-caliber guns of the P-40Es vastly improved the appearance of enemy river craft, in the eyes of the Flying Tigers. The P-40s sped away, leaving all four boats on their way to the bottom.

June gave way to July, and the end of an era was inexorably approaching, as the Flying Tigers' days drew to a close. For the few that were staying, it was difficult to watch their comrades preparing to depart, going back to the United States and the comforts that they had all missed for so long. Tex felt the pull of home as well, unable to keep his thoughts from the warm Texas evenings that would have been perfect to spend swimming in the Guadalupe River, or tracking wary game through the parched scrub brush of the hill country. He told himself his own return would come.

On the evening of July 3rd, the Flying Tigers gathered at the estate of Lin Sen, the elderly president of China, in Chungking. H.H. Kung, Madam Chiang's brother-in-law and China's Minister of Finance, was "laying on" a party for the Tigers. The food was excellent, and the facilities breathtaking; but somehow, the melancholy drizzle outside reflected everyone's mood. Even Madame Chiang's games of musical chairs couldn't raise the men's spirits much. After speeches by the Generalissimo and Chennault, the Flying Tigers whiled away the time as the evening wore on. There was a hush as the clock neared twelve; the men who had worked and fought together for so long looked morosely at the floor. They were about to lose something, and they could feel it slipping away.

When the clock struck the hour of midnight, the American Volunteer Group passed into history.

The Flying Tigers, and their weathered leader, had written a unique page in the annals of war. Nineteen of their pilots would never return home; but only four of them had been lost in aerial combat. Only a dozen of their trusty P-40s had been shot down; sixty-one had been lost on the ground to strafing, accidents, and the demolition at Loiwing.

For that price, they had bought for China the destruction of two hundred ninety-nine Japanese aircraft (confirmed), and some fifteen hundred enemy airmen dead. And far more planes than those lay strewn in the trackless jungle between Rangoon and Thailand, wrecked on the rugged hills below Paoshan, and mired at the cold bottom of the Gulf of Martaban. No one would ever count the hulks of twisted metal that silently bore witness to the Tigers' valor on the face of the Salween Gorge, or the bodies of marauders sinking into the rice paddies beside the highway from Loiwing to Lashio. It was impossible, too, to estimate the effect on the spirits of the Chinese people—rising from despair to relief when Japanese bombs never fell, bullets did not kill, enemy soldiers failed to arrive. There was no measuring the strength lent to battered China by the AVG's effort—strength that kept the nation from crumbling when things were darkest.

On the 4th of July, 1942, the sun rose on a new organization. The China Air Task Force was born, cobbled together from the newly arrived Army Air Corps personnel and the long-suffering remnant of the Flying Tigers who had agreed to stay. Adam and Eves' leader Bob Neale was to command the fighter pilots of the CATF for the two weeks he would remain in China. On the day it came into existence, the strength of the CATF was scattered in various places. The 74th Fighter Squadron, now commanded by Frank Schiel, was at Kunming; Tex had been given the 75th Fighter Squadron at Hengyang; and Ed Rector took the 76th at Kweilin. These three formed the 23rd Fighter Group, the only such unit ever to stand up in the field under combat conditions. They had only fifty-one aircraft, all beat-up P-40s inherited from the AVG. If the eighty-three Tigers had not volunteered to stay two weeks more, those would have simply been left sitting on the field; no Army had shown up to operate or maintain them. The CATF also included the 16th Fighter Squadron, which the Old Man had acquired through "tactical deception" and stationed at Lingling; and the 11th Bombardment Squadron, equipped with a handful of B-25 bombers.

At Hengyang, "official" establishment of the 75th Fighter Squadron's headquarters was anything but official. Tex walked into a sparsely furnished shack one day with a young airman who had just arrived at the base, and gestured at the empty desk.

"That's all we've got," said Tex. "You're now the squadron first sergeant. If you can get whatever we need to run this outfit, I'd appreciate it. I don't know a thing about Army regulations, so I'm counting on you to take care of paperwork and things."

The airman, whose name was "Red" Irwin, scratched his head for a minute, then chuckled, "Well, this will be something. Don't worry, sir—we'll get into business all right."

Within days, Irwin had acquired a stack of typing paper from a nearby missionary, along with permission to use his typewriter once a week. With this "vast array" of office equipment, the headquarters of the 75th lurched into operation. Not long after, a phone was smuggled in from someplace; and then a call came from Chennault at Chungking, asking for the 75th's commander.

"I've got a problem back here, Tex," the Old Man explained when Tex got to the phone. "Have you met "Ajax" Baumler?"

"That's the guy they call the 'Foaming Cleanser,' right?"

Tex hadn't met Captain Albert Baumler, though he had heard of him, and told Chennault as much.

"Well, here's the problem," the Old Man continued. "He's a very experienced guy—knows a hell of a lot about Army regulations—and a good pilot. But he gets in a lot of trouble when he drinks."

That fit in with what Tex had heard, all right. During his first week in China, Baumler had stuck a .45 in the ribs of AVG crewman Preston "G.I." Paull when Paull wanted to call it quits at the bar and go to bed. Ajax had threatened to shoot him unless Paull stayed up and drank with him; and Paull responded by laying Baumler out on the barroom floor with one punch to the eye. It was an inauspicious beginning.

"I heard about him going a round with G.I. Paull," Tex told Chennault on the phone.

"Right. I'm going to have to deport him from the country for that," replied the Old Man, "unless...I wondered if you might be willing to take him there in the 75th, maybe work with him a little."

Tex ran his fingers through his hair and thought. He could certainly use a good combat pilot, and Baumler was already an ace from the Spanish Civil War. The man's knowledge of Army operations and regulations would be a strong asset as well. Finally, Tex told Chennault that he'd do it; but he wanted to fly up and meet Ajax first. Chennault agreed.

In a jeep beside the flightline at Kunming, Tex and Baumler had a man-to-man conversation. Tex explained what was probably going to happen, and a contrite Baumler vowed that if he were only given another chance, he would never touch another drop of whiskey. In the end, Tex agreed to take him into the 75th, and Baumler was beside himself with gratitude. To take advantage of the man's administrative skills, Tex also assigned him the duties of squadron adjutant. Baumler went to work with a will; and for a long time, Tex thought he had made the right decision.

There was now no hiding the fact from the Japanese that the Americans were in East China. The enemy had also known for months that the long-awaited breakup of the Tigers had occurred on July 4th. Enemy pilots had counted the days with eagerness, expecting to reap a glorious harvest of inexperienced P-40 pilots as soon as the AVG bowed out. Just after dawn on the 4th, they opened by sending a dozen I-97 fighters low and fast over Hengyang, ready to start racking up easy victories.

Instead of the "duck shoot" they anticipated, half of the six P-40s they faced were occupied by Bob Neale and Tex—the top two AVG aces—and Ed Rector. The Tiger veterans whaled away on the shocked Japanese, turning five "Nates" into fireballs before the rest got away to bring word to their comrades: whoever the P-40 pilots were now, they must have learned a thing or two before taking over. It was most unwelcome news.

Two days later it was the 75th's turn to strike, with Caleb Haynes' B-25s anxious to get into action. The bombers were going south to the industrial city of Canton on the coast, planning to hit an oil refinery with 500-pound bombs. Tex took six P-40s up from Kunming into an overcast sky to escort the B-25s, and together the strike force made a three-hundred-mile run to their target. Tex watched from above as the *Mitchells* laid down a hard-hitting bomb run on Canton's storage tanks and warehouses; then everyone turned northward again for the return trip.

It wasn't going to be that easy. A few minutes later, someone called out "bandits" below. There they were: a dozen angry I-97s rising to punish the raiding party. Tex thought the "Nates" should have known better, but he signaled to the bombers to continue on to safety, and dove toward the enemy fighters along with the other P-40s.

As always, Tex was looking for an opponent who was concentrating on someone else; and in a few seconds, he had his man. Pulling around in as tight a turn as the P-40 could manage, he dropped easily behind the little fighter and let go a barrage with the deadly .50s. Tracers sheared through the left wing and walked back along the fuselage. It was over for the Jap as he plummeted into an uncontrollable spin. Tex glanced right to see his wingman still hanging with him. John Petach burned a second Japanese fighter. However, the P-40s had little fuel to stay and dogfight; so with superior speed, they turned for home and outdistanced their opponents. All eventually landed safely at Hengyang.

The fighter pilots of the 23rd were becoming skilled at escorting the bombers, and the men of the 11th Bombardment Squadron were unquestionably satisfied with the arrangement. Tex kept his escorting fighters out in front, having learned from the disastrous Japanese method of keeping their fighters far behind their bombers. In front, the P-40s would meet any enemies first; and if the Japanese attacked from behind the formation, the P-40s had only to turn, and they would be back past the bombers in seconds. It would work to near-perfection: in the history of the 23rd Fighter Group, only a single B-25 would be shot down by enemy planes while the fighters escorted them.

Three days after the oil refinery raid on Canton, Tex took an escort mission up to Hankow again. After dropping their bombs, the B-25s headed for home as usual. Things had been uneventful, and the bombers would not likely encounter any Japanese fighters on the way home; so Tex decided to take his four-ship of P-40s "hunting" on the wide Yangtze. While the bombers watched with interest from high above, the fighters cruised southwest along the river with their eyes peeled. Soon enough, they identified four dark forms on the water—Japanese gunboats. These were not exactly the "cream" of the Imperial Navy, being mostly converted wooden-hull vessels with a few gun emplacements affixed to the deck. But they were more than sufficient to bully helpless Chinese rice boats, and they excelled at that.

Tex made a final check for enemy fighters, then went into a long power dive from sixteen thousand feet. As his engine RPMs climbed, he watched flashes of fire begin to reach up for him from the gunboat decks below. The Japs had already learned what would happen when the shark-nosed planes found them on the river. The P-40's airspeed was as high as Tex had ever seen it when he finally hauled back on the stick, feeling the G-forces press him into the seat, leveling out right on the water. His flight was spread out behind him, picking their targets. Tex lined up on the nearest gunboat and fired.

The designers of the P-40E had well thought out the precise alignment of its wing guns. They did not fire exactly straight ahead; instead, the barrels were angled slightly inward. That way, at a point hundreds of yards ahead of the plane, the streams of ammunition would meet, then fan out beyond as they approached the end of their accuracy and effectiveness. As Tex opened up from long range, he used the wide spread of his bullets at their extreme distance to clear the deck of the boat, spraying a hail of lead that cut sailors in half and ripped the superstructure to shreds. As he got closer, Tex nosed downward slightly to put the conversion point of the bullets right on the waterline. The concentrated .50-caliber storm blew gaping holes in the hull; pieces of wood flew in every direction. When no one remained on deck to return fire, Tex pulled around hard and distanced himself to make another pass.

For the bombers above, it was a treat to behold. The fighters had one vessel burning and sinking after the second pass. They needed only a few more attack runs to put the entire flotilla permanently on the riverbed. The victorious P-40s climbed from the Yangtze once more, overtaking the bombers for a final escort into Hengyang. It had indeed been good hunting.

That evening, word came to the 75th that the Chinese wanted a small, enemy-occupied village near their front lines dive-bombed the following day. As Tex studied the map, he realized that there could be no substantial air opposition on this one; the village was relatively insignificant, and far from any airfield. In fact, the mission would likely provide good training on dive-bombing a real target for some of the new Army pilots. He scheduled John Petach to lead the mission, with new Lieutenant Leonard Butsch on his wing to "learn the ropes." Rounding out the flight of four would be Arnold "Red" Shamblin and Ajax Baumler. It looked like a "milk run."

It turned out to be a nightmare. As the four-ship arrived over the target area, anti-aircraft fire from numerous hidden batteries sprang up toward them. The explosive shells were already bursting around them, and Petach realized immediately that this target was much more important than it had seemed.

"Stay high, you two—above the flak," he barked tersely at Baumler and the wide-eyed Butsch. "Red, let's go get that building and get out of here."

The target was the principal building in the town, which the Chinese had identified as the local headquarters and communications center for the Japanese. Petach arrowed toward it, with Shamblin behind him; the guns moved to track them. The fire was heavier than either Flying Tiger had seen before. Nevertheless, Petach took his P-40 down to six thousand feet—a range at which he could hardly miss—before releasing the bomb slung on its belly rack. Seconds later, the big demolition weapon detonated right on top of the headquarters.

At the same instant, John Petach's luck ran out. As he leveled out to get away from the target area, a well-aimed gun battery sent a 20mm shell directly into the midsection of the speeding plane. The shell exploded; the left wing sheared off, fluttering earthward. The P-40 lurched into a skid. In seconds, Petach was enveloped in a fireball from which he could not escape.

Hardly believing what he had just seen, Shamblin pushed his stick left and lined up directly on a concentration of the deadly AA guns. They would pay for that one. He released his massive bomb and peeled away—but the fire was too intense. Shamblin's P-40 took several cannon bursts, beginning to trail smoke. From high above, the last thing the shocked lieutenants saw was Shamblin bailing out, rolling on the ground, and heading for cover. Later tortured and killed by the Japanese, he would never be heard from again.

The news hit Tex like a ton of bricks. Both men, his friends, had agreed without hesitation to stay for the extra two weeks when he had appealed to them; and they had only been eight days away from leaving for good. Petach had left behind his new bride "Red," and a child he would never see. Tex's certainty that he had not purposely put his friends at risk did nothing to soften the blow; it was almost too much to bear. That night, he stared at the ceiling, unable to sleep. It would not be for the last time.

* * *

As Tex watched the fresh, youthful Army faces file into East China, one in particular caught his eye. The chaplain assigned to the 75th Fighter Squadron had just come from missionary work farther east in China; he had accepted a commission when the Japanese burned his mission to the ground. A devout patriot who spoke several dialects of Chinese fluently, he began to operate as a field intelligence agent, identifying important targets for the CATF's planes to hit. His name was John Birch.

As the two-week volunteers headed home, Charlie Bond and Bob Neale took recently widowed "Red" Petach into their care for the trip back to the States. It was to her everlasting credit that, even while still grieving her loss, "Red" realized that nothing could have changed the course of events. Never for a moment would she blame anyone for her husband's brave sacrifice—a fact for which Tex would always be grateful.

Chapter 21

"YOU'RE NOW MAJOR HILL"

Tex's "promotion ceremony," if it could be called that, had none of the traditional formality and pomp. In a muggy tent, with only the members of the Army induction board to observe, someone handed him a pen and a sheet of paper with the oath of commissioning printed on it.

"Please read the oath and sign," intoned Colonel Homer Sanders, commander of the 51st Fighter Group and president of the board.

Tex signed. An NCO whisked the paper into a folder, while Sanders pumped Tex's hand and smiled. "Congratulations! You're now Major Hill, commander, 75th Fighter Squadron."

Tex blinked uncertainly, trying to think of an appropriate response.

"Great," was all he could manage.

As he left the tent, he realized it really was that simple: he was going to "put on a different hat" and continue to do the same thing he'd been doing yesterday.

Only in China, he thought with a grin.

On the same day, Colonel Robert L. Scott took over command of the 23rd Fighter Group. His men would learn over time that "Scotty," as they called him, was fiercely loyal to those whom he led. In addition, he had two characteristics that generated their respect immediately.

The first was his eagerness to fight. Since his initial meeting with Chennault months before on a transport flight, Scott had not ceased attempting to wheedle a P-40 from the Old Man. He wanted to use it to protect the Tenth Air Force airbases in India's Assam Province. That group of bases was the western end of the treacherous air supply route over the Hump—now China's only lifeline, since the Burma Road had been lost. At last, Chennault had relented, and Scott had a field day as he put the aircraft through its paces against enemy targets. Nothing motivated him like the prospect of combat against the Japanese.

Scotty's other strength, in Tex's view, was the wisdom to realize what he didn't know. The colonel was a relative newcomer to China when he assumed command of the 23rd. Although he had gone along on a raid or two with the AVG for experience, he was not an "old hand" by any means. Realizing that, Scotty put many of his early mission assignments from Chennault on the table before the group, asking the veterans how they thought it ought to be executed. When they outlined a coherent strategy, the colonel agreed, and took a wing slot on the mission. Scotty was a fast learner, and it wouldn't be long before he picked up the finesse required to be an effective combat leader on many later missions.

Some of the leadership "ropes" Scott learned were from Tex, whose standards of integrity were so high, it was almost comic at times. On one occasion, as Madame Chiang pinned the Chinese 6th Order of the Cloud Banner on him for action over Burma, she looked up at the towering Texan and gave him a half-joking order.

"Now Tex, the next time you shoot down a Jap, I want you to think of me and say, 'This one is for the Madame.'"

Tex's brow wrinkled. After an awkward pause, he shook his head.

"I'm sorry, ma'am, but if I do, it would be the first time I ever thought about a woman when I was combat," he admitted.

Two days before Tex's commissioning, the only serious mishap in the AVG-to-Army transition had occurred. With only a couple of days left until the two-week AVG volunteers departed, five B-25s flew up to strike Hankow once more, with P-40s escorting them. Over the target, all the planes plastered the docks and warehouses. Then the formation turned toward Hengyang—only to learn that an alert was underway there for incoming enemy aircraft.

Tex was on the ground at Hengyang, frowning at the plotting boards, which showed Japanese fighters following hot on the heels of the returning bombers. Worse, a heavy rainstorm to the north was closing in on the field. Tex quickly launched the available fighters at Hengyang to take care of the Japanese. He knew that if the bombers landed at Hengyang (they had never been there before), they would likely be unable to take off again in time to escape the fighters—especially with the storm approaching. He quickly raised the B-25s on the radio, advising them not to refuel or take off again once they landed.

"If you don't stay put," he explained, "you'll get up into the altitude where the Jap fighters are. The warning net can't tell the difference between you. Let our guys take care of the Japs."

His concerns proved well founded. Fearing to be caught on the ground by enemy fighters, three B-25s took off in spite of Tex's instructions. They turned north, straight into the sector where the radio warning net was reporting Japanese aircraft. The *Mitchells* stayed low, but the intercepting P-40 pilots—who had never seen a B-25—thought they were Japanese, just as Tex had feared.

AVG pilot Freeman Ricketts made a firing pass from the rear on one of the *Mitchells*, assuming it was an enemy. Facing down Ricketts was the bomber's rear gunner; he opened fire on the oncoming P-40, thinking it was a Japanese plane. Ricketts shot the B-25 up and down, one of his bullets smashing into the rear gun canopy and neatly parting the hair of the gunner (whose name was Stubblefield) right down the middle. Then Ricketts' guns jammed. He came around for another pass, trying to clear them, and saw five parachutes blossoming from the crippled bomber. It was then that he noticed—with a sickening shock—the Army Air Corps star on the side of his target.

"I...I think I just shot down one of our airplanes," Ricketts mumbled numbly into his radio.

But the whole crew survived. It was the only telling example of confusion in the transition weeks from AVG to CATF.

With the Siang and Yangtze Rivers within easy reach of the CATF's fighters, as well as Tungting and Poyang Lakes, strafing of river-going vessels became a frequent mission. The Japanese relied heavily upon river traffic to speed the flow of their ill-gotten supplies to their forces on the coast, for shipment back to Japan. There were gunboats, sampans, steamers, junks, and other craft in plenty to do the job; so the 23rd Fighter Group found no shortage of floating targets.

Occasionally, there was something bigger. As July wore on, intelligence reports began coming in about enemy shipping activity farther down the Yangtze. The town of Kiukiang was a major point of concentration; from there, the enemy could sail supplies northwest up the Yangtze toward Hankow, or move them south across Poyang Lake to Nanchang. In addition, thirty thousand enemy soldiers were moving through the area, to reinforce their positions at the battlefront against the Chinese.

In spite of the heavy flak they would certainly encounter, the 11th Bombardment Squadron determined to hit the Kiukiang staging area; and Tex was only too happy to take some of his boys along. He hadn't been feeling well for almost a week, but didn't have much time to think about it.

By then, the bombers knew their work well. Over the target, they scored direct hits on docks, warehouses, and rail yards, deftly avoiding the worst of the flak. One of the *Mitchells*, however, whose radio operator was Ted Kaveny, suffered a direct hit from the explosive AA shells. It lost power, beginning a long dive toward the Yangtze River below. Tex watched as parachutes began to pop out of the stricken B-25. One by one, the crew bailed out safely, all eventually touching down near the river.

Just then, Tex noticed a Japanese ground patrol snaking its way through the undergrowth toward the wreckage, intent on capturing and killing the Americans. Kaveny and his comrades, completely unaware of their danger, were detaching their chutes and looking for cover. Tex winged over and sent his P-40 zooming toward the enemy patrol at treetop height—startling the downed B-25 crew, who briefly thought Tex's plane was a *Zero*. Tex lined up and fired on the Jap patrol, which dove for cover to avoid being strafed to death. As he made several passes, pinning down the enemy, Kaveny and his crewmen made haste to lose themselves in the undergrowth. Friendly Chinese quickly picked them up, escorting them back to Allied lines by a long, circuitous route. By the time Tex departed and the Japanese resumed their search for the Americans, a shattered B-25 was the only sign of them.

Tex wasn't finished for the day. When the bombers turned for home, he and the fighters peeled off to strafe the vessels moving about on the northern edge of wide Poyang Lake. There were five ships; and as the fighters dove, Tex could see the vessels were all much larger than the wooden gunboats he'd attacked on the Yangtze earlier in the month.

The largest, in particular, was a different "breed of cat." The others were obviously supply ships; but as the big one mushroomed in Tex's vision, he could see that it was an enormous gunboat of some two thousand tons—virtually a small destroyer.

Anti-aircraft guns were mounted on the big ship's deck, and puffs of smoke around him heralded the arrival of their fire. It was heavier than he had guessed; some of the explosive shells detonated uncomfortably close. Nevertheless, Tex leveled out and began to blaze away, working up and down the vessel to cause as much damage as possible. The ship was sizable enough that any fighter plane was going to have difficulty crippling it; it took the concentrated fire of all three P-40s to accomplish the task. As they made pass after pass in the face of the anti-aircraft barrage, smoke gradually billowed from various quarters of the ship. The ponderous vessel began to list, then to sink. Low on ammunition, the pilots finally broke off the attack, leaving the destroyer sinking and two other supply steamers ablaze. As they climbed once more, one member of the flight called out enemy fighters he had sighted, climbing from the airfield at Nanchang. The Americans searched for them, but thick clouds in the area prevented the two groups from finding each other. For his actions during the long and eventful mission, Tex later received the Distinguished Flying Cross.

Touching down at Hengyang, Tex found himself so exhausted he was hardly able to climb out of his cockpit. Worse, he was shivering with chill, despite the summer heat of the river valley. What was wrong? He'd flown plenty of hair-raising missions before, and they would certainly have tired anyone out; but he could not account for the leaden malaise he felt now. Summoning all his strength, he managed to stumble into the alert building.

As the days went by, Tex found that his "condition" came and went. Some days he didn't feel too bad; other days, it was all he could do to get out of bed with fever, headache, and fatigue. Fortunately, Tex was able to depend upon an outstanding deputy for the day-to-day running of the squadron: John Alison, recently transferred from the 16th Fighter Squadron at Lingling. Next to Tex, Alison was the most senior man in the 75th; and he proved to be as capable a "strong right arm" as Ed Rector had been in the AVG days.

What Alison lacked in stature, he made up for in flying skill and motivation—and they came with a sense of humor. On a return mission to Kiukiang, six days after the 75th had sunk the destroyer, Alison led a flight of six planes to the target when Tex had to turn back with engine trouble. The fighters were intercepted by a formation of Japanese "Nates," and without hesitation, Alison led the P-40s into the fray.

At one point in the swirling dogfight, he called out cheerfully to Lieutenant Henry Elias: "Say, Elias, who's that flying formation on you with his wheels down?"

It was a Japanese I-97 (which had fixed landing gear), already firing at the unfortunate lieutenant; Elias had to maneuver violently to get the enemy in his own sights and blast him. Alison's unflappable outlook was an asset to the group—to say nothing of his other talents.

Another strength of the 75th, like all the squadrons in the 23rd Fighter Group, was Chennault's leadership. The Old Man knew his veteran AVG hands had learned to discern Japanese patterns of activity well in their long seven months of combat. Instead of managing their missions with a microscope, he allowed Frank Schiel, Ed Rector, and Tex wide latitude to lead. Chennault provided them with guidance on the kinds of targets that would hurt the Japs the most, and then turned his squadrons loose in the hands of those three. They repaid him with results. The 23rd's presence was felt far and wide along the eastern China battlefront, and well into enemy territory. Commanding the 75th was the most satisfying, enjoyable job Tex would have in his life.

When night fell over Hengyang, Lingling, and Kweilin, the enemy once again resumed his old tricks. It wasn't long before Japanese bombers in ones and twos began coming high overhead, dropping a few bombs that had no effect—except to disturb the Americans' badly needed slumber. Tex had seen it all before, in the muggy final days of Rangoon. This time, he resolved, it would not go unchallenged.

Late in July, Tex settled upon a plan to give the Japanese a taste of their own medicine. In the wee hours of the morning, he buzzed away from Hengyang, alone in a solitary P-40, winging his way to the north. A nearly full moon lit the sparsely clouded night, its pale light turning the Siang River into a shimmering serpent below. Following the now-familiar course up to Tungting Lake, he cruised high above the water to the mouth of the Yangtze, then proceeded northeast toward Hankow. It was strange to see the Chinese landscape illuminated by moonlight, and stranger still to be moving further into enemy territory with no one at his side.

Navigating by moonlight did not let him down; from far away, he saw the glow of lights on the docks at Hankow. There, enemy soldiers sweated around the clock in the glow of tung oil lamps, loading and unloading the plethora of material they needed. Night had always been an ideal time for the Japanese to work, since it was sure to be free of interference from American bombers and fighters—until now.

After surveying the scene, Tex went into a dive to conduct his business. He had equipped his P-40E with a 570-lb demolition bomb, reserved especially for those docks. Spotting a likely looking building, he lined up on it and let the belly bomb go. As it crashed through the roof of the structure and detonated, Tex was already swinging back for another pass.

Now the Japanese knew something was up, and the sleepy anti-aircraft batteries came groggily to life. It was fortunate they couldn't see any target to hit, for their concentrated wrath would have been too much for any single plane. Tex sped unmolested back over the wharves, where he dropped two strings of fragmentation bombs, and then peeled back around to strafe. The docks came alive with explosions that made short work of soldiers and crates of equipment. Flames began licking hungrily at the warehouses lining the waterfront. As a farewell gesture, Tex made a strafing run on a small boat, starting a fire aboard and holing it many times at the waterline. As he banked the P-40 toward home, climbing for altitude, he couldn't help but smile. *We can get you too*, he thought. *Try that on for size*. The raid earned him the Silver Star—and earned his men a good night's sleep, as the Japs were kept too busy for their usual nighttime nuisance bombing run.

By the end of July, the Japanese were fed up with losing ships, aircraft, men, and supplies to the infuriating CATF. The enemy finally mobilized for an aerial effort to drive the Americans forcibly out of the East China Bases—especially Hengyang and Lingling, from where most of the damage had come.

The opening round of the battle over Hengyang came with a report from the warning net that engine noise was headed toward the field. Normally, that news would have been greeted with groans, as the men knew they would lose some sleep—but this night was different.

A short time before, Tex had held a conversation with Chennault about Japanese night bombings over the erstwhile Chinese capital of Nanking, some years earlier. On one occasion, the Old Man had explained, he had been able to break up the enemy attack by sending up fighters at split altitudes, getting them both above and below the bombers' position in order to find them. It was a long shot, but it had worked at least once. At Chennault's suggestion, Tex had decided he was going to try it the next chance he got—and now seemed to fit the bill. He had previously explained his intentions to two others, who wanted "in" on the attempt as soon as they heard about it: Ajax Baumler and Johnny Alison.

"Johnny, you get up to twelve thousand feet," Tex now addressed his deputy. Tex was still in his sleeping attire, a Burmese *sarong*. "Ajax, you stay around nine thousand. Those bombers have got to come right across the field somewhere between you; and then, you can get them."

The two pilots needed no further explanation, and took off immediately. As they climbed to altitude, Tex grabbed a radio and took up position in a nearby earthen dugout by the runway, along with a few other "spectators." The moon was almost full; there was good visibility of the cloudless sky from their vantage point on the ground. Before long, Tex heard engine noise, and then he picked out three bombers in the sky to the north.

"Johnny, they're coming. They're making the run from north to south across the field—"

"I got 'em in sight," piped up the excited Alison. There was a pause, and then he continued, "Watch for the fireworks!"

Within a few seconds, everything seemed to happen at once. Tex and the others watched a stream of tracer bullets emerge from the darkness—but they were coming from one of the three bombers, not from Alison's six .50's. In the air, Alison saw the dim outline of the right bomber's rear turret suddenly explode with brightness as the Japanese gunner opened up on him. Alison immediately let go with his own guns, but heard his aircraft being riddled in the engine and cockpit as he flew straight up the stream of deadly fire to deliver his own ordnance where it would do the most good.

On the field below, Tex and his companions flinched instinctively as a sudden blast of .50-caliber fire ripped into space directly overhead. It was Alison's second burst, and was followed by an immediate explosion as the center bomber turned into a fireball, weirdly illuminating the second bomber in the formation for a few seconds before falling directly toward the runway. Then Tex and the others scattered for cover; the stricken bomber was coming down nearly on top of them. The dying aircraft was a spectacular sight as it sailed earthward like a meteor, finally slamming directly onto the end of the runway, shaking the earth beneath Tex's sprinting legs only a hundred yards away.

In the air, Johnny Alison knew that the front-to-back raking of his P-40 had damaged it greatly. The engine was sputtering (later inspection revealed a five-inch exit hole in its crankcase); the radio was shattered; and he had a bloody scratch along one arm, where a bullet had grazed him. The P-40 was on its way down.

Fighting to stay engaged for a few more seconds, Alison exerted his matchless flying skill, slipping his P-40 sideways, adjusting his sights onto the lead bomber, and firing another burst. It was all he could manage—but his bullets sheared into the left engine of the big plane, and flames shot out behind it. That one, too, would be going down.

Tex and company saw Alison's third burst of fire—but were nearly flattened an instant later, as unseen bombs exploded less than a hundred yards from them. The lead bomber had dropped its load unobserved; the shock wave from the bombs' detonation staggered the men on the ground. Then Tex saw another burst of several hundred .50-caliber rounds, two or three miles to the north; apparently, Ajax had found a target in the darkness.

In the silence that followed, Tex's pulse quickened as he heard the sound of Alison's engine dying. With a *blup-blup-blup* it sputtered and coughed; and they could all see the flames shooting back along its fuselage, as their deputy commander fought to coax a few more seconds of control from the P-40. (Miles to the north, Ajax Baumler's guns blazed to life again.) Alison was trying to make a controlled descent onto the airfield. He purposely approached high, conserving precious altitude, planning to throttle back at the last second and literally stall the aircraft just before touching down—a desperate technique known as "slipping off" altitude. Knowing the long odds against success no matter what his skill, he forced the canopy back to allow a quick bailout, if it came to that. Wind shrieked into the open cockpit.

Alison was a magnificent pilot, but the crippled P-40 couldn't meet his demands. He was already too high over the field—he was going to overshoot. He had made up his mind to get out of the aircraft, and prepared to do so—when suddenly he stopped himself. There were pitifully few flyable planes at Hengyang, and the squadron needed every aircraft and part it could get. If he bailed out, only wreckage would remain of his P-40. He was too low to bail out safely in any case.

With a supreme effort, Johnny Alison forced himself to sit back down in the cockpit. He poured the coal to the engine and aimed for the Siang River, trying to avoid crashing on the field.

It was too much; the mangled engine quit suddenly. Tex's blood froze as he watched Alison stay with the plane, hauling the nose up to maintain altitude. *He'll never make it.*

"Johnny, get out! Dammit, *bail out!!*" yelled Tex into the radio, expecting any moment to see his deputy's small figure drop over the side of the aircraft.

It did not. The stricken P-40 disappeared behind a low hill toward the Siang, precisely where Tex thought a bridge would be. There was no sound; his friend was gone.

When Ajax landed, flushed with victory after a second bomber had fallen to his guns, he found Tex still glowering at the horizon that hid the river, waiting for word of Alison.

Soon he could wait no longer, though, because the Japanese were just warming up. It was 3:30 a.m. when another air-raid signal jolted him back to alertness. Still clad only in the *sarong*, Tex charged out to the flightline toward his aircraft. He threw the P-40's throttle open and roared down the runway, intent on getting airborne before the raid was overhead. Moments after his wheels left the ground, yellow phosphorus bombs detonated directly beneath him on the runway. He instinctively shoved the stick right—a maneuver that nearly spun him in, with his speed still low and landing gear still down.

A second wave of enemy bombers had just completed their run on the field. Tex settled quickly on a course of action. He climbed to altitude in the darkness and turned north for Hankow, guessing that the bombers had come from the airport there. If he were right, they would get a surprise when they came home to land.

Unfortunately, Tex's guess was off the mark. The bombers must have come from Yochow, beause when Tex got over the field at Hankow, there were no signs of activity. Cursing his luck, still overwhelmed by Alison's loss, he turned wearily back toward Hengyang.

As he approached the field, he noticed with dissatisfaction that no landing lights were set up. It was not quite five a.m., still quite dark, so he radioed to the ground for help.

"Tex, this is Ajax," came a voice in reply. "We weren't sure when you were coming back in, and that last group of Japs pounded us pretty close to the runway. The damn Chinese that were supposed to set the lights up disappeared; I've got "Red" Irwin working on it right now."

Low on gas, Tex was relieved as lanterns began lighting up, one by one, on the field below. Finally there were enough to set down safely, so Tex lined up his approach.

What none of them knew was that a third wave of enemy bombers, of which they had no warning whatever, was now directly overhead. As Tex throttled back, lowered his wheels and flaps, and neared the ground, a "stick" of bombs detonated directly in front of him. Once again he nearly crashed for lack of power, as he broke left to avoid the explosions, pulling up and cursing into the microphone.

"Ajax! What the hell's going on down there?" he shouted.

For a few seconds, there was nothing. Then he heard Baumler using a few choice words himself.

"There's another wave up there!" Baumler yelled the obvious conclusion. A moment later, he added, "Irwin got hit by some shrapnel, but it doesn't look too bad."

Tex pulled up once more, with a concerned glance at the gas tank. He searched the sky as it began to lighten in the east, but couldn't see any enemy aircraft. In quick radio conversation with Ajax, he learned that almost one hundred fifty yards at one end of the runway had been so badly damaged by bombs as to be unusable. The nine-hundred-meter strip was short already; and making some quick calculations, Tex realized he would have to wait until there was enough light to land safely between craters. It was going to be a race against running out of fuel; but if he tried to put down immediately, he would certainly crash.

Tex sweated it out, circling at low power, "leaning out" the engine's fuel mixture, and doing everything possible to conserve dwindling gasoline. As sunrise neared, he decided there was just enough visibility to put the P-40 down. Studying the ground, he planned to land on the damaged end of the runway just past the bomb craters, rolling off the other end if necessary, where a hard-packed field could support his plane as it came to a stop.

It worked. Safely on the ground at last, Tex wobbled away from the plane in exhaustion, heightened by the strange malady he still hadn't figured out.

Some of the men had come out to greet him. His *sarong* drew a few stares; he didn't care.

"Alison?" he inquired hoarsely.

"Tex," Baumler said, unable to hide his grin, "the Chinese fished him out of the river awhile ago. He made it."

Tex tried to keep himself calm as relief flooded through him.

"By golly," he mumbled, with a grin of his own, not trusting himself to elaborate without great emotion. "By golly."

Hungrily consuming a makeshift breakfast and some tea, Tex tried to unwind from the night's activities as the sun climbed above the horizon. Bert Christman, John Petach...he was more than a little grateful that Johnny Alison's name did not have to go on the end of that list of friends that were gone. It would have been difficult to take.

He was only halfway through his second cup of tea when yet another huge wave of fighters was reported heading toward the field. It was mid-morning, and the men's faces were drawn with fatigue after the long night. This was obviously an all-out enemy attempt to force the 75th out of Hengyang; and with enough time, it would inevitably succeed. However, Tex jogged to his P-40 with some renewed energy, buoyed by Alison's escape from death.

Twenty-seven fighters and thirty-four bombers were on the way, the main strength of the Japanese effort. Tex was not alone this time; ten P-40s climbed aloft with him. Some of them, from the 16th Fighter Squadron at Lingling, had just arrived. The warning net had spotted the enemy a good distance out, allowing the pilots to don oxygen masks and get into position at nineteen thousand feet. The Americans spotted the enemy fighters approaching the field at about the same altitude. With surprise, the Army pilots realized they had not seen planes of this type before.

The unfamiliar aircraft were Nakajima Ki-43 *Habayusa* fighter-interceptors, which translated to "Peregrine Falcons." The Allies had nicknamed them "Oscars," encountering them frequently elsewhere in the Pacific. More maneuverable than even the *Zero*, the small fighters were markedly more dangerous than the I-97 "Nates" the 23rd Fighter Group usually encountered. The Ki-43 had about the same firepower as the I-97—but better speed, range, and ceiling. On paper, as usual, the "Oscar" made the P-40 look sharply disadvantaged. Fortunately, combat did not take place on paper.

The Japanese hoped that their bombs during the previous night had made the runway at Hengyang unusable. So it would have been, but for hundreds of Chinese coolies who tirelessly filled filled craters around the clock to erase that possibility. When the "Oscars" spotted the P-40s at their own altitude, they swarmed angrily toward the Americans.

Tex felt more than ready for them. Here were those responsible for the near-death of Johnny Alison; heaven help them when he got within range. Leading the American pilots as they raced toward the enemy was Tex's P-40, its throttle wide open. The leader of the Japanese "Oscar" formation moved out in front of his own group; and the two men singled each other out as their aircraft rushed together.

On the ground, everyone held a collective breath at the sight. The two combatants streaked toward one another at a closing speed of ten miles a minute. Neither showed the slightest sign of maneuvering. Out of the corner of his eye, Tex saw Major Gil Bright, formerly of the Panda Bears, destroy a Japanese fighter off to his right. Almost simultaneously, Tex and his opponent fired, sending tracers tearing through the air that separated them. Tex saw 12.7mm bullets race toward him; he watched his own tracers saturate the front of the enemy plane. He heard his P-40 being hit, but did not care. He wasn't turning. If the other pilot got him, it was going to be through a hail of lead right down his throat.

In the end, the tremendous firepower of the P-40E's six .50's determined the contest. Tex sustained many hits to his engine and cockpit; but that was nothing compared with the Japanese pilot's ordeal. The .50-caliber slugs ripped chunks of metal from the little Japanese plane like a buzzsaw, blowing through the light armor and hammering into the pilot's body before burying themselves in the rear of the cockpit. The Jap held his suicidal head-on pass for as long as possible, but a split-second before collision, the "Oscar" slumped into a shallow dive. Tex arrowed through the airspace that the enemy plane had occupied a second before.

A roar went up from the men on the ground when they saw their leader, still airborne, climbing out of the duel. The Japanese plane streamed fire and smoke, drunkenly circling several times right over the field—and then pushed straight down into a near-vertical dive. In his final seconds of life, the shattered pilot was aiming his aircraft toward what looked like a group of planes parked near the end of the runway. As the "Oscar" disintegrated, it impacted the ground less than fifty feet from its target, spreading fragments all over the area. It was the first kamikaze attack the 23rd had witnessed.

One of the 75th's ground crewmen elbowed a speechless companion.

"Good thing those were dummies," he said, smiling and jerking a thumb at the bamboo P-40s the Jap pilot had been aiming for.

What followed that opening act was the greatest aerial battle that ever occurred over the town of Hengyang. The fighter groups stormed into each other; bullets arced all over the sky as the pilots locked into combat, their pulses hammering. Gil Bright was having the fight of his life, flaming a second "Oscar" and putting bursts of fire into a third.

But it was not easy to get the drop on the relentless new Japanese fighters. At last, their sheer numbers forced the P-40 pilots, low on fuel, to land at Lingling rather than risk being strafed while attempting to land at beleaguered Hengyang. Just when it seemed the Japanese would never stop coming, the "Oscars" finally broke off the dogfight and turned for home. All the 75th's planes, including Tex's riddled P-40, eventually returned to Hengyang safely.

When he landed, Tex stepped out of his cockpit in a cold sweat, his face thin and eyes bright with fever. He strode slowly toward the end of the runway and the burning wreckage that was the funeral pyre of his opponent. A few ground crewmen were gathered around to look, and Tex studied the pieces of what had once been the enemy pilot. Without a word, he extended a boot and rooted the corpse around a bit. What made these men so ready to die? It was a question the Jap couldn't answer; and Tex walked away.

When he stepped through the doorway of the operations building, Tex stopped abruptly. A smile spread over his face. Standing before him, his bandaged face wrinkling with a grin of his own, was Johnny Alison.

"Let me tell you about it, Tex," he began. "You're not going to believe what happened..."

* * *

As the non-inducted members of the AVG made their way home, they received no help in their travels from Army leadership; but Army troops themselves, who knew and appreciated the AVG's contributions, lent considerable assistance. Three days before the big fight over Hengyang, the War Department drafted orders to Tenth Air Force headquarters in India directing them not to allow ex-AVG men any priority on planes or ships returning to the States. This left the group who had volunteered for the two extra weeks of duty to assist the Army, along with pregnant widow "Red" Petach, stranded in India. Many of them had to wait for weeks before purchasing their own passage on commercial ships bound for America.

Chapter 22

FAREWELLS

"So I put the P-40 down in the river," Alison explained to a beaming Tex as the men gathered around, "just as neat as you please. I felt like hell from the landing, but I made it to the shore all right. Then some Chinese almost shot me—they thought I was a Jap."

The men laughed, declaring they weren't surprised to hear it, for they often ribbed Alison about his short stature.

"Anyway, once they *didn't* shoot me, they took me to a Catholic missionary's house, there in the town. He sewed up my head," Alison continued, indicating the bandage wrapped around his cranium, "but he wouldn't let me leave the house for anything. Said I was still in shock. I did convince him to let me go out on the roof and watch the action, though," he said, winking at Tex, "and that's when I saw your little duel, and the free-for-all afterward. What I wouldn't have given for a movie camera!"

But in spite of their heroic efforts in the skies over Hengyang, it was eventually impossible for the handful of 23rd Fighter Group pilots to sustain their defense of the field. Fewer and fewer planes remained intact and flyable after each wave of enemies. Two more raids of "Oscars" came that day, forcing the weary defenders into contests in which they were badly outnumbered.

By now, the Army pilots were gaining experience born of "battlefield necessity," and gave a good accounting of themselves. Lieutenant "Mack" Mitchell earned the Silver Star that day, making repeated diving passes on a pack of nine "Oscars," taking fire from all of them. Others claimed their first aerial victories, too; but amid the peril of continuous combat, there was no time to celebrate.

By the time the third wave of Japanese attackers sailed in, the exhausted pilots could not put down at Hengyang. The enemy was strafing the airfield continuously, forcing the ground crews to stay in the slit trenches—where they opened up on the strafers with a "homemade" anti-aircraft barrage of .30-caliber machine guns, Bren guns, and pistols.

The defending P-40s diverted to Lingling, the 16th Fighter Squadron's base, which was also sustaining heavy raids that day. There, Tex himself was forced to land mere yards behind an enemy fighter who had just made a strafing run on the field. Out of gas, Tex had to hope the Jap didn't see him and pull around for another deadly pass to finish him off (he didn't).

At the end of the long night and day, both sides had to admit little success: the Japanese could not sustain their attacks to prevent the 23rd from re-occupying the bases; but the Americans were reduced to a handful of aircraft—not enough combat effectiveness to stave off the Japs.

Tex's unidentified illness had gradually worsened to a point at which he could hardly function. Something had to give. When he could keep up the pace of alert and combat no longer, Tex was finally persuaded to fly back to Chungking and visit a hospital.

At the wartime capital, a Chinese nurse silently took a blood sample from his earlobe and put it under a microscope. She couldn't speak a word of English, but beckoned him over to look into the instrument. While Tex studied the array of microorganisms uncomprehendingly, she opened an English medical encyclopedia and pointed to a picture that looked nearly identical.

It was under the heading MALARIA. Tex had fallen victim to that dreaded tropical malady. Treatments for it were only partially effective, especially once the disease had progressed for any length of time. In all likelihood, it was the final vengeance of a Burmese mosquito, come back to haunt him. For the remainder of his days in China, malaria would be another opponent Tex had to battle. Right now, he was losing.

There was nothing for it but to submit to hospitalization and recovery. In his present condition, he was doing the men of the 75th absolutely no good. He knew they would be in good hands under Alison's leadership. Tex was flown to Chengtu, a town some one hundred fifty miles northwest of Chungking in Szechwan Province, to stay with a missionary family and recover his health.

Situated on a high plateau with mountains rising to the northwest, Chengtu was a beautiful location with a cool, dry climate. Tex took to his bed in the missionaries' home, and they administered regular quinine treatments to battle the bacteria that had laid him low.

For a week or more, he was barely conscious of activity around him, sleeping most of the time while his body fought the fever that ravaged it. Finally the fever broke, and in the peaceful surroundings, he slowly began to improve. At length, he could leave his room and walk about the surrounding area.

More than three hundred thousand Chinese coolies were hard at work on nearby Sinjen airfield. They were building it up to accommodate the heavy B-29 *Superfortress* bombers of Twentieth Air Force. Once the runway was complete, and the aircraft arrived, the Allies intended to bomb Japan from this very spot. Chennault himself would have preferred to stage the bombers into his eastern airfields, where fighters could escort them; otherwise, he maintained strongly, the missions to Japan would be suicidal. But "Hap" Arnold was keeping the project in his own hands, and Chennault did not have Arnold's ear. Watching the coolies, Tex was amazed to see such a mass of humanity combining its efforts with single-minded intensity on the vast project.

When he was well enough to want news of his comrades, he learned that the 23rd Fighter Group had expended the main reserves of their strength and materiel fending off the Japanese effort to wipe them out. Lee Minor, a 75th pilot, had become the first Army

Air Corps casualty in China when "Oscars" swarmed him over Hengyang in the final Japanese assault. AVG veteran Charlie Sawyer had earned the Distinguished Flying Cross, taking on six enemy fighters to protect a group of B-25s he was escorting back from Canton, shooting one Jap down and scattering the rest. Lieutenant Patrick Daniels had been awarded the Silver Star for making repeated dangerous strafing runs on the docks at Haiphong, in Indochina. Three days later, Ed Rector had led 76th Squadron fighters and some of the 11th's bombers back to Haiphong, where they set afire huge piles of coal supplies the Japanese had hoarded for shipment back to their home islands.

But by the 12th of August, Chennault had had to acknowledge the entire group had virtually lost its combat effectiveness operating from the advance bases. He had pulled them back. They had been reduced to a few gallons of gas and a pittance of operational aircraft, and were glaringly vulnerable to renewed Japanese attack. The 75th had relocated to an airfield at Chanyi, some eighty miles northeast of Kunming. Ed Rector's 76th had pulled back to Kunming itself, to join Frank Schiel's 74th; and the 16th Fighter Squadron had withdrawn to Peishiyi. From these locations, the Old Man waited impatiently to bolster his numbers of planes and equipment, so he could put forth his strength once more. The Japanese had failed to drive the 23rd from East China; but lack of spare parts and flyable airplanes had temporarily accomplished the enemy's mission for him.

When he had been recovering for nearly three weeks at Chengtu, and felt almost human once again, Tex received a visitor: a Chinese general named Lim. After politely inquiring about Tex's health and expressing pleasure at his recovery, Lim had an offer for him. Would Tex like to fly a captured Japanese fighter plane?

Tex could hardly believe his ears as he listened to General Lim's explanation. Some time before, a Japanese I-97 "Nate" had gone down over free Chinese territory without exploding (a rarity). The Chinese had captured the plane nearly intact, and engineers had restored it completely. Lim was looking for someone, besides himself, qualified to take the "Nate" for a test flight; and he offered Tex the opportunity. Tex jumped at the chance.

The two men rode out to Sinjen Airfield, and Tex looked the little airplane over. As far as Tex knew, no American had flown a Japanese fighter before; he would be the first. When he climbed up on the wing and looked into the cockpit, he had difficulty believing he could possibly get himself into the tiny compartment. It would certainly be impossible to take a parachute with him—which certainly put an interesting spin on things. Once he had looked it over, though, Tex gave Lim his decision: he wanted to fly it.

With a feat rarely equaled in the history of contortionism, six-foot-three Tex somehow managed to cram his lanky frame into the pilot's seat. His knees were so bent, they were back at his ears; he looked for all the world like a grasshopper as he fumbled with the seat belt. Strapped in, he looked carefully over the controls, while General Lim stood on the wing and offered instruction. Lim himself (a much shorter man) had been up in the "Nate" a few times already, and indeed was one of the most accomplished pilots the Chinese had produced.

The I-97's instrumentation required little explanation: there was a fuel gauge, an oil temperature gauge, and a needle-and-ball to indicate the aircraft's attitude. Only a few other gauges were in evidence; it was a very rudimentary setup. At Tex's feet was a horizontal bar that served the same function as rudder pedals. There were no brakes at all.

Lim showed Tex how to start the engine. The plane carried two types of fuel: in addition to regular aviation gasoline, there was a gallon of high-octane mixture for takeoffs and landings. Once the engine was purring, Lim shouted a caution to him about the throttle; but Tex couldn't quite hear it.

Tex was ready, so he cracked the throttle open "just a hair" to get the aircraft rolling. When the plane lurched suddenly into motion, Tex instinctively "cut back" on the throttle—and then realized what Lim had been trying to tell him.

The throttle worked in the opposite direction of the P-40's. Tex thought he was cutting it back, but he actually threw it wide open—and the plane leaped ahead with a roar. There was nothing for it but to ride it out. He was airborne in what seemed like little more than a hundred yards.

Once in the air, Tex found the plane simple to fly. It would have been much more enjoyable if his knees were not in his ears; but he was able to put the "Nate" through its paces anyway. As he began to maneuver, he noticed that there were no trim tabs; the controls built up a tremendous pressure when the pilot adjusted the aircraft's attitude. Nevertheless, the I-97 had an incredibly light wing loading; Tex was able to turn and loop with agility that the P-40 could never approach. However, he knew that such amazing maneuverability came only by sacrificing armor plating, self-sealing gas tanks, and firepower; and on the whole, Tex considered it not worth the price. But it was nice to "wring out" the little fighter, with moves that would have been unheard-of in an American plane.

After his last few stalls and aerobatics, Tex was ready to set the I-97 down. His legs were starting to cramp up. He had no problem with the landing, the tail skag (there was no wheel) dragging him gradually to a stop. Getting out with some relief, he gratefully thanked General Lim for the opportunity. *Wait till I tell the boys in the 75th*, he thought.

Within a few more days, Tex was ready to leave Chengtu. The quinine treatments had worked, and his malaria had gone into remission. Thanking the missionary family for their care and hospitality, he headed to Chanyi to join his squadron once more.

The town of Chanyi was isolated in a valley surrounded by mountains, some eighty miles northeast of Kunming. Even in August, the air was noticeably cooler than at Hengyang, so the Americans liked the climate a good deal better. The facilities and food were a considerable improvement too, with clean hostels and an alert shack making up the buildings allotted to the 75th Squadron. The airfield had only a single grass strip that served as a runway, which was surrounded by a large dike to keep runoff from the monsoon rains from flooding it. The arrival of the 75th marked the first time most of the townspeople had ever seen a westerner, but the Americans were treated very well.

The standdown of the 23rd Fighter Group for lack of fuel and parts was nearing its end; with the precious trickle of supplies coming over the Hump, Chennault had been carefully shepherding those resources back to operational levels. On the first day of September, Tex and his squadron mates flew east once more, to the familiar base at Hengyang. It was time to let the Japs know that the 75th was back.

From Kweilin the next day, Col Robert Scott took eight P-40s of the 74th and 16th and sped northeast, to join eight more of the 75th that Tex was leading. The sixteen planes, a veritable armada by 23rd Fighter Group standards, headed east to Poyang Lake and the city of Nanchang. There, they intended to hit targets on the lake and in the town.

"Hit targets on the lake" proved to be an understatement. Tex's flight of eight peeled off and spotted some twenty-six junks and sail barges. Japanese operated all the vessels, having confiscated them from their original owners to aid in moving Japan's supplies. With Lieutenant Henry Elias on his wing, Tex began to make strafing passes on the rice-laden vessels, which were moving into Nanchang to deposit their cargoes for Japanese troops. Soon, barges were burning and capsizing everywhere, their sails afire, drifting aimlessly to shore, where Chinese peasants waited hungrily to grab the supplies. By his fourth pass, Tex was ready to move on—but he noticed that Elias was no longer on his wing. Checking the sky and calling on his radio yielded no response from the lieutenant, so Tex pressed on.

The other P-40s were going through the area like a whirlwind. Hal Pike and his 16th Squadron planes shredded motorboats on the Kan Kiang River, while Frank Schiel and other 74th pilots hit river steamers elsewhere on the lake. "Scotty," as the men called their group commander, pounced on a lone Japanese fighter and downed it in flames. John Lombard flew south to the town's railroad station and riddled a locomotive.

It was two days after the mission that Tex sadly learned the fate of Henry Elias. He had veered off to join in a dogfight against some enemy planes he had spotted. Elias got the worst of it, though, being shot up enough to force him to bail out; and when he did, the Japanese ruthlessly strafed him to death in his parachute. Tex shook his head bitterly, remembering Bert Christman's fate at Rangoon some eight months before.

On the same afternoon after the Poyang Lake raid, the 23rd returned to the area for another go; but this time, only eight planes could make the trip. Mechanical or electrical failure of the P-40s' worn-out parts was chronic, and the ground crew couldn't replace them—they had no spares.

The following morning, Japanese fighters winged up from Canton to take revenge upon Hengyang, Lingling, and Kweilin. They showed up at seven a.m.; wave after wave of "Nates" came through the area for hours. The Japanese knew how badly the 23rd could hurt them from those forward-deployed bases, and weren't about to tolerate its return.

Tex was in the air several times during the six-hour running fight; the combat stretched across a huge swath of landscape, extending north and west all the way to Chihkiang and Chanyi. The Japanese were making themselves elusive, trying to strafe the airfields and catch P-40s on the ground while avoiding them in the air. Nevertheless, Tex finally got the drop on one of them, maneuvering purposefully; and then it took only several short bursts to send the "Nate" spinning down.

It was another long day of aerial combat. When it ended, the Americans still held their bases in defiance of the Japanese—who had five fewer planes than they began the day with.

After that, the 23rd held the three forward bases with only five flyable aircraft. Dozens of P-40s sat idle, awaiting a critical part that was unavailable, doing the group absolutely no good until they could be repaired. Chennault was unwilling to let the Japanese attack again—nearly unopposed—and strafe the aircraft into uselessness; so, once again, he ordered a pullback to Chanyi, Kunming, and Peishiyi. Some of the aircraft awaiting repairs were evacuated on trucks.

Chennault's pattern of pushing eastward when the group's strength was built up, then pulling back when they lost their effectiveness, would become a familiar one. Without sufficient supplies, there was simply no other way they could operate. Years later, the Old Man would write about this period: "the China Air Task Force, unbroken in combat, was facing death from acute starvation."

It would be more than a month before the 23rd would have enough strength to return to their trio of forward bases. The monsoon season, now in progress, prevented much aerial combat anyway; and in the interim, there was little to do but "sit alert" and play cards. At Chanyi, the game of choice was Red Dog, a variant of poker that tended to amass huge "pots" of money on the table.

Therein lay a nasty potential for some to lose a lot of dough. Tex and Johnny Alison observed the games with concern, as several of their young airmen gradually found themselves so far in debt, they could hardly see daylight. The two leaders discussed the problem. They knew that such situations between the men would inevitably lead to hard feelings, eroding the morale of the squadron.

Finally, they settled upon a unilateral solution. One morning, Tex announced a "jubilee" on all debts from playing Red Dog—they were forgiven, and everyone now had a "clean slate," by order of the commander. With this came a moratorium on playing the game; the men would have to restrict themselves to poker, acey-deucey, or some other hand of cards.

It was also during these "recovery" times at Chanyi and Chungking that Tex became acquainted with Colonel Merian C. Cooper, Chennault's Chief of Staff. After World War I, in Poland's war for independence against the Soviet Union, Cooper had organized the Polish Kosciusko Squadron to resist the Soviet drive on Warsaw. That squadron later evolved into the predecessor of the USAAC's 303rd Bombardment Group in the Second World War.

After the Great War, Cooper had spent years in the movie business, serving as the executive vice president of RKO Pictures before it went bankrupt in 1932. A mechanical genius, he had then begun work on a technique of miniature projection that was used to make the movie *King Kong*. He patented the cutting-edge technology under the name "Cinerama," which became familiar to moviegoers everywhere. When the Second World War arrived, he sold the business and entered the Army, where his creativity and visionary thinking made him a singularly outstanding military planner.

Late at night, long after planning sessions ended at the group headquarters in Chungking, Cooper and Tex would sit outside and talk for hours. Tex was fascinated by the man and his intelligence, listening to stories of his service in World War I, Poland's war against the Soviets, and his movie-making days. When Cooper began to bend his planning genius to the missions of the 23rd Fighter Group, good results inevitably followed.

As September and October slipped away, dominated by monsoons, action occurred only sporadically for the 23rd. In a massive enemy raid on Hengyang after the 75th had pulled back, Lieutenant Burrall Barnum won the Distinguished Flying Cross when he single-handedly staved off sixty-six marauding fighters from strafing the field where crippled airplanes were being repaired. Two days later, Lieutenant Thomas Smith earned the Silver Star when he downed an enemy Ki-46 "Dinah" reconnaissance plane over Kunming—the first aerial victory for Frank Schiel's 74th Fighter Squadron. In late September, twenty pilots from the 6th Fighter Command in Panama arrived in Kunming to augment the 23rd. Among them was a likeable kid by the name of John Hampshire, whose star would quickly be on the rise.

Standouts Ed Rector and Bruce Holloway were awarded the Silver Star when they staged out of Yunnanyi to hit trucks and vehicles moving up the Burma Road above Lashio. Holloway was hit by ground fire and forced to bail out, emerging from the jungle five days afterward. Rector blasted vehicles and staff cars, continuing south to the enemy encampment at Chefang to give it a thorough going-over. Three days later, Rector topped that with a Distinguished Flying Cross for valor during an escort mission: he fought a solo rearguard action against a half-dozen Ki-45 "Nicks" over Gia Lam Airfield near Hanoi, while the remainder of his fighters escorted 11th Squadron bombers to safety.

As October wound down, Merian Cooper spent long hours at headquarters, poring over Chinese intelligence reports on Japanese shipping activity in Hong Kong's Victoria Harbor. A big Japanese naval task force was moving in, and Cooper was figuring out a way to render a "proper greeting" from the 23rd. Chennault called the squadron commanders up to Chungking, and Cooper briefed them on his plan for a strike on the shipping and docks. On the evening of the 24th, Tex and other pilots slipped surreptitiously into Kweilin, one by one.

Before dawn the next morning, twelve B-25s and ten P-40s were ready to depart. That group represented almost every operational aircraft in the 23rd Fighter Group. "Scotty" led the fighters into the air, while Tex took an element of four on his commander's wing. Below and behind them, Caleb Haynes' *Mitchells* droned purposefully toward their target.

It was the first strike on Hong Kong, and it caught the Japanese completely by surprise. When the B-25s opened their bomb bay doors, high explosive ordnance fell like rain toward the docks below. While Tex and the fighter pilots watched, the weapons found their marks, and the whole area came alive with smoke and debris. Haynes and his boys "sowed" destruction up and down the shoreline, wreaking untold damage on the offloaded goods below.

The initial surprise did not last, however. Already, a score or more of Japanese fighters were rising from Kai Tak Airdrome below. Tex and the others watched their silvery forms as they climbed angrily to altitude and made for the bombers.

"Let's go get 'em," Tex called into the microphone; and ten P-40s dove to the attack.

As he shot earthward, Tex executed a split-S and pulled back while inverted, gaining even more speed on the descent, watching the enemy aircraft grow rapidly larger. There were at least twenty Mitsubishi A6M *Zero* fighters, old standbys of the Imperial Japanese Navy that the Allies had long since nicknamed the "Zeke." Tex watched the enemy's reaction as he screamed into range; quite a few noticed his P-40 and turned defensively, but some did not. He leveled out of the dive and lined up on one of the latter, notching his seventeenth enemy plane destroyed when he blasted it from the right rear quarter. A satisfying explosion followed.

Tex had been the first to reach the enemy, but now others were coming in. "Scotty," John Hampshire, and Morton Shear all achieved aerial victories in the opening seconds of the battle. As they pulled up from their attack passes, though, the persistent Japanese fighters continued to gain on the bombers; and Tex knew that the Americans' top priority must be to prevent the enemy from reaching those B-25s.

Instead of concentrating on one Jap fighter at a time, the P-40s would have to take on the whole group to allow the bombers to escape cleanly. On his next pass, Tex began a series of turns and dives, snapping off short bursts at every *Zero* he could find; he did not expect to shoot any down, but it forced them to turn away from their intended prey to avoid Tex's fire. In this way, he damaged three more *Zeros*, and with his comrades' help, prevented the Japanese from getting through to the bombers.

There was one exception: as Caleb Haynes and his pilots made a formation turn, one B-25 lagged behind, and was set upon by half a dozen *Zeros* before the P-40s could prevent it. The *Mitchell's* gunners brought two of the Japs down, but the bomber sustained enough damage to doom it. The crew of five bailed out. Two were rescued by Chinese and led safely back to the 23rd bases, but the other two were captured and killed by the Japanese. Incredibly, that was the only bomber lost to enemy fire in the history of the CATF.

There were other enemy fighters in the air that day that Tex never saw, including a number of the twin-engined "Nicks," but the results of the battle were familiar. Besides the one B-25, all the Americans made it back to Kweilin; and they left some twenty enemy aircraft in smoking ruin around Hong Kong. Two days later, the Japanese retaliated for the strike by sending a large fighter force to raid Kweilin; but they were rewarded with only a single aerial victory—and they lost sixteen of their own fighters to the guns of the Army Air Corps pilots. Cooper's plan, combined with the fighting prowess of the 23rd, had struck a telling blow.

As the 75th retired once more to Chanyi, Tex realized he was not completely over his malaria. He didn't have the stamina that he was used to relying upon, and a slight fever came and went at times. That was the trouble with the tropical bacteria: it held on tenaciously, sometimes forever. It could not be stamped out without extended treatment over a long period of time.

There came a night at Chanyi when a ground crewman shook Tex awake.

"Major! Major, come quick. Ajax has fallen off the wagon!"

The airman was already leaving the room; Tex pulled on some rumpled clothes and hurried out toward the flightline. He was just in time to see a P-40 roaring down the runway at full throttle, while a group of men ran behind it, waving wildly. Moonlight illuminated the scene as the plane bounced crazily along the runway, veering first one direction and then the other, before finally achieving takeoff speed and lurching into the air.

"He's up, sir," puffed one crewman as Tex ran up, "drunk as a skunk. By the time we saw what he was doing, we couldn't stop him."

There were curses all around as Ajax Baumler, the "Foaming Cleanser," pulled sharply left, nearly falling out of his takeoff climb. Somehow he kept the plane in the air, a dark shadow against the moonlit sky, and brought it once around the pattern. Apparently it was to be a short flight, for Baumler now appeared to be lining up for a landing. As he descended, there were anxious murmurs from the men—who on earth could land a plane while completely drunk?—but Baumler did it, putting down with much more grace than he had displayed on takeoff. When his wheels touched down, everyone let out a pent-up breath of relief as he coasted down the runway.

Sadly, Ajax was not through. As he turned the P-40 around to taxi back, one of the crewmen wailed, "His engine's at full power. He's almost at takeoff speed! What the hell—is he going up again?"

There was no telling. Baumler returned down the runway so fast that his rear wheel was off the ground. At the last minute, the large dike that surrounded the airfield loomed in his vision—and Baumler realized what was about to happen. Engaging full left rudder, he made a spectacular ground loop—right into a row of seven just-repaired P-40s that Johnny Alison was planning to lead on a mission later in the morning.

Groans and shouts of anger rose from the onlookers, including Tex. Dazed but unhurt, Baumler slid back the canopy and stood swaying unsteadily in the cockpit for a second. Then he stared wildly at the faces coming toward him, leaped to the ground, and took off running across the runway. The ground crew was in hot pursuit, and soon one of them felled Baumler with a flying tackle from behind. It was over.

Many hours afterward, a sober Ajax Baumler could remember nothing of his nighttime antics. He had begun drinking the evening before, breaking his promise to Tex, and the rest was a blur. He listened with shock and amazement as others grimly recounted the incident; he shook his head in disbelief.

"I just can't understand it," he repeated morosely, over and over.

Three of the P-40s were "cracked up" and required repair, so Alison was left with only five to run the mission.

Tex and Johnny Alison discussed how they should deal with the situation. What made it so difficult was that Ajax Baumler was a terrific pilot, having already shot down six Japanese planes in China. The prospect of losing him was almost intolerable. The two leaders mulled over their options, and finally hit upon a solution: they would write it up as a "taxi accident." It was the truth as far as it went; and they figured that even with three cracked-up P-40s, they were coming out ahead, six to three.

"I don't need this kind of headache, Johnny," sighed Tex, after the two submitted their report.

Over the next few weeks, the Japanese air force and the 23rd Fighter Group traded blows like boxers in a vast ring. The enemy focused his efforts on Kweilin, from which the stinging raid on Hong Kong had come. Time after time, the Japs threw fighter armadas at the base, sometimes two or three in one day. The 16th Fighter Squadron bore the brunt of these assaults, rising to defend it again and again. The Americans always gave better than they got in the wild melees; but the strain of constant combat wore men and aircraft to a frazzle.

Later that month, in return, the 23rd ranged far and wide, hitting a vast array of targets across eastern China in a brilliant display of combat power. Merian Cooper was right in the thick of the planning. Three dozen P-40s and twelve B-25s plastered the port of Hongay in Indochina, sending a twelve-thousand-ton freighter to the bottom of the harbor. The following day, CATF bombs rained on barracks and ships in Sanchow Island near Haiphong. B-25s put a shellacking on Tien Ho Airdrome near Canton, turning forty-two Japanese aircraft into scrap. At nearby White Cloud Airdrome, P-40s zoomed low over the field to put fragmentation bombs into parked enemy planes. More *Mitchells* sunk an eight-thousand-ton freighter on the crowded Whampoa docks. Johnny Alison hammered the airport at Hankow with a flight of P-40s, afterward leading them out onto the Yangtze River to thrash wharves, steamers, and gunboats. Sienning, Tungting Lake, Yochow, Poyang Lake, Hsinning, Lungling: the list of Japanese-packed targets was long (and distinguished).

In the grand finale before the CATF ran out of gasoline, Chennault sent twenty-two P-40s and ten B-25s over Canton to deliver an extraordinary performance. After six- and eight-thousand-ton freighters were sent into oblivion by the bombs of the *Mitchells*, the P-40s plowed into forty-odd intercepting enemy fighters, and lambasted twenty-seven of them within ninety seconds. Some of the triumphant pilots would call it "the greatest dogfight of the war."

After this supreme effort, the 23rd was spent; and Tex was nearly in the same state. Chennault had refused to let him participate in many of the most dangerous raids during this period, for a good reason: at long last, Tex had received leave orders back to the United States. Staring at the papers numbly, Tex had reflected that he'd almost forgotten what the States looked like. Chennault didn't want to lose Tex on the eve of his return, so he kept him on a "short leash" while the 23rd ravaged the enemy far and wide for six days. Tex had no idea what his future assignment would be; he knew only that he was to be allowed some leave before reporting to Washington, D.C. He later learned that he was supposed to have gone home in October; but General Bissell had held up Tex's transfer orders for an additional two months.

At Chanyi, Tex said goodbye to Johnny Alison, who would be taking command of the squadron upon his departure. The men gathered around their leader one more time, and Tex declared that he would like to return to the 75th when his leave was over.

In early December, as the first frosts formed in Kunming, Chennault held a small farewell dinner for Tex and Ed Rector at his home. Rector was also going on stateside leave, and the two friends got a look at each other for the first time in weeks. The fight with malaria had left only one hundred forty-seven pounds on Tex's lean frame; Rector showed all the signs of combat stress and extreme fatigue. Joining them in Chennault's house were Frank Schiel, Scotty, and Tom Gentry, Chennault's surgeon from the AVG days. Tex was introduced to Colonel Clayton "Casey" Vincent, Chennault's new executive officer. The Old Man himself presided over the subdued festivities. It was obvious he was sorry to see them go.

"You boys have done a fine job out here," Chennault declared, "but you need a rotation out. You deserve it."

There were murmurs of agreement.

The next day, the two friends boarded a Douglas C-47 *Skytrain* transport and lifted off from Kunming in the chilly morning. Three P-40s, led by Major Bruce Holloway, escorted them for some distance, finally turning back with a wave of farewell. As the big airplane climbed out of the mist, Tex settled back in his seat and closed his eyes. He was going home.

* * *

Although the Battle of Midway was a turning point in the Pacific campaign, the Japanese nevertheless completed their conquest of the Solomon Islands and New Guinea on the same day Johnny Alison was presumed dead. Six days later, as Tex lay wracked by malaria in Chengtu, U.S. Marines began the heroic recapture of the Solomons with an amphibious landing on Guadalcanal.

As Tex lifted off the runway at Kunming to return to the States, overwhelmingly superior numbers of British and Australian forces in North Africa began to push their way westward across German minefields toward Axis positions near El Alamein. In five days of heavy fighting, they forced Field Marshal Erwin Rommel's famed armored forces to retreat, with only a handful of tanks remaining; it was the first decisive victory, at long last, over the famed German "Desert Fox."

In the town of Victoria, Texas, nineteen-year-old Mazie Sale flipped idly through a copy of "Time" magazine one evening. She paused when an article caught her attention. It was about young Major David L. "Tex" Hill, one of the most decorated heroes of the war at the time. After reading down the list of his medals, she looked at his photograph, thinking he looked awfully young to have turned in such a performance. She turned the page and resumed flipping.

Chapter 23

THE HOME FRONT

It took Tex the remainder of the year to reach United States soil. The C-47 carried him and Ed Rector back over the Hump, then refueled and flew on to New Delhi. There, the two friends learned of a tragedy they had barely missed: Frank Schiel was dead. Their fellow squadron commander and comrade throughout the AVG days, Schiel had slammed into a mountain near Kunming in bad weather, returning from a reconnaissance flight over the Japanese-occupied island of Formosa. It had happened just hours after Tex and Rector had departed. Schiel had been flying an F-4A, a photoreconnaissance version of the Lockheed P-38 *Lightning*, when it happened. He had flown dozens of those dangerous missions, in stripped-down planes at high altitude, hundreds of miles deep in enemy territory with no way to defend himself. He had already earned the Silver Star and Distinguished Flying Cross for his bravery, and the news was a bitter blow to the group. Ed Rector was already feeling miserable enough, and thought he was coming down with the flu.

It wasn't the flu, as Rector learned after he and Tex reached Bombay by train. It was pneumonia. Tex's friend spent the next few weeks battling the illness in a British hospital, very nearly dying before his high fever broke and the point of crisis passed. An "old girlfriend"—Rector seemed to have them everywhere—took him into her care, and nursed him slowly back to health.

With Rector thus in "capable hands," Tex had to move on; and after a plane trip to Karachi, he began the long trek across Africa. He hopped from city to city across the continent in a variety of transport planes, finally ending up somewhere in Eritrea, awaiting a final flight to the United States.

At that point, who should show up in a DC-4 but ex-AVG man Bob Prescott, now flying for Trans-World Airlines? After a happy reunion and Prescott's gratefully accepted offer of a lift, Tex settled in for the long trip across the Atlantic, finally touching down in Miami on New Year's Eve, 1942. As he walked down the steps and set foot on the ground—thirty-two pounds lighter, battle-tested, and much wiser—he almost couldn't believe it.

Tex was anxious to complete the journey and get to his Texas hill country home, but there were several things to accomplish first. He had been ordered immediately to Washington, D.C. to make a report on the China situation to the Joint Chiefs of Staff, including Chief of the Army Air Forces General Henry "Hap" Arnold. Also, he carried diplomatic messages from Generalissimo Chiang Kai-Shek to President Roosevelt. These were weighty tasks; so in spite of his weariness, he took the next flight north and made his way to the nation's capital.

After delivering the messages from the Generalissimo, Tex visited the War Department. Shortly, he found himself sitting in front of more generals and admirals than he had ever seen. Tex was in a unique position to report accurately, since he was one of the first USAAC pilots to return from the China-Burma-India Theater, and had been in a command position. Other than the highly stylized write-ups in the press, little detailed war news emerged from that part of the world.

Tex was a little nervous in front of the brass, but it didn't deter him one whit from giving a straightforward account of things. He described the operations of the China Air Task Force, spending plenty of time on his observations of the capabilities of the Japanese. He praised Chennault and his effectiveness as a leader. He told them about the outrageous supply situation—how the CATF had to scrape, scrounge, and wring every rivet and spark plug across the Hump from Tenth Air Force headquarters in India. Tex eagerly described what might be accomplished if the CATF were given a higher priority on supply.

The military leaders listened carefully. They had long since determined that the European Theater of Operations was going to have first priority in the war—a "Germany First" Allied strategy—but they nevertheless wanted to understand the situation in China. They might not be willing to free the CATF from the shoestring it operated on; but they cared enough about it to take interest in its accomplishments—which were inspiring, to say the least. After the briefing, there was a promotion ceremony for Tex himself, at which he received the silver oak leaves of a lieutenant colonel. He was twenty-seven years old.

When that was concluded, the War Department ran Tex through intelligence debriefings for several days. Then it gave him his next assignment. After his leave at home, he was to spend a few weeks at the Air Force Tactical Center, abbreviated AFTAC, in Orlando, Florida. Before he departed Washington, World War I ace Eddie Rickenbacker visited Tex at his hotel room; and Tex thoroughly enjoyed Rickenbacker's company.

As he moved about the capital during his short stay, Tex noted with interest that a massive construction project was nearly complete on the banks of the Potomac; the huge structure was soon to house all seventeen offices of the War Department. The single gargantuan building had been assembled virtually on top of a swamp, in a staggeringly short time. It would bear a name to match its enormous shape: the Pentagon.

At long last, Tex boarded a train, and watched Washington disappear over the horizon as he rolled south toward Texas.

His homecoming was pure joy. Instead of going directly to the family home in Hunt, he traveled to Victoria, Texas, where his brother Sam was now pastor of a Presbyterian church. Sam had temporarily suspended his pastoral duties when he had joined the Army Air Corps some time before. Happily, his assignment was to train pilots at nearby Matagorda Island; and he was often able to return to Victoria for short stays. In the meantime, Dr. Hill himself had come out of retirement in the hill country to take up the pastorate at Sam's church in Victoria, and he and Miss Ella lived there during this period. There were many back-slappings and embraces when Tex was reunited with them once more.

The weeks before his report date to AFTAC were relaxing and enjoyable. Tex made several hunting and fishing expeditions with his father, reminding him fondly of the excursions they used to take when he was a boy. He spent a great deal of time outdoors, not taking things very quickly. His spirits lifted; the break had a wonderful effect upon him. He began to put on weight again, and to look more like himself. His body gradually recovered from long illness and combat fatigue, and his old smile began to flash readily.

There were times, though, that other emotions flashed as well. While in Victoria, Tex learned of a coal strike in progress that threatened to restrict the operation of factories producing equipment for American troops in combat. He was infuriated by the audacity of men who would quit working when their country was at war, no matter what their grievance might be.

On one occasion in Austin, Tex addressed a joint session of the state's Senate and House of Representatives. Shortly after Governor "Coke" Stevenson introduced him, Tex was asked for his opinion about the coal strike.

"It's a tremendous letdown for guys like me when they get home," he said, with an edge of steel in his voice. "I don't know if those strikers realize that their actions are costing lives out there. If I run into any of these guys, I'll probably get thrown in jail. I'd treat them like enemy agents."

Nobody had to ask him what he meant.

One of Tex's longtime ambitions had been to own a good piece of land. As a Squadron Leader in the AVG, he had earned a salary of $750 per month; and he had collected a $500 bonus twelve times, for each of his aerial victories. Out of all this, Tex had kept only $50 each month for incidental expenses. There was precious little to spend the money on in war-torn Burma and China—and in any case, all the cash in the world wouldn't have bought the AVG the things it really needed. Tex had sent the vast majority of his AVG earnings, along with most of his Army salary later, back to Dr. Hill, who put it in a savings account for his son. By the time Tex came home, there was a good-sized "nest egg" in the account; and he had decided to invest it in buying a ranch of his own.

Dr. Hill and Tex searched around for the right kind of place. Dr. Hill suggested his son check out a sixteen-hundred-acre ranch that a friend, Mr. Alfred Kott, was offering for sale. Tex had met Kott years before, when he spent summers working on the Duderstadts' ranch. The ranch was near the town of Mountain Home, Texas, some fifty miles north of Kerrville.

When he saw the place, Tex knew immediately it was exactly what he was looking for. The ranch was nearly a mile off the highway, quiet and isolated, accessible only through the property of a Mr. Elmer Real. Unfortunately, even the down payment on the ranch was greater than the sum of Tex's carefully shepherded funds; but an oilman friend of Dr. Hill's, admiring Tex's accomplishments, wanted to help. The oilman put up an additional $3500, and arranged an excellent interest rate on a loan note, so that Tex could purchase the place. Although he was still in the Army, the young man was now a Texas rancher, at least in name.

When his leave finally ended, it was with considerable reluctance that Tex boarded a plane bound east, for Florida.

The Air Force Tactical Center, near Orlando, represented a new concept for the United States—and it was a good one. Pilots who had returned fresh from combat were taken into the unit and checked out in the latest fighter aircraft, equipment, and weapons. The pilots, in turn, would pass on their own experience and proven tactics learned in the heat of battle. AFTAC coordinated closely with the Overseas Training Units (OTUs) that prepared new pilots for combat flying in Europe or the Pacific; it was an excellent way to disseminate the knowledge and experience of veterans to pilots in training.

Charlie Bond, formerly of the AVG's Adam and Eves, was already assigned to AFTAC (having returned to USAAC service after his return home), and he greeted Tex happily. Bond had the job of checking Tex out in the P-47 *Thunderbolt* (before which he offered his opinion of the fighter's size: "I always feel like I'm crawling on an elephant!") In turn, Tex passed on to the Center the experience and tactics that had punished the Japanese in the air over China.

During his tenure at AFTAC, Tex did notice one shortcoming in the OTU program. Given only a short time to work with pilot trainees, the program could not possibly teach them thorough, effective tactics for fighting opponents in both Europe and the Pacific. Since a pilot could only be going to one theater or the other, Tex approached Major General Gordon Saville to recommend that the OTU curriculum be split into two tracks: one for pilots assigned to Europe, and another for those assigned to the Pacific. It would allow the men to focus exclusively on learning how to combat the enemies they would be up against. Saville considered it, but eventually decided not to take Tex's advice.

As his time at AFTAC drew to a close, Tex received orders directing his next assignment. He would be taking command of the Proving Ground Group, a division of the Army's Proving Ground Command, at Eglin Field. Eglin was only a short hop from AFTAC, being situated well up in the Florida panhandle—right next to Pensacola, in fact, where Tex had attended Naval flight training. He looked forward to his new station.

The Proving Ground Command was a massive operational "test bed" for the Army Air Corps' planes, armament, and munitions. One of the command's groups concentrated exclusively on evaluating new projects that emerged from the laboratories at Wright-Patterson Field, in Ohio. Pilots had learned that the Wright-Pat engineers, in their zeal to give life to their latest inventions, sometimes declared them more "combat-ready" than they actually were. At the Proving Ground, such gadgets and weapons could be thoroughly tested in conditions as close to aerial combat as possible.

Tex's group, on the other hand, focused on prototype aircraft and performance comparison between airframes. The latest models from aircraft production lines nation-wide were brought into Eglin to be "wrung out" in the Florida skies, and "stacked up" against each other to see which would be winners and which would not.

The Proving Ground Commander was Major General Grandison Gardner, who greeted Tex warmly upon his arrival. Gardner was easygoing, a good man to work for, and Tex had all the latitude he wanted in leading the Proving Ground Group. The group itself consisted of five sections, representing four different aircraft types and one "skunk works." The Fighter Section had every fighter type in the Air Corps inventory—an awe-inspiring array of planes. A-20 *Havocs* formed the bulk of the Light Bombardment Section; B-25s and Martin B-26 *Marauders* made up the Medium Bombardment Section; and Boeing B-17 *Flying Fortresses* and Consolidated B-24 *Liberators* comprised the Heavy Bombardment Section. Finally, the Special Weapons Section featured aircraft specially outfitted for unorthodox missions—such as B-25s equipped with a 75mm cannon in the nose. Tex realized with satisfaction that he was going to be checking out in just about every USAAC aircraft imaginable.

Two weeks after taking command of the Proving Ground Group, Tex flew a P-40L from Eglin into the little airport in Victoria, Texas for a weekend visit with his mother and father. His brother Sam was in town from Matagorda, and it would be a good chance to spend time with the family. Sam took the opportunity to preach a sermon at his own First Presbyterian Church on Sunday, and Tex attended. But when he spotted beautiful Mazie Sale sitting in a pew across from him, he forgot all about the sermon.

* * *

Back in China, the CATF was suffering through a miserable winter. The quantity of supplies coming from Tenth Air Force headquarters in India was pitiful; and despite Chennault's pleas, they did not include basic necessities such as razor blades, soap, and toilet paper. No uniform items were forthcoming either, though General Bissell was quick to complain about the non-regulation attire of CATF personnel.

In spite of this, the men themselves continued to perform. Ajax Baumler took over the 74th Fighter Squadron after Frank Schiel's death, changing its role from training to combat, and sending his P-40s out to maraud enemy forces whenever he had enough gasoline. The 75th, led by Johnny Alison, relieved the 16th at Yunnanyi. The 16th had been pounded by Japanese counterair attacks, and the 75th took up the defense while also escorting bombers on missions into northern Burma. In early January, the steely-eyed Bruce Holloway took over the 23rd Fighter Group from "Scotty," and as Merian Cooper headed stateside, Casey Vincent replaced him as CATF Executive Officer. At age twenty-eight, Vincent was the youngest Colonel in the Army Air Forces.

Meanwhile, a British counteroffensive from India back into Burma was running into heavy resistance as it moved along the coast. By February it ground to a halt, still short of Akyab; and the stubborn Japanese proceeded to throw the British Army back out of the country with over two thousand casualties. More successful at first was eccentric British general Orde C. Wingate, who snaked into Burma with three thousand specially trained "Chindits" to wreak havoc upon Japanese lines of communication from elusive jungle bases. This force, too, eventually crumbled as it succumbed to starvation and disease, eventually losing three men in ten before hacking its way back out into India.

By mid-January, the CATF was again out of gas, and Chennault grounded them for a period that would stretch to over a month. During this time, an uncomprehending Stilwell tried to further cut CATF fuel supplies by half, stockpiling them for his planned return invasion of Burma. When Chennault curtly informed Stilwell that the CATF could not fly another combat mission if such an order was enforced, Stilwell relented—but snapped to Chennault, "You've got to learn to do without things!"

When Tex had been at the Proving Ground for a week, the CATF was disbanded and Fourteenth Air Force formed, with General Claire Chennault named as commander despite the objections of the War Department and the Army brass. In spite of great difficulties during its short lifetime, the CATF had managed to destroy one hundred forty-nine Japanese aircraft—while losing sixteen of its own—to say nothing of the ships, vehicles, installations, troops, and supplies that had disintegrated under its bombs and guns.

Chennault had mixed feelings about his new command as he wrote: "...the CATF passed into history with its planes still grounded from lack of gas and its personnel huddled around charcoal stoves all over Yunnan, still cursing Delhi for the lack of supplies...during that grim period the CATF was the only tangible evidence of American aid and American offensive spirit to millions of Chinese, whose courage and determination to continue the war had reached its lowest ebb...

"The CATF was probably the smallest American Air Force ever to be dignified by the command of a general. It certainly was the raggedest. Its paper work was poor, and salutes were scarce, but when the signals were called for combat, it never missed a play."

Tex drives while Johnny Alison seizes the moment at Chanyi, late 1942.

Tex during his visit to the Pentagon, where he briefed the Joint Chiefs of Staff on the state of the war in China.

Tex and others around the rudder of a downed Japanese aircraft. (L to R: Tex Hill, Noel Bacon, Tom Cole, Ed Rector, Frank Lawlor, Frank Schiel.)

P-40 restored and flown by Jerry Yegan. Markings are for number 108, which Tex flew to lead the famous Salween Gorge mission, May 7, 1942.

Portrait of Mazie Sale Hill, 1943.

Chapter 24

"I HAVE TO MEET THAT GIRL!"

All seemed normal as the Hills returned to Sam's home after the Sunday morning service. But after dinner, Tex cornered his brother in the kitchen.

"Sam," began Tex, "there's a girl I saw at church—"

"You mean Mazie Sale?" Sam broke in with a smile.

"How do you know who I'm talking about?"

Sam chuckled. "Brother, you were staring at her the whole service. If I didn't know better, I'd take it unkindly—like something was lacking in my sermon."

"I have to meet that girl!" exclaimed Tex, ignoring the jibe. "I wonder..."

But Sam was steering Tex toward the stairs. "You're still getting over that malaria," he said gently. "I'd suggest you stretch out for a bit. You've got to go back to Florida tomorrow." Tex nodded and retired to his room, lost in thought.

Meanwhile at the Sale house, Sunday dinner was a much grander affair. Dr. Walter Sale and his family gathered at their large dining room table, along with the usual eight or so Army aviation cadets from Foster Field whom Dr. Sale customarily invited for dinner. His was an open home, and many young men enjoyed tarrying there to socialize with his four beautiful daughters.

Mazie was the third oldest of the Sale girls, and the cadets generally agreed that she was a knockout. Her chestnut hair fell to her shoulders, curling in waves around her pretty face. She had sparkling blue eyes and a perfect complexion, with a slim figure to match. Mazie's brilliant, ready smile lit up her striking features.

With her good looks went a wonderful disposition, for Mazie's spirits were naturally buoyant; she never complained, and was quick to compliment. In her childhood years she had been quite a tomboy, sustaining more bruises and skinned knees than any boy in her classes. Now she displayed that same energy during frequent evening parties and dances in the Sale home. She would leap up onto tables, tap-dancing the night away in a high-heeled good time. Nevertheless, she was every bit a graceful young lady; and so, with all these charms, she had no shortage of beaus and admirers. Mazie was having the time of her life.

As Sunday dinner wound down, Dr. Sale's cook, Lucille, told Mazie she had a telephone call. "It's the Reverend Sam Hill, miss," she said.

Mazie hurried into the next room and picked up the phone. "This is Mazie Sale," she said, wondering what it was about.

"Mazie, this is pastor Sam Hill," Tex's brother replied. "How are you this afternoon?"

"Why, I'm just fine, thank you. How are you?"

"I'm doing fine. Listen, I'm calling because my brother Tex is in town for the weekend, and he'd like to come over and meet you this afternoon. Would you be up for that?"

Mazie paused. "Oh, Sam, I can't possibly. I'm sorry, but I have a date. We're going on a picnic, and I just can't do it today."

At that moment, the figure of Dr. Sale was framed in the doorway.

"Mazie, what are you talking about to Reverend Hill?" he asked with a frown.

Mazie covered the receiver. "Oh, Daddy, he wants to bring his brother over to visit, but I was telling him we're going on that picnic."

Dr. Sale's frown deepened, and his words were stern. "Mazie, tell him to come on over. If his brother wants to visit, that's your patriotic duty!"

He turned and left, and Mazie put the phone to her ear once more.

"Well...sorry about that, Sam. Well, if you want to visit, I guess that's fine. When will you be coming over?"

"Since you have plans, we'll be over right away," Sam replied. The conversation ended. Mazie walked out into the dining room and addressed the cadets.

"I'm sorry, you all, but we're going to have to be a little late picking up the others for the picnic," she announced.

"What's up?" asked one of the boys.

"Well, pastor Sam Hill and his brother Tex are coming over for a visit."

Half of the cadets almost dropped their forks at this news. They all knew about Tex Hill from *Time* and *Life* magazine features, or from the movie *The Flying Tigers*, and "hero" was very nearly an understatement of their regard for him.

"You're kidding!" said one. There were grins all around.

As Tex and Sam arrived at the Sale house and walked up to the front door, Tex found himself arguably more nervous about meeting Mazie than he had been in aerial combat. Sam rapped the knocker and Dr. Sale opened the door, shaking hands and greeting the men. When he had invited them inside, Tex looked up, and saw Mazie standing at the top of the stairs, smiling.

As she began to descend, he thought: *Man, that's it. That's all she wrote.*

Mazie, too, felt unaccountably stirred when she looked at Tex, who still bore the effects of long illness on his features. Behind his handsome face she could discern suffering, but also that he faced it with resolute courage.

"Hi, I'm Tex Hill. How do you do?" he asked with a smile.

Mazie introduced herself, thinking: *If he asked me to marry him right now, I'd say yes.* It was the kind of love at first sight that only happened in stories.

Seconds later, Tex was surrounded by the cadets, who wanted to know all about the Flying Tigers, the war in China, and how many Japs he had shot down. With Sam and Dr. Sale, they moved into the living room, where Tex talked a long time about operations in the Far East. It was nearly time to leave when he was able to visit with Mazie again, and they got no further than to exchange a few pleasantries. But each of them had seen enough.

When Tex and Sam returned to the parsonage, Tex had an announcement for his brother and parents. "I'm going to marry that girl," he stated decisively.

There was a silence. All three looked at him with raised eyebrows, wondering what on earth had occurred. Tex had never mentioned even having a girlfriend before, and he had certainly seemed far too busy to think about one now. But somehow, they could tell, he had made up his mind.

Mazie's picnic was held some thirty miles to the southeast in Port Lavaca, a beautiful seaside town on the Gulf of Mexico. When she returned home late in the afternoon, Mrs. Sale had a message for her.

"Mazie, Tex Hill called you," she said.

"Oh," said Mazie in surprise, "what did he say?"

"Not a thing. Don't worry," her mother added with a smile when she saw the anxious look on the girl's face, "he'll call back."

She was right. When the phone rang, Mazie made sure she was the one to answer it.

"Sale residence, Mazie speaking."

"Hello, Mazie, this is Tex Hill. How are you?"

"Well, hello, Tex! I'm fine, thank you. Are you doing all right?"

"Yeah, fine. Say, I was wondering if you might like to go to church with me this evening," he drawled.

"Oh," Mazie replied, somewhat subdued, "well, Tex...I'm afraid I have a date this evening."

"Oh, I see. Well, how about going to eat Mexican food after church then?" he asked.

Mazie thought quickly. She knew her date would probably last most of the evening, and there was no way she could see Tex and still keep it. Suddenly she made up her mind.

"Well, all right, Tex. That would be fine."

"Great!" replied Tex, and he made arrangements to pick her up.

As Mazie hung up the phone, she wondered: *What have I done?* She knew that William Fly, a naval aviation cadet, was supposed to fly into Victoria from Corpus Christi and pick her up in less than two hours for the date—and she had just agreed to stand him up.

Mazie's conscience bothered her. On countless occasions she had "preached" to the girls at the University of Alabama's Kappa Kappa Gamma House, "Don't ever stand up a boy. If you don't want a date with him then don't accept one, but don't ever break your word and stand him up. That's just dreadful." Now, here she was, doing exactly that. But despite some guilty feelings, she was ready when Tex came around a short while later. His brother Sam was with him.

The three of them had delicious fare at a Mexican restaurant, and Tex and Mazie rapidly became better acquainted. Afterward Sam, fulfilling one of his pastoral duties, made the rounds of his parishioners at a nearby hospital. Tex and Mazie waited in the car and talked at length, completely captivated by each other's company.

"You know, Mazie," Tex said half-jokingly, "those aviation cadets you keep around for company are a bad influence."

"Oh, *really*, Tex," Mazie chuckled.

"No, no—I'm serious. They'll corrupt you completely. You don't know it, but you're a helpless pawn in the toils of Beelzebub!" The two of them laughed out loud.

The next day Tex had to return to Eglin; but he resolved to come to Victoria again as soon as he could. He found his thoughts constantly turning to Mazie. His mind had not changed about marrying her; he just had to figure out a way to do it.

Within a few days he was back in San Antonio, keeping a speaking engagement to relate his experiences in China at the city's Municipal Auditorium. Mrs. Hill called Mrs. Sale to ask whether Mazie wouldn't like to accompany the Hills. Afterward, the family would be driving up to Dr. Hill's home in Hunt, Texas to spend a day or two; and Mazie was invited along for this trip as well. Mazie accepted both invitations when her mother passed them along, and quickly packed her things.

Sam gave her a ride up into the hill country, and Mazie got a look at Tex's childhood "stomping ground" for the first time. She did not feel like a stranger as the Hill family gathered for meals and fellowship, for their honest friendliness overcame any case of nerves she might have had. She enjoyed the visit a great deal.

The trouble was, thought Tex, there was too much family around for him to get any time alone with Mazie. How could he make his intentions known while the place was crawling with Hills? On top of that, neighbors kept dropping by to talk with Tex and congratulate him on his accomplishments in China. At any other time, the visits would have been gratifying; but for Tex just now, they were maddening. When Richard Frederick, owner of a nearby ranch, came by to greet him one afternoon, Tex pulled him aside with a purposeful look in his eye.

"Mr. Frederick, I've brought Mazie up here to get to know her a little better, but we haven't been alone two minutes around here. Do you think we might be able to come over to your place for dinner or something, so I can get some time alone with her?"

Frederick chuckled and patted Tex on the shoulder. "I understand perfectly, son. Happy to help."

Frederick extended the invitation. That evening, as Tex and Mazie prepared to depart, Dr. Hill emerged from the house. He, too, was dressed for dinner and ready to go.

"Daddy," Tex smiled, "I don't think...I think just the two of us are invited."

"What?—oh," his father replied with some embarrassment, as realization dawned on him, "I see. Well, you two have a nice time then." He waved to Tex as they departed down the drive.

It may have been the shortest dinner on record. As Mrs. Frederick was whisking the supper dishes off the table, Dick leaned back and looked at his watch.

"Whew! Seven o'clock...well, I'm about done in. Come on, Gertrude, these kids want to be alone. Let's go to bed." They tramped up the stairs together, leaving Tex and Mazie stifling laughs.

They sat for a long time in the living room, talking, on a bearskin rug in front of the fireplace. Tex kissed Mazie for the first time.

"Mazie, will you marry me?" he asked quietly.

"I...I don't know," the flustered girl replied, "I'll have to ask my Daddy!"

"I'll ask your Daddy," Tex replied with a grin. "Do you want to marry me?"

"Yes, I do." They were the best three words Tex had ever heard in his life.

The following morning, as the Hills were preparing to return to Victoria, Sam sidled up with a knowing grin on his face.

"So, brother," he asked, "how did things go last night at the Fredericks' place?"

"Well," replied Tex with a straight face, "I proposed to Mazie on a bearskin rug."

Sam had to steady himself on the back of a chair.

Not long after Tex returned once more to Eglin, Dr. Sale called his daughter into his downtown office in the National Bank of Victoria building. Mazie knew that such a summons meant a serious matter, and approached her father's "inner sanctum" with trepidation.

"Mazie, I want to talk to you," he said, not unkindly, motioning her into a chair and getting right to the point. "Mazie, you've had a lot of boys fall in love with you before, and I know you've broken a lot of their hearts."

Mazie wasn't convinced this was quite true, but she did enjoy having a number of sweethearts.

Dr. Sale continued, "Let me tell you something about Tex. He's not a boy; he's a man, and that's different. If you hurt him," her father said, pausing and looking hard at her, "I'll never forgive you as long as I live."

They were hard words, but meant for good. Mazie knew her father was serious, but it was all right. She knew Tex was the one for her.

Tex himself shared this view wholeheartedly, and saw no reason why they couldn't be married by the end of the month. On his next trip back to Victoria—unscheduled—he placed a long-distance call just before taking off to let Mazie know he was coming.

Near panic ensued in the Sale household. At the moment Mazie was not wearing her false fingernails, which she always did for visitors, especially *this* visitor. *Oh, Lord, he hasn't seen me without my nails on!* She made a beeline for the ten-cent store to buy a kit. Tex was already in the air, so it would have to be a "rush job." When she returned home, she quickly coated the insides with glue and pressed the nails on. To help things go more quickly, she wrapped a rubber band around each finger to hold the nails in place. Putting on make-up and changing clothes without using any fingers was a miracle of dexterity, but somehow she managed it. She heard Tex entering the house downstairs just as she was putting the finishing touches of polish on. Waving her hands frantically to dry the polish, she decided at last that she was ready to meet her fiancée, took a deep breath, and went downstairs.

Tex sat in the living room, wearing the uniform the Army called "pinks": an Eisenhower jacket, beige trousers, and brown shoes. He rose when Mazie entered, and kissed her.

"I brought you something," he said with a smile, as the two sat down.

"What is it?" Mazie asked.

In reply, Tex pulled a small box out of his pocket and opened it, revealing a beautiful diamond ring. Mazie's eyes were wide.

A more romantic scene could not be imagined than the young officer slipping an engagement ring onto the finger of his bride-to-be-until the false fingernail came off Mazie's ring-finger with a small *pop* and landed, glue-side up, on Tex's "pinks." For several seconds, they both stared at it—Tex in puzzlement and Mazie in horror.

"What on earth is *that*?" asked Tex, leaning forward to examine the fingernail. It was too much; Mazie lost her composure.

"Well you might as well know right now: I wear false fingernails!" she exclaimed in despair.

Tex looked back and forth from the glue-coated fingernail to Mazie, then smiled at her. "Anything else?" he said with a sardonic grin.

His easygoing manner disarmed her; they were both laughing in a moment.

On Saturday, March 27th, 1943, Tex and Mazie were married in the First Presbyterian Church in Victoria. Only thirteen days had passed since they had first laid eyes on each other. Dr. Hill and Sam shared the ceremonial duties, "tying the knot" fairly tightly; and Dr. and Mrs. Sale held a wonderful reception in their Victoria home. That magnificent house, set far back amid lush grass and trees on grounds that occupied an entire city block, was easily one of the area's most storied buildings. Colonel Sam Houston had made it his headquarters for a time during Texas' struggle for independence; and it was commonly acknowledged that the benevolent ghost of Judge Alexander Hamilton Phillips, the house's master after its construction in 1851, could occasionally be heard striding heavily along the upstairs hall. Sixty years after their wedding day, Tex and Mazie would be as much in love as on the day Mazie descended the stairs to greet her handsome visitor.

After the wedding and festivities, both were exhausted. They drove through the darkness in a borrowed car from Victoria toward San Antonio. It was a hundred-mile trip; and by the time they reached Cuero, only twenty-eight miles out of Victoria, the newlyweds' eyelids were drooping. Tex slowed the car as he passed a three-story, European-style hotel next to the town's movie theater.

"The Muti Hotel," he mumbled, reading the sign. "Let's just stop here for the night, Mazie."

Tired as she was, his bride looked at him aghast.

"I am *not*," she declared, "spending any honeymoon night in a place called the 'Muti Hotel!'"

That was the end of discussion on the subject. Seventy-two miles later, Tex pulled the car up to the Gunter, one of the oldest and poshest hotels in San Antonio.

Tex turned to Mazie as a valet approached the car. "Now, don't act like we just got married," he admonished.

Mazie nodded—but as the valet opened her door, hundreds of rice kernels spilled in all directions.

Following a night in their complimentary bridal suite, the newlyweds boarded a train for Washington, D.C. Tex, as usual, had orders—to report to the War Department. The train ride lasted for three days, during which Mazie and Tex had to share an upper berth in a passenger car. It wasn't what she might have imagined for a honeymoon. When at last they stepped onto the platform in the capital, both were thinking: *If we can survive that trip, we've got it made.* They were right.

The train station was a swarm of activity. The young bride watched wide-eyed as crowds moved in all directions on untold business. She and Tex got in a crowded line to speak to a porter about hailing a cab, but people were elbowing their way to the front from every direction. After some time, an exasperated Tex told Mazie to stay put while he himself pushed through to speak to the porter.

"Excuse me, I've got to get a cab," Tex raised his voice over a number of other jostling patrons. "I have orders to report at the War Department, and I can't possibly be late."

The jaded porter looked at him in annoyance. "Yeah, buddy, you and everyone else. Ain't you heard? There's a war on!"

Tex turned crimson; *This is it*, Mazie thought. She didn't hear what her husband said as he leaned close to the porter and spoke; but in very short order, a cab was pulling up, and Tex was beckoning her to get in.

After he had reported for duty, many officers continued to approach Tex to learn about events in China; and he was happy to relate what he knew. For a few days in the capital, Tex's time was occupied by sitting for a portrait; the War Department had commissioned an artist named Baskerville to paint a number of them, and Tex was one of the selected subjects. Mazie came down each day to watch the sittings. The work still hangs in the Pentagon today.

One evening, the Air Corps held a formal banquet. Scores of generals and their wives attended, and nineteen-year-old Mazie found herself seated beside Tex right in the middle of them, at the head table. Somehow, the conversation turned to West Point.

Back in Victoria, Mazie had occasionally met West Point cadets at social events or Sunday afternoon dinners. To her, they had seemed snobbish and full of self-importance, and she didn't have much liking for them.

When the subject came up, Mazie remarked without hesitation to everyone within earshot: "Well, I've never met anyone from West Point that I liked."

Dead silence fell over the table. Wondering if she had said something amiss, Mazie looked at Tex. He was scowling. After a few seconds the conversation picked up again, and it wasn't until hours later that she had a chance to find out what happened.

"Mazie," said an exasperated Tex, "every woman in that room was wearing a miniature!"

"What's a miniature?" asked Mazie innocently.

Tex explained how West Point graduates traditionally gave their fiancées distinctive miniature engagement rings, which they wore ever after along with their wedding rings. Mortified, Mazie realized that every woman she'd seen that evening had indeed been wearing one. She was sure that Tex would be "drummed out of the service" without delay.

He was not, of course; and their marriage survived such rocky first steps with grace.

* * *

Shortly after Tex's and Mazie's wedding, the pace began to pick up in East China. Once again, Chennault had finally stored up enough fuel and spare parts for the group to advance to their eastern fields and renew the offensive. Johnny Alison led the 75th out to Lingling, while the 16th moved into Kweilin. Hengyang remained unoccupied for a time, and the 74th and 76th stayed in western China at Yunnanyi and Kunming.

The Japanese responded immediately to the move. On the first day of April, they sent ten "Oscars" and two of the new Nakajima Ki-44 Shoki fighters, nicknamed "Tojos," to strafe Hengyang and Lingling. Rising in defense, 75th Squadron pilots shot down five of them in flames; but Lieutenant Burrall Barnum was killed when a Japanese fighter collided with his P-40 in midair.

At Chungking that week, Chennault had a second star pinned upon his shoulders, reflecting his recent promotion and broader command. He was now a Major General, commander of the Fourteenth Air Force.

Over the Hump from India, new aircraft began to arrive for the Fourteenth. These were B-24 Liberators of the 308th Bombardment Group; the massive bombers were going to give Chennault's forces a punch that had been missing for a long time. Unfortunately, the monsoon rains of early spring had turned all but one of the western Indian airfields into a morass of mud and water. Gasoline and supplies flown over the Hump for the B-24s shrank woefully in March, and were only a pittance by early April.

The beautiful Sale family home, Victoria, Texas, built in 1851.

Tex and Mazie's Wedding Day.

Chapter 25

PROVING GROUND

When Tex and Mazie flew from Washington to Eglin Field a few days later, Tex discovered that there wasn't much of a "base" to speak of; it was missing basic amenities (such as an officer's club). There were quarters for married officers, but the ones Tex and Mazie were to take were undergoing renovation. In the interim, they did what many of the single officers were doing: rented rooms in a large frame house in the nearby town of Valparaiso, from a Mr. Mears. The place was in an area called Shalimar, right next door to a lively nightclub, and was already occupied by several other bachelors, some of them—much to Tex's delight—old "China hands." Tex and Mazie occupied the place's attic, sleeping on pallets, while the lower floors were left to the bachelors. It was a strange arrangement, nearly driving the other men crazy while it lasted. At last, Tex's and Mazie's base quarters were renovated, and they moved in—to everyone's relief.

At that time, the panhandle coastline of Florida was practically virgin beach; Fort Walton consisted only of a few seaside shacks. From Eglin, it was only an eight-minute drive to the Gulf of Mexico. Tex and Mazie often sat out on the wide, idyllic strand, watching and listening to the wheeling gulls and crashing waves. Occasionally a Navy ship could be seen, far out on the water.

Their quarters at Eglin were across the street and several houses down from the residence of the base commander, General Gardner. Other officers' wives had quietly informed Mazie that when she had an opportunity, it would satisfy proper etiquette to call upon the commander's wife. One warm spring morning, as Mazie was gardening in the yard with her usual energy, she noticed Mrs. Gardner's car pull into its driveway, and thought: *What a perfect time to go over and visit!* Dropping her spade and hastening barefoot across the street, she hailed Mrs. Gardner just as the chauffeur was closing the car door behind her.

"Mrs. Gardner! Hello, Mrs. Gardner, I'm Mazie Hill, Tex Hill's wife. We've just arrived; Tex commands the Proving Ground Group," she announced, beaming.

The base commander's wife turned toward her slowly, showing little indication of a smile as she looked over the sweating young woman before her. Mazie was clad in shorts and had her hair pulled back in a ponytail. Smudges of dirt from her gardening were everywhere. A few seconds of silence passed.

"Come in the house," intoned the older lady.

Mazie followed her, smiling, imagining Mrs. Gardner had a nice little visit in mind. When they stood in the immaculate entrance hall, Mrs. Gardner turned to face her young neighbor. She gestured to a "low boy" table sitting against the wall; on it was a silver tray, containing a number of calling cards.

"Do you see that?" she asked.

"Yes," replied Mazie.

"When you call on the commanding officer's wife, young lady, you wear white gloves, and you leave your card."

That was all. Mazie felt her face flush, and nearly burst into tears on the spot—but she did not. Leaving the house, she resolved not to call on the commander's wife again. When she later met General Gardner, he was very friendly and—Mazie thought—a little apologetic. Apparently he had learned of the incident, probably from the chauffeur, who had overheard every word. As was her nature, Mazie did not let it bother her for long.

Tex, meanwhile, was finding his new command very satisfactory. Within a short time, he had checked out in every major variety of Army fighter plane and then some: new models of his beloved P-40, the Lockheed P-38 *Lightning*, the Bell P-39 *Airacobra*, the Republic P-47 *Thunderbolt*, the British *Spitfire*, and the brand-new North American P-51 *Mustang*. It did not take him long to become familiar with all of these.

Tex was especially impressed with the P-51, which represented a revolution in fighter aircraft design. This fact was even more amazing since North American, a company that had never tried its hand at building fighters, had designed it. Rushing from design to production in just over one hundred days, the P-51 "A" model was equipped with the trusty Allison V-1710-81 engine that had serviced the P-40 so well. With a laminar flow wing and radiator "scoop," however, the early *Mustang* could hit 390 mph and top thirty-one thousand feet without any trouble.

Those impressive numbers turned out to be just the beginning. Before Tex left Eglin, the "B" model arrived. The Allison engine had been replaced by a Rolls-Royce Merlin, another liquid-cooled power plant that delivered 1380 horsepower. Armament consisted of four .50-caliber wing guns, and reinforced racks beneath the plane could carry 1000-lb. bombs. An 85-gallon extra fuel tank nearly tripled the aircraft's range, to a whopping 1300 miles. Best of all, the Merlin engine allowed the P-51B to soar to forty-two thousand feet and hit a top cruising speed of 440 mph in a "clean" configuration. Tex couldn't wait to meet the Japanese in one of these.

Part of his duties included flying the "heavies" as well; and among the bombers Tex learned to pilot were the Douglas A-20 *Havoc*, the Boeing B-17 *Flying Fortress*, the Consolidated B-24 *Liberator*, the North American B-25 *Mitchell*, and the Martin B-26 *Marauder*.

After some time, Tex was able to plan and execute a landmark event in inter-service cooperation. Although Eglin Field was only a short distance from Pensacola, the Army and Navy had almost never allowed their aircraft to participate in joint aerial activity of any kind. Part of the reason was the old rivalry between the two services, dating back to their beginnings. But with Tex's Navy background and current Army position, he was able to bridge that gap; he knew many officers throughout Naval aviation by the time he left the fleet for China. After talking to a few old acquaintances at Pensacola, Tex convinced them to bring a number of Navy aircraft to the Proving Ground.

None other than Charles Lindbergh, the man who had crossed the Atlantic non-stop in the "Spirit of St. Louis" some years before, provided the impetus for the joint exercises. Lindbergh was now a top man in the United Aircraft Corporation, which had contracted with the U.S. government to build a new "super fighter." To accomplish this, United wanted to compare the performance specs of as many aircraft as possible, picking out the best characteristics to work into the planned new aircraft. That was where the joint Army-Navy air exercises came in. When the training event concluded after many test flights and mock dogfights, it was assessed as a huge success. Afterward, though, the planned United "super fighter" never materialized; Tex never figured out why.

Five of the former AVG ground crew, upon their return to the States, had decided to enter Army aviation training. When Tex learned of it, he approached General Gardner and asked for permission to get them assigned to the Proving Ground Group when they graduated. Gardner agreed, and Tex was able to secure three of them: former radiomen William Sykes and Rolland Richardson, and armorer Don "Rode" Rodewald, who had been so instrumental in working on the dive-bombing project back at Kunming. Tex believed the men would make fine test pilots, and he was absolutely right. Tragically, however, Bill Sykes crashed to his death in a trainer aircraft, on the day of his graduation from flight school.

A more difficult decision confronted Tex when Ajax Baumler returned from his combat tour in China that spring. Learning that Tex was at the Proving Ground, Baumler contacted him and asked if Tex could bring him into the unit. After thinking it over, Tex felt he had to refuse. He knew Ajax was an outstanding pilot and administrator, literally talented enough to be Chief of the Air Force. But his disastrous drinking incidents were too much to bear. Tex was amiable enough toward Baumler, but he wanted no part of the inevitable consequences of taking him in.

Spring gave way to a gloriously hot Florida summer, and Tex and Mazie spent plenty of time on the beach. Relaxing there with friends one Sunday afternoon, Tex was surprised to see a lone P-51 winging its way over the water. He squinted, blocking the sun with his hand to get a better look. The *Mustang* had to be from Eglin—which meant it was one of his.

Suddenly the aircraft went into a dive, leveling out right on the water and doing a barrel roll just above the ocean swells. Then it climbed again, beginning a series of loops, turns, and spins worthy of any air show in the country.

Tex couldn't believe it. Whoever the guy was, he was an amazing pilot. He was also breaking every rule in the book. The P-51A was a new aircraft, still in testing; and it was only to be flown by designated test pilots. Solo stunts at wavetop height were definitely taboo, but none of the test pilots in Tex's group could have put on a performance like this anyway. When he found the nearest telephone, Tex called base operations, telling them to ground the unknown pilot immediately upon landing and figure out what was going on.

The following morning, Tex's curiosity was satisfied. The mystery pilot was Major John C. "Pappy" Herbst, a hotshot aviator assigned to a specialized Arctic-Desert-Tropic unit. He had been attached to the Proving Ground Group to get his flying time. While Tex appreciated the man's skill in the cockpit, he couldn't simply let the incident pass. He approached Colonel Winslow "Winnie" Morse, General Gardner's deputy, and recommended that Herbst be grounded for thirty days—essentially a "slap on the wrist" for the pilot. Morse agreed, and Tex thought no more about it—until later, when he returned to China.

The Proving Ground Group's Special Weapons Section was often the most interesting to observe in operation; intriguing new equipment arrived constantly to be tested. That summer, a number of curious-looking crates were unloaded at Eglin from a Consolidated C-87 *Liberator Express* (a transport version of the B-24) and toted into the hangars. When crewmen opened them up, they discovered the crates contained prototype models of the new M-9 rockets.

For the next several months, the section tested the rockets extensively. They proved to pack quite a wallop on their target—if they hit the target. The rockets' erratic flight reminded Tex of the old naval torpedoes he used to drop from the TBD. Occasionally, the M-9s did a complete about-face and zoomed back in the direction they came from. Launching them in combat would be a gamble, to say the least. The early models were fired from metal tubes that would weigh down a fighter plane, greatly reducing its speed and maneuverability. Plastic tubes were designed shortly thereafter, which were an improvement, but still not satisfactory. Eventually, the engineers got rid of the tubes altogether and mounted the rockets on rails; this "zero rail" configuration proved most effective.

Late in the summer, one of the more unique airplanes arrived at the Proving Ground: the Culver PQ-8 *Cadet*. It was the product of early experimentation with remote-control aircraft; several PQ-8s could be remotely "flown" from an airborne "mother ship." A pilot remained in the PQ-8 in case there were any problems, and could take over the controls if necessary. When Tex checked out in the PQ-8, he was somewhat nervous; the aircraft proceeded to take off down the runway, while he sat and did absolutely nothing. During flight, he continued to ride "hands-off" as the plane performed some basic maneuvers, then came in for a tolerable landing, without Tex having even touched the stick. He shook his head. The PQ-8 might be an engineering triumph, but it didn't *feel* right to a combat pilot.

Whenever he got the chance, Tex flew from Eglin back to Kerrville to visit his family. Sometimes he took Mazie along and drove to Victoria as well. They enjoyed those visits, with Tex especially welcoming the chance to range out into the hill country for some hunting. It was the pastime he had missed most in China; and in the Florida lowlands, there wasn't much game running around either.

Occasionally, Tex was ordered up to Washington, D.C. for official business or a formal function. For those trips, he usually took a B-25 or stagger-winged C-43 *Traveller*.
He became well versed at flying the "heavies" on the overland hops.

On one occasion, retired Major James Edgerton, one of the first Airmail pilots in 1918 and now assigned to the Proving Ground Group, approached Tex with a request.

"I'm supposed to be the guest of honor at the 25th Anniversary of the Air Mail Dinner in D.C.," Edgerton explained. "Any way you could take me?"

"Sure," Tex replied.

He had just checked out in the C-43, a light transport aircraft, and figured this would be a good chance to get some cross-country flying time in it. As the two neared Atlanta in the air, however, they encountered dreadful weather; the sky was "socked in" all the way up the eastern seaboard.

"Well, I can get you there anyway," Tex said, looking at Edgerton, "but it's going to be a pretty hairy ride."

Edgerton indicated he'd take the chance. Tex sent the aircraft down onto the deck to fly "contact." Hundreds of very rough miles later, they landed in pouring rain in Washington D.C., and caught the first transportation available to the banquet. They made it—but the weather had delayed them enough that Edgerton was too late to deliver his speech.

It was also during this time that Tex had a chance to view the 1942 motion picture "The Flying Tigers." It was a gory, over-stylized, cornball story of the AVG. It starred John Wayne, whose character was based upon Tex himself. The film's script was written with "technical advice" from two dishonorably discharged members of the Flying Tigers; it came across as highly positive, if thoroughly "corny." Moviegoers loved it. They were desperate for any portrayal of American success in the war, which, at the time, the Allies were losing on every front but China. Tex knew the filmmakers' intent, but he still had to chuckle and shake his head at the "over-the-top" acting.

Summer passed, and fall moved quickly by. Tex asked General Gardner to acquire Ed Rector, who was looking for a new assignment, having been stateside for some time. When Rector arrived, the two friends had another joyous reunion; Tex could think of no one he was happier to work with. The Proving Ground was starting to look like a collection of old China hands.

There came a night in November when Tex and Mazie were awakened by someone knocking urgently on their front door. Tex fumbled for the light and looked at a clock. It was eleven p.m.

"What on earth?" wondered Mazie aloud, as Tex pulled on a robe and padded out into the entrance hall. He opened the front door.

"I'm sorry to disturb you, sir, but General Gardner sent me," the orderly standing on the porch said. "He's just had an urgent wire, and requests that you meet him at his quarters."

Tex looked down the street at the general's house; sure enough, the light was on. At this hour, it must be important; so Tex didn't bother putting more clothes on as he thanked the orderly, slipped on some shoes, and walked over. Gardner was waiting for him.

"Take a look at this, Tex. It's from Chennault," said the general, handing him a copy of a message.

Tex read it with growing excitement: Chennault was requesting that Tex be transferred back to Fourteenth Air Force, asking General Gardner to release him.

"Looks like...the Old Man needs me back in China," Tex said quietly, looking up at his commander and offering back the paper.

"You can keep it. I'm guessing you want to get going as soon as possible," replied Gardner, with a knowing smile.

"Yeah...yeah, I do. I appreciate that, sir," said Tex. His mind was already spinning. *Back to China—!* But it was time. He had enjoyed his assignment at the Proving Ground;

but if Chennault needed help, Tex was ready.

* * *

Two weeks after Tex's and Mazie's arrival at Eglin, Allied codebreakers learned of a Japanese bomber flight scheduled to carry Admiral Isoroku Yamamoto on a tour of his Pacific bases. A flight of P-38s intercepted it. After a short chase, the man responsible for masterminding the attack on Pearl Harbor was shot down in flames by Captain Rex Barber.

In spite of the lack of fuel coming over the Hump, Fourteenth Air Force aircraft strength was growing as more planes, mostly well-used P-40Ks, bolstered their numbers. Chennault put Casey Vincent in charge of the East China Task Force (Forward Echelon), responsible for all operations east of Chungking. The Rear Echelon covered the area from Kunming westward into northern Burma.

Near the end of April, the Allies' Trident Conference convened in Washington D.C., with both Stilwell and Chennault in attendance. The two had conflicting views of how the war should proceed in their theater; so each was given a chance to present his plan. Stilwell called for a troop buildup to invade and retake Burma, thus reopening a land route into beleaguered China. Chennault believed this would take too long, arguing instead that supplies over the Hump be sharply increased and heavy bombers moved into China to hit Japanese shipping and—eventually—the home islands themselves. Roosevelt decided in favor of Chennault, and ordered that Fourteenth Air Force be given priority on supplies coming over the Hump.

At Lingling in China, a rising star in the 75th Fighter Squadron named John Hampshire was shooting down Japanese planes as fast as he made contact with them. As his victory totals soared, many considered him the most brilliant fighter pilot to fly in the theater. Hampshire had racked up an incredible twelve aerial kills in his first six missions—when one day, three dozen enemy fighters descended upon Lingling. Hampshire had his finest day yet, knocking down his thirteenth and fourteenth planes and damaging three more.

Then his number came up: swarmed by enemy aircraft, he was hit in the stomach by 12.7mm bullets that punctured his cockpit. Hampshire crash-landed on a sandbar in the Siang River, trying to stay alive while flight surgeon Ray Spritzler, at tremendous personal risk that earned him the Soldier's Medal, stuffed himself in the baggage compartment of Joe Griffin's P-43 and lifted off at night to save Hampshire. Word came in while they were en route: John Hampshire was dead. The 75th had lost one of its best.

In May, the ground front in East China came suddenly to life as the Imperial Japanese Army opened a campaign from their Tungting Lake bases. One force drove westward toward the capital of Chungking and the airfields at Chengtu, while another pushed south down the Siang River to capture the troublesome Fourteenth Air Force bases. Battle was joined on both fronts, and Chinese troops resisted furiously. Fourteenth Air Force fighters flew close support missions for them day and night, while bombers hit strategic targets behind Japanese lines. By the end of May, the enemy offensive had ground to a halt, and the American aircraft continued to pound Japanese troops as they retreated back the way they had come.

During the summer of 1943, the eastern China sky seemed filled with fighter aircraft. The Japanese 3rd Air Division mounted an effort to drive the Fourteenth Air Force once more from their three forward bases on the Siang River. Time after time they sent dozens of "Oscars," "Tojos," and improved "Nates" to engage and strafe the Americans; but each time, the Japanese were sent home with losses and scant success. During the heaviest fighting, the enemy extended his attacks to Kunming, and ranged out to the satellite Fourteenth bases of Suichwan, Kanchow, Chihkiang, and Shaoyang. But at summer's end, they had to admit failure: even the commander of the Japanese Army Air Forces himself had been shot down and killed by a P-38.

For its part, the Fourteenth Air Force spread out to carry the offensive to the Japanese whenever they had enough gasoline and flyable aircraft. In Indochina, they blasted Hanoi and Haiphong Harbor, and long-range B-24s raided previously unreachable Hainan Island. Canton was a favorite target, with P-40s and B-25s regularly hammering Tien Ho and White Cloud Airdromes, and Liberators sinking ships and ravaging the wharves at the Whampoa and Kowloon Docks. To the north, the Americans strafed sampans on Tungting Lake and enemy troops at Changsha, ranging as far as Ichang and Kingmen to frag-bomb Japanese trucks, tanks, and trains moving to the battlefront. Up the Yangtze they flew, raiding Pailuchi and Hankow time after time to devastate Jap supply areas, skimming across Poyang Lake to bomb ships at Kiukiang and locomotives at Nanchang.

As the monsoons arrived in October and the Fourteenth paused to regroup, Tex passed command of the Proving Ground Group to Ed Rector, and headed for Miami to catch his flight overseas.

Tex and Mazie (on Tex's right) during sittings for a portrait by Baskerville at the Pentagon, 1943. Also shown is Lafayette Escadrille pilot Chuck Kerrwood. The portrait still hands in the Pentagon today.

Flying Tigers Charlie Bond, Tex Hill, and Ed Rector. Original photo taken 1943 in Washington, D.C. when Lord Halifax awarded the trio the British Flying Cross for gallantry in Burma. Decades later, "coincidental" photo taken and superimposed by Gordon Johnson.

Chapter 26

THE HAMMER FALLS

"Tex! By golly, it's been a long time. How are you?"

Tex turned to see a man in an Army uniform—a Colonel—approaching him. He looked familiar, but Tex couldn't place him. He stopped, and the two shook hands.

"Well, I'm fine, thank you, sir," Tex replied.

He was usually good with names, and his mind was racing to recall the other man's identity. In his mind, he pictured his old home at Hunt, his sister getting ready to go on a date, a cadet walking through the door—

"Bill Fisher!" Tex exclaimed, and the other man's smile widened. Tex continued, "Well, I'll be darned. Every time I go to the Far East, I seem to run into somebody who used to date my sister." The two men chuckled.

"The Far East, eh? It so happens I'm going that way too," said Fisher. "I've got to report to General Chennault over at Fourteenth Air Force."

"Is that right! Well, I'm doing the same thing!"

Before long, the pair was deep in conversation, filling each other in on the whereabouts and doings of mutual friends. The two of them were about to board a transport plane in Miami, and once their long flight was underway, they would appreciate each other's company.

The transport flew south to Belém, a Brazilian city at the mouth of the Amazon River, then out into the Atlantic. They refueled on Ascension Island before continuing on to Africa; and from there, Tex found they were retracing his steps of eleven months before. In Karachi, India he crossed paths with Bruce Holloway, who was awaiting transport back to the States. Holloway had a tip for Tex.

"I've done some reconnaissance work on Formosa," he declared, fixing Tex with his ice-blue eyes. (Holloway was referring to the Japanese-occupied island off the southeastern coast of China that would one day become Taiwan.) "Let me tell you, that place is jammed with Jap aircraft. If there's any way you can get a raid over there, it could really hurt them."

On the 3rd of November, Tex and Fisher touched down at Kunming. Stepping from the C-47, Tex sucked in a breath of chilly mountain air. He had returned to China.

As the two made their way to Chennault's headquarters, Tex was amazed at the number of Army Air Forces administrative personnel that moved back and forth on hurried errands. It looked like the operation had grown many times in size since the year before; and he found it somewhat disquieting. Were all these "paper-pushers" really necessary?

They walked into a planning room in one of the buildings, where a handful of people moved about at various tasks. Charts and maps were everywhere, and stacks of orders and memoranda festooned the place. It was a far cry from the humble headquarters of the AVG. Chennault was there, discussing something with several officers in front of a huge wall map; but he turned with a smile when Tex approached.

"Good to have you back, Tex," the Old Man said, with a hearty handshake. Tex thought Chennault looked a little more careworn than he remembered, but the same old glint flashed in his eye. Tex introduced Bill Fisher, whom Chennault had not met. Then, without preamble, the Old Man directed their attention to the map and launched into a briefing. As ever, he was all business.

"Now, Bill, you're going to have the 308th Bomb Group—that's a heavy group with B-24s," said Chennault, barely glancing at Fisher. "We're going to start bombing Japan from these bases," he added, touching several locations on the map.

Bill Fisher sat blinking in incomprehension. He had no concept of the operation in China, and this "fire hose" briefing was like being thrown into the deep end of a pool. Tex tried to suppress a grin; Fisher would get along all right, when he had time to talk to some of the old hands to catch up.

"Tex, you're going to have the 23rd Fighter Group," Chennault was saying. "A few days ago, we got some intelligence from the field about a big Jap ground offensive building up in the Tungting Lake area. The boys in the 23rd are already hitting the enemy on the ground wherever they find them." Chennault went over a few more points, then turned Tex and Fisher loose to make arrangements for getting to their forward-deployed locations.

"I'm sure we'll be seeing plenty of each other," said Tex, shaking Fisher's hand in parting.

The command structure, Tex soon learned, had been rearranged since his previous tour. The 23rd Fighter Group now consisted only of its three original squadrons. The 74th, commanded by Captain Paul Bell, remained at Kunming to attack targets in northern Burma and escort 11th Bomb Squadron B-25s on their missions. Major Elmer "Rich" Richardson led the 75th, Tex's old outfit, from Kweilin, which was also the site of the 23rd's headquarters. The 76th was split between operations at Hengyang and Suichwan, a recently completed forward base less than a hundred miles southeast of Hengyang.

P-51As had already begun to trickle into China, and pilots of the 76th were gradually checking out in the first two dozen or so. The 76th's commander, Capt John "Willie" Williams, was plenty proud to have the first squadron in China flying the *Mustang*.

The 51st Fighter Group, which had remained so long in India, had moved into China by then as well. It mainly supported Rear Echelon operations to the west, and included the 25th and 26th Fighter Squadrons, as well as the veteran 16th and P-38-equipped 449th. Bill Fisher's 308th Bombardment Group was operating mostly out of Chengkung and Chengtu to the northwest.

Such was the array of Fourteenth Air Force strength at Chennault's command; when compared to the freewheeling days of the AVG, it was vast indeed.

Tex soon learned that his worries about the size of the expanded headquarters in Kunming were well founded. There were very nearly more personnel there than in all the operational squadrons combined. Considering the monumental difficulty of getting enough supplies over the Hump to support fighter and bomber operations alone, Tex wondered how the Old Man could allow himself to be saddled with scores of orderlies, clerks, and other administrative personnel. Chennault had always disliked paperwork before; maybe, Tex speculated, he was feeling pressure from "higher up" to put more effort into it.

The supply situation in China remained a cause of great concern. With a good deal more aircraft, and especially the B-24s, Fourteenth Air Force's gasoline consumption and requirement for spare parts had "spiked" enormously. Mercifully, the tonnage transported over the Hump had also expanded after the Trident Conference decision. The net result was roughly the same as it had been a year before: there was rarely enough of anything. China was still on the end of the world's longest, most bottlenecked supply line; until the very end of the war, "doing more with less" would be the watchword of Chennault's men.

In another day's time, Tex had checked out in a P-40 once more, and flown into 23rd Fighter Group headquarters at Kweilin. Chief and southernmost of the three forward bases, Kweilin was located a short distance from the Li River, straddling the seemingly endless railroad that ran from Hangchow on the shore of the East China Sea to Hanoi in Indochina. The town's particular locale in Kiangsi province featured unique geography: the region was studded with curious limestone hills that looked like the tops of giant ice cream cones. Anyone who had been there could immediately recognize that part of China. Bored into the base of one of those hills was a large natural limestone cave, which had served as an operations room for Chennault in days gone by; now, it was the "war room" for the Forward Echelon and 23rd Fighter Group.

After moving into his quarters at Kweilin (a short process indeed), one of Tex's first priorities was to visit each 23rd Fighter Group base. He wanted some idea of the status of operations at each one of them. As he "toured" the familiar sites, he was amazed at how young the airmen looked. Were these kids old enough to enlist? Tex wasn't sure. The men, in turn, seemed to view Tex as something of a legend suddenly incarnated before their eyes, and were thrilled to shake hands and get a look at him. Tex saw immediately that while the faces might be new, the 23rd was full of eager troops who seemed ready to follow their veteran commander. Tex would be especially impressed, then and afterward, with the squadron commanders: men like Johnny Alison, Bob Liles, John Lombard, Phil Loofbourrow, Elmer Richardson, Ed Goss, Don Quigley, and Grant Mahony. They were the backbone of the 23rd's fighting spirit. No one, it seemed, was a "sorehead"; everyone pulled together, and it would make all the difference in the months to come.

There were a few "bad apples," unfortunately. One was a pilot in the 449th, who had crashed flying a B-25 while assigned to a unit in the Middle East. He had bailed out, but the rest of the crew never got the word; they were found dead still strapped into their seats. Later in China, he was shot down in a P-38 north of Hengyang, and had the good fortune to be rescued by Chinese villagers, who secreted him back through enemy lines to safety. When he returned to the States, the pilot was interviewed by the press—and, to the shock and horror of his companions back in the theater, he revealed the name of a village along the escape route he had used in China. Sure enough, Japanese intelligence picked up the story and sent troops into the village, where they butchered every man, woman, and child.

As Chennault had predicted, the Japanese were advancing out from their battle lines around Tungting Lake, on the offensive again. John Birch, Tex's onetime chaplain from his 75th Fighter Squadron days, had been a key agent in gathering intelligence on the campaign. Indications were that the enemy was sweeping south from Tungting Lake into the "Rice Bowl" of China, to forcibly confiscate food supplies needed for their armies. Tex's 23rd pilots began to bomb and strafe Japanese soldiers as they wound their way south by locomotive, truck, or foot. At the same time, a nearly opposite enemy offensive was driving from Indochina toward the recently completed auxiliary airbase of Liuchow. Tex had not been in China a week before he was "neck-deep" in planning missions to resist these moves.

One of the disappointments of Tex's group command was that his knowledge of strategic plans and future Allied moves made him, in the eyes of Chennault and Casey Vincent, too valuable to risk on every combat mission. On his previous tour, Tex's mode of operation had been to get in a plane and lead missions himself. Now, he was ordered to be more selective about when and where he flew—a mindset that did not come easily for him. On many occasions, he found some "reason" to be out in front of the most dangerous missions anyway; there was no stopping him.

Tex's methods of leadership remained the same as in his 75th Fighter Squadron days: getting around to meet and know his people, taking care of them, being the first in line for a tough job, and valuing combat performance above paperwork. Newcomers to his office in Kweilin took one look at his desk and scratched their heads; Tex's "In" box contained whole peanuts, while his "Out" box contained shells. When he was at the desk (which wasn't often), his feet were usually up on top of it. But when a hazardous mission came up, it was a good bet that Tex would be right in the middle, finding—or inventing—some reason to get involved.

He "warmed up" to combat flying again by leading a couple of fighter escort missions for bombers over Hankow. There, the Japanese were staging supplies for their siege of Changteh, up the Yangtze on the southwest shore of Tungting Lake. At Changteh, Chinese General Hsueh Yueh's starving defenders were desperately holding on as enemy troops tightened a noose around the city. On the missions over Hankow, Tex flew a new P-51A that had just been assigned as his personal plane; his crew chief decorated it with shark's teeth (impressive, though lacking the same effect as on the old P-40), and painted the name "The Bullfrog" along the side of the engine. It was one of Tex's pet names for Mazie.

As he escorted the 308th bomber crews on their missions, Tex began to get to know them. In spite of Bill Fisher's lack of experience in China, he was an outstanding bomber pilot who knew his work. His squadrons were full of standouts like Jack Edney and Jack Carey, who were a credit to combat flying. Fisher was also a man who enjoyed life's amenities, and he immediately got comfortable at Kunming. When he decided he wanted a tennis court next to his headquarters, Fisher sent miniature bulldozers to level the most likely spot—a Chinese graveyard. Bones flew in all directions.

One definite advantage of a bomber, Tex reflected on one visit to Fisher's headquarters, was that it could *carry* things. While Tex's fighter pilots were scraping by without basic PX supplies, the 308th was hauling in whatever it needed from India, in the cargo bays of its B-24s. After some head-scratching one day, Tex approached the 308th's commander with a proposition.

"Hey, Bill, I've got a deal for you," he said.

"What's that, Tex?"

"Well, I've got to hand it to you; you and your boys are living pretty "high on the hog" up here. But if you'll bring in some "rations" every once in awhile for my guys, I will personally escort you on any mission you choose. I'll fly right over your head."

Fisher was no dummy, and he jumped at the deal. "Hell, yes, Tex," he replied with a grin, shaking his hand.

In the months ahead, both men would feel sure they had the better end of the bargain.

Tex's boss was the commander of the Forward Echelon, Colonel Casey Vincent. The two had barely met the year before, on the eve of Tex's departure for the United States. Now they would work closely together in planning the operations of the 23rd. Vincent was one of the greatest officers Tex had ever met. He was strong and solidly built, sharp as a tack, and fearless. The following spring, Vincent would be promoted to general at the age of twenty-nine, carrying the burden of the entire air war in eastern China on his shoulders. Yet he would handle the position with outstanding aplomb, producing results of which anyone could be proud. Before long, Vincent moved Tex into his own house, a very small but well-constructed dwelling (it even featured indoor plumbing) near the airfield at Kweilin. Tex was vice wing commander for Vincent as well, and often took over Forward Echelon operations when Vincent was called to Chunking, New Delhi, or Washington, D.C.

On the 22nd of November, as his staff meeting convened at Kweilin, Vincent stood before a "blown-up" photograph of an airfield on the wall. Tex studied the photo with a practiced eye, noting that there were a lot of enemy planes on the field.

"Gentlemen," said the smiling Vincent with a gleam in his eye, "you see before you a photograph of Shinchiku Airdrome on the island of Formosa. There are eighty-eight bombers of the Imperial Japanese Navy lined up here, wingtip-to-wingtip." He looked around the room as the officers goggled, finally resting his gaze on his second-in-command.

"Tex, do you have any suggestions?" Vincent asked with a wink.

Tex smiled. "Let's get 'em!"

They needed no further discussion on that point; and the men put their heads together to decide what aircraft could make such a mission. No P-40 had the range to reach Formosa, even with extra fuel hung all over it; Suichwan, the closest Fourteenth Air Force base, was nearly three hundred miles from the island. In the end, the men figured that fourteen B-25s, eight P-38s of the 449th, and eight P-51As of the 76th were all of the airplanes in China that could make the trip. The Allies had never struck Formosa; Vincent's reconnaissance pilots had been taking pictures of it for months, trying to figure out a way to put a raid on it. Now, the arrival of the P-38s and P-51s in the theater provided that means; but they would still be "sailing into uncharted waters."

On the 24th of November, the day before Thanksgiving, a special camera-equipped F-4A took another snapshot of Shinchiku airdrome. Tex and Vincent practically drooled as they counted fully one hundred Japanese bombers on the main strip, with an even larger number of fighters parked on a side runway. Before the mission aircraft staged into Suichwan that evening, Vincent pulled Tex aside for a word.

"Tex, I want you to take charge of this mission," he said soberly. "It's got to be a secret. Don't even tell the men where you're going until you're about to take off. This one can't leak out to the Japs."

Tex nodded. He could well understand Vincent's concern, for the raid presented some particularly dangerous possibilities. The aircraft would be operating at the extreme limits of their range, even taking along extra fuel tanks to augment it. They would barely have the gas to make a couple of passes on the airfield before turning for home. If the Japanese were alerted and got airborne, drawing the raiders into a fuel-burning dogfight, not a single one of the Americans would make it back. Also, the mission would be navigating through an area with unpredictable weather patterns that created particularly rough crosswinds. On top of all that, in order to avoid detection, the final one hundred miles of the trip would have to be on the deck, right across the watery Straits of Formosa. Life preservers were about as common in China as Cadillacs—there were none. However, there were plenty of Japanese fighters who dreamed of catching the Americans at that altitude and "chewing them up."

"One more thing," Vincent continued. "When you get close to home, give me a call on the radio. If the mission fails, the code will be 'New York.' If it succeeds..."

"How about 'San Antonio?'" Tex said, grinning.

"'San Antonio' it is," Casey agreed.

As Tex prepared to depart from Suichwan the following morning, Thanksgiving Day, he went over the plan in his head. The B-25s, with their crews' navigation skills and equipment, were the best choice to take the lead on the way to the target. Once there, the P-38s would go in first with their heavy firepower to strafe the field. The *Mitchells* would follow them, dropping fragmentation bombs. The P-51s would cover the group in case of air attack, following the others in strafing runs if the coast was clear. After that, everyone had better be on the way back.

At nine a.m., after receiving a good weather forecast, Tex called the pilots together. They knew something big was in the wind, noticing the number of aircraft that had been collected at Suichwan, and they watched Tex intently. When he briefed them on the target, they could hardly wait to get off the ground.

The B-25s took off first. Eight of them were from the 11th Bomb Squadron, with Colonel "Preacher" Wells their leader; the remaining six, led by Colonel Irving "Twig" Branch, hailed from the newly-formed Chinese-American Composite Wing. In the nose of Wells' lead bomber rode *Life* Magazine correspondent Teddy White. Then Major Sam Palmer, commander of the 449th Fighter Squadron, led the eight P-38s off the ground. Finally, Tex took off with the eight P-51s of the 76th. When the formation was assembled, they headed out—first vectoring northward to deceive any enemy intelligence spotters below, then curving around to fly southeast.

In strict radio silence, Tex led the force of thirty aircraft toward the China coastline. After a couple of hours, they reached the coast and skimmed out across the Strait at a hundred feet altitude. The weather was good, and they had seen no enemy air activity. Tex eyed the water below, knowing that two U.S. Navy submarines had been alerted to the mission and were patrolling beneath the waves, ready to pick up American pilots if they were shot down or forced to "ditch." After twenty minutes over the water, the dark coastline of Formosa appeared on the horizon. The pilots took deep breaths and moved about in their seats, trying to shake the stiffness of the two-and-a-half hour flight. The fighters jettisoned their empty external fuel tanks. The "curtain" was going up; the mission was about to get much more interesting.

The planes pulled up to a thousand feet, and Formosa spread out before them. Shinchiku Airdrome was closer to the north end of the island, and the B-25s had pulled off near-perfect navigation: they were headed directly toward it. As the formation crossed the coastline, the P-38s accelerated away in front, and Tex dropped behind the bombers with the rest of the P-51s.

Suddenly the Americans spotted a plane coming up the coastline from the south. It was too big to be a fighter, and it couldn't possibly be American. Tex dispatched Sam Palmer in one of the *Lightnings* to vector in that direction and take it out. The pilot of the Japanese transport plane—for so it was—must have assumed the formation ahead of him was friendly, for he made no attempt to maneuver as Palmer blasted him with all five nose guns. Tex could imagine the look of numb surprise on the pilot's face as the aicraft turned into a fireball.

By the time Palmer rejoined the formation, Shinchiku Airdrome was coming into view. It looked just like the photographs: scores of airplanes crammed together in long rows. Now Tex could see, in the air north of the field, a flight of Japanese bombers strung out, just coming in to land. Ground crews awaited them on the runway with gasoline trucks and ordnance to be loaded. Also visible were enemy fighter crews, who apparently had just received warning of the incoming Americans; for they were running toward their cockpits and taxiing for takeoff.

Tex quickly directed the P-38s to take the bombers that were landing, while the B-25s pressed on with a run over the field. Tex himself adjusted course slightly and, with the rest of the P-51s, lined up to make a pass on the field right behind the *Mitchells*.

The fireworks were not long in coming. Sam Palmer's P-38s pounced on the Jap bombers, which were stuck helplessly in their landing pattern. Each *Lightning* opened up with four .50-caliber machine guns and a 20mm cannon in the nose, shredding the lumbering enemy aircraft one by one, right up the line. Bomber after bomber exploded and fell spinning to earth. When there were none left, the P-38s wheeled toward the main field.

Tex and the P-51s roared in behind the P-38s. Suddenly a Japanese *Zero* loomed up just ahead of Tex, flying directly away from him. A few Japanese pilots had somehow managed to get into the air. Tex raised his nose and lined up a relatively simple shot, directly into the rear end of the fighter, which was in the unenviable position of being barely airborne, slow, and fighting for altitude. Tex sent his tracers streaming into the enemy's tail and cockpit. Flames erupted from the *Zero* as Tex zoomed under it, and he barely avoided the now-falling fighter by breaking hard to the right. Behind him, Captain Paul Bell tore a second *Zero* to pieces; and as five more lifted off, they were each met by an avenging P-51. Seven *Zeros* soon lay in smoking ruin off the edge of the runway.

As Tex banked his *Mustang* around, he watched the *Mitchells* drone over the runway at a thousand feet altitude and release their fragmentation bombs. The hundred or so Japanese ground crewmen stared up open-mouthed, not believing the Americans could actually be overhead. When the frags hit the runway, the enemy's world came apart in a hellish maelstrom of exploding gasoline and flying shrapnel. Planes disintegrated in all directions, as the bomblets tore them up in a whirlwind of fury. The field became a sea of dark smoke, punctuated by flashes of detonating ordnance. Shinchiku was taking a pounding.

Tex picked out two bombers parked on the near side of the field that had escaped destruction. He walked the fire of his four machine guns right up to them and poured lead into both; but as he whipped past, they did not burn. The rest of his flight was right behind him.

The B-25s had already turned, winging their way back out toward the Straits; but the P-51s and P-38s weren't finished. They turned for another pass on the stricken airfield, eyes peeled for anything that still looked intact. Tex spotted another bomber on the far side, and held a medium-length burst into the fuselage until its fuel ignited and the plane erupted in fire. Other American fighters were descending like birds of prey upon various aircraft, expending their ammunition in a paroxysm of destruction before turning out to sea.

Tex was low on ammunition himself by now, but there was no reason to save any; he had no gasoline for a dogfight. As he made a final turn away from the field, he spotted a group of Japanese troops who had been bathing in a river that ran by the airdrome. Diving a final time, he raked the group with .50-caliber bullets; then he finally turned for home, his guns nearly empty. Behind him, smoke blackened the sky from scores of burning planes and vehicles, and Shinchiku was strewn with bodies.

At that moment, a round of ammunition "cooked off" in Tex's overheated guns. The sharp *bang* made him jump, and he instinctively "jinked" right, nearly putting the P-51 into the river. He looked around frantically to see who was shooting at him. When he saw no one and realized what had happened, he had to laugh.

All thirty planes touched down at Suichwan; incredibly, a lone bullet hole in one of the P-38s was the only damage they sustained. They had been five hours in the air, and their guns and gas tanks were empty; but they didn't care. Tex headed to the nearest radio to contact Vincent and the others listening back at Kweilin.

"San Antonio—in a big way," he drawled.

It had been a perfect mission, and Tex had become the first P-51 pilot to shoot down a Japanese aircraft.

Shortly after the raid, Casey Vincent sent a photoreconnaissance aircraft over to assess the damage. When the pictures came back, he was beside himself. Forty-three enemy bombers could be clearly counted burning on the runway; and between the bombers landing and the fighters taking off, another fifteen had been shot out of the air. The strike on Formosa was the most successful raid the Allies had made in the China-Burma-India Theater. Angry Japanese radio broadcasts announced that "all but one of the American planes were shot down" in the action; the Americans knew that when the whoppers got that big, the Japs must have been hurt badly. Not missing the fact that it was Thanksgiving Day, Tex and his companions celebrated far into the night.

* * *

As Tex and the pilots of the Fourteenth Air Force were pounding Formosa, the Sextant Conference convened in Cairo. There the Allies, including Generalissimo and Madame Chiang, announced their support for Operation Twilight, a plan to bomb Japan from bases in China with new Boeing B-29 Superfortresses. *The only catch: Chennault* would lose his priority on Hump tonnage as supplies built up for the B-29s.

Thousands of miles out in the Pacific Ocean, U.S. Marines made a bitterly contested landing on Tarawa in the Gilbert Islands. Near the Solomons, a huge contest was taking place for Rabaul and New Guinea. For the first time in their Pacific campaign, the Japanese were suffering setbacks on land.

Within a month after the Formosa raid, Tex was promoted to full Colonel, making him one of the youngest in the Army Air Forces at twenty-eight. When the Forward Echelon became the 68th Composite Wing in January, Tex assumed the duties of vice wing commander as well. For his leadership of the raid on Formosa, Casey Vincent requested that Tex be awarded the Distinguished Service Cross; but Stilwell's headquarters rejected the proposed decoration, and "knocked it down" to yet another Distinguished Flying Cross.

Back in the United States, Mazie kept busy performing volunteer nurse's aide work at the hospital in Victoria. On an extended summer visit to her cousins in Louisville, Kentucky, she took a course in an experimental form of treatment for victims of polio, which was rampant in children at the time. Mazie spent many hours in the Crippled Children's Hospital, pressing steaming rags onto the degenerated muscles of the disease's small victims, telling them stories during the procedure to ease their discomfort. The treatment eventually proved ineffective, but the children never forgot Mazie; for years afterward, she received letters from them communicating heartfelt thanks for her care.

Newly promoted to Colonel at age 28, with Ed Rector. Tex and Casey Vincent were responsible for the entire eastern China air campaign.

Photo of Shinchiku Airfield, Formosa, immediately after Tex led the strike mission, November 25, 1943.

Chapter 27

ICHI-GO

Tex cruised south at twenty thousand feet in the "Bullfrog," down the railroad from Hengyang to Canton. Behind him were three P-51As of the 76th Fighter Squadron, and they were looking for a scrap. After touting the virtues of the *Mustang* to these pilots as they checked out in it, Tex was leading them toward Hong Kong and enemy territory to see if he couldn't demonstrate how good the new fighter was.

In the early part of 1944, it was easy for the 23rd Fighter Group to goad the Japanese into an aerial battle. It was becoming rare for the Japs to go on the offensive and raid Fourteenth Air Force bases; but they could always be counted on to protect their staging areas at Hankow and the docks at Canton and Hong Kong. If the Fourteenth showed up, they would soon have a "welcoming party."

The quartet of P-51s began to fan out and look for enemy aircraft. One flight officer stayed on Tex's wing, while 76th Squadron commander "Willie" Williams and Lieutenant Bob Colbert paired off together. As they sped south over Canton, Williams suddenly "called out" three Japs, off to their left and slightly above them. Tex looked— and looked again. They were Japanese fighters all right, but he had never seen the type before. It was his first glimpse of the new Ki-44 *Shoki*. The four *Mustangs* broke left neatly and bored ahead in a shallow ascent. Then the "Tojos" saw them—and pulled straight up into vertical climbs.

Tex hadn't seen any Japanese fighter do *that*, but he was sold on the P-51's capabilities. He pulled straight up after them, and his three companions did the same. It was a bad idea: the *Mustang* began to lose speed quickly as the Allison engine struggled, and soon Tex realized he was going to stall out any second. With a curse, he "bent it over" to turn his ebbing climb into a screaming dive; but that was just what the enemy fighters had been waiting for. They flipped over and charged downward like birds of prey on the diving P-51s. The "Tojos" had sprung their trap beautifully.

Colbert was the first to go, pieces of his aircraft flying in all directions as it was riddled by enemy bullets. The young man "hit the silk" just before his plane exploded. Williams had not much longer to stay in the air, bailing out as tracers blasted through his canopy. Finally the flight officer on Tex's wing bailed out too, his *Mustang* taking fatal damage. Then Tex was alone, with his three enemies feverishly intent on killing him. He twisted and rolled, using every trick he knew, plunging earthward all the while, watching tracers shoot past his airplane only feet away, desperately trying to make himself a difficult target. Checking six, he realized incredulously that the enemy pilot behind him was trying to overrun him in a *dive!* What were these things?

Bullets slammed into the fuselage and tail of his plane. His altimeter showed less than eight thousand feet, the minimum he needed to get back over the mountains to the north. As he was trying to decide whether to stay with the aircraft or bail out, the tracers suddenly stopped. Looking over his shoulder, Tex could see...nothing. The planes had vanished.

He leveled out, craning his neck in all directions. There was no sign of the enemy aircraft. They had miraculously broken off the attack, just when they had him dead to rights. *Thank you, Lord.*

Tex's P-51 was functioning more or less normally, but he had no idea where his other pilots were. He flew cautiously around the area to see if he could spot Williams or Colbert, but without success. There was certainly nothing salvageable about the mission; so he headed glumly back north, up the railroad toward Kweilin.

The *Mustang* was looking a bit like Swiss cheese as Tex, soaked with sweat from the close call, put it down on the runway. As he made his report and related the combat with the dangerous new fighters, concerned pilots of the 76th gathered around to listen.

"What did they look like?" asked one.

"Look like?" Tex echoed, managing a weak smile. "Well, they had a hell of a big engine, and big red balls on the wings!" It was all the description he could think of.

Williams and Colbert were both rescued. Williams had unhappily parachuted directly into the airport in Canton, but quick-thinking Chinese had immediately whisked him away to a hiding place. He returned to Kweilin a week later. Colbert had landed some distance to the north and sustained a bad bullet wound in his leg, but he too was returned in good time. Tex decided to fly over to Kunming and talk to Chennault about the disastrous dogfight.

"Sir, they've got a new fighter down there," he told the Old Man. "It whipped our P-51s pretty good. I don't know if we're going to be able to beat them in the air."

Chennault was nothing if not matter-of-fact, always boiling problems down to the simplest possible solution.

"Tex," he replied, "get them on the ground. Then you don't have to fight them in the air."

As usual, he was right.

Even if his headquarters had expanded to near-unmanageable proportions, the Old Man himself was still a master of the practical and the positive. He simply refused to consider the possibility of defeat. One time, just after Tex's return to China, he and Chennault took a transport to Kweilin to survey the site for operations. After hiding the aircraft in a revetment, the two men walked along a ridge above the airfield. They approached a battery of Chinese 40mm anti-aircraft guns concealed in the trees. Just as Tex and Chennault arrived, an air raid sounded, and the Japanese attacked. Finding no targets to strafe on the field, the enemy pilots decided to put on a little "air show" for the Chinese they knew were watching below. The Japanese aircraft began making acrobatic passes on the field, zooming right over the AA guns in the process; but the battery commander did not fire a single shot.

Amazed, Chennault stalked up to him. "Why don't you shoot those aircraft?" he asked.

"Honored Sir, we have orders not to shoot them," the commander replied politely.

"Why not?"

The man hesitated. "If we shoot at the planes, they will come back and attack us heavily. We cannot afford to lose these guns."

"Don't you realize," Chennault shot back emphatically, "that if you shoot that plane down, he *can't* come back?!"

Two days after Tex's brush with death over Hong Kong, Vincent sent him to Hengyang to take over fighter operations in support of the defense of Changteh. With Tex went the 74th Squadron, joining the 75th already at Hengyang. The siege of Changteh, on the southwest side of Tungting Lake, was not going well. Japanese assaults had worn the Chinese defenders past the point of exhaustion. The day Tex arrived at Hengyang, the Japs finally forced their way into the city and captured it.

That wasn't about to deter either Tex or the Chinese. The 74th and 75th began a series of strafing and bombing attacks that caught the Japanese off guard, hitting their equipment and vehicles throughout the city and all the way back along their supply lines. B-25s of the 11th knocked out troop and supply concentrations, while P-40s skimmed over Tungting Lake to strafe enemy sampans supporting the offensive. The P-40s also dropped food supplies, carried in specially constructed bamboo "belly tanks," to Chinese defenders on nearby Mount Tchsan. When the Japanese wavered under the aerial flurry, the Chinese armies rallied and counterattacked, recapturing the city in a rush five days after losing it. Throughout the rest of the month, the P-40s continued to hound the retreating Japanese troops; and by the year's end, the enemy had been driven back to the positions from which his offensive had begun.

The Japanese struck back at Hengyang two days later, sending a force of the new Kawasaki Ki-48 "Lily" bombers, escorted by Ki-43 "Oscars." The 74th and 75th met them with twenty-one P-40s; they shot down three of the bombers and several more fighters, sending the Japs home with no success to report. At Lingling, another enemy raid caught and burned several P-40s on the ground, but paid for it with several "Oscars" shot down in the air. For the next two days, the enemy kept returning to Hengyang, trying hard to deal a telling blow to the Americans; but the warning net performed admirably, and the Japanese had trouble catching the 23rd on the ground. In the air, though, several American pilots lost their lives, and then-Lieutenant Don Lopez lost half a wing in a mid-air collision with an "Oscar." But on the whole, the 74th and 75th gave much better than they got.

Christmas at Kweilin felt strange; the weather was hot, and the alert pilots kept one eye on the sky for enemy raids. But that evening, the men managed to throw a party all the same, bolstered by holiday "rations" from Bill Fisher and the 308th Bomb Group. As the hour grew late, Tex found himself in a game of dice with a few other officers. Eventually, Casey Vincent walked up.

"Pull up a seat, Colonel," said one of the men.

"Naw, it's late. Besides, as your C.O., I'd have a conflict of interests in this game.

Not to mention," he continued with a wink, "being a better player than any of you. I can't take your money."

Hoots and challenges sounded from the group, and they pulled their commander toward the floor and into the game. Vincent chuckled in resignation, and proceeded to join in.

He rose from the floor some time later, having cleaned the group out for some five hundred dollars in workmanlike fashion. Vincent laughed as he reached for his hat.

"I'd just like to say that I *did* warn you," he said.

The month of January passed in mostly foul weather, with little aerial activity. Tex led the 23rd's only major mission, escorting B-25s to Hong Kong, where they hit enemy shipping at the Kowloon docks. The *Mitchells* had begun to use a new technique called "skip bombing," which proved highly effective. They would dive from altitude and level out on the deck, firewalling the engine, heading directly toward an enemy vessel. After firing a few bursts with their heavy forward guns to clear the decks and suppress fire from the ship, they would release a bomb at top speed. As the B-25 would break away, the bomb would "skip" right across the water, crashing into the side of the ship to detonate. The results were tremendous, and it was fascinating to watch.

By the last week in January, the Fourteenth Air Force's intelligence personnel were buzzing. Field operatives had been observing a sharp increase in enemy troop strength around Hankow on the Yangtze River to the northeast; and at the same time, a similar buildup was occurring in Canton to the south. Chennault promptly warned Stilwell about the possibility of a large offensive later in the year; but at the general's headquarters, as usual, the Old Man's reports were virtually ignored.

The frantic pace of ground attack missions from Hengyang had tapered off with the recapture of Changteh, and the 23rd was afforded a bit of a "breather." When he was summoned to Casey Vincent's staff meeting one day, Tex took off from Hengyang and vectored southwest down the railroad toward Kweilin. As he neared Lingling, the weather was worsening, with the overcast descending steadily below a thousand feet. At best, he could traverse only one narrow pass between the mountains to reach Kweilin. Tex was weighing his options when he noticed a B-24 lifting off from the runway at Lingling.

In such weather, a fighter pilot would be foolish to enter the overcast. He could break out "on top," where the sky would be clear—but there would be no way to "let down" safely through the solid clouds below at his destination. On the other hand, the *Liberator* had navigation instrumentation on board that enabled it to do exactly that. Thinking himself fortunate, Tex listened to the radio conversation between the bomber and Lingling, then raised the other plane.

"Oboe Victor, this is Red Leader. Where are you headed?" Tex spoke into the mike.

"Red Leader, our destination is Point Gold." *That's Kweilin*, noted Tex with satisfaction.

"Oboe Victor, mind if I join you above the weather?" replied Tex.

"Glad to have you along," came the answer.

Tex started to move into position on the B-24's wing. He would have to "fly contact," keeping the other plane in sight at all times, to avoid becoming lost in the clouds.

Just as he was sidling up to the big bomber, Tex had the strangest feeling that he was making a mistake. G*et back down on that iron compass*, a voice seemed to say. *If you can't get through, go back and spend the night at Lingling*. Wondering if he was going crazy, Tex thought he'd better go with the sudden conviction.

"Oboe Victor, this is Red Leader. Ah...you guys go ahead. I'm going to stay down on the railroad after all."

"Suit yourself, Red Leader. Over and out." The bomber faded from view immediately as Tex winged over and dove back into the valley to pick up the railroad that led southward into Kweilin.

Less than sixty seconds later, every man on the B-24 was killed when it plowed into a mountain, not ten feet from the peak. The bomber had ascended in a straight line upward, rather than a safer spiral. Tex learned of the accident when he touched down at Kweilin, and the news dazed him. Someone had spared his life once more; it did not take profound wisdom to know Who it was.

On a day in early February, Tex was out near the runway when he noticed a number of familiar-looking crates being unloaded from a transport plane. They were the M-9 rockets, come to China at last. When he got a closer look, Tex saw that they were the earlier and more unreliable models that shot from a tube; but the 23rd Fighter Group couldn't afford to be choosy. After a few weeks of practice, the rockets became another weapon in the group's arsenal; the pilots blasted locomotives, buildings, and vehicles with them. The M-9s were just as unpredictable as Tex remembered, and thus limited in effectiveness. Wind and g-forces often combined to prevent them from releasing at all, causing them to "hang up" in the tube. When they did release, though, they were fairly accurate, and inflicted far more damage than a fighter's .50-caliber machine guns.

On the 5th of March, Tex and three of his pilots flew back over the Hump to India to retrieve a flight of P-51 "B" models that had just arrived. The extra fuel tank and improved engine would provide a large boost to the combat capability of the 76th Fighter Squadron. While there, Tex stopped in at Malerkotla to see an old friend. It was none other than Johnny Alison, back in the theater as deputy commander of the 1st Air Commando Group. Tex caught Alison on the eve of the 1st's massive glider lift operation into Burma. They were preparing to lift twelve thousand of General Orde Wingate's "Chindits" behind enemy lines; the jungle-wise troops intended to carry out an expanded version of Wingate's earlier guerrilla operation. Alison was happy to see his old commander, and gave Tex a briefing on the impending mission. The operation was fraught with danger, and would see great loss of life in the end; but Alison's confident eagerness had not diminished a bit.

On another ferry trip to fetch more P-51s, Tex learned firsthand how Chennault's immense headquarters staff was undermining the Old Man himself. As Tex's flight was preparing to return to China, he received a call from an officer in Fourteenth Air Force's operations division. The man told Tex that "the Old Man wanted" him to stage immediately out of Nanning and escort a force of B-25s on a raid of Sama Bay, on the shore of Hainan Island.

"I don't think that's real smart," Tex replied. "We're not a combat unit here. These guys just flew over to ferry the planes back to China. Hell, the planes haven't been boresighted, or maintained, or anything yet. This is not a good idea."

"I'm sorry you think so," came the reply. "The Old Man wants this mission run."

It didn't sound to Tex like anything the Old Man would have planned; he was sure that some "clown" up at headquarters had dreamed it up himself. Nevertheless, he reluctantly agreed, and led his flight southeast toward the auxiliary field of Nanning, rather than to Kunming for the inspection and maintenance new aircraft always received. When they landed at Nanning, Tex learned that the bombers were to show up the following day at a certain time.

As the hour approached the next day, Tex and his comrades played baseball while their planes sat ready to take off upon the B-25s' arrival. When a *Mitchell* emerged from the horizon and descended toward the field, the fighter pilots dropped their mitts and ran for their P-51s. But something was amiss: there was only one bomber. It taxiied in, and the pilot got out, shaking his head.

"We ran into some bad weather," he said glumly. "The other guys got scattered in it. They should be along soon."

Nanning's tiny airfield had no lights, and everyone knew a combat mission would have to return before dark in order to land safely. Time passed, and the bombers were nowhere to be seen. More time went by, and Tex was eventually certain they could not get to the target and back in daylight. There would be no way to see the field when they returned. Tex was not about to risk any of his planes and men so foolishly. He said as much to the crew of the single bomber that had made it, and lifted off with his entire flight to fly northeast—back to Kweilin.

Chennault was initially unhappy about the scrubbed mission; but when Tex gave him a full report, the Old Man realized it had been ill conceived. Unfortunately, it was not the only occasion that his staff failed to give him good information. Part of the problem was that his Chief of Staff, General Edgar "Buzz" Glenn, didn't take the time to visit the various Fourteenth bases to see what was going on. A good chief of staff in that position would have had his "finger on the pulse" of Fourteenth Air Force operations, able to pass along firsthand reports of issues and problems to his commander. Glenn preferred to stay at headquarters and let the men come to him. The result was that Chennault could not stay on top of the complex operation as well as he would have liked.

With the middle of April came events that permanently changed the face of the war for the Fourteenth Air Force. That spring, the Japanese high command considered their strategic position carefully. American carrier-based aviation and General George Kenney's 5th Air Force were operating in the southwest Pacific; that curtain of Allied airpower was moving steadily toward the South and East China Seas, and would exact a murderous toll on the Japs' precious shipping lanes. The medium and heavy bombers of Chennault's Fourteenth Air Force were already making life in that sector miserable, sinking hundreds of thousands of tons of shipping, month after month. To mitigate the vulnerability of her lifeline, therefore, Japan resolved to create a land route of supply that stretched from Indochina in the south to the old capital of Peiping in the north. Once it was in place, demands on their ocean shipping arteries could be relaxed somewhat.

The Japanese knew exactly what the primary threat to such a land supply route would be: the marauding pilots of the Fourteenth. That "thorn" had to be removed from their flesh. With good fortune, Japan's strategists calculated, she could accomplish three goals at the same time: clear the countryside of the infuriating Fourteenth Air Force bases; create a wide, safe line of supply all along the Hanoi-Peiping railroad (which ran through Hengyang, Lingling, and Kweilin); and force China into a long-sought surrender. The strategy's first step was already underway: an offensive from Burma toward the Hump bases in India's Assam Province, to tie down potential reinforcements for China's armies.

Top priority in the plan was given to the eradication of the Fourteenth Air Force bases, and this was reflected in the name the Japanese chose for the operation: *Ichi-Go*—

"Number One." The first phase of *Ichi-Go* called for the clearing of the northernmost segment of the railroad, from Hankow to Peiping. Being out of range of Fourteenth Air Force planes, this fifty-mile-wide lane was easily secured by the middle of May, with little effective Chinese resistance.

In the north, the main Japanese staging area for *Ichi-Go* was at Yochow, on the north side of Tungting Lake. Chennault knew from his intelligence agents that unprecedented levels of Japanese materiel were stockpiled there for use in the upcoming offensive; the field operatives had pinpointed exactly where these were. The Fourteenth conducted what raids it could on those massive stores; but the sheer quantity of supplies was so enormous that B-25s and P-40s hardly made a dent. Even the group of B-24s caused only moderate damage.

Chennault thought immediately of another option. The new B-29 *Superfortresses* were finally arriving in Chengtu. They were to be the instruments of Operation Matterhorn, the revised plan to bomb the Japanese home islands from China (still without fighter escort). To keep them out of Chennault's hands, "Hap" Arnold had assigned the heavy bombers to Twentieth Air Force, under his own direct command. Now, Chennault requested that they be used to put a saturation raid on Yochow. He knew the damage these aerial behemoths could inflict would be plenty to stop the coming offensive in its tracks, with a few good raids. One of those who agreed with the Old Man was Curtis LeMay, a Colonel who had just arrived with the first of the B-29s. But Arnold denied Chennault's request, flatly stating that the 20th was a "strategic air force," and would not be used on "tactical targets." The fate of East China inched closer.

On the same day the first B-29s arrived at Chengtu, Tex led the longest fighter escort mission in history up to that time. Jack Carey, an outstanding leader in the 308th Bomb Group, was taking a flight of B-24s far north of their usual targets, to knock out the only railroad bridge in the region that crossed the Yellow River. The bridge was four hundred miles north of Hankow; but with the extra 75-gallon fuel tanks on the P-51Bs, Tex and his fighters could just make the seven-hour round trip. They were mildly disappointed not to run into any aerial opposition, and had to be content to watch the show as the *Liberators* dropped several spans of the bridge with well-placed bombs.

It was too late to stop the first phase of *Ichi-Go*, but when miserable weather cleared on the 6th of May, the Americans countered the second phase's opening moves. Tex led a veritable armada of fighters (by China-Burma-India standards) on the mission, including P-51s, P-38s, and P-40s of the 76th, 449th, and 75th respectively. Along with the B-24s, there were fifty-four aircraft. Chennault was doing everything he could to hammer the Yochow staging areas before it was too late.

As usual, Tex and the fighters arrayed themselves in front of the bombers, to take on any enemy interceptors. As they cruised over Tungting Lake in heavy haze, Major Charles Griffith suddenly called out enemy fighters above and to the east. The P-51s turned toward them, lacking their accustomed altitude advantage, and engaged. Tex was flying a P-51B painted just like the old "Bullfrog" (which the "Tojos" had shot nearly to pieces over Hong Kong).

The haze gave the fight a spectral feel; enemy fighters appeared suddenly in the mist, and then were gone. Tex recognized them as "Oscars"; at full throttle, he snapped several shots at one that arced quickly through his field of view. Some of his .50-caliber bullets hit their mark; but apparently not fatally, as the Jap banked away into the haze.

In a patch of clearer sky, Tex spotted another enemy fighter, whose pilot must also have been trying to pick out the Americans in the eerie fog. Tex arrowed straight at him in a slight dive, approaching from the beam and opening fire before the "Oscar" could make an evasive maneuver. Bullets slashed into the canopy and fuselage, and Tex held the burst, closing on the Jap at over 400 mph. In another second, the enemy's engine caught fire and the right wing disintegrated; the little fighter entered a broken series of spins that ended in Tungting Lake below.

The haze made it difficult for Tex to rejoin the other fighters after the dogfight. The bombers had pressed on toward Yochow, plastering it with good results. Tex returned to Hengyang. That day's action would be his final aerial victory.

On the ground, the Japanese Army was about to explode south down the railroad out of Hankow any day. Their large-scale troop movements and preparations were unmistakable. At the same time, just as Chennault's men would require unprecedented quantities of fuel and supplies to counter the offensive, Fourteenth Air Force's share of the supply tonnage coming across the Hump was steadily dropping.

There were two reasons for this disastrous situation. First, the B-29s at Chengtu—and the four squadrons of gas-guzzling P-47s that came along to protect them—were unable to "fly in their own supplies" as originally planned, even with the conversion of some of the *Superfortresses* to tankers. Instead, Chennault was ordered to share his own fuel reserves with them. Second, General Stilwell repeatedly helped himself to the gasoline and equipment that was earmarked to be flown in to the Fourteenth; he wanted it to support his foundering campaign to retake Burma. In April, gasoline delivered to the Fourteenth Air Force was a small fraction of the allocated amount. There was even less in May.

Chennault knew what was coming from the Japanese, and he pleaded with Stilwell to send more fuel for his aircraft to defend eastern China. Stilwell refused to believe there was any "emergency," and declined to do so.

On the 26th of May, two hundred fifty thousand Japanese soldiers roared south from Hankow and engulfed Changsha. That city, defended once more by the redoubtable Hsueh Yueh, was all that stood between the Japanese and the first Fourteenth Air Force base in their path: Hengyang.

* * *

Along the India-Burma border, three days after Tex's trip to ferry back the P-51Bs, Japanese troops swarmed out from behind their fortified positions for a massive attack. Driving swiftly toward the Indian cities of Kohima and Imphal, they took Stilwell and the British completely by surprise. The enemy sped up the Chindwin River toward the Ledo road, still under construction by Stilwell's troops, and halted just short of the Assam-Bengal Railroad. Besieged but holding tenaciously at Imphal, the British were supplied by a hastily organized airlift operation called Stamina. *Other transport planes airdropped the 5th Indian Division into the area to relieve the defenders. On the first of June, British reinforcements finally broke the siege at Kohima.*

Virtually trapped in Burma by the sudden northward thrust of the enemy behind him, Stilwell pressed on with his own southeastward advance, cutting the Ledo Road out of the jungle. At the same time, General Frank Merrill led three thousand men on an incredible drive toward the key Burmese city of Myitkyina, capturing its airfield on the

17th of May in bitter fighting. His regiment-sized outfit afterward bore a nickname that would become one of the proudest titles in the history of combat: "Merrill's Marauders."

Meanwhile, to the west, the Japanese were on the verge of chopping the last supply route into China as they greedily eyed the plain of Assam Province spread out before them. Dotting that region were the precious airbases that comprised the western terminus of the Hump air supply route; only the stubborn British were in the way.

Far to the east at the Salween River gorge, the stalemate between the Chinese and Japanese was broken at last. Chinese forces on the eastern shore, designated "Y Force," crossed the river and attacked the surprised Japanese, pushing them back with initial success.

On the 6th of June, thousands of miles away, the shores of Brittany came alive with fighting on a scale rarely seen in history. The Allies were conducting the largest combined air, land, and sea operation in history, striving to gain a foothold in France. By the end of that hard-fought day, one hundred fifty thousand Allied troops were ashore at Normandy; the liberation of Europe had begun.

Texas 23rd Fighter Group commander, climbing into the "Bullfrog."

At a refueling stop before a bombing mission to the Yellow River Bridge, April 1944 (the longest fighter escort mission in history up to that time). L to R: Y.P. Tom, Jack Carey, Pavlasec, Link, Tex, Lewis. Carey, commander of the 375th Bombardment Squadron, wrote of this mission: "To Tex Hill, who shepherded our lumbering B-24s to the target in the hostile skies over China in WWII. Words cannot express the relief that we felt when we were told at the briefing that Tex and his boys would be riding 'shotgun.' The entire 308th Bombardment Group will be forever indebted to Tex. Many bomber crew lives were saved by your valiant protection. We, the survivors, say Thank You and God Bless."

Chapter 28

THE ROAD HOME

The city of Changsha was falling. Flying low over it on his way to Tungting Lake, Tex could observe the crumbling town and some of Hsueh Yueh's miserable defenders, making the best of their situation. The Chinese general had begun his defense with nearly one hundred fifty thousand men; but there were fewer each day, as the enemy's assaults took their toll. Against the Chinese pressed five divisions of the Japanese 11th Army, themselves only the spearhead of a much larger force that spread out on ether side of the city to surround it. The Japanese had artillery, armor, and enough firearms and ammunition to go around; the Chinese did not. In spite of Yueh's spirited reports to Casey Vincent that he would hold the city, Tex didn't see how it was possible. It was the 12th of June, and the handwriting seemed to be on the wall.

Tex's wildest dreams of horrible flying weather could not beat the soup the "Bullfrog" was cutting through at the moment. Rain washed down in sheets. The ceiling loomed at three hundred fifty feet, leaving airspace flat as a pancake in which to operate. Visibility was down to a few hundred yards. More or less on Tex's wing was Lieutenant Ted Adams, flying his first combat mission as a member of the 74th Fighter Squadron. Adams was incredulous that they would fly in such weather, but there was no alternative. The Chinese defenders at Changsha needed support so desperately that the 23rd Fighter Group couldn't afford to be grounded. Tex was taking Adams up to Tungting Lake to show him how to strafe enemy targets. He had learned in the Navy that it was possible to fly contact over water in bad weather without being severely affected by weather fronts, and was putting the knowledge to good use.

The Japanese, on the other hand, were grateful for the foul weather. It grounded their aircraft, but it was ideal for their soldiers and vehicles to move in concealment. The pouring rain brought the Japanese out in all manner of lake- and river-going vessels, in which they could slip southward along the route of advance with impunity.

Such at least was their belief; but they were mistaken. Tex and Adams stayed low on the Siang River, flying contact on the water and watching their prop wash kick up spray from the surface below. All at once, as they rounded a bend, a fifty-foot motorboat loomed out of the deluge before them, cutting slowly south against the current. The boat was packed so tightly with standing Japanese troops, Tex thought they resembled cordwood stacked on end.

Tex and the Japanese both reacted instinctively. Tex thumbed his gun switch on as he banked right, opening fire. At the same time, the jam-packed enemy soldiers struggled to raise their guns and take aim at their shark-mouthed attacker. The crack of rifle reports filled the air.

The P-51's machine guns churned the river's surface as Tex "walked" his fire right into the front of the motorboat. Slugs tore through the wooden bow and began to slam into the front ranks of the helpless Japanese soldiers. Adams watched in amazement as Japanese infantrymen flew out of the boat like matchsticks, Tex's .50-caliber gunfire bulldozing them right down the line. When the length of the boat was strafed and sinking, only a few survivors clung to floating chunks of wood or lay on the shattered deck. The whole thing had happened in seconds.

But Tex had problems of his own. As his fire reached the end of the boat, several Japanese bullets impacted his canopy—and a second later, it flew off into space. Instantly a torrent of rain lashed him at 250 mph, and the suddenly howling wind lifted the map that had been on his lap and slapped it onto his face as if it were glued there.

Tex knew he was vectoring straight for a high bank on one shore of the river. He pulled up sharply, completely blinded, feeling a brief jolt as something scraped his P-51's underbelly. Knowing he was now clear of the bank, he reached up and tore the map away. He saw with relief that he was more or less in level flight, heading away from the river. He throttled back. Rain was soaking him and the cockpit, his airspeed causing it to sting his eyes painfully. Craning his neck around, he could just see Ted Adams, still with him through the downpour; so he banked southward toward Hengyang. For today, the hunt was over.

When the two touched town at the base, Tex got out and examined his plane in the relentless rain. There were pieces of brush caught in the P-51's air scoop; he had come within mere inches of plowing into the riverbank. Ted Adams was aghast when he saw his commander's plane, with missing canopy and added greenery; and almost as shocked when he looked at the sopping Tex himself, who still carried the shreds of his map. Tex strode over and put a dripping hand on the young man's shoulder.

"I'll tell you one thing, Ted," said Tex with a grin, "nothing keeps you on your toes like getting shot at."

It was not the last mission for Tex that day, or for many days afterward. The entire group was pulling together in a massive effort to interdict Japanese troops as the enemy drove on buckling Changsha. In rotten weather, the men of the 23rd sped off their muddy runways four or five times a day, hunkering below the overcast and skimming up the river in pouring rain to blast the enemy wherever they could find him. They frag-bombed columns of soldiers moving along high roads between rice paddies, blowing them to bits as they looked for cover. With innumerable strafing runs, they sent every conceivable variety of junk, sampan, steamer, and motorboat to the bottom of the Siang River and Tungting Lake. There was no way for the aircraft to maintain large formations in the soup; so they flew contact on the river or railroad in ones and twos to hunt for the

Japanese. They shot the new M-9 rockets into larger water transports, blowing them to pieces; then emptied their guns into troops that clung to the wreckage. In conditions that were considered nearly suicidal for aircraft, they flew mission after mission, exacting a heavy toll upon the advancing enemy.

The Japanese fought back. Their strategy of moving in the bad weather was worthless, so they took to shooting everything they could at the approaching American planes. The danger of flying into the face of such ground fire to strafe was extreme; but the men of the 23rd did it again and again—because their leader did it without hesitation. They lost dozens of pilots; four squadron commanders were killed by ground and gunboat fire in thirty days. It was perilous, miserable work; but the 23rd Fighter Group knew the importance to China of slowing the Japanese offensive, and they did not shrink from it.

In spite of their supreme effort, Changsha fell on the 18th of June; Yueh's defenders could hold out no longer. The victorious enemy pushed on through the city and continued their drive toward Hengyang, while Chinese troops retreated reluctantly before them. The determined advance of the Japanese in the face of murderous losses from Tex's 23rd Fighter Group astounded Casey Vincent, who wrote in his diary: "Don't see how they can keep coming—but—they do!"

Another consequence of the city's loss was the collapse of the radio warning net for Hengyang. Tex realized this one day when Japanese aircraft showed up unannounced over the field. Because of that, he knew he would have to evacuate soon. Chinese ground resistance was stiffening once more as the enemy moved southward, though; and two days after the fall of Changsha, the Japs were forced to a halt at Hengshan, a few miles from Hengyang airfield.

Tex reluctantly gave the order to evacuate the base. While Chinese troops hastily prepared defenses within the city itself, the ground crew of the 23rd prepared to burn the airfield's facilities. The following morning bore witness to a strange sight: P-40s dropping one-thousand-pound bombs on their own airstrip to demolish it. Tex hated to see the base go, knowing what a linchpin of the Fourteenth's operation it had been; but there was no other choice. The Japanese were approaching when the last planes finally evacuated to Lingling a few days later. They had hung on until the last possible hour, repeatedly making the ten-minute flight to the front lines to bomb and strafe enemy soldiers. On the 28th, the airfield fell; but the Chinese stopped the enemy there, and prepared to defend the city of Hengyang to the last.

Events were moving so quickly that it was difficult to keep track of everything. The 118th Tactical Reconnaissance Squadron, flying special camera-equipped P-51s, arrived in China as Tex was evacuating Hengyang. When they were attached to the 23rd Fighter Group, Tex promptly made another fighter squadron out of them. The cameras would come in handy; but a couple dozen more P-51s gunning for the enemy, he reasoned, would come in a lot handier.

Casey Vincent was promoted to Brigadier General in the final week of June, becoming the second youngest officer in the Army Air Forces to hold that rank. Vincent hardly noticed, busily orchestrating the hundreds of daily strikes against the advancing enemy. The men of his 68th Composite Wing were taut-nerved and combat-weary, but they kept fighting.

A day or two after evacuating Hengyang, Tex touched down in Liangshan on an errand. Shortly after he landed, a transport plane came in, and out of it stepped a fellow with a vaguely familiar face. It was John "Pappy" Herbst, the daredevil Tex had grounded at Eglin on a Sunday afternoon many months before. Remembering who he was, Tex greeted Herbst warmly.

"What are you doing here?" asked Tex, after shaking hands.

"I'm supposed to report to General Morse," replied Herbst. "I guess I'm to take the 3rd Squadron of the CACW."

"Winnie" Morse, who had concurred with Tex's recommendation for grounding Herbst back at Eglin, was now in China, commanding the Chinese-American Composite Wing. The CACW was a new outfit, formed on the assumption that American pilots could train Chinese flyers more effectively if they were in the same unit. So far, it was working well.

Tex recalled the amazing daredevil flying he had witnessed standing on the beach at Eglin. He knew immediately that with Herbst's piloting skills, Tex needed him far more in the 23rd than General Morse possibly could. The 23rd had also lost numerous good squadron commanders in the brutal effort to stop *Ichi-Go*.

"Wait a minute," he said to Herbst, thinking quickly. "I'm short as hell of squadron commanders right now. Don't report in yet. Let me see if I can get you over with me."

That was fine with Herbst, and he waited while Tex paid a call on his old boss. Tex considered how to couch his request, deciding that a little "tactical deception" was in order. Once in Morse's office, he got right to the point.

"General, do you remember that damned "eight-ball" we had down at Eglin that time—when we ended up having to ground him for running wild in that P-51?" asked Tex.

Morse's face clouded over. "Yeah, I remember," he replied. "Why?"

"Well, he's back," Tex continued, "and he's here to join *your* group."

He watched as Morse's jaw set. If there was anything the general was allergic to, it was an "eight-ball." Tex could already "see the wheels turning" in Morse's mind, as he tried to figure a way to get out of the situation.

"You know," said Tex, in as offhanded a manner as he could manage, "I'm real short of squadron commanders right now. At this point, I'd even take this guy off your hands, if you'd rather do that." He watched the General out of the corner of his eye.

"Hell, you can have him!" Morse exclaimed immediately, his face betraying his relief.

The matter thus settled, Tex departed to make the arrangements, and "Pappy" Herbst promptly re-boarded the transport and winged his way back to Kweilin. When Tex arrived there some time later, he gave Herbst command of the 74th Fighter Squadron. Herbst would soon prove to be the greatest leader that unit had ever seen.

Tex's own style with his men was a curious mix of discipline and camaraderie. When new men reported to the group, he would call them into his office—but not for the usual formal session on "commander's expectations." Instead, he'd put his feet upon the desk and relax, talking about what was going on with the war and outlining the conduct he hoped for from them. When he led a mission, it was often with a pre-briefing no more complex than: "Y'all follow me."

In the air, on the other hand, Tex maintained strict discipline that was reminiscent of Chennault. His men knew their mission and the targets they should look for, so Tex gave them wide latitude in pursuing them. Because Tex demonstrated the qualities that were important to him, he got those qualities from his men.

The Japanese advance from Changsha had continued until they surrounded the city of Hengyang. At that point, a second offensive opened far to the south; the enemy began to push northward from Canton. Their ultimate aim was to drive their two armies together, clearing the long north-south supply route as they went. Dug in among the buildings of Hengyang were ten thousand troops of General Fong Hsieng-Chien, a field commander of Hsueh Yueh. To hold the city, General Fong had only three 75mm artillery pieces, a few mortars, and a rifle for every two or three soldiers. His troops were starving and outnumbered; but as they sat astride the junction of the two major railroads that crisscrossed Eastern China, they were determined to hold out.

The Japanese themselves were in poor shape to assault the city immediately. Their supply lines were overextended, reaching all the way back to Hankow. Many of the troops that first arrived at Hengyang had run a month-long, withering gauntlet of Fourteenth Air Force air attacks to get there. While the Japanese ground assault paused to await fresh men and supplies, the Americans proceeded to hammer it once more with P-40s, B-25s, and B-24s.

In addition to walloping the usual lake and river traffic, they scoured the railroad that ran south from Changsha and the road that paralleled it, frag-bombing and strafing trucks and trains attempting to carry supplies forward. The *Liberators* unloaded tons of bombs onto supply depots in villages along the way, and dropped flares at night to illuminate truck convoys for the guns of the fighters. The frustrated Japanese around Hengyang awaited supplies that never came; it was a long while before enough materiel found its way past the vigilant pilots of the Fourteenth.

When the Japanese siege turned into an assault once more, Chennault requested transports from India to drop food to the stalwart defenders within the city. Stilwell refused, absorbed with his lengthy siege of Myitkyina; and so Chennault sent his few available planes to do the job. Once more, crewmen rigged up the bamboo "belly tanks" for the P-40s, filling them with rice and pork to be dropped into the city perimeter for the hungry troops. Yueh's stand at Hengyang against the hugely superior Japanese Army would be beyond outstanding: it was epic.

Unbelievably, against incredible odds, the Chinese resisted for over six weeks. Their defense recalled the one made by the Filipino and American troops on Bataan two years before, or the Alamo's defenders. When the enemy broke through at long last on August 8th, there was no "death march" for the Chinese, as at Bataan. Japanese slaughtered the half-starved defenders to a man, piling their skulls into a mound on a hillside overlooking the city. A host of bodies floated silently down the Siang. At Kunming, Chennault wrote bitterly: "The fate of East China is sealed."

Hengyang was lost, but the enemy had paid dearly for it. In the Fourteenth Air Force's two-month, all-out effort, they had flown well over five thousand sorties, mostly in prohibitive weather, usually against murderous ground fire. Some thirteen thousand enemy soldiers lay dead on the route of the southward advance, or washed up downstream on the Siang. They had burned or sunk a thousand boats, and destroyed five hundred trucks. In the air, the Fourteenth had shot down over a hundred Japanese planes. For all this, they had sacrificed forty-three aircraft, and almost as many pilots.

After a two-week pause to recover their strength, the Japanese renewed their relentless advance down the Siang River valley. With the fall of Hengyang, the warning net collapsed for Lingling and Kweilin; so by the first week in September, the 23rd had to evacuate Lingling. The Japs rolled in on the 7th with little resistance—and three days later, Casey Vincent began evacuating the 68th Composite Wing's headquarters at Kweilin. He complained bitterly in his diary about the lack of gasoline, which hamstrung 68th Wing operations continuously, including an excruciating five-day period of complete grounding in late July. With enough fuel, Vincent believed, the tide of battle in East China could literally have been turned.

Some time before the Japanese arrival at Kweilin was imminent, Vincent had moved non-essential personnel and equipment southwest down the railway to Liuchow. Gradually, the base had been stripped down to its bare minimum of men and materiel; the fighter squadrons stayed, continuously running missions over and beyond the Japanese battle lines.

September 14th was evacuation day for Kweilin. The regular Chinese guard had pulled out, and refugees swarmed over the field. Japanese subversives emerged after sunset as well. As Tex and Casey Vincent packed up their things in the small house they had called home, the crack of firearms sounded sporadically from several locations.

"This place sounds like a shooting gallery," Tex chuckled.

"Yeah," Vincent agreed. "Hey, Tex, what do you think we should do about this commode? It's the only one within two hundred miles that I know of. I bet some Jap general is sitting on it pretty soon."

Tex nodded, scratching his head. "Well, the boys are out burying dynamite and stuff in the runway. Let's see if we can't get a little something to booby-trap it with." Casey agreed, and before long, laughing, the two had rigged their precious toilet to blow sky-high the next time someone flushed it. Tex was taken back to the prank-pulling days of his boyhood.

"My only regret," said Vincent, near tears from mirth, "will be not getting to see this thing go off."

The demolition of Kweilin proceeded apace, the ground crew detonating one-thousand-pound bombs under the runway's surface to put huge craters in it. They fired the buildings (all the equipment had been pulled out some time before). Just before dawn, the last personnel lifted off the single remaining usable strip in the "Silver Slipper," Vincent's own B-25, and watched the sun rise over ruined Kweilin. General Chang Fei-Kwei's 4th Army was digging in inside the city, and off to the southwest stood General Chay Lo's 9th Army; but they would be paltry forces to stop the Japanese juggernaut, concentrating its strength some thirty miles up the railroad. The "Silver Slipper" droned off southwest to Liuchow, the next base down the line.

All the 23rd's fighters at Kweilin had also moved to Liuchow—with the exception of one group. "Pappy" Herbst's 74th Fighter Squadron flew two hundred miles northeast, setting up operations at a group of bases located in a pocket of Chinese-held territory that was actually *behind* the Japanese advance. These "pocket" bases included Suichwan, the primary airfield, and Kanchow, Namyung, and Changting.

For four months, the 74th and 118th Fighter Squadrons operated as guerrilla units from these bases, inflicting heavy casualties during the later Japanese drive from Hengyang south to Canton. Right in the middle of it was Herbst, whose quiet leadership and unbelievable combat skills combined to make him, in Tex's words, "one of the greatest fighter pilots I ever saw." He racked up a formidable score of eighteen *official* victories; but long after he was ordered to abstain from combat, Herbst continued to blast enemy aircraft out of the sky on "observation missions." He was unquestionably one of the Fourteenth Air Force's all-time greatest.

There was another man, however, whose contribution was less than spectacular. As October moved on, Tex began to ground his pilots who had racked up more than one hundred missions in China. The constant stress of flying low-level missions in the face of withering fire from enemy ground troops, anti-aircraft batteries, and Japanese fighters wore on the pilots, until they began to slip and make mistakes. The signs of such combat fatigue became pronounced in men with over one hundred missions, and fatalities increased markedly after that point. The flight surgeon insisted upon giving these pilots medical "tags" and grounding them, and Tex concurred. But when General "Buzz" Glenn, Chennault's Chief of Staff, heard about it, he was not pleased. Later, while Tex was staying with Chennault and Glenn on his way back to the States, Glenn confronted him on the issue.

"Tex, what's this about grounding the pilots who've got a hundred missions?" Glenn asked over dinner one night, his voice betraying his annoyance.

"Yes sir, I was doing that," replied Tex.

"What for?"

"It's the right thing to do," replied Tex. "They can only run themselves so hard before they make some careless mistake and get killed. They've got almost no chance to survive another ten or fifteen missions. I've seen them die that way too often. I was not going to fly those guys."

"Look, Tex," said Glenn, "we're already short enough on good pilots. You're telling me that you're going to take the most seasoned veterans and pull them out of the fight? It's not going to happen. You tell the new group commander to fly them," Glenn directed sternly.

Tex's features hardened. "General, I'm sorry, but I'm not going to do it. You can fly them if you want. They're wearing medical tags, and they've all been grounded by the flight surgeon, but if you want to fly them, it's your call. These guys should not be flying. Matter of fact, I've noticed you've got plenty of fighter pilots running around here at headquarters. Doesn't seem like they've got a lot to do—how about sending some out to the 23rd? We sure could use the support, and right now it doesn't seem like we're getting any."

Glenn was angry, but knew he could not coerce Tex further. Glenn himself had to order the 23rd's new commander, Major Phil Loofbourrow, to fly the combat-fatigued pilots after that—which he did—for Tex was now headed in a new direction. Kweilin was to be his final evacuation.

Tex received orders in early October to return to the States once more. He would be leaving at a bitter time, with base after base falling to the Japanese and China teetering on the brink of disaster; but that was the way of things. Phil Loofbourrow, Tex's deputy, would take the reins of the 23rd Fighter Group for a few short weeks before the next commander—none other than Ed Rector—arrived.

On his return trip, Tex passed Rector in Cairo before beginning the now-familiar passage across Africa and the Atlantic. When Tex was delayed in the Azores, a former classmate from Texas A&M offered to give him a lift on a Naval Air Transport Service cargo plane. Tex touched down at Washington's National Airport in late October and checked his orders once more. He was to report for duty in Fighter Requirements at the new Pentagon.

* * *

The months of June and July were a blur of activity in both the Pacific and Europe. The western press was full of news of the Allied breakout from the beaches at Normandy, culminating in the liberation of Paris on August 25th. From there, Eisenhower's armies swung eastward and advanced toward Germany and victory—but not without a long and difficult fight. Fourteen weeks after the D-Day landing, Operation "Market Garden" commenced in an effort to open a route around the imposing German West Wall defenses. An entire airborne corps was dropped behind enemy lines near Arnhem; but the operation eventually ended in failure, with most of the British paratroopers captured.

In the Pacific, Douglas MacArthur continued the "island-hopping" campaign that inched closer to the Japanese home islands. After securing the Solomons and Gilberts, the Navy and Marines turned north to the Marshall and Mariana Islands. One after another, they fell in costly assaults: Kwajalein, Eniwetok, Saipan, Guam. Massive aerial battles preceded some of these: in the most decisive air victory of all time, Navy and Marine fighter pilots lambasted two hundred forty-three Japanese carrier-based planes, and another fifty-eight from Guam. The beating was dubbed the "Marianas Turkey Shoot."

From Chengtu in China, the great B-29 Superfortresses lifted off at last to bomb Japan itself on June 15th. Seventy-five of them droned over the Imperial Iron and Steel Works at Yawata, but their bombs failed to cause any significant damage. Chennault cringed when he calculated how many thousands of gallons of precious gasoline the B-29s had used in the attempt.

In October, the B-29s had better luck against Formosa, when they teamed up with Admiral Halsey's Task Force 38 to give the Island the pounding of its life. What Tex and his comrades had achieved by surprise a year before, the Army and Navy bombers surpassed by sheer mass throughout a three-day aerial assault.

In Burma, staunch British and American resistance at Imphal and Kohima finally broke the Japanese offensive toward the plain of Assam; the enemy left thirty thousand dead in the jungle and mountains as they fell back to their original positions. Chinese soldiers of Stilwell's Mars Force finally captured Myitkyina after a two-and-a-half month siege, opening a land route into China once more for the first time since the fall of Rangoon. On the 7th of August, Stilwell was promoted to full general, receiving his fourth star.

In Washington D.C., a group of AVG veterans lobbied a bill into Congress that would afford them veterans' benefits for their service in Burma and China. Secretary of War Stimson wrote a letter to the legislature opposing it, urging Congressmen not to confuse the men of the AVG with "those who actually served." The letter was full of incorrect information, including the crucially wrong statement that 220 out of 250 AVG members had stayed on in China to become the 23rd Fighter Group—thereby becoming entitled to benefits without the need for legislation. Reading that, Congress was misled into thinking that only a small handful of ex-AVG personnel were seeking veterans' status. The bill was defeated. Fifty-one years later, the situation would finally be rectified, with the American Volunteer Group becoming fully recognized among America's veterans.

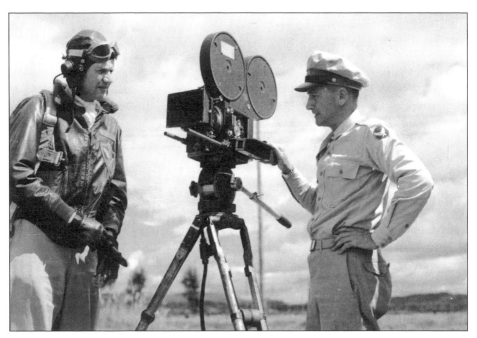

Army Air Forces photographers take shots of Tex by the "Bullfrog," Kunming, 1944.

Tex with titular chief of the Chinese Air Force General Zhou Zhi-Rou and a CACW commander during an inspection of the CACW at Kweilin, 1944.

Group photo of 68th Composite Wing headquarters personnel at Kweilin, 1944. Tex is in row 2, middle.

Chapter 29

JET AGE

On New Year's Day of 1945, the Rose Bowl was a shutout: the Trojans of the University of Southern California blanked the Tennessee Volunteers in a lopsided twenty-five-to-nothing contest. Although Tex attended the game, he barely remembered any of it. He was brooding over an argument he'd had that morning, during a pre-game brunch party.

One of those present at the party was the Chief of the Army Air Forces, General Henry "Hap" Arnold. At one point during the festivities, Arnold had engaged Tex in conversation.

"Tex," he said, "I want you to know I'm disappointed with the way things went over in East China. I thought you guys said the Fourteenth Air Force could hold onto those airfields out there. Chennault promised me he could."

Remembering the bitter evacuations of Hengyang and Kweilin, which were only two of the many bases that had by now been abandoned, Tex felt his collar get a little warm.

"General," he replied, "the Old Man told you the truth. We could have held them all right—if we'd had anything to do it with."

"What do you mean?" Arnold frowned.

"I mean aircraft and pilots, and supplies. Chennault was promised that he would have a hell of a lot more combat power than he ever got. My fighter group had no replacement pilots—"

"No replacement pilots?!" Arnold broke in, incredulous. "We've got thirty-five hundred surplus pilots in the Army Air Forces right now!"

"Well, if you don't get them into the hands of people who can use them, what the hell are you training them for?"

Tex was suddenly conscious of dead silence from the guests in the immediate area; but at that moment, he didn't care. In his mind's eye, he could see the faces of the boys who had died under his command, too combat-fatigued to fight at their best, succumbing to mistakes, driving themselves to the point of exhaustion. No, Tex was just warming up.

"We didn't have any new replacement aircraft, either," Tex continued. "The planes we got—hell, my guys recognized the serial numbers on them from flight training in Barstow, Florida! That second-hand junk was flown halfway across the world with no maintenance. And we had no facilities to do decent maintenance in China, that's for sure."

"Listen," Arnold growled, "we have *never* given second-hand aircraft like that for replacement purposes."

Tex shook his head. "General, I don't know where you're getting your information, but I sure as hell know what I got."

At that moment their host, C.C. Mosley, stepped in and separated the two. Tex was hot, and he knew it; he realized bitterly that Arnold had not had an accurate picture of the situation in China.

"Tex," Mosley advised him soberly, when the two had adjourned to a quiet corner, "General Arnold isn't going to forget what you told him. You wait." The incident faded, and the group went on to the football game.

A couple of days later, at five a.m., Tex's phone rang. The call was from Washington, D.C.; "Hap" Arnold wanted Tex to report there without delay. When he arrived, Tex learned that the Chief had investigated what Tex had told him, and found it to be true. An aggressive investigation had ensued, and Tex was called in to testify about the activities of the Fourteenth Air Force Chief of Staff and Operations Officer.

The Chief of Staff was General "Buzz" Glenn, who had taken little pains to learn what was happening at his forward operating bases in East China, preferring to stay at Kunming. As a result, he was virtually ignorant of the conditions of the planes and pilots doing the fighting. When queried about it, Tex replied to the investigation board that he had not seen Glenn at any of the forward bases in Tex's entire tenure as 23rd Fighter Group Commander.

In the end, "Buzz" Glenn was relieved and demoted to Colonel. Tex felt sorry for him, but knew that Glenn's poor management of Fourteenth Air Force operations had caused losses, and even deaths, as Chennault was not provided critical information.

From that time forward, "Hap" Arnold took steps to virtually flood the China Theater with planes and equipment; but the damage had been done already. The Fourteenth Air Force bases were lost, the war was nearly over, and it was too late to do much good. Tex reflected on the series of events with a heavy heart, wishing things could have turned out differently.

The next month was full of activity for Tex. At the end of it, he stepped from a plane onto the runway at Bakersfield Municipal Airport, California, with a feeling of relief. After only a week or so at the still-new Pentagon, he had narrowly escaped what turned out to be an antiseptic, paper-pushing "red tape" assignment in Fighter Requirements. For the operationally tuned Tex, it was "torture."

Following some leave back in Texas, he had managed to secure a group command of P-38s at Van Nuys. There, he had run into old AVG hand R.T. Smith, and prepared to settle in—only to receive yet another set of orders, which brought congratulations from all quarters. He was to transfer to Bakersfield, to assume command of the 412th Fighter Group. What made the assignment enviable was that the 412th would be the United States' first combat group equipped with jet aircraft.

Tex would be assuming command of the 412th from Col Homer Boushey. The group was to provide cutting-edge fighter muscle for the 319th Wing of Major General James Parker's Fourth Air Force, headquartered in San Francisco. It consisted of the 445th Fighter Squadron located at Bakersfield, along with group headquarters; the 29th at Palmdale; and the 31st at Oxnard, which was being equipped with twenty of the new Bell P-59A *Airacomets*.

Tex and Mazie arrived in February, finding that the California desert reminded them in some ways of Texas. It was hot and dry, with scrubby plants and small trees dotted across the plains and low hills. Modest mountains of the Greenhorn, Tehachapi, and Temblor ranges lay east and south of the town, and the vast Sequoia National Forest began a short distance northeast. Nearby Lake Buena Vista was the best bet to find any water closer than the coastline—if it wasn't dried up. The area's climate was more desolate than Texas, however, and Tex and Mazie didn't care for it much. The town was small, and the rented apartments that would have to serve as their home were decidedly "no-frills."

Before his report date to the 412th, Tex was due for a few weeks of "R&R" from his China tour; and he was to take it at the AAF's Santa Monica Redistribution Center. A few weeks into it, just before Christmas, an invitation from a Major C.C. "Mose" Mosley broke the monotony. "Mose" had been a World War I combat pilot, and he took a liking to Tex from their first meeting. After the Great War, Mosley had started up his own company, Western Air, along with an overhaul outfit called Grand Central. In 1939, "Mose" had contracted with the Army Air Corps to operate six schools around the country to train pilots. (One of the Air Corps' representatives at his schools had been Robert L. Scott.) Now, Mosley's holdings included the only open, non-union shop on the west coast—and it stayed that way, because "Mose" took extremely good care of his employees. Mosley wanted to know if Tex and Mazie would like to move from their hotel in Santa Monica, to stay at his estate in Beverly Hills over the holidays.

It didn't take Tex and Mazie long to accept the tycoon's offer, along with a flight on his personal DC-3—dubbed the "Full House"—to Beverly Hills. They stayed in gorgeous guest rooms in the mansion for the remainder of Tex's R&R; and during that time, they got an up-close look at the glamour of the Hollywood scene.

Mosley was fond of throwing parties for the area's rich and famous (it was at one of these, two months before, that Tex had had his encounter with "Hap" Arnold). Tex and Mazie mingled in amazement with dozens of movie stars, politicians, and wealthy businessmen. They met Ronald Reagan and Jane Wyman, Robert Taylor and Barbara Stanwyck, directors Lawrence Stallings and King Vidor, and a host of others. Twenty-year-old Mazie absolutely could not believe it. When it eventually had to end, the couple bid a fond goodbye to their host and departed for San Antonio. Soon afterward they flew to Bakersfield, and Tex was finally able to take stock of his new command.

The 412th was out of the mainstream, a bit reminiscent of the 23rd Fighter Group in China; very few PX supplies were available for its men. There was plenty of space for a golf course or two, though, and Tex took up the game with relish in his spare time. Joining him on most occasions were Major Rex Barber, who had shot down Japanese Admiral Yamamoto, and two of the 412th's squadron commanders: Major Bob Pettit, recently of the 1st Air Commando Group, and Major Wynn Miller, whom Tex's children would later affectionately nickname "Uncle Wynn."

The Bell P-59A *Airacomet* was America's first attempt at a production jet fighter. Tested in extreme secrecy at Muroc Army Air Field in the California desert, only eighty miles from Bakersfield, it was later shipped to the 412th for combat evaluation. Tex and his men would find that the P-59A wasn't really suited for combat—but it was a start. The twin General Electric I-16 engines that powered it, delivering 1650 lbs. of thrust apiece, represented promising technology, based upon the British Halford engine. The P-59A had a top speed of 450 mph, and ceiling above forty-three thousand feet—but its range was painfully short, at only 440 miles. The 412th immediately began to evaluate the jet's performance against enemy planes.

With Germany fading fast by the spring of 1945, one of the most prominent match-ups in the group's evaluation was to pit the P-59A against the latest model of Japanese *Zero*. Before Tex arrived, he had heard that the jet was supposed to be able to turn inside a *Zero*—something he had to see to believe. Several of the Japanese fighters had been captured by this time; so once he checked out in one, Tex lost no time going up against the P-59A in early April.

A furious dogfight ensued over the desert as Tex—in a *Zero*—and a pilot of the 412th in a P-59A strove to get on each other's tails. After numerous white-knuckled gyrations, Tex found himself nearly there, though flipped into an inverted position. His Japanese-built engine, equipped with a "float" carburetor, chose that very moment to quit cold.

Sailing through space in sudden silence, Tex tried to restart the engine. Nothing happened. He wrestled the aircraft into a level glide and took a look below. There was just room to make a dead-stick landing on the runway. It was hardly a prospect to inspire confidence; but he certainly wasn't going to embrace the *bushido* code of the real Jap pilots and "ride it in."

Somehow, he made it onto the ground without killing himself. When he emerged shakily from the cockpit, two things were accomplished. His reputation was made with his pilots, who had watched the near-fatal landing with amazement; and he resolved never to get into a Japanese aircraft again for the rest of his life.

"What a hell of an irony that would have been," he told the pilots later with a grin, "getting killed in a Jap airplane."

Two days later, an exceptionally interesting aircraft touched down on the runway at Bakersfield. Its designation was the MX409. Seeing its experimental paint and markings, the pilots of the 412th immediately understood why Lockheed's engineers had dubbed it the "Green Hornet." It featured the new GE J33-A-11 jet engine, and it had been tested out at Muroc even more quietly—if possible—than the P-59A. It was, in fact, a prototype of the brand-new P-80 *Shooting Star*.

The P-80 was designed to be a high-altitude interceptor. It had raised eyebrows among test pilots when the new engine rocketed it through the California sky at an unprecedented 580 mph in level flight. It could more than double the range of the short-legged P-59, representing a major step forward in U.S. jet technology. The P-80 would become America's first operational combat jet, seeing extensive action within a few short years over the barren mountains of Korea. For now, it had been turned over to the 412th to "wring out" in simulated combat conditions.

One downside to the new jet was its single engine, based upon the British Halford turbojet, which delivered less thrust than the two engines on the P-59. Also, the poorly balanced bucket wheels on the turbines shook fan blades loose after only some ten hours—often, disastrously, while in flight. But by summer, a few of the first P-80As, equipped with the improved I-40 engine and six .50-caliber machine guns, and able to carry 5-inch rockets or a ton of bombs, began to trickle into the squadrons of the 412th Fighter Group.

Tex offered his not-overly-technical assessment upon checking out in the Green Hornet: "That thing's a real boot in the butt."

The dawn of the jet age was attracting attention from many circles, and several enthusiasts approached Tex, seeking any hands-on experience they could get. Jack Frye, president of Trans World Airlines, was one man who talked Tex into "checking him out" in the P-80; Glen Oderkirk, chief pilot for the Hughes Aircraft Company, was another. Though not strictly legal, Tex didn't mind the checkouts. He could see what was coming, and knew that these men were eager to get in on the "ground floor" of the revolution in aircraft design.

Tex commanded more senior leaders in his group than he really needed; still, there were plenty of field-grade officers looking for a job at the time. When Major Robin Olds appeared in Tex's office one day and announced he was "happy to be on board," Tex was at a loss.

"How the hell did you get here?" Tex queried.

"Well...I won't bore you with the details, sir, but I'm here," Olds said with a grin.

"All right. I'm up to my eyeballs in Majors. Go find yourself a job," Tex directed. Olds did.

In July of 1945, two months after Germany's surrender to the Allies, Tex relocated the headquarters of the 412th from Bakersfield to Santa Maria Airfield, a hundred miles southwest and close to the Pacific. Tex and Mazie lived at the *Rancho Marsalia*, a group of houses rented by some dozen members of the 412th—an improvement over the Bakersfield apartments. But by the end of November, the group had moved again, to March Field near the town of Riverside; and Tex and Mazie took quarters on the airbase.

At March, Tex took on another China veteran that he knew would be a sure winner: Lieutenant Colonel "Pappy" Herbst, fresh from command of the 74th Fighter Squadron. Herbst was now one of many "China hands" that Tex had collected, one by one; the 412th was becoming nicely full of them. While the group was still training in Santa Maria, all had wondered whether they would be returning to the Far East; Tex had even received a report date to deploy the 412th for combat, even though they were not really ready. When the atomic bomb dropped, however, the face of the war changed entirely; all possibility of the group going overseas evaporated.

A day came when Tex received a call from his friend Gerhard Neumann, whose story was a long and fascinating one. Born in Germany, Neumann had been assigned to China to investigate possible German production of *Messerschmitt* aircraft. When the war began, he was interned for a time; then he defected, and went to work for CNAC, later becoming attached to the AVG and joining the Army Air Corps.

Neumann was an engineering genius, a man who could build, disassemble, and rebuild anything. On several occasions, he had single-handedly restored crash-landed Japanese aircraft to full operational condition; flying them, the 23rd's pilots had learned a great deal about the enemy's capabilities. Shortly after Tex returned to America, Neumann (then a Master Sergeant in the USAAC) had reconstructed a downed Japanese

Zero for transport back to the United States. But when Neumann himself arrived in America and it was learned that he was not a U.S. citizen, government officials immediately planned to deport him. With his prospects looking poor, the German had phoned his former commander, to see if there was anything Tex could do to help.

In response, Tex wrote the government's Immigration and Naturalization Service, describing Neumann's contribution to the American war effort, his outstanding character, and his unique accomplishments in China. Tex also called Tommy "The Cork" Corcoran, Roosevelt's legal advisor who had been so instrumental during the startup days of the AVG. Soon afterward, the INS granted citizenship to Neumann on Tex's recommendation (and a phone call from Corcoran sealed the issue). Tex also wrote a letter to General Electric's Aircraft Engine Division, asking about employment for the German and describing his capabilities. GE agreed to take him on. (Years later, with his genius and work ethic, Gerhard Neumann became president of that same division.) "Herman the German," as he called himself, was forever grateful for Tex's efforts on his behalf. Every Thanksgiving Day for the rest of his life, he tracked down and telephoned Tex to thank him again—and to talk about the "good times," especially the (literally) groundbreaking raid on Formosa.

By the end of 1945, with World War II ended, Tex found his thoughts turning once more to his native hill country. The ranch he had bought in Mountain Home was still there, waiting only for its owner to take up residence and begin to work it. Tex and Mazie found life in California "all right," but not what they were used to. Tex enjoyed command of the 412th; but after hostilities ceased, he found peacetime service didn't carry the same satisfaction. Ranching was something he'd always wanted to settle down to; it looked like the time had come to try it.

If he was going to leave, Tex knew just the man to take over his job. He called Bruce Holloway, who had also commanded the 23rd Fighter Group, and was now working at the Pentagon.

"Tex! How's life back in California?" asked Holloway, pleased to hear from his friend.

"Great. What are you up to these days?" Tex replied.

Holloway sighed. "Well, you know, flying this desk, shooting down wall posters. What can I do for you?"

"Well, I don't know how much you know about the group I've got out here, but I think it's right up your alley," Tex began. "I've got all the old China hands already here in the 412th."

He described to Holloway the setup of the group, and their mission to evaluate the latest jets. Holloway was a pioneer of the jet age himself, having studied under the rocketry genius Dr. Robert Goddard; so his interest was aroused immediately. In the end, he decided to take the command.

Holloway took over the group at a time when the War Department was trying to fit a plethora of excess Colonels into any available position, and he found himself saddled with no less than eight of them in the group. With men like John P. "Jack" Flynn, Jack Bradley, and Jay Robbins, they were far from "dead weight"; but Holloway couldn't possibly have squeezed in any more.

When Bruce Holloway set aside his Pentagon desk and headed west to California, Tex and Mazie were at last free to return to the state they both called home. The opportunity had been a long time coming.

***

When Tex departed China for the second time, events in the theater continued at a furious pace. The same day Tex flew back over the Hump, President Roosevelt relieved General Stilwell of command in the China-Burma India Theater, replacing him with General Albert C. Wedemeyer. The Japanese ground offensive in East China resumed, and eventually culminated with the fall of Liuchow, Nanning, and every other Fourteenth Air Force base between Hankow and Indochina. Operation Ichi-Go was successfully completed (though the cost would prove too heavy in the end).

The Japanese were already showing signs of cracking. After a long siege, the British finally captured Akyab on the Burmese coast. Allied forces flowed southward from northern Burma along three corridors, forcing the now-bedraggled enemy into a springtime retreat down roads and rivers. They hammered the Japanese back from Meiktila and Mandalay in March; and by the first week of May, they liberated the port of Rangoon once more. The Ledo Road, finally completed at a massive cost in resources and manpower, opened to the north—but its benefits turned out to be a mere footnote, as airlift tonnage over the Hump into China outstripped the road's deliveries by a factor of ten.

Just before scores of AAF B-29s began to firebomb Japan, U.S. Marines made heroic, bitterly contested landings on Bougainville, Iwo Jima, and Okinawa, "stepping" ever closer to the Japanese home islands. On the Chinese mainland, then-starving Japanese forces loosened their grip on the territory they had wrested from Chennault's men; the tide had turned. The Chinese counterattacked successfully along a wide front, reversing the gains of Ichi-Go, and the invaders retreated toward the coast.

Realizing that victory was at hand, the War Department began to make sweeping changes in the command structure of the China Theater. "Hap" Arnold ordered Chennault's Fourteenth Air Force to relocate to northern China, where there was almost no significant action. Tenth Air Force, which fell under the hastily-organized command of General Stratemeyer, would replace the Fourteenth in East China to achieve final victory against the Japanese.

The switch was all too obviously born of malice and politics. Chennault was also stripped of his most veteran fighter and bomber units, and these given to Stratemeyer. Old grudges died hard within the Army brass, and Chennault was finally feeling the spite of men who did not happen to like him. Despondent, he resigned his commission on July 14th, and took a last tour of the nation he was primarily responsible for saving. Millions flocked to the streets of Kunming and Chungking to pay homage to the Old Man. He returned to his native Louisiana to the biggest ticker-tape parade in the history of New Orleans (Tex was there too).

After the war, Japanese General Takahashi, in charge of the armies occupying central China, made a telling declaration: "Without their air force, we could have gone anywhere we wished."

On August 6, the nuclear age dawned in atomic fire as the uranium-based "Little Boy" propelled the war toward an abrupt conclusion in the skies over Hiroshima. Twenty-six days later, Japanese foreign minister Mamoru Shigemitsu signed an unconditional surrender on the deck of the battleship *Missouri*—with Chennault conspicuously absent. The war was over.

Colonel Tex Hill and his young bride, Mazie.

Chapter 30

MOUNTAIN HOME

Tex wasn't sure he had heard correctly. He looked carefully at the three impeccably-dressed men facing him. One was Carr P. Collins, chief executive officer of a Dallas-based insurance firm. To his left sat Dan Harrison, one of the richest oilmen in the Houston area. Rounding out the trio was D.K. Martin, overseer of the vast Kokernot Ranch in western Texas. They were all seated in Dr. Hill's study, their earnestly serious gazes bent upon Tex.

"Governor?" Tex managed to ask after a brief silence, glancing at his father, who sat beside him.

"It sounds harder than it is," said Collins with a smile. "With Governor Stevenson moving up to the U.S. Senate, we're looking for a good candidate. You don't have a lot of past political affiliations; and you're a decorated veteran who people respect. The legislature was impressed with the address you gave down in Austin awhile back."

Tex remembered the occasion, but didn't recall anything particularly noteworthy about his speech. Now, here were three of the most important men in the state, appearing on his father's doorstep to ask Tex to consider running for governor of Texas! It was a little hard to take in.

"Frankly, we think you'd be a shoe-in," interjected Harrison. "Nobody's even heard of the other guy, who'd be your opponent."

He looked at Dr. Hill, who seemed to be lost in thought.

Tex pondered the life that was being offered to him, wondering what it would be like. He had never considered a political career before; at thirty-one, he would be the youngest governor in state history. Was he prepared to take such a step? There would be no going back. Looking out the window at the hill country spring afternoon, Tex thought of the other life he'd always wanted—the ranch waiting at Mountain Home. He thought of Mazie, now only a few weeks from childbirth. He looked again at his father, wondering what he was thinking.

"I'm going to have to think about it," Tex said finally, looking from one man to the next. "It's really an honor, you know, for you to give me that opportunity. Let me talk to Mazie and do some thinking."

The men rose, shook hands with father and son, and departed. Tex discussed the prospect of the governorship with his father; Dr. Hill was obviously pleased, but did not try to influence his son.

"You're going to have to make your own call on this one, David," said Dr. Hill.

Mazie was startled when she heard the news. After thinking it over, she, too, told Tex it was up to him.

"Do you want to do it?" she asked.

"I don't know," replied Tex, frowning. "It's a great offer, but...I'd love to finally settle down on that ranch for awhile. I just don't know."

Tex's separation from the Army Air Forces had been approved. He had turned over command of the 412th Fighter Group to his friend Bruce Holloway with little fanfare; then he and Mazie had returned from California to Victoria and Hunt, Texas. They were visiting their families before heading out to the ranch at Mountain Home.

On April 11th, Mazie gave birth to a daughter at the Nix Hospital in San Antonio. She was christened Mazie Lee Hill, greeted with joy by the whole family. Dr. Hill would walk about his home, patting the infant girl on the back, waiting for her to fall asleep, and chanting a snatch of homemade doggerel:

> *Chant the name, chant the name of Mazie Lee, Mazie Lee,*
> *Wherever she is found, she shall have great renown,*
> *Because she is our precious Mazie Lee, Mazie Lee, Mazie Lee.*

Not long afterward, Tex and Mazie drove out to Mountain Home at last. As they talked about the future, Tex recalled a conversation just before they had been married.

"I'll tell you, Mazie, the thing I really want to do, whenever I leave the service, is work a ranch," Tex had said. "That's how I've lived most of my life, growing up—working on ranches. What would you think of that?"

"Oh, that's wonderful!" Mazie had exclaimed, radiant. "I just love ranching myself, you know."

Mazie had been thinking of the golden daylong excursions she had often made with friends to the Welders' or the O'Connors', who lived in grand plantation style, close to Victoria. Those "ranches" were set amid a "wilderness" of gorgeous homes and swimming pools, where beautiful white-faced cattle grazed among oil derricks. Pool parties, dancing, and barbeques were the order of the day. *If that's ranching*, she had thought, *count me in!*

Tex had wondered just how Mazie knew enough about ranching to "love it," but he soon forgot the matter. Now, they headed down the road on the short drive out to Mountain Home. He felt a growing excitement as they left the Guadalupe River valley and went up the highway toward the ranch—*his* ranch! It was like coming home all over again.

The "town" of Mountain Home, Texas was little more than a gas station at the dusty intersection of State Roads 41 and 27, on the Edwards Plateau between Fredericksburg and Junction. The couple rumbled through it and ranged out into what looked like the middle of nowhere, seeing only occasional fences to mark property borders.

Occasionally they spotted scattered groups of sheep, goats, or cows in the distance. Tex was feeling more enjoyment by the minute, back in his native element; but poor Mazie's spirits were sinking into her shoes as she surveyed the empty landscape. There was only one road, and several times, Tex had to stop the car and get out to open a gate in a fence line before proceeding. The trip seemed much longer than its actual thirty minutes. When it ended, Mazie got out of the car to look at the ranch for the first time.

It had several buildings, the walls all made of the rock-and-mortar combination Mazie immediately dubbed "peanut brittle." One structure was obviously a barn, meaning that the smaller one—Mazie frowned—must be the main house. Inside it was a fireplace in the living room, a wooden cooking stove in the kitchen, and very little else. It certainly bore no resemblance to the Welders' palatial dwellings; and Mazie felt growing trepidation as she looked around. Nevertheless she resolved, as always, to make the best of it.

When they had moved in along with little Mazie Lee, life began to settle into a routine. Along with the seventeen hundred acres of land, Tex had bought small herds of cows, sheep, and goats; now, he spent a considerable amount of time caring for them. He had to "de-horn" the cattle, shear and worm the sheep, farm fodder for the livestock, and feed and pasture all the animals. His three types of livestock were ideal for the hill country, for they ate different fodder, and their market prices tended to balance each other out. When not occupied with his herds and flocks, Tex spent hours on horseback riding the fence line, or hunting deer and rabbits in the brush. Mazie, too, took to the saddle to get around a bit. Tex found himself able to relax at last, and it wasn't long before he decided with finality that he wasn't going to run for governor of Texas.

But while Tex settled comfortably into the rancher's life of his dreams, Mazie struggled to enjoy it. She had spent her whole life in a completely different environment, and missed her accustomed surroundings a great deal. Taking care of Mazie Lee presented no problem; but chores like churning butter from fly-infested milk were another matter. She found her days as a rancher's wife dreary and dull.

For excitement, if it could be called that, she played jokes using the eighteen-party telephone line that serviced their remote area. Tex and Mazie had made fast friends with Willie and Callista Collins, whose ranch was several gates away. Mazie would call up Callista and wait until she heard all sixteen "clicks," telling her that everyone else was silently listening in. Then she would begin an impromptu "tall tale," while Callista would play right along.

"Well, hi, Callista! I just wanted to call and make sure you were all ready for that fancy party in San Antonio on Saturday night," Mazie would say, oozing sincerity.

"Oh, why yes, I think we are," Callista would reply.

"That's wonderful. Now, Callista, this is *real* fancy. Willie will have to wear a tuxedo." As she said it, Mazie smiled, thinking: *Willie wouldn't any more own a tuxedo than the man in the moon.*

"Oh, well, Willie doesn't have a tuxedo," would come Callista's reply.

"Well, he'll have to get there early and rent one, because this party is the 'Ritz,'" Mazie would say.

Of course, there was no party—there never was; and the thought depressed Mazie. Most of the neighbors were not as friendly as Willie and Callista, and a number of them looked critically upon Tex's marriage to Mazie. Why couldn't he have married one of their native hill country girls? Who was this city girl, anyway, who didn't know anything about ranching? As time passed, Mazie wondered how long she could keep her spirits up.

As the Texas autumn turned to winter, events at the ranch took a drastic turn. A day came when a harsh wind shrieked down from the north, bringing an icy chill and clouds heavy with precipitation. The temperature dropped, and kept dropping, until it was breaking records across the region. Ranchers stood close to their fires and perused their almanacs, perplexed. It was the coldest weather in over a century.

Then a freezing rain began, surpassing anything in recent memory. The sleet poured from the sky in wind-driven sheets, covering the ground, building into an ice storm worthy of the eastern seaboard or the Great Lakes region. Trees cracked; barbed-wire fences groaned and snapped under the tremendous weight of ice. The goats shivered, dragging their heads along the ground, unable to lift them because of the ice caked on their horns and beards.

At the height of the storm, Tex returned from a quick check of the animals, coming through the house's front door with a blast of cold air. He quickly shut the door behind him, and began to knock the ice crystals off his hat.

"Mazie...the chickens broke," he said. Mazie came into the room carrying their daughter, thinking she had misheard.

"What's that, Tex?"

"I said the chickens broke." Tex was shaking out his coat now, trying to hide a slight smile from his wife.

"Broke? What do you mean?" asked Mazie, perplexed.

Tex looked at her. "You know how they roost up in the trees. Well, the ice built up on them, and they froze to death, and fell out of the trees, and...they broke."

Mazie tried to smile, but she had news for Tex too. "Well, Mazie Lee's diapers are freezing solid when I change her—in the pail I put them in beside the bed." They looked at each other for a long moment, and Tex read the unhappiness in Mazie's face. *She's had enough*, he thought. He was right.

It was not the winter alone that made things difficult for Mazie. Every day, she had watched Tex carry buckets of slop around for the animals and perform the myriad of laborious tasks that constituted ranching. Tex enjoyed the occupation as though born to it, but Mazie saw only a smart, charismatic, capable leader "wasting his talents on a few goats." Then there was the financial debt on the ranch itself, which Mazie thought would be difficult to repay, though Tex was very happy with the 30-year, low-interest note he had obtained. It didn't help, either, that the livestock *were* dropping dead, taking with them the source of the young couple's livelihood. Mazie felt that Tex was destined for something more in life than paying off the ranch and shearing sheep. When the time was right, she told him so.

"Tex," Mazie said to him one winter day, when he had come in from outside, "please sit down a minute. I want to talk to you."

"All right," he replied, removing his coat and stretching out his legs in a living room chair.

"Tex, I'm going to tell you something. When I married you, everyone in Victoria was talking about it—saying it wouldn't last. They thought I was getting married because you were a big war hero, with lots of medals, and that it was the glamour I was attracted to. I want you to know that that isn't true."

Tex nodded as he pulled his boots off, wondering where this was going.

"But I also want you to know," Mazie continued, a note of desperation in her voice, "that when I watch someone like you feeding those pigs, and when I think about spending the next twenty or thirty years skimming the bugs off the milk and churning butter... well, it just does something to me."

She stopped, and Tex looked at her carefully. He had known Mazie wasn't particularly happy at the ranch. However much he might have enjoyed it—and he enjoyed it a great deal—he wanted Mazie to be happy. He made up his mind immediately: they were moving.

One morning, during the worst of the cold weather, when they were completely "trapped" in the house with the phone lines dead, Mazie was staring morosely out the front window. Suddenly she saw a huddled figure moving up the driveway in a long coat. She blinked, thinking she was seeing things—but there it was all the same.

"Tex!" she exclaimed, gripping the sill. "There's a man out there!"

Tex didn't even look up. "You're hallucinating," he drawled, with some sarcasm.

"He's in uniform," Mazie continued in wonder. "Well, I never! It's a General Officer!"

At that, Tex got up and came to the window. Sure enough, a general was struggling and staggering through the ice directly toward the house.

"What in the world!" Tex expostulated, striding to the front door.

By the time he opened it, the man was only yards from the door, and he looked up at Tex with a weak smile. His face was red with cold, and he shivered visibly. Noticing the three stars on the man's shoulder, Tex immediately ushered him inside and over to the fire.

"Tex Hill?" the general croaked, extending a nearly frostbitten hand. "I'm General Fred Walker. My gosh," he paused, panting, "I asked someone how far it was to Tex Hill's place, and they said 'right up the road.' So I parked my car when I couldn't get it past one of those gates, and started walking." He shook his head ruefully. "It must have been three miles!"

Tex and Mazie waited for their mysterious visitor to warm up, before asking him about his errand. Mazie brought him something hot to drink. When he was finally ready to speak, the general pulled a folded piece of paper from his pocket, and handed it to Tex.

"Tex, this is a letter from Governor Stevenson. On behalf of him and General Knickerbocker, I'm to ask if you'll consider joining the Texas Air National Guard. He'd be honored to have you assume command of the 58th Fighter Wing. It's headquartered at Ellington Field, near Houston." General Walker waited for the message to sink in, while Mazie read the letter over Tex's shoulder. Sure enough, Governor Stevenson was asking exactly that. Tex had received a similar letter some time before, but had decided he wasn't interested. Now, however, he was looking for some way to leave the ranch behind, for Mazie's sake.

With the imminent organization of the Air Force as a separate branch of service, the Air National Guard was in its formative stages throughout the country. The "Texas branch" would actually encompass Arkansas, Louisiana, Mississippi, and Alabama as well; though at this point, it had only a command structure, without any airplanes. Tex was being offered a chance to get in on the "ground floor"—and with the command would come a commission as a Brigadier General. Tex was intrigued, drawn by the chance to get into the cockpit once more. In the end, it didn't take him long to accept— a decision that Mazie wholeheartedly endorsed.

The job was not full-time. Before Tex and Mazie could move from the ranch, guardsmen would commute from San Antonio to Mountain Home to pick up their commander and take him to the airport. Tex flew a Beechcraft C-45 *Expeditor* transport, which had been assigned to him for the purpose, out to Ellington to perform his weekend duties—which were not especially challenging.

Before long, Tex and Mazie moved to San Antonio for good. After renting several apartments, they bought a "G.I. house" on Garraty Road in Terrell Hills, near the Army base of Fort Sam Houston. Mazie was thrilled to be back in "civilization"; and even Tex had to admit that some things about it weren't so bad.

One of the first things attended to was obtaining federal recognition for the Texas branch of the ANG. The governors of all five states signed a document granting their approval of the organization, and Tex was to personally present the endorsement in Washington, D.C. On his way to the capital, he stopped at Maxwell Field in Montgomery, Alabama to see a friend—General Casey Vincent. Vincent pinned his own silver general's stars on Tex; then, after talking over "old times" for a while, sent him on his way.

In Washington, Tex quickly accomplished his errand, and the Texas Air National Guard became officially recognized. While Tex was at the Pentagon, a general suggested that he take the examination for a regular commission in the soon-to-be-formed U.S. Air Force. Tex figured it couldn't hurt, so he put in his application and took the exam. General Grandison Gardner, Tex's old commander from the Proving Ground, let him know that he would "support" Tex's application; so it looked like a sure thing. The results, Tex learned, would be some time in coming. Meanwhile, it made sense to resign his National Guard commission; he would have to do so anyway, when he received the regular commission. So resign he did, shortly after returning to San Antonio. Sure enough, the regular commission was later approved—but on that occasion, Tex was nowhere to be found.

* * *

After the Second World War ended, the men of the AVG began to make their mark in almost every imaginable walk of life. Some, like Charlie Mott and Charlie Bond, stayed in military service and rose to become flag officers. Freeman Ricketts and "Buster" Keeton, along with a score of others, piloted for Pan American or one of the other airlines. Bob Prescott, Dick Rossi, and ten other ex-AVG pilots put up $10,000 apiece and started up Flying Tiger Lines, which soon became the largest all-cargo air carrier in the world. (Prescott and Rossi also founded the Hungry Tiger restaurant chain.) Chuck Older became a federal judge, later presiding in the famous Charles Manson case. Ken Jernstedt served as an Oregon state senator for over twenty years. "Red" Petach remarried and took up politics, becoming president of the Maryland Women Republican's Association. Bob Layher took up wheat farming in Kansas.

AVG armorer Don "Rode" Rodewald was a top Air Force test pilot, until a crash landing in 1954 cost him the use of his legs. But "Rode" didn't even slow down: thirty years later, in a Piper Comanche, he became the first and only paraplegic to fly solo around the world. Among the other ex-AVG were a doctor, a lawyer, and one who was both. There were a Hollywood movie scriptwriter, a state aviation director, a jet engine pioneer, and an Olympic diving coach. Far from sinking into obscurity, the Flying Tigers made their presence felt wherever they fared.

In China, although the war was over, the situation in the countryside remained in dire straits. Conflict between Chiang Kai-Shek's Nationalist forces and the slowly growing Communists immediately threatened to escalate, with the Japanese threat removed. The United States was making a misguided attempt to negotiate a cease-fire between the two parties, to avoid civil war. General Albert Wedemeyer quickly airlifted Nationalist troops into key positions throughout the country, to prevent crucial cities from being overrun by Communist forces in the wake of Japan's surrender. In some areas, pockets of scattered Japanese troops continued to hold out for days after their country had given up.

Lieutenant John Birch, who had worked so tirelessly as a field agent for Chennault against the Japanese, heard about a group of American prisoners of war being held by one such force of Japanese troops near Hsuchow, north of Nanking. The pocket of Japanese resistance was behind Chinese Communist lines, but Birch took a band of Chinese soldiers into the area under a U.S. Army banner to negotiate the Americans' release.

As Birch approached the Japanese-held area, he found the route guarded by Chinese Communist troops. Speaking excellent Chinese, Birch explained to the junior officer that he would like to approach the cornered Japanese troops and engage in negotiations for the American prisoners. The officer hesitated, saying that Birch would have to ask permission of his commander. Birch and a single Chinese aide were escorted the short distance to the commander's headquarters, while the rest of the party remained behind.

When John Birch repeated his request to the Communist commander, the other man took offense at a perceived lack of formal courtesy in the American's address. The commander shrugged off Birch's request, instead demanding to know by what right he was bearing arms in China and desiring passage through the Communist lines. Birch quietly stated that he represented his commanding officer, but the Communist was not impressed. He became loud and abusive, declaring that the United States "had no authority here." When he demanded that the American surrender his sidearm, Birch refused. The commander promptly turned to a couple of nearby soldiers and ordered them to shoot the two emissaries through the legs.

"Now do you know who is in charge here?" the commander sneered, as the men fell to the ground.

Bleeding profusely, Birch and his Chinese aide were dragged outside the village and thrown into its dump, where Communist soldiers repeatedly bayoneted the American. Later, an elderly woman from the vilage surreptitiously helped the wounded Chinese aide escape to safety. John Birch died from loss of blood amid the piles of waste; his grave was never found.

But the worst crime was still to come. When the aide's story reached the ears of the U.S. State Department, it was discredited—in spite of clear photographs the aide had managed to take of John Birch's body. The State Department did not want anything to upset the "delicate negotiations" going on between the two factions in China; even now, there was more than a little sympathy within the department's ranks for the Chinese Communists. They quietly brushed the matter aside, doing nothing to exact restitution.

Much later, when Chennault found out about the incident, he wrote: "...if I had still been in China, there would have been a squadron of B-25s blasting that Communist position with no further questions asked." It was a shameful mark on the record of the government of the United States.

Claire Chennault returned to China in 1946. Nine long years of war had left the nation in a shambles. Starvation and disease ravaged the interior, along with crop failures and famines on a scale never before seen. The Old Man resolved to form a civil airline, one that could move food from the interior to the coastal cities and return with manufactured goods. By May, with the help of Fiorello LaGuardia, Tommy "the Cork" Corcoran, and Whiting Willauer, Chennault had raised enough funds to purchase some twenty Curtiss C-46 Commando and C-47 transport aircraft. China Air Transport was born, with headquarters in Shanghai. While Tex and Mazie were enduring the great ice storm in Texas, the first cargo flight flew from Canton into China's interior. Chennault was back in the business of saving China.

Tex, Mazie, and little Mazie in front of the "peanut brittle" stone house on the ranch at Mountain Home, Texas, 1946.

Mazie riding "Nellie" on the ranch at Mountain Home, Texas, 1946.

Chapter 31

HEART OF AFRICA

When Tex returned to San Antonio from Ellington Field one day, he had received a letter from none other than Merian Cooper, Chennault's Chief of Staff from the early days of the CATF. Tex remembered the part Cooper's creative genius had played in some of the CATF's most effective strikes, and later in masterminding General Kenney's Fifth Air Force assault on Wewak. Scanning the letter, Tex noted Cooper was back in the movie-making business, producing pictures in Hollywood. He wanted to know if Tex would like to come out and work with him—"team up again, like the good old days in China," it read. Tex had to smile at that. He wasn't sure what Cooper had in mind, but it might be fun. With ranching no longer occupying Tex's time, he thought he might at least go for a visit.

Before long, he flew out to Hollywood to meet Cooper once more. It was a pleasant reunion, and "Coop" was eager to fill Tex in on his current film projects; there were three of these. One was a "remake" of a documentary called *Grass*, a silent film that followed the annual migrations of several nomadic Afghan and Asian tribes to mountain pastures. The tribes' journeys were difficult, and they always suffered some loss of life along the way. The second picture was a fictional story about a girl that grew up among a family of gorillas. The third was an action film that starred John Wayne.

Cooper introduced Tex to John Ford, his director, and to John Wayne himself. Ford had helped Wayne become famous as the "Ringo Kid" in *Stagecoach*; and although Wayne was an actor, he was a genuine rifleman and horseman *par excellence*. When he shook hands with Tex, recognition dawned in the eyes of "The Duke."

"I played you in a picture awhile back!" the actor exclaimed. "Your name caught my eye, there, in the script; that's what made me decide to do that one."

Tex had to smile, recalling the corny action in *The Flying Tigers*. His natural honesty wouldn't let the opportunity pass.

"Yeah, I saw it," he replied. "That thing was so corny! You know, the situation over there really wasn't anything like that picture."

"Well, it did all right, anyway," Wayne replied, "and I really enjoyed doing it."

The two hit it off, beginning a friendship that would last until the actor's death many years later.

Cooper's excitement about his filmmaking projects was infectious, and it wasn't long before Tex found himself agreeing to go to work for the producer, signing a contract to assist in all three pictures. "Coop" explained what he wanted Tex to do first, as soon as it could be managed.

"This movie about the girl that grows up with the gorillas," he explained, "is called *Mighty Joe Young*. I want to make the scenes of the girl interacting with the baby gorillas very convincing. For that, we really need a live baby gorilla...that's where you come in, Tex."

Tex frowned, trying to make the connection. Cooper did it for him.

"You're a hunter, and this is going to be quite a hunt. How would you like to go to Africa and get us a baby gorilla?"

It certainly wasn't a routine first assignment. With some excitement, Tex began to make plans for the trip. Back in San Antonio, he scrounged around to collect information on gorillas. The highest concentrations of the primates, he learned, were to be found in the Belgian Congo; that was the place to begin his search.

"Just be back before the baby comes," admonished Mazie, who was expecting their second child in the fall.

After a long flight on a Pan Am carrier, Tex touched down in Leopoldville, the Belgian Congo's capital. It was the first time he had been in sub-Saharan Africa; and as usual, Tex was fascinated by a part of the world he'd never seen. During his short stay in the city, Tex located a qualified cameraman (a Belgian), who had made a number of documentaries and was quite experienced. If Tex ever could manage to come up with a gorilla but have difficulty getting it back to America, he figured the Belgian could do the shooting for the picture. It would save Merian Cooper the trouble of shipping a crew all the way from Hollywood.

During the day, Tex began to visit local officials, trying to secure permission to organize a gorilla hunt. The dark-skinned men would greet him warmly enough and listen patiently; but they shook their heads when Tex explained his intentions. The chief game warden, speaking English with a heavy French accent, told Tex his government had just placed Congonese gorillas under the very strictest form of legal protection. Trying to merely capture one would likely enrage the others in a pack, provoking them to attack the hunters—who might then have to kill some of the primates in self-defense. Because of that possibility, the warden insisted, no hunt could take place.

After a few days of continued attempts to convince him, Tex realized the warden wasn't going to relent. The only option was to search for gorillas elsewhere. He recalled from his research that there was a species of coastal lowland gorilla native to the nearby French Cameroons; he decided that a visit there would be his next step. The lowland gorillas did not have the hairy crest found on those in the Congo, but otherwise, there was little difference between the two species to the untrained eye.

Tex boarded an Air France flight bound for Douala, the port of entry for the French Cameroons. The city was only a few degrees off the equator, and the June air was humid and muggy. On his first evening in Douala, he decided to dine at what looked like the finest restaurant in the city. The waiter brought out a plate of biscuits, a welcome sight for Tex. He picked one up. It looked like it was made from rye bread—until one of the "rye" pieces moved. Tex nearly dropped the biscuit in surprise. The dark-colored bits were weevils.

Tex began to pick out the insects with great care, but it was nearly impossible. Surreptitiously peering around, he noticed that other customers were eating the biscuits without a second thought. He couldn't believe it. But within a couple of days, Tex was no longer bothering to pick out the weevils, either—it was too much trouble.

Shortly after his arrival in Douala, Tex encountered a red-haired Irishman named O'Hara in one of the city's bars. The man spoke several African dialects fluently. He described to Tex how, during the war, he had stepped in to command some Nigerian troops in India when their British commander had been killed. Tex in turn related his own exploits in India and Burma; and he and the Irishman hit it off. O'Hara invited Tex to stay at his place in town, which sounded very nice compared to most of the available lodging. Tex accepted, happy to find that the accommodations were indeed pleasant. O'Hara's house was made of brick, and very musty inside. Because of the moisture, leather turned green virtually overnight—*but*, Tex reflected, *I've certainly seen that before*. When he told his Irish host about his intention to hunt for a baby gorilla, O'Hara's face lit up.

"Ah! Tex, it so happens that I've a friend in Yaoundé, a Greek, who might be able to help you get a little safari organized."

"No kidding," Tex replied with interest.

"No kidding. Let me drive you up there, and I'll introduce you to him." It was settled, and without further ado the men departed.

Yaoundé was a hundred and twenty miles inland to the east, and the drive in O'Hara's car took half a day. Tex was concerned about dealing with the French officials; but with a wink, O'Hara assured him that for enough money, he could bribe them for "darn near anything."

When they arrived, O'Hara looked up his friend and arranged a rendezvous. The man's name was Joe Devulakous, and Tex learned quickly that the Greek had plenty of expertise to organize the little expedition. O'Hara gave Tex a friendly salute in farewell, and rumbled back down the road to Douala.

Devulakous was a veteran of many safaris into the "bush," and soon secured all the official permission Tex needed. Supplies, though, were more difficult to obtain. The French government routinely took all of the Cameroons' exports, paying their colony in "soft" French *francs* that had no purchasing power outside the French Empire. Thus, the colonial nation found herself able to buy almost nothing but wine and perfume imports from France, resulting in a critical shortage of many things they desperately needed. Tex didn't see how wine or perfume would help him catch a gorilla (by any conventional method), so it was some time before he and Devulakous were able to scrounge up the food and equipment they would require while "up country."

Finally, their expedition was outfitted. Devulakous loaned Tex his own truck and driver, and the two men loaded up their supplies and drove into the bush toward a native village. There, they collected some half-dozen native hunters, who volunteered more out of curiosity than anything else. Devulakous had explained to Tex the usual method of catching one of the young gorillas—which seemed to Tex rather cruel. A hunting party would sneak up on a pack of the primates and shoot one of the females with a poisoned dart. The pack, including the female, would immediately grab their young and take off in flight. After a long chase through the jungle, the poison would go to work on the mother. She would lag a little behind the others at first, eventually becoming separated from them. When she finally succumbed and went down, the hunting party quickly approached and took the baby gorilla. Tex didn't like it, for occasionally, the mother died; but he decided to go ahead with the hunt anyway.

The safari eventually located a pack of gorillas, and everything worked just as Devolakous had described. Within a few days, they had captured three young primates of varying sizes. The next step was to get one back to Hollywood, but Tex ran into another obstacle: primates were a species protected by the United States government as well. For a sufficient bribe, there would have been no problem getting one *out* of the French Cameroons; but upon arrival in America, the "little fellow" would have been confiscated promptly. It just wasn't going to work.

Tex cabled Merian Cooper, informing him of the situation, explaining that there was no problem, since the Belgian cameraman he had discovered in Douala could do the job. But Cooper was nonplused, fearing that the Belgian wouldn't have the right kind of experience. "Coop" insisted upon shipping his own cameraman from Hollywood to do the filming, at great expense. Tex shook his head, having no choice but to wait until the cameraman arrived. He watched the calendar, knowing that Mazie was nearly due to give birth, wondering if he could make it back in time.

There was a second reason to finish up quickly and get back to the States as well. Tex had received a wire informing him of the results of his application for a regular Air Force commission, which he had almost forgotten. He had been accepted. With the commission came an assignment to active duty, of course, and Tex was required to report by a certain date. The wire had arrived just as his expedition was preparing to head up country, and he doubted he could make it back to America in time. He cabled in reply, asking for a thirty-day extension of the report date.

General Anderson, in charge of Air Force personnel, granted Tex's request, informing him that the new date would have to hold firm; otherwise, the regular commission would be withdrawn. When the African trip dragged on into its third month, and the cameraman was just arriving from Hollywood, Tex realized he wasn't going to make the extended report date either. His days of active duty service really were at an end.

Cooper's Hollywood cameraman was quite a character, fitting nearly every stereotype in the book. He was flighty and easily offended, with no experience in African living conditions. Harboring a phobia of germs, he took regular baths in alcohol and never ventured far from his tent. He refused to touch anything or go near the natives, sourly studying the production sketches Cooper had sent over for some time before proclaiming he was ready to begin. The cameraman took over, and Tex's job was finally done; he boarded the next flight for home.

As things turned out, Cooper would have been better off taking Tex's advice and using the Belgian cameraman. Good lighting for outdoor filming was hard to come by in that part of Africa during that particular season. The Hollywood man got plenty of good footage of the gorilla playing around a bed; but he used a plain white sheet as a backdrop. The contrast between the dark gorilla and the sheet was extreme; when the film was later developed, the gorilla looked like nothing so much as a lump of coal moving about in snow.

Mazie had been in Victoria, Texas, staying with her parents as her delivery date approached. Tex made a beeline there when he touched down in the U.S., striding into Dr. Sale's home just as Mazie began having labor pains. She smiled to see him—but made it quite clear that she took a dim view of his idea of "returning in time for the baby." They hurried to the hospital with only a short while to spare. On the evening of September 17, 1947, David Lee Hill, Jr., was born to the proud parents.

While Mazie recovered, Tex thought long and hard about his recent adventures. Eventually, he decided that the movie business really wasn't for him. He enjoyed the thought of traveling around the world to work on pictures; but Mazie had "put her foot down" after his near-absence from his son's birth. Tex called Merian Cooper and explained why he couldn't complete the contract for all three pictures. "Coop" understood.

"If you ever change your mind, Tex," he said, "give me a call."

It was time to take stock of things. Tex had declined to run for governor of Texas, sold his ranch, resigned his general's commission in the Texas Air National Guard, missed the reporting deadline for a regular commission, and canceled his contract to work for "Coop" in the movies. In the eyes of some, those might seem like missed opportunities—and maybe they were. But Tex still felt he would discover something out there to "get into," something that would prove to be exactly what he was looking for. He began to turn over ideas in his head.

Wildcats, Inc. in action. (L to R: Phil Loofbourrow, Tex, Johnny Mitchell, and a promoter.)

Captain John Hampshire in the cockpit, Chanyi, 1942. Hampshire had an incredible 14 victories in 7 missions before being shot down and killed.

Tex greets Chennault upon his arrival in New Orleans from China, 1945. Picture taken just before the largest ticker-tape parade in the city's history, in honor of Chennault.

Chapter 32

OIL AND ORE

Shortly after Tex's return from Africa, a bug—the "oil bug"—bit him. While he searched for something to do, he had a chance visit with Mike Jarman, an old friend of his mother's family from Virginia. Jarman was in the business of drilling oil wells, and was quite the promoter of his line of work. When Tex asked curiously what was involved, Jarman began to describe (with great enthusiasm) the process of locating oil and putting down wells.

Tex found it fascinating. Jarman explained the different ways and formations in which oil could be found in the earth. He talked about rigs and pipes, pressure and barrels, and the excitement of hitting the "gusher." By the time the visit ended, Tex found himself eyeing the oil business with interest. It looked like an exciting occupation; but it wasn't something he could put up the resources for alone.

A day came when he got a call from Wynn Miller, one of his old squadron commanders (and a golf partner) from the 412th Fighter Group in Bakersfield. "Uncle Wynn," as the Hill children came to know him, came out to visit, and Tex told him about his new interest in oil. It wasn't long before Tex had Miller primed to go prospecting for the stuff in the nearest sandy patch. When the two collected a third partner, drilling expert Joey McCartney, they had the team they needed. Meanwhile, Tex had convinced several of his friends from the movie business in California—including John Wayne—to invest some money in the project. The independent oil operation of Wildcats, Inc. was born.

A short time earlier, Mike Jarman had told Tex about a singularly interesting character in the oil business. The man's name was T.J. Drews, and he operated a piece of equipment known as a "doodlebug." The device looked and seemed to function much like an old-fashioned divining rod, a forked instrument that was held out in front of the operator; it "tugged" downward when oil was below. It was difficult indeed to subscribe to such "mumbo-jumbo," but Jarman had related Drews' sure-fire record of success to Tex with conviction. Enlisting the services of T.J. Drews seemed as good a way as any for Wildcats, Inc. to determine a location for their first well.

When they met, Tex saw immediately that Drews was an eccentric fellow. An elderly man with a shock of white hair and drooping moustache, he peered suspiciously at the three partners. He was reluctant to answer any questions about the "doodlebug," clutching it under one arm as if protecting a prize treasure.

"It operates by electronics," he stated tersely, and would add no more.

Shrugging, Tex and the team boarded a truck and prepared to head out into open country. They were near Cedar Creek, Texas, a dusty town situated along a tributary to the lazy Colorado River, some twenty-five miles southeast of Austin. There was no ongoing oil production whatever in that area, so the men were in uncharted waters. Drews had directed Tex to drive around in a large circle, occasionally indicating that he should stop the truck along the route. At the stops, he would get out and listen intently on his headphones, making a mark on a small map and jotting down a bearing next to it. The others were intrigued, but could make nothing of Drews' curious methods. After enough halts and bearing checks, the old-timer was able to triangulate whatever it was he was listening for. He circled a spot on the map in pencil and looked at them.

"That's your best bet," he said. "Try about seventeen hundred feet deep, right there."

The others were amazed—and more than a little skeptical—but Drews seemed confident. After some discussion, they decided to give it a try.

The project got underway in earnest then. They had to purchase oil-drilling machinery and equipment, transporting it out to the remote area. Tex couldn't help wondering if it would all be for naught; but he pitched right in with a will. When the drilling rig was finally in place, the team fired it up and watched; large quantities of earth began to pile up to the side as the drill pushed ever downward. The earth gradually turned to mud.

At last, just as the drill approached the depth described by Drews, small black globs began to appear in the mud. Sure enough, the "Travis Peak" rock formation they had reached, which had never been found to carry oil before, was there saturated with it. Drews had been right on the money.

They "sat back" on the small well for some time, wondering what would develop. In time, they learned that their "strike" would not produce enough oil to be commercially viable; but it did prove to Tex and the others that T.J. Drews was onto something. It was time to move on and look for bigger things.

The next stop for Wildcats, Inc. was Coleman, Texas, a small town south of Abilene. Drews went at it again with the "doodlebug," his arcane procedures indicating oil could be found in a particular spot at a depth of thirty-seven feet. The team sank a well in and watched. As the cuttings came out, Drews checked some of them under an infrared light, which would cause hydrocarbons to fluoresce. The cuttings glowed, so the men knew they were getting close. At just under forty feet, they stopped the drill and conducted a drill stem test, attaching the test tool onto the end of the drill and lowering it down so it could expand. The test was positive. Next they deepened the well, extending it to a level below where they thought the oil might be, running pipe down to that depth. The next step was to "perforate" the well—a delicate operation intended to allow oil to enter the pipe, but not anything unwanted, like water. Success required a good cement job on the pipe.

But the cement job didn't hold. Minutes afterward, the team had the beginnings of a first-class salt water well on their hands. Disappointed, they shut the machinery off, realizing that with the capital they had sunk into the operation, they were nearly broke. Then someone pointed out that their situation might be salvageable. Texas was struggling through a statewide drought that summer, and the town of Coleman was being forced to import water from Brownwood, a small town to the east. The well that Wildcats had put down could be very useful to the residents of Coleman.

Tex approached Sam Gray, a wealthy banker in the area, with a proposal. Recently, in another town further south, oil drillers had found fresh water (and occasionally oil) when they reached a rock formation called a "hickory," which lay beneath the Ellenberger layer. Tex and the others knew that there was also a chance for oil in that kind of formation, though to date, only water had been found in "hickorys" around Coleman.

"If you'll give us five thousand dollars," Tex told Gray, "we'll push the well we've started eight hundred feet deeper, down to the hickory. If there's oil there, it's ours. If it's fresh water, why, it's all yours."

It was a tempting offer in light of the drought, and the banker called a town meeting to discuss the issue with the residents. Eventually, however, he declined.

It wasn't long afterward that Wildcats, Inc. had to fold. They were out of capital. (Strangely, an offer had come in from a Chicago businessman to put up $300,000 behind T.J. Drews; Tex couldn't believe it when the eccentric "doodlebug" operator had declined, exclaiming, "That's peanuts!") But the end of Wildcats was not the end of Tex's interest in the business. By now, he had learned quite a bit about drilling for oil, and he intended to put that knowledge to good use.

In the "boondocks" of Texas, at the intersection of La Salle, McMullen, Webb, and Duval counties, a lone oil well sat in the middle of nowhere. It was in an area called Old Rodriguez Field, and had been created using a standard rotary-drilling technique. The well produced a paltry gallon every day. Tex knew the place, and had a feeling that there was more oil to be had beneath the parched earth. He had learned from other oilmen about a dry percussion drilling technique using an earth socket cable tool; oil operators around Old Rodriguez knew nothing about it. Tex believed that if he could get into the field with an earth socket and go to work, a lot more oil would be forthcoming.

Approaching the lease owner, a man named Rowden, in a café in Hebbronville one day, Tex offered him ten thousand dollars for the well along with the thousand acres of land upon which it sat. Rowden agreed; it didn't look to him like there would be enough oil to make it worth keeping.

Tex got to work, drilling down through the mud with standard equipment until he reached the top of a particular loose sand formation at about four hundred feet. Then he brought in the earth socket, which represented a significant departure from a standard oil drill. Instead of a rotary-type action, the earth socket was a hollow, slotted steel tube that repeatedly slammed downward into the well to cut a cylinder-shaped chunk of earth from the bottom, which was then lifted out. The percussive action compressed the edges of the hole and prevented water from coming in, a persistent problem when performing rotary drilling into loose rock.

Tex's earth socket bit into the sand formation. Four hundred feet below its surface, he hit the jackpot—twenty barrels of oil came welling up in short order. It was the beginning of prosperity for Old Rodriguez Field, where Tex eventually put down thirty-seven wells, starting a miniature "boom" in the area. Each barrel brought a market price of $2.50.

After a few years in the operation, Tex made a mistake. Bob West of ABC Oil Company, an expert in secondary oil recovery, convinced Tex that the end of his primary yield from Old Rodriguez was near. A significant investment, said West, would be necessary to maintain pressure on the wells and transition to secondary recovery. Would Tex be interested in selling it to ABC instead?

Tex wasn't in a financial position to make such an investment in secondary recovery on his own. He resisted West's offer for about a year, but then sold the field to ABC for the seemingly fair price of $100,000. He kept no residual interest in the operation—a big mistake, as he would later learn.

It turned out that Old Rodriguez Field was just warming up. West and his team quickly recouped their investment while the wells continued to yield primary oil; then they sold it to Texaco. The massive corporation implemented a fire-flooding secondary recovery technique, forcing another 1.4 million barrels from the depths over the ensuing decades, while the price rose past $20 per barrel. It was a "gold mine." Some wells on Old Rodriguez would still be producing at the turn of the century. Tex could only shake his head at the turn things had taken, but—who knew?

As time went on, Tex began to find his niche in the business. He was becoming a first-class field operator—someone who could buy up a low-production operation, examine it, and determine what was needed to increase the yield, or where new wells should be put down. When production increased, he would sell the operation at a profit and move on, applying the same process elsewhere. There were many lonely nights spent out in the "boondocks" throughout the state, sitting around a well to monitor its operation and fine-tune any possible improvements. The solitude didn't bother Tex a bit, though; to him, it recalled the nights long ago on camping trips with his father.

While Tex was coaxing oil from the Texas limestone, Mazie turned her energies in another direction. One day she went to visit a former sorority sister from the University of Alabama, whose husband was a former Doolittle Raider, now in the real estate business. His partner was the mayor of Galveston. Knowing Mazie's outgoing personality, her friend suggested that she get into the real estate business herself.

"You already know everyone in San Antonio," she pointed out.

Mazie put the idea to Tex a short time later.

"Tex, what would you think of me getting a real estate license?" she asked.

Tex thought long and hard about it before giving his answer.

"If you'll quit volunteering to run every Boy Scout, Girl Scout, Little League, Junior League, and every other kind of league event," said Tex, with a twinkle in his eye, "and quit working every charity fund drive that comes along in San Antonio, and running in all directions—yeah, I think you could turn that energy into something like real estate."

Mazie studied for and passed her exam, and received her license. She went to work for Agnes Sullivan, a wonderful lady who taught her a great deal about selling houses. The first house Mazie sold was on the corner of Wilshire and Eldon Road, and she never looked back. When Agnes died, one of her partners, Lillian Roberts, started her own firm and invited Mazie to work for her. Lillian retired years later, and offered to sell the company to Mazie. Mazie bought it, seeing for the first time her name on the company sign: "Mazie Sale Hill, Realtor."

Mazie rose to the top of her profession, eventually becoming the first woman to be elected president of the San Antonio Board of Realtors. After many years, she allowed herself to be bought out with a handsome offer from Charlie Kuper, for whom she went to work as a senior member of the Kuper Realty Company. After fifty-five years in the business, she would remain an active, top-notch realtor.

While keeping his hand in the oil industry, Tex occasionally worked in other circles. Once, during the course of his travels, he found himself in Mexico City, and ran into a fellow named Charlie Poulliot. Poulliot was a French Canadian, a veteran of the First World War who had served in the Black Watch, later becoming a first-rate mining engineer.

One evening, as Tex and Poulliot visited in a hotel room in the heart of the sprawling city, there came a knock on the door. A dark-skinned young man stood outside, holding a small cloth bag. He spoke little English; but when he pulled a large chunk of ore from the bag and showed it to Poulliot, the Canadian was immediately interested. After some examination, he explained to Tex that the ore was almost pure galena, and would fetch a handsome market price if it could be obtained in quantity. Turning his attention to the Indian, he got out a map and began to ask him where the ore had come from. The Indian indicated a location in the state of Oaxaca, just north of where the country narrowed into the Isthmus of Tehuantepec.

Tex and Poulliot studied the region. It was extremely mountainous, and would be difficult to reach—impossible, in fact, without a hundred-mile walk from the closest place an airplane could drop them off.

"How on earth would we get the ore out of there, even if we could find it?" Poulliot wondered with a frown.

"I could help you there," said Tex. He explained how gliders could be carried into the valley in pieces, assembled, loaded with ore, and "snatched" out by an aircraft flying overhead using a hook-and-cable system. It was something Tex had seen practiced in China with success. Poulliot was impressed.

"Think you're up for this?" Poulliot asked him with a smile. Tex nodded; it looked like an adventure.

He was not wrong on that score. A short time later, Tex and Poulliot were standing near the mouth of the Rio Verde, where it emptied into the Pacific, watching the aircraft they had just exited disappear into the sky.

"Sure hope they remember to come get us at the other end," said Tex.

They would have to hike inland for a hundred miles to reach the ore site, then continue an equal distance further to rendezvous with another airplane.

It was the beginning of a trek that lasted several weeks, over rugged and beautiful terrain. The paradisiacal country flowered in a perpetual spring reminiscent of Coleridge's *Xanadu*; and Tex had walked off some twenty pounds by the time they arrived in the mysterious valley. He never felt better in his life. Along with the two men went the Indian who had showed them the ore and a group of native helpers called *mosas*, leading several horses loaded with bedding and spartan equipment. The expedition carried only a little food, for they could stop frequently at mountain villages along the way to eat. The natives were curious, and willing to share their simple fare of tortillas, beans, and the occasional egg or chicken.

Tex found the varied ethnic characteristics fascinating. In one village, the natives were so dark-skinned as to resemble Africans, and Tex immediately recognized the "beehive" huts they lived in; he had indeed seen such dwellings on his trip to Africa. He later learned that several Spanish slave ships had run aground in the area three hundred years before, and the survivors had settled on the very spot.

As they neared another village in a region called the "Land of the Pintos," the *mosas* became fearful, insisting that the group give it a wide berth.

"*Muy feo, muy feo,*" they repeated, indicating something extremely ugly.

Tex caught sight of the inhabitants of the village. Their bodies were covered with large orange and blue splotches of pigmentation, giving the "paint people" a fearsome appearance indeed.

In a third village, the natives had eyes as blue as the sky, in sharp contrast to the brown found in most of Mexico's inhabitants. It was a result of their ancestors' association with Spaniards from the region of Andalucía.

Eventually, the expedition reached the ore site, and Charlie Poulliot turned his expert eye upon the rock formation. After a few experimental digs, he groaned in disappointment. The galena had come to the surface in a "float," a section of pure ore that had broken off from a larger piece that lay far deeper. It was maddening; the fact was, there was not enough in the "float" to be of any commercial value. There was nothing for it but to pack up and trek the second hundred miles, where they boarded the plane for Guadalajara and Tex returned to the United States. If he was no richer, at least he had enjoyed the trip immensely.

Tex's second try at mineral mining in Mexico came on a tip from Bill Kane, another mining engineer whom Tex had met through Poulliot. Kane had done extensive mineral surveys in Mexico early in the war for the U.S. government, and knew where most of the viable mines could be found. (Mexico, Tex was learning, was the most mineral-rich country in the Western Hemisphere.) Kane pointed out a location one hundred miles southwest of Guadalajara in the state of Jalisco, near the town of Autlan de Navarro.

"This," said Kane, "is the biggest manganese prospect in this hemisphere."

Manganese was a mineral used in hardening steel, and it was in great demand by U.S. manufacturers.

Tex and drilling tycoon Fred Hamilton set out for the spot, and were amazed at what they found. The manganese was spread throughout a *mantos*, a horizontal blanket-like formation of rock. At three separate locations around a large hill, they found deposits of the ore open to the sky. It was reasonable to assume that the whole hill was full of the stuff—and that meant a lot of profit. Tex then tracked down the land's "owner"—or the closest person he could find—and settled on a deal with him to mine the ore.

When Tex returned to the U.S., he set up a contract with a company in Washington D.C. The U.S. government was stockpiling manganese, and Tex's sample was the finest they had seen. The whole legal process took several months; Tex took pains to make sure he did it correctly.

When he returned to Mexico, Tex was surprised to find the whole area blocked off by men carrying pistols, who wouldn't let him near the place. The "owner" whom Tex had negotiated with was decidedly nervous when he met them, and began to vacillate about selling the property. Tex hinted that they might pay him more money, but the man finally admitted the problem: he had no claim to the deposit whatsoever, which was actually on government land. The shifty character had hoped to buy it from his government and sell it to Tex at a profit, but he had failed. Disgusted, Tex and Kane had to fold up shop.

But it still wasn't his last expedition in Mexico. Bill Kane got him involved in one more operation, this time to acquire zinc for the U.S. government. At that time, American industry had a great demand for the mineral, which was used in all kinds of manufacture. Kane and Tex blocked out a zinc ore deposit in western Mexico, near Hermosillo. The high-grade ore had been removed from the area some time before, but the "tailings" still contained quite a bit of the mineral. As the price climbed with demand, these tailings could be re-processed for a profit; and that was exactly what Tex and Kane had in mind.

Alas, the project was not to be successful. The two partners had no trouble setting up the operation and processing the ore, but just as they began shipment back to the U.S., disaster struck: the British dumped a huge stockpile of zinc onto the world market. America jumped at it; and in the suddenly flooded market, Tex and Kane found their painstakingly orchestrated operation would bring only a tiny fraction of the price they had anticipated. For the third time, Tex saw his "south of the border" plans crumble.

There was a lesson in it all, and Tex learned it well. There was no easy way for a foreign businessman to make a profit in Mexico. Wheels could be greased for a time with *mordillas*, or bribes; but eventually, the government would move in to stop a steady profit from leaving their country. There was nothing entrepreneurs like Tex could do about it. The sole exception was for a man to move into the country and become part of it; then a profit could be realized (and Tex knew several friends who did precisely that). But moving to Mexico was a sacrifice Tex wasn't ready to make. He returned to San Antonio, to pick up the oil business where he had left it.

Near the end of the Korean War, Tex felt the urge to get back into the cockpit and "get some flying in." He was accepted for a commission into the active reserve as a Colonel, and assumed command of the 8707th Flying Training Group, under General Jack Foster's 8707th Wing, at Brooks Air Force Base. The Air Force's primary single-engine jet trainer at the time was the North American T-28 *Trojan*, a stable, acrobatic airplane that Tex enjoyed flying. The mission of the 8707th was to train a sudden influx of pilots in jet combat, should such a surge become necessary. The outfit was top-notch, full of outstanding instructors; Tex could see in short order that they were ready to carry out their program on a moment's notice. Later, the Air Force changed the group's mission, and the 8707th transitioned to the Fairchild C-119 *Flying Boxcar* transport.

Then, in early 1955, Tex transferred to command of the 433rd Troop Carrier Group, which also flew the C-119 (and later the C-5 *Galaxy*). The reserve duty was enjoyable, and Tex liked the feeling of being back in the air behind the controls. In early 1957, he resigned his commission and bid farewell to active military service—though not to the cockpit. He would stay in the ready reserve until 1968.

Tex and Mazie were well on their way to four children. On September 26th, 1949, Ann Shannon arrived, with Lola Sale following some four years later. The family reached its full complement of six, with the result that life in the Hill household was never dull. Mazie had begun her career in real estate, and with her engaging personality and hard work, business was flourishing.

In his own work, Tex spent plenty of time out on the plains with only the oil wells for company; but occasionally, something out of the ordinary occurred. One day, one of his men brought Tex a big sack with something wriggling inside. It was a baby javelina, a wild pig. Tex thought he would bring it home for Shannon—the "Florence Nightingale" of the four children—to see. His daughter was delighted, and promptly took "José the javelina" under her care. The flea-bitten creature (very shortly "de-flead" at Mazie's insistence) would follow Shannon around, fetch the newspaper on command, and even sleep in her bed, becoming as much an obedient pet as a dog or cat. The sight of a "heeling javelina" brought double-takes every time.

Eventually, however, José began to reach his full-grown size, becoming decidedly unfriendly to anyone but Shannon. Eventually, there was nothing for it but to donate him to the zoo in Victoria. That winter was particularly cold; and poor José, possibly the most well brought up wild hog in the world, froze to death.

Shannon maintained a virtual menagerie of creatures, and Tex took delight in adding to it. He might, for instance, bring home a tarantula for the girl's "show and tell" at school. On one occasion, he spotted a tree snake while golfing at the Oak Hills Country Club. Quickly nabbing it, he slipped the reptile inside the zipper pocket on his golf bag for safekeeping. When he got back home and opened the pocket, however, there was no snake. Shrugging, Tex figured the little fellow must have escaped—until one day, he spotted the snake in his rearview mirror while driving, stretched out and sunning itself on the back seat.

"That thing is living somewhere in the car," he told Shannon.

But no amount of his daughter's searching could locate it.

One evening, as Tex and Mazie were late for a fancy dinner at the San Antonio Country Club, a light changed to red ahead of him, causing him to hit the brakes suddenly. Immediately he hollered, scaring Mazie half to death, as his shoes filled with water. Shannon, feeling sorry for the snake, had put a pan of water and some food for it under the driver's seat. That was the end, Tex decided, of helping with "show and tell."

By 1957, oil prices had dropped to such lows that independent operators were being forced out of the market. Huge stockpiles of equipment were being sold for scrap, or left to rust on the vast oil fields of west Texas. Tex found that his particular specialty—improving production—was in far less demand, as drillers and workers folded up shop all over. Although he kept some financial interest in the industry, Tex sold most of his assets too.

He was sorry to see it all go, having drilled over one hundred wells and enjoyed the work immensely. At the time, Tex held the record for more oil and gas discoveries in south Texas than all other oil operators combined. He had conducted joint ventures with Humble Oil (later Exxon), Mobil, Sinclair, and a host of other, independent firms. It was the end of an era in his life; but new doors were about to open—back into the Far East.

* * *

After the withdrawal of American forces from the Republic of Korea in 1949, eight divisions of Communist troops from the northern People's Republic of Korea invaded the country in June of the following year. The scale and efficiency of their opening drive was such that Seoul was overrun in three days, and Russian-built T-34 tanks of the PRK were racing toward Taejon by month's end. U.S. troops of General Welton Walker's 8th Army were hastily airlifted in from Japan; but Communist forces threw them back from Taejon, and they retreated into a small pocket around Pusan.

In mid-July, General Douglas MacArthur led an amphibious landing halfway up the peninsula at Inchon, two hundred miles behind the communist lines. Six battalions of the 1st Marine Division went ashore and secured the port, where the Army's 7th Infantry Division joined them before driving quickly inland to recapture Seoul. It was a complete strategic surprise. When 8th Army forces counterattacked from Pusan, the enemy was quickly shoved back past the original border of the 38th parallel.

MacArthur then kept going, as U.S. leadership now envisioned a Korea united in democracy. The 8th Army took the capital of Pyongyang in late October; advance American forces were already halting at the Yalu River that separated Korea from China. At this point the Chinese, newly under Communism, launched a massive counterattack with three hundred thousand foot soldiers. As 1950 ended, the 8th Army found itself forced back over ground it had just won. Seoul was lost again in January to the hordes of Chinese; but the Communist forces were running out of supplies. General Matthew Ridgway rallied the 8th Army to recapture Seoul yet again, and the front stabilized at the 38th parallel once more. Armistice talks began and dragged on for two years, during which little significant fighting occurred between the deadlocked American and Chinese armies.

On July 7, 1953, the combatants signed a general cease-fire (though not a treaty) that left the ideological stances of North and South Korea much the same as they had been before the war. American and ROK dead numbered just under five hundred thousand; North Korea and China had lost some two million soldiers. The fruit of China's loss to the Communists four years before was bitter indeed; and it was America's young fighting men, not State Department bureaucrats, who had to taste it.

In May of 1952, the first reunion of the Flying Tigers took place in Los Angeles, California. Seven years earlier, just before the end of the war, George "Pappy" Paxton and others had secured incorporation papers for the group. Now Bob Prescott sent aircraft of his Flying Tiger Lines far and wide across the country to collect the Tigers and their families. The Old Man himself flew in, and a grand reunion of old friends ensued, to everyone's great satisfaction.

Casey Vincent congratulates Tex at Kweilin after the raid on Formosa, November, 1943.

Montage of pictures of Tex and Clayton "Casey" Vincent, Kweilin, 1943.

Tex and Doreen Davis, Chennault's Secretary, at Kunming, November 1943.

Chapter 33

LOSING CHINA

The United States has no current relationship in the international arena as painful as that with the People's Republic of China—and no more disappointing legacy than the failed policy that brought us to such a point. Five decades after the nation's fall to Communist forces, China is beginning to awaken economically, industrially, and militarily. She is becoming daily a more powerful player on the world stage. It is all the more tragic, then, that instead of an ally, America is faced with a stirring behemoth of a billion and a half souls who consider the United States mainly an enemy. It is well worth examining the miserable road taken to arrive here, in the hope that such colossal mistakes may never be repeated.

The humble beginnings of the Chinese Communist Party came just four years after the great October 1917 revolution in Russia, which saw the Russian Communists overthrow the rule of the Tsars and establish the United Soviet Socialist Republic. The connection is inescapable, and ties between the two nations' Communist groups have been present from the start. Both Sun Yat-Sen and later Generalissimo Chiang Kai-Shek recognized the Chinese Communists for what they were, and never made a single concession to the group's aspirations of power. Chiang especially prosecuted them, striving to stamp out their threat to China's *Kuomintang* (National People's Party), under which the republic was finally becoming unified. By the late 1920s and on into the 1930s, large numbers of Nationalist Chinese forces were engaged in suppressing the militant Communists and silencing their bankrupt dogma.

A charming and charismatic character named Mao Tse-Tung led the Communists. In 1931, Mao announced the formation of a "Chinese Soviet Republic," making obvious the group's ideological ties with their northern neighbors; and he gathered his forces around him to operate out of Kiangsi Province. The resourceful Mao was able to keep the movement alive—never having enough strength to commit to a decisive action against the Kuomintang forces, always managing to tie them down with elusive guerrilla operations in the mountainous province. When the Japanese invaded Manchuria in that same year, Chiang could not resist them with his full military might; for substantial Chinese forces were engaging the Communists.

Much later, during the Second World War, when Chiang faced a similar dilemma, many westerners somehow saw this "two-front war" in China as evidence of a mere half-hearted commitment on Chiang's part to fight the Japanese. (The propaganda of a few prolific Americans who had attached themselves to the Communists' camp, commanding large audiences in the State Department, the War Department, and the press, essentially created this view.) But Chiang Kai-Shek knew exactly what he was about. The Communists presented a threat that was insidious and powerful, a blight that lurked constantly in the internal organs of China, patiently awaiting its chance to seize national rule if given the slightest opportunity. This was no bogeyman of Chiang's; it was manifestly evident in the stated and written goals of the Communists themselves. A greater danger than even the Japanese invaders, Chiang knew, was the threat to the republic from within. Looking back, it is easy to see that he was correct.

The beginning of World War II was not in 1939, as most written history states, but 1937. After being content for years with holding Manchuria and industrial areas along the East China coast, growing Japanese imperialism prevailed. Japan began a systematic campaign to take China's major cities; and in short order, she captured Shanghai, Canton, and the capital of Nanking.

At no time during Chiang's leadership of China was the country so united as when faced by the suddenly renewed Japanese threat. Even the warlords, who usually acted independently though they were nominally loyal to Chiang, came to Chungking to pledge allegiance to the Generalissimo. Popular support for him was high; the Chinese people believed Chiang was the man to drive out the Japanese aggressors. The Communists bided their time, waiting to see what would happen. They made negligible efforts to take up arms and fight the Japanese, paying lip service to that "common cause"; and their perpetual conflict with the Nationalists was quiet for a time.

By the time of General Stilwell's arrival in China, Mao Tse-Tung and his deputy Chou En-Lai had long since settled upon their party's strategy to discredit Chiang's Nationalist government. All they needed was to enlist a "voice" to proclaim their message. Stilwell came to China knowing nothing of the long and troubled relationship between the Nationalists and the Communists, nor of the latter's ties to the Soviet Union. But before long, he was recommending that American Lend-Lease supplies be issued to Communist troops, which he saw as a viable force to resist the Japanese. Mao and Chou were only too glad to encourage this view, loudly proclaiming that they would surely strive against the invaders with all their powers "if only we were properly equipped."

Chiang himself had studied in Communist institutions in Moscow, and he knew the Communist *modus operandi* inside and out. He saw right through the thin rhetoric, consistently refusing to allow his internal enemies to be armed further. Where Stilwell (and, through press releases from his headquarters, most in the United States) saw only a "domestic squabble" between the Kuomintang and the Communists, Chiang Kai-Shek knew that the ultimate aim of the Communists was to liberate the *entire world* from Capitalism. Helping the Communists, therefore, could only hurt the United States in the long run. They were a threat to the world fully as dangerous as the Empire of Japan.

The U.S. government initially had no intention of helping the Chinese Communists. China was one of the Allies, and the Generalissimo a respected head of state; and though the Pacific Theater took a back seat to Europe in the grand strategy, America directed all of her efforts in China toward support of the Nationalist government. It took the efforts of a small number of individuals, carefully placed, to throw doubt and confusion on the issue, and eventually change U.S. policy toward that great nation.

In the early summer of 1943, several incidents involving the Communists in Sinkiang Province brought the group's political activities to the attention of the U.S. government. Stilwell soon contacted John P. Davies, a former consul who had served in Kunming, and whom the general knew from his previous China tour ten years before. Stilwell instructed Davies to select several men to be Stilwell's "command political advisors," and with this team, to study intelligence reports on the Communists. Davies picked John Stuart Service, John K. Emmerson, and Raymond P. Ludden. Secretary of State Hull agreed to the loan of the four men only on the condition that they remain subordinate to the U.S. ambassadors to China, and that they report their activities to the same. Those conditions were broken almost immediately.

What few outside this team knew was that the men were heavily sympathetic to Communism. They began to foster close relationships with Mao Tse-Tung and Chou En-Lai, making extended visits to Communist headquarters in Yenan, writing skilled and biting reports from Shensi Province, and bending the ear of anyone in a position of power to quietly promote the Communists and slander Chiang. The team's access to Stilwell's command intelligence reports, as well as message traffic between the Generalissimo and Washington, put them in an ideal position to damage the credibility of the Nationalists and sabotage U.S.-China relations using pro-Communist messages of their own. It was a well-organized, very effective campaign.

Davies and Service worked especially tirelessly. Their numerous eloquent reports on the Communists painted a picture of them that was difficult not to like. They were not true Communists, wrote the two men, but "agrarian reformers." All they wanted was a chance to study Western democracies, in the hopes of someday promoting such self-government in their own country. Their group's young men and women represented the best and brightest China had to offer. They had no ambitions to overthrow Chiang Kai-Shek, who had surely misjudged them from the start. They had no ties to Soviet Union. If the U.S. would only give them arms, they would be willing and able to fight the Japanese alongside the Allies.

At the very least, went the "analysis" of Davies and Service, America should regard the Communists with "an attitude of sympathetic support." The Communists, they said, were the heirs apparent to power in China, even if they claimed no such ambitions. The only feasible solution was to promote a coalition government in China, with equal representation from both groups. If the U.S. persisted in aiding only the Nationalists, the Communists might approach the Soviets in desperation for assistance—and what would America do when faced with a Communist China?

In addition to heaping praise upon the Communists for their virtues, Davies and Service slandered Chiang and the Kuomintang at every turn. Chiang's government was full of nepotism and corruption, they wrote, a throwback to the old tyrannical warlord era. The Kuomintang was a dinosaur, a dying regime with no popular support that was soon to be cast off in favor of the "new Democracy." By blockading the positions of Communist forces, Chiang had broken his "promises" to maintain a united front against Japan. He would not fight the Japanese, and was instead preparing for civil war as soon as the Allies achieved victory. He was stealing and hoarding American Lend-Lease supplies, and even selling them to the Japanese, with whom he was in secret contact to form a clandestine peace. The list of wild accusations went on and on.

Mao Tse-Tung and Chou En-Lai had found their "voice," and in their wildest dreams, they could not have imagined how successful it would be. The poignant Davies-Service reports circulated throughout Washington in the State Department, War Department, Treasury Department, Office of War Information, and Office of Strategic Services. Sadly, they found a fertile field, swaying the hearts and minds of a number of men in key positions—especially in the State Department—toward sympathy for the poor "agrarian reformers" oppressed by an "incompetent old tyrant." The seeds sown there on Mao's behalf would not be in vain.

The truth was, of course, far different. Chiang's policies were not universally popular—no leader's would have been, whose country had been locked in a protracted war for seven years. Famine, disease, and armed conflict inevitably created conditions of social and political upheaval within the nation. But on the whole, China resolutely hung together under Chiang. The Communists, on the other hand, were dyed-in-the-wool disciples of the Soviet line, as even a casual glance at Mao Tse-Tung's writings and correspondence would have revealed. Millions of Chinese soldiers' graves, and hundreds of press reports of battles in China, exposed the falsehood of the view that the Generalissimo would not fight the Japanese. (However, there was scant evidence indeed of Communist resistance to the invaders.) The "stolen and hoarded Lend-Lease supplies" about which Davies and Service trumpeted were in fact Chennault's stores of aviation gasoline and equipment at his strategically placed airfields—bought and paid for long before Pearl Harbor. Not a single Lend-Lease rifle or bullet had even been issued to Chinese soldiers within China—other than to the Yunnan Expeditionary Force, which Stilwell needed for his Burma campaign.

Regrettably, Davies and his group led Stilwell himself down the same road to Communist sympathy. Davies and his team were, after all, Stilwell's political advisors; and they were becoming expert at promulgating their own brand of political advice. Stilwell's military disagreements and personal differences with the Generalissimo—he called Chiang "the Peanut"—undoubtedly made it all the easier for the general to be persuaded into sympathy for the Chinese Communists, and hatred for Chiang Kai-Shek.

As time went on, Stilwell began to openly disobey and attempt to coerce Chiang, his own Supreme Commander in the theater. He threatened to withhold from China desperately needed Lend-Lease equipment, unless the Generalissimo agreed (among other things) to arm the Chinese Communists. He repeatedly lobbied the White House, through General George Marshall and the War Department, to take a hard line with the Generalissimo unless his demands were met. Incredibly, he finally even ordered his assistant, General Frank Dorn, to draw up plans for possible assassination of Chiang, supposedly upon directions from President Roosevelt.

Eventually, Chiang had enough. He tolerated years of such behavior from his Chief of Staff for the sake of relations with the United States. But as the military situation in

East China grew desperate in late 1944, and Stilwell continued to ignore it at the expense of his Burma campaign, the Generalissimo knew he must have someone else in position, in whom he could place his confidence. He insisted that Stilwell be recalled from his mission and replaced with another officer. Reluctantly, Washington agreed.

In time, Stilwell became still more openly polarized in his admiration and support for the Communists and disdain for Chiang Kai-Shek and the Nationalists. Upon his death from liver disease in 1946, the Communist *Daily Worker* published a letter from the general that referred to one of the leading Communist leaders: "Isn't Manchuria a spectacle?...It makes me itch to throw down my shovel and get over there and shoulder a rifle with Chu Teh."

Stilwell's attitude toward the Chinese Communists is significant because until the time of his recall, his headquarters was the major source of press releases and message traffic that emerged from the China Theater to make its way back to the United States. Unfortunately, it was common for him and his staff to suppress or edit news that did not paint the picture they thought best, while releasing ample coverage of items that supported their view. When the Communist Party in America pitched in with their own war of words about China, the damage was done: many in the U.S. government, and in the public, assumed that the likes of Davies, Service, and Stilwell must have the "real picture" of things. When Stilwell was recalled, it touched off a storm of anti-China publicity in the press. Fed by Communist propaganda, Americans saw Stilwell as an honest, homespun American soldier, "victimized" by the Oriental conniving of Chiang Kai-Shek and the Kuomintang.

Not surprisingly, then, even before the end of the war, the State Department was already advocating Kuomintang negotiations with the Communists. Vice President Henry Wallace strongly proposed the idea in a visit to Chungking in the summer of 1944, much to the delight of Mao and his followers. Chiang refused, wondering how western leaders could be so shortsighted as not to see the consequences of allowing a Communist foothold in the government of China. But Chiang had not reckoned with the propaganda machine that was in full swing. It was at work in his own country as well, in Communist radio broadcasts and publications; and the war-weary Chinese couldn't help but listen. The Communist promises of a bright future sounded too good to be true, for good reason: they were.

The Communists continued to husband their strength in 1944 and 1945, while the Nationalists spent their efforts and lives in resisting Japan's *Ichi-Go* campaign. The Communists' numerical strength was growing; as Japan's surrender neared, they boasted some one million troops under arms. When the war ended suddenly, with the advent of the atomic bomb, the Communists found themselves in a position of immediate opportunity. Most of Chiang's troops were concentrated in the south and west of China, where they had been battling the Japanese. Communist forces along the Yangtze River realized that they could move into many of the key ports and industrial centers of northern China before Chiang could react.

General Albert C. Wedemeyer, who had replaced Stilwell as commander of the China Theater, recognized the danger and moved to counter it immediately. With a massive airlift operation, he flew whole divisions of Nationalist troops from their fighting positions in remote parts of China to the major cities in the north, right over the heads of the Communist troops. In this way, the Nationalists were able to solidify their control before a sudden initial Communist coup could take place. But Communist sympathizers in the State Department ruthlessly suppressed Wedemeyer's subsequent report, which detailed a blueprint to reorganize the war-torn country with American aid to the Nationalist government. (These same State Department "experts" were busy convincing the White House that placation of and cooperation with the Soviet Union was necessary, a policy whose magnitude of error would only be revealed with the passing of years.)

With each entreaty from Washington for Chiang to embrace the Communists in a bipartisan government, Communist determination to hold out grew stronger, and the Generalissimo's task of dealing with them more difficult. It certainly looked to the Communists like they had the U.S. on their side at heart. Emboldened, they touched off civil war anew in the country mere months after the Japanese surrender. The State Department sent General George Marshall hurrying to Chungking with orders impossible to execute: end the civil war and form a Nationalist-Communist coalition government over the country. Before leaving, Marshall received most of his China indoctrination from Stilwell, which did not help matters.

But the Communists had made a serious mistake in opting for renewed civil war. They faced superior numbers of Nationalist troops, which were equipped with U.S. arms and veterans of fighting the Japanese. Chiang's forces began mopping up the Communists wherever they encountered them; and the war would have come to a speedy conclusion, but for one thing: Marshall and his mission from the State Department. Following his orders, Marshall brought immense pressure to bear upon the Generalissimo to call a cease-fire. Like Stilwell, he threatened to cut off all American supplies, including a proposed $500 million loan and an already-promised air force of eight fighter and bomber groups.

The price was too high for Chiang to defy such coercion, for he well knew the suffering among his people that the United States' aid could alleviate. He reluctantly agreed to the cease-fire. Hundreds of thousands of Communist troops, which had been on the verge of obliteration, were allowed to walk out scot-free from under the noses of their Nationalist enemies. They all headed in the same direction: the vast, northernmost Chinese province of Manchuria.

There, Russian troops that had invaded China in the final days of the war had seized a gold mine: the colossal armament stockpiles of the Japanese Kwantung Army. There were enough guns, mortars, artillery, and even armored vehicles in this bonanza to supply one million troops for some ten years—and the Soviets gave it all to the Communists, upon their arrival in Manchuria. What had been a rag-tag horde of militants on their last legs was suddenly transformed into a fighting force with first-rate equipment. (The Russians later claimed, quite truthfully, that they had not given a single Soviet gun or bullet to the Chinese Communists.)

Nationalist troops, on the other hand, were suffering under a ten-month embargo of American supplies to China, which Marshall had imposed as a measure to exert pressure and force the cease-fire. The general had also made Chiang promise not to use his air force—a hugely potent weapon—against the Communists. Month after month, State Department policy continued to hamstring the Kuomintang and favor the Communists in the struggle. In the summer of 1947, when the two armies clashed for control of

Manchuria, the Nationalists found themselves mowed down by Communist troops wielding and driving brand-new equipment—the same troops they had pushed to the brink of collapse only months before.

For their part, the Nationalist troops had had no replacements for their American armament since 1945, and now they were fatally outmatched. In a series of decisive battles, the core of Chiang's forces was lost in the cold north of China. The Communist armies picked up momentum, and by the following summer they roared southward in an offensive that would eventually end in the capture of Chungking. Marshall's mission returned to the United States when it became apparent that things had backfired beyond his worst nightmares. In late 1949, Chiang's Kuomintang government fled to Formosa, and the Communists assumed complete control of the nation. The State Department "experts" faded quietly back into the woodwork, unwilling to face any consequences for their folly. China was lost.

To his credit, it did not take General Marshall long to understand the true nature of the struggle going on in China. In his subsequent cabinet position as Secretary of State, he sought to reverse the tide of Communist expansion, which by then had become a worldwide menace. The failure of his mission in China had been inevitable, given the impossible orders that—true to his soldierhood—he had sought to carry out to the best of his ability. What Washington continued to view as an "internal Chinese problem" was revealed, once it was too late to stop it, as the fundamental struggle against universal Communist expansion. Seeking a "coalition government" was a standard early Communist political maneuver; when it became apparent they no longer needed such machinations, the Chinese Communists had dropped the charade and taken complete power by force of arms.

The magnitude of the State Department's misjudgment was revealed in the aftermath of the Communist takeover. Mao Tse-Tung promptly began a ruthless extermination of any Chinese who had held a position of significance in the Kuomintang government. Formosa—later renamed Taiwan—was only large enough to hold limited numbers of Chiang's people; millions of Nationalists had no choice but to remain in China and face the consequences of their defeat.

History grimly reports the atrocities of Adolf Hitler and the bloody purges of Joseph Stalin; but they were the work of amateurs in comparison to what followed in the ensuing years of Communist rule. In his effort to consolidate power and impose the "new Democracy" on a shocked Chinese people, Mao slaughtered some *sixty million* Chinese—equivalent to nearly half the population of the United States at the time. The "agrarian reformers," the "best and brightest" that China had to offer, showed their true colors at last—when it was too late to do anything about it.

It is staggering to think that America could have lost, in the space of only four years, a country of China's stature that had been a staunch ally throughout the previous five years of world war. China is the linchpin of the Far East and the Pacific Rim, a nation of supreme strategic importance; and it began the decade of the 1940s in a strong, friendly relationship with America. Through Communist subversion and consistently weak foreign policy in Washington, China ended the same decade under the control of America's enemies—men who embraced ideological doctrine indistinguishable from that of the Soviet Union. There has been no greater disaster in international relations in our nation's history.

If that had been the end of the matter, things would have been grim indeed; but the U.S. could not escape the consequences so lightly. It is because of China's loss to the Communists that every subsequent American political and military failure in the Far East has occurred. Communist North Korea could never have stood upon its own two legs without Red China's backing. The price for that conflict was over fifty-four thousand American soldiers dead, many times that number of Korean and Chinese casualties, and a necessary garrison of U.S. troops on the peninsula that has been under continuous threat of war for over five decades. In Indochina, Viet Minh rebels under Ho Chi Minh and Vo Nguyen Giap would never have obtained massive supplies from Red China. They used those to arm themselves and overthrow the French, setting in motion the chain of events that led to more than a decade of U.S. involvement in the Vietnam War. The price: some fifty-eight thousand Americans dead—and countless Vietnamese. It is impossible to determine the precise effects of a free China upon the years of the Cold War between East and West; but it is easy to know that things would have been far different.

Today, the People's Republic of China continues to dominate the region; periodic military exercises and rhetoric between Beijing and Taipei are all that remain of the old clash between the Nationalists and the Communists. Some among the Mainland Chinese people still remember Chennault and the AVG, and secluded monuments to them remain, scattered throughout the countryside. But the nation is not America's ally, and the gulf that separates their ideology from that of the U.S. is wide indeed. It will not likely be bridged, until the day the curtain is pulled on this world, and the Author comes onto the stage, and all wrongs are made right.

Tex in the cockpit of a T-28 jet trainer, as 8707th Flying Training Wing commander, Brooks AFB, Texas, 1952.

Chapter 34

SUNSET

In 1958, Tex lost the two most important men in his life.

Claire Lee Chennault, newly promoted to Lieutenant General, died on July 27th. He was sixty-eight. At the burial service in Arlington National Cemetery, reading the list of Chennault's honors took some time; five nations and three of the U.S. military's branches of service had decorated him.

As Tex and Ed Rector stood at the graveside, they observed their companions. Part of the Old Man's legacy could be seen in the faces present, looking on in silence: icons of airpower like Albert Wedemeyer, George Kenney, Nathan Twining, Curtis LeMay, Thomas White, Bedell Smith, and Carl Spaatz. They were losing one of their own.

Another part of Chennault's legacy hung invisible in the air. It was the farewell of a grateful Chinese people, for whom Chennault had bought a great measure of the victory over Japan.

Finally, there was the grief of the men who had fought with him, flown for him, and would have followed their flint-eyed leader anywhere. Tex was one of these.

Later in the year, Tex's father, Dr. P.B. Hill, also passed away with his family around him at the Nix Hospital in San Antonio. The venerable chaplain of the Texas Rangers lay in state for several days at First Presbyterian Church, while his comrades gathered from far and wide. The Rangers conducted a twenty-four-hour vigil over Dr. Hill's body; and when the time came to bury him, they would suffer no one else to perform the task. No other person had influenced Tex Hill's life like his father. The loss was a sore one.

Tex was mostly out of the oil business by that time, and had resigned his commission in the active reserves. He remained in a ready reserve status until 1968, occasionally finding time to get back into the cockpit of a fighter jet or two to check out in them. In the course of time, he flew the Cessna T-37 *Tweet* and Northrop T-38 *Talon* trainers, and even the McDonnell-Douglas F-15 *Eagle*, still the USAF's premier air superiority fighter decades later. Tex remained in touch with many of his former friends and associates in the Far East, and soon had occasion to put those relationships to good use.

In the early 1960s, conducting business in Southeast Asia was a difficult prospect for a Western firm. Most organizations within the various nations—including China, Taiwan, South Korea, Thailand, Malaysia, Singapore, and others—were hidebound and hierarchical, from governments to companies. It was characteristic of these that no matter the nation, ethnic Chinese largely held their positions of power and influence. American corporations wanting to build economic inroads to the Far East typically found their representatives dealing with some fourth- or fifth-rate official, who, however polite and ingratiating, had no real decision-making power. The "Yankee" businessmen had great difficulty even getting an audience with the Chinese having authority to really help them. It was simply the way things worked in that part of the world.

As a result, Tex unexpectedly found himself in a particularly advantageous position. Because of his long association with many Chinese officers and statesmen during the war, he had close personal friends scattered throughout Southeast Asia in high places—especially in Taiwan, but even in Communist China. When that word got out, a number of companies began to beat a path to Tex's door to see if he could help them open commercial doors into the Far East.

In this way, Tex discovered that he had something few other non-Chinese did: access to, and the respect of, the region's "power players." At first, he merely made a contact or two on behalf of friends like Flying Tiger Lines founder Bob Prescott, putting them in touch with the right person to help them with a project or deal. For these favors, he neither asked nor received any sort of "finder's fee"; but he soon developed a reputation for being an "inside authority" on Southeast Asia. Before long, larger and larger firms began to contact Tex, seeking to retain him as an expert consultant on their foreign business ventures. Such work eventually became Tex's occupation, and he made dozens of trips to the other side of the world and back throughout the 1960s and 1970s.

One of the earlier requests he received was from Gerhard Neumann, the German whom Tex had helped with immigration into the U.S. Now president of General Electric's Jet Engine Division, Neumann explained that the corporation was in a tight spot in the Far East. They had just lost a lucrative contract in Singapore, and now were in a similar struggle in Thailand. Thai Airways was preparing to purchase a fleet of Boeing 747 aircraft, and both Pratt and Whitney and GE were competing to build the engines for the planes. The man whom GE had sent to represent them in Thailand, explained Neumann, had made a singularly poor showing to date. Would Tex be willing to take over the effort?

Tex agreed, and before long was on a plane to Thailand as GE's "expert consultant." When he took over, the wheels began to turn, as he was quickly able to contact the very man who was to make the contract decision. Tex made such a good impression that the Thai Airways executive invited him to live in his own house for several weeks, where Tex basked in the hospitality and culture of a wonderful people. He enjoyed his stay immensely—and General Electric got its contract. Tex had rescued the firm from nearly being out of business altogether in Southeast Asia.

That success soon led to another position. The president of Thai Airways, Danish-born Niels Lumholdt, hired Tex as his own special assistant. Tex became an ambassador for the airline throughout the region, cementing business agreements and maintaining contacts that fostered great commercial success for Thai Airways. The ride ended when the airline was sold to a group of Texas businessmen.

On another occasion, Northrup Aviation enlisted Tex's services. They were trying to sell fighter aircraft to the South Korean military; but without the proper credentials, the military wasn't listening. When Tex arrived, he was able to get an immediate audience with General Chang Chi-Rang of the South Korean Air Force. Tex explained the proposal, and Chang agreed that the aircraft would meet his nation's needs. The general told several of his officers to expect contact from representatives of Northrup to work out the details; and Tex departed Korea with the skids successfully "greased" once again.

When Northrup later made efforts to market its F-5 *Freedom Fighter* jets to Taiwan, the firm turned to Tex a second time. Arriving in Taipei, Tex found that the numerous Northrup representatives already there took plenty of hot baths and talked to low-ranking officials, but had no conception of how to conduct business in the Orient. Tex's assessment was that the company should approach Chiang Kai-Shek about building a joint aircraft production facility on the island itself, where workers from both nations could manufacture the fighters until the Taiwanese were able to accomplish it on their own. Northrup jumped at the idea, and, with Tex's help, made the arrangements to do exactly that.

There were occasions when, despite Tex's best efforts, things didn't work out. One time he was hired by "E" Systems, a company that specialized in high-tech equipment like that found on Air Force One, the President's plane. "E" Systems already operated an aircraft maintenance facility on Taiwan, but the Taiwanese government wanted to shut it down for a number of reasons. The corporation knew they were finished in the region anyway, but they wanted Tex to try and salvage what he could. After taking stock of the situation, he realized the facility could remain open if certain parties in the U.S. government would step up to the plate and make the legal effort to protect it. However, they did not; "E" Systems lost their facility, and the U.S. lost a potentially valuable strategic base of operations.

At times, Tex engaged in a little business of his own in the region. With the help of Moon Chin, a Chinese associate and beloved friend, Tex bought up ten T-28 *Trojan* trainer aircraft—the same planes he had flown on reserve duty with the 8707th Flying Training Wing at Brooks. These particular T-28s had been sitting in crates in Louisiana, disassembled, for years. They were in restorable condition, and Tex and Moon were able to sell them to the government of Taiwan as training aircraft for their Air Force.

As he ran one "rabbit trail" after another, Tex was careful to make time for the reunions of the AVG. By the end of the 1950s, these were regularly being held every other year at a secluded resort in Ojai Valley, California, and were always well attended. It was at these, years after their exploits in China, that some of the men really got to know each other for the first time. While fighting the Japanese, they had been too busy to lean back and talk about their hopes and dreams. Many of them hardly knew at all the comrades-in-arms who weren't in their own squadron, because they had rarely been located together after training at Toungoo. As they continued to hold reunions in places like New York, Taipei, San Diego, Mallorca, and San Antonio, the AVG men found that the new friendships were just as good as the old. And even among his fellow fighter pilots, Tex seemed to gravitate to positions of leadership. He was elected president of the Flying Tigers Association and the American Fighter Aces, serving honorably in both positions.

* * *

Sixty-three years after sailing to high adventure on the Bloemfontein, Tex Hill has slowed his pace somewhat. For him, there are no more enemy fighters to duel in the sky, no ground targets to strafe, no wars to win. Others will have to see to those things. But his ears can still catch the call to duty, and America has no more loyal son. If he cannot dive out of the sun with a wide-open Allison engine roaring ahead of him, at least he can regale the young pilots of this different era with the tale of what it was like. If he need not lead men to fight beyond their physical limits, at least he can say with conviction why such determination will someday be needed again. If he did not pay for the Allied victory in the Second World War with his life, he can tell the stories of many who did.

Nowadays Tex still shoulders a rifle, heading into the scrub hills and hunting grounds of his beloved south Texas whenever he can. Wild hogs and deer are the usual victims of his still-expert marksman's eye, and the joy of the hunt sings a familiar chorus in his soul. As he strides along beaten tracks and through waist-high prairie grass in search of prey, it is easy to mistake him for his father. The idea, if you told him, would bring his familiar smile.

The list of honors conferred upon David Lee "Tex" Hill, along with certificates presented, speeches sought, articles written, awards given, and endorsements requested, is long and—he would say—"not real important." What is important, Tex will assert, is that men who deserve honor and respect, veterans whom he knows—or knew—are appreciated for their efforts. What's important is that young men and women know their stories, understand their sacrifices, and carry on where they left off. What's important is for the nation to remember and uphold the freedoms such patriots paid so dearly for. Without these men, Tex will point out, we could not hope to live as we do. Their lives, and too often their deaths, mean too much to simply brush aside.

Never forget, whisper the giants of a fast-disappearing generation. *Never forget.*

* * *

On May 11, 1988, a few elderly gentlemen stood with a grinning group of U.S. Army aviators in front of a vicious-looking AH-64A *Apache* attack helicopter for a few pictures following a ceremony. The veterans were Flying Tigers; so were the youngsters. Tex and his comrades had just officially bestowed the name and insignia of the Flying Tigers on the just-activated 4th Aviation Battalion, 229th Attack Helicopter Regiment, at Fort Hood, Texas. To this day, the 229th is still the only U.S. military unit to hold that honor.

The 23rd Fighter Group passed its legacy on as well, to the leering, tank-destroying A-10 *Thunderbolt IIs*—better known as "Hogs"—in the group of the same designation at Pope Air Force Base, North Carolina. That fighter group still contains the 74th and 75th Fighter Squadrons; and to members of his beloved 75th, Tex is still the honored "Shark One." The 76th Space Control Squadron, at Peterson AFB, Colorado, carries the torch passed from Ed Rector in the heat of battle to the limitless horizon of space with pride. Men and women in these outfits have not forgotten their amazing history.

In December of 1996, at the AVG reunion in Dallas, surviving members of the Flying Tigers walked slowly across the stage, one by one, to thunderous applause. They were receiving Distinguished Flying Crosses and Bronze Stars from the Chief of the U.S. Air Force, General Ronald Fogleman. It was the first time the Department of Defense had ever approved individual awards for the Flying Tigers. Before presenting them, the Chief declared what everyone in attendance already knew: "These are long, long overdue."

Tex with members of the 229th Attack Helicopter Regiment. (L to R: SFC Kenney, CPT Deon, CSM Johnson, CW4 McNamara, Tex Hill, CW4 Clemens, CW4 Phelps, SFC Voeltner, CW4 Kristen, SFC Svab. On helicopter: CW4 Flick. Kneeling: CW4 Jack Pike.

Tex in front of an A-10 "Warthog" with pilots of the 23rd Fighter Group. The 23 FG flew two of the "Hogs" to Lexington, KY to honor Tex's induction into the Kentucky Aviation Hall of Fame, November 2003.

*Tex deciding whether to destroy damaged P-40s at Loiwing as Japanese troops advance on it, spring 1942. (*Life *Magazine photo)*

"Pappy"

Late afternoon in May I found him resting out in back,
Reclined in that old hammock, while the sun shone through a crack
Of trees and cloud, now sinking on its steady earthward fall.
I watched the shadows lengthen, casting grey upon the wall.
My gaze came then to rest on my grandfather, lying there
With half-closed eyes, the hammock swaying in the lazy air.
His lean, tall frame was for a while surrendered to the time
When day has spent its heat, and waits for evening's cool sublime.
The ebbing sun touched on his face, revealing lines of care
From days uncounted, years on years, a lifetime written there
In trackless paths on cheek and 'round the eye. It seemed to me
The two had known each other very long, the day and he.

The sky remembered him from afternoons long gone away,
When no line graced his handsome face, and time had yet no sway
On eyes that pierced the heart, and booted feet that strode with pride
Across the earth—and where feet would not go, on wings he'd ride.
His Texan voice was often heard in anger or in jest
To right some wrong, or warmly tell a joke that he loved best.
In those young days, the peace he sought would only come with toil,
A hard and bitter day of war on unforgiving soil.
To aid a friend, to do as Jesus would: these were his ways,
So duty pulled him from his home and comfortable days
To lead his warrior comrades in the trenches of the sky.
Such paths are never easy; not a few fell there to die.

I thought as daylight waned and gave way to a quieter hour
He'd not have chosen war to learn, if peace lay in his power;
But roads he'd walked were often hard from doing what was right.
I knew a time must come at last when days would close in night,
And turn from night to endless day anew in other lands
Where cares will cease, and we await the Father's loving hands.
There he will find undying essence of beloved things
In this old world: the truest friends; the shining silver wings
That never fail; the wedding feast with perfect-seasoned meal;
The solace for his soul that drink could never truly heal;
And answer to the joy of hunt, and salve for earthly ill.
The need was never known that heaven's Master cannot fill.

The sun was going swiftly down when I turned to the door
And entered into laughing faces, thinking of how poor
Our lives must be when measured with the glory that awaits.
For God's true sons, they'll shout a welcome at the deathless gates.

- Reagan Schaupp

Tex in the cockpit of his P-51A, the "Bullfrog." Note the condition of the 23rd's "replacement" aircraft (pilots recognized their tail numbers from training at Barstow, Florida!) This later led to Tex's argument with "Hap" Arnold.

Tex after "checking out" in an F-5 at Randolph AFB, Texas, 1983.

Bob Hoover, Chuck Yeager, and Tex at the Oshkosh Air Show, 1986.

General Henry "Butch" Viccelio awards the Distinguished Service Cross (second only to the Medal of Honor) to Tex in San Antonio, Texas, 2002.

ACKNOWLEDGEMENTS

God, for the words;
Dawn, Jonathan, Charles, and Hannah, for patience;
Pappy and Munna, for the story and legacy;
All veterans, for the sacrifice and example.

The 15,000th and final P-40 to roll off the Curtiss-Wright assembly line in Buffalo, New York. Tex was on hand for the event, December 1944. Photo signed by company founder Burdette Wright: "To Tex Hill, with our appreciation of the fine work you did in China."

Official Roster of the American Volunteer Group "Flying Tigers"

Note: asterisks (*) denote AVG members who did not fulfill their contracts or were not honorably discharged when the Flying Tigers were officially disbanded, July 4, 1942. (Does not include USAAF personnel attached to the AVG before disbandment.)

NAME	Unit	Position
Adair, C.B. "Skip"	HQ	Staff, Ops & Supply
Adkins, Frank W.	3rd	Flight Ldr
Allard, James L.	HQ	Auto Mechanic
Alsop, Joseph W., Jr.	HQ	Staff Historian
Anderson, Frank A.		Crew Chief
Armstrong, John Dean	2nd	Wing Man
Atkinson, Peter W.	1st	Wing Man
*Bacon, Noel R.		Flight Ldr
Bailey, George R.	2nd	Crew Chief
Baisden, Charles N.	3rd	Armorer
*Bartelt, Percy R.		Flight Ldr
Bartling, William E.	1st	Flight Ldr
Baughman, Edmund C.	HQ	Comm.
Beaupre, Leo A.	HQ	Clerk-Transp.
Bell, Donald	HQ	Clerk-Transp.
Bent, Morton "Twisty"	2nd	Clerk-Operations
*Bernsdorf, Donald R.		Wing Man
Bishop, Lewis S.	3rd	Vice Sqdn Ldr
Blackburn, John Ed., III	1st	Wing Man
Blackburn, William J.	1st	Crew Chief
Blackwell, Harold	2nd	Crew Chief
*Blaylock, Glen O.		Crew Chief
*Bohman, Morris P.		Wing Man
Bolster, Harry R.	2nd	Wing Man
Bond, Charles R.	1st	Vice Sqdn Ldr
Bonham, Ernest O.	HQ	Comm.
*Boyington, Greg		Flight Ldr
Brady, James E.	HQ	Clerk-Transp.
Breeden, Kenneth V.	HQ	Clerk-Admin.
Brice, George	2nd	Crew Chief
Bright, John G.	2nd	Flight Ldr
Brouk, Robert R.	3rd	Flight Ldr
Brown, Carl K.	1st	Flight Ldr
Bruce, Everett W.	HQ	Dental Surgeon
*Bryant, Alfred W.		Clerk
Buglar, Carl F.	2nd	Chief-Admin.
Burgard, George T.	1st	Flight Ldr
*Buxton, Richard H.		Clerk-Med. Orderly
Callan, Michael R.	1st	Crew Chief
Carney, Boatner R.	HQ	Staff
Carter, John B.	1st	Line Chief
Cavanah, Herbert R.	3rd	Flight Ldr
Ceder, Melvin E.	HQ	Staff-Police
Chaney, Charles	2nd	Crew Chief
Chennault, Claire L.		Group Commander
Christensen, Keith J.	3rd	Armorer
Christman, Allen Bert	2nd	Flight Ldr
Clouthier, Leo P.	3rd	Clerk-Operations
Cole, Thomas J., Jr.	2nd	Wing Man
Colquette, Leon P.	3rd	Crew Chief
Conant, Edwin S.	1st	Flight Ldr
*Cook, Elmer J.		Wing Man
Cornelius, Jack	1st	Crew Chief
Cribbs, Charles D.	HQ	Clerk-Med. Orderly
*Criz, Albert		Wing Man
Croft, John S.	1st	Flight Ldr
Crookshanks, Jesse R.	3rd	Crew Chief
Cross, Harvey G.	HQ	Comm.
Cross, Jim	1st	Flight Ldr
*Crotty, John D.		Clerk-Operations
Curran, George F.	1st	Crew Chief
Cushing, Albert D.	HQ	Clerk-Operations
Daube, Otto W.	2nd	Crew Chief
Davis, Doreen	HQ	Steno-Typist
Davis, William H. S.	HQ	Asst. Operations
Dean, John J.	1st	Flight Ldr
Dolan, Walter J.	1st	Crew Chief
Donovan, John Tyler	3rd	Wing Man
Doran, Francis R.	HQ	Clerk-Admin.
Dorris, Carl E.	1st	Clerk-Admin.
*Dudzik, Francis P.		Clerk-Admin.
DuPouy, Parker S.	3rd	Vice Sqdn Ldr
*Durbin, Estill E.		
Durrall, Eugene C., Jr.	HQ	Clerk-Intelligence
*Dyson, James P.		
Engle, Charles	3rd	Crew Chief
Engler, John R.	HQ	Comm.
Ernst, Richard J.	HQ	Comm.
Farrell, John W.	1st	Flight Ldr
Fauth, John Edward	3rd	Crew Chief
Fish, William H., Jr.	2nd	Wing Man
Fobes, Edwin L.	HQ	Clerk-Admin.
Foshee, Ben Crum	3rd	Wing Man
Foster, Emma Jane	HQ	Nurse
Fox, Harry E.	2nd	Line Chief
Francisco, Charles H.	3rd	Comm.
Frillmann, Paul W.	HQ	Chaplin
Fritzke, Henry W.	2nd	Armorer
*Fuller, Henry W.		Instructor
Gallagher, Edward F.	3rd	Crew Chief
Gasdick, Joseph	HQ	Chf Sheet Metal Wrkr
Gee, Chun Yuen	HQ	Engineering Helper
Gentry, Thomas C., M.D.	HQ	Chief Surgeon
Geselbracht, Henry M.	2nd	Flight Ldr
Gilbert, Henry G.	3rd	Wing Man
Gorham, Lloyd L.	2nd	Crew Chief
Gove, Irving P.	1st	Crew Chief
Goyette, Edger T.	HQ	Det. Cmdr Point A
*Graham, Richard E.		Crew Chief
Greene, Paul J.	3rd	Flight Ldr
Greenlaw, Harvey K.	HQ	Staff-Operations
Greenlaw, Olga S.	HQ	Clerk-Admin.
Groh, Clifford G.	3rd	Flight Ldr

Name	Sqdn	Role	Name	Sqdn	Role
*Gunvordahl, Ralph N.		Wing Man	Linton, Jack R.	1st	Armorer
Hall, Lester J.	2nd	Wing Man	Little, Robert L.	1st	Flight Ldr
Hammer, Maax C.	2nd	Wing Man	Loane, Ernest W.	1st	Wing Man
Hanley, Lee D. (Leo)		Armorer	Locke, Robert P.	HQ	Propeller Specialist
*Hardesty, Martin L.		Crew Chief	Loomis, Elton V.	3rd	Comm.
*Harpold, Clayton M.		Mess	Losonsky, Frank S.	3rd	Crew Chief
Harrington, Jasper J.	1st	Line Chief	Lum, George L.	HQ	Engineering Helper
Harris, David H.	HQ	Staff	Lussier, Joseph E.	1st	Comm.
Harris, Edward J.		Chief-Admin.	Martin, Neil	3rd	Flight Leader
*Hastey, Raymond L.		Wing Man	McAllister, Gale E.	3rd	Crew Chief
*Hauser, John B.		Crew Chief	McClure, Edgar B.	1st	Crew Chief
Haywood, Thomas C., Jr.	3rd	Flight Ldr	*McDowell, Mark H.		Crew Chief
Hedman, Robert P.	3rd	Flight Ldr	McGarry, William D.	1st	Wing Man
Heller, John E.		Clerk-Transp.	*McGuire, Maurice G.		Wing Man
*Henderson, George G.		Clerk	McHenry, Sharon L.	HQ	Clerk-Engineering
Hennessy, John J.	1st	Flight Ldr	McKinney, Eugene R.	1st	Armorer
Henson, Thomas M.	HQ	Clerk-Med. Orderly	McMillan, George B.	3rd	Flight Ldr
Hill, David Lee	2nd	Sqdn Ldr	Mangleburg, Lacy F.	3rd	Wing Man
Hodges, Fred S.	3rd	Flight Ldr	Martin, Neil G.		Flight Ldr
Hoffman, Louis	1st	Flight Ldr	Merritt, Kenneth T.	2nd	Wing Man
Hoffman, Roy G.	HQ	Armorer	*Metasavage, Frank G.		Crew Chief
Hooker, Burton L.	HQ	Parachute Rigger	Mickelson, Einar I.	1st	Wing Man
*Houle, Leo J.		Wing Man	Milhalko, Alex	2nd	Comm.
Howard, James H.	2nd	Vice Sqdn Ldr	Miller, Arvold A.	HQ	Comm.
Hoyle, Daniel J.	3rd	Clerk-Admin.	Misenheimer, Charles V.	1st	Crew Chief
Hubler, Martin R.	HQ	Clerk-Operations	*Moore, Lawrence C.		Clerk
Hurst, Lynn A.	2nd	Wing Man	Moss, Kenneth R.	HQ	Clerk-Meterology
Jacobson, Frank	1st	Crew Chief	Moss, Robert C.	2nd	Flight Ldr
*Jaeger, George B.		Auto Mechanic	Mott, Charles D.	2nd	Flight Ldr
Janski, Edwin A.		Propeller Mechanic	*Mundelein, Charles D.		Crew Chief
Jernstedt, Kenneth O.	3rd	Flight Ldr	Musgrove, Willard L.	1st	Crew Chief
*Johnston, Leon H.		Clerk Operations	Musick, James H.	2nd	Armorer
*Jones, Jack D.		Armorer	Neal, Robert J.	1st	Armorer
Jones, Thomas A.	2nd	Vice Sqdn Ldr	Neale, Robert H.	1st	Sqdn Ldr
Jordan, Joe T.	HQ	Clerk-Finance	*Newell, Ferris D.		Clerk-Admin.
Jourdan, Walter C.	HQ	Clerk-Meterology	Newkirk, John V. K.	2nd	Sqdn Ldr
Kaelin, Albert V.	1st	Clerk-Admin.	Neumann, Gerhard	HQ	Propeller Specialist
Keeton, Robert B.	2nd	Flight Ldr	Older, Charles H.	3rd	Flight Ldr
*Kelleher, John P.		Wing Man	Olson, Arvid E., Jr.	3rd	Sqdn Ldr
Keller, Daniel W.	3rd	Crew Chief	Olson, Henry L.	3rd	Crew Chief
Kelly, Thomas D.	HQ	Telephone Lineman	Osborne, Harold L.	3rd	Crew Chief
Kemph, Merlin D.	1st	Crew Chief	Overend, Edmund F.	3rd	Flight Ldr
Kenner, Charles D.	1st	Crew Chief	Overley, John L.	2nd	Crew Chief
Kepka, George B.	3rd	Crew Chief	Paull, Preston B.	2nd	Crew Chief
Kiner, Melvin W.	HQ	Telephone Lineman	Paxton, George L.	2nd	Flight Ldr
King, Robert J.	HQ	Comm.	Peeden, Joseph N.	1st	Crew Chief
*Knapp, Donald R.		Wing Man	Peret, Richard C.	HQ	Group Engr. Officer
Kustay, Stephen	1st	Armorer	Perry, Paul J.	3rd	Armorer
Kuykendall, Mathew W.	1st	Flight Ldr	Petach, John E., Jr.	2nd	Flight Ldr
Kwong, Lawrence C.		Staff	Pietsker, Joseph H.	HQ	Photographer
*Lancaster, George R.		Clerk	Pistole, Herbert	2nd	Armorer
Laughlin, C.H., Jr.	3rd	Flight Ldr	Pon, Kee Jeung	HQ	Engineering Helper
Lawlor, Frank L.	2nd	Flight Ldr	Poshefko, Joseph A.	3rd	Armorer
Layher, Robert F.	2nd	Flight Ldr	*Power, John D.		Crew Chief
Leaghty, Charles C.	HQ	Parachute Rigger	*Power, Robert H.		Wing Man
Lee, Joseph S., M.D.	HQ	Flight Surgeon	Prescott, Robert W.	1st	Flight Ldr
Lee, Pak On	HQ	Engineering Helper	Prevo, Samuel B., M.D.	HQ	Flight Surgeon
Liebolt, Edward J.	1st	Flight Ldr	Probst, Albert E.	1st	Flight Ldr
Lindstedt, Robert K.	HQ	Comm.	Quick, Carl	2nd	Crew Chief

Name	Sqdn	Role
Raine, Robert J.	3rd	Flight Ldr
*Rasbury, James D.		Mess
Rasmussen, Robert P.	1st	Crew Chief
Rector, Edward F.	2nd	Vice Sqdn Ldr
Reed, William N.	3rd	Flight Ldr
Regis, James E.	HQ	Photographer
Regis, Stanley J.		Crew Chief
*Reynolds, George B.		Crew Chief
Richards, Lewis J., M.D.	HQ	Flight Surgeon
*Richardson, Charles A.		Crew Chief
*Richardson, Randall S.		Clerk
Richardson, Rolland L.	HQ	Comm.
Ricketts, Freeman I.	2nd	Flight Ldr
Ricks, Wayne W.	HQ	Propeller Specialist
Riffer, Clarence W.	3rd	Armorer
*Ringey, Joseph E.		Auto Mechanic
Roberts, Carson M.	2nd	Comm.
Rodewald, Donald L.	1st	Armorer
Rogers, Robert W.	HQ	Crew Chief
Rosbert, Camile J.	1st	Flight Ldr
Rossi, John R.	1st	Flight Ldr
Rumen, John N.	2nd	Armorer
*Rushton, Edwin H.		Wing Man
Sandell, Robert J.	1st	Sqdn Ldr
*Sanger, Kenneth C.		Comm.
Sasser, Ralph W.	HQ	Comm.
Sawyer, Charles	1st	Flight Ldr
Schaper, Wilfred E.	1st	Crew Chief
Schiel, Frank, Jr.	1st	Vice Sqdn Ldr
Schiller, Ralph F.		Armorer
Schramm, Leo J.	3rd	Crew Chief
*Schur, Carl E.		Crew Chief
Seamster, Loy F.	HQ	Comm.
Seavey, Edward H.	HQ	Comm.
Seiple, Wilfred R.	3rd	Crew Chief
Shamblin, Arnold W.	2nd	Wing Man
Shapard, Van, Jr.	2nd	Wing Man
*Shapiro, William D.		Clerk
Shaw, John E.	HQ	Clerk-Med. Orderly
Shee, George Leo Wing	HQ	Engineering Helper
Shields, Milan R.	HQ	Propeller Specialist
Schiller, Ralph	2nd	Armorer
Shilling, Eriksen E.	3rd	Flight Ldr
Shreffler, Roger	HQ	Comm.
*Smith, Corbett J.		Mess
Smith, Curtis E.	HQ	Group Adjutant
*Smith, George		Admin.
Smith, Robert A.	3rd	Crew Chief
Smith, Robert H.	1st	Flight Ldr
Smith, Robert M.	HQ	Comm.
Smith, Robert T.	3rd	Flight Ldr
*Sommers, John T.		Clerk-Operations
Stewart, Jo B. (Miss)	HQ	Nurse
Stiles, Edward L.	3rd	Crew Chief
Stolet, Irving J.	3rd	Crew Chief
*Stubbs, Gail L.		Instructor
Sutherland, William L.	HQ	Auto Mechanic
Swartz, Frank W.	2nd	Wing Man
Sweeney, Joseph H.	3rd	Comm.
*Swindle, Estes T., Jr.		Wing Man
Sykes, William A.	HQ	Comm.
Terry, Julian E.	3rd	Line Chief
Towery, William H.	HQ	Mess Supervisor
Trumble, Thomas C.	HQ	Secrtry to Grp Cmdr.
Tuley, Chester A.	2nd	Crew Chief
Tyrell, George	2nd	Crew Chief
Uebele, John J.	1st	Crew Chief
*Unger, William H.		Armorer
Van Timmeran, Frank E.	3rd	Line Chief
Vaux, Morgan H.	HQ	Comm.
Viverette, Hugh J.	HQ	Clerk-Med. Orderly
Wagner, Earl F.	2nd	Armorer
Wakefield, Manning, Jr.	HQ	Crew Chief
*Walker, Harold H.		Crew Chief
*Wallace, Stanley H.		Wing Man
*Walroth, Robert H.		Wing Man
*Walsh, Andrew A.		Clerk
Walters, George F.	HQ	Clerk-Admin.
*Watson, Eugene A.		Wing Man
Whelpley, Donald A.	HQ	Clerk-Meterology
*White, John E.		Crew Chief
*Whitehead, R.G.		Asst. Gp. Ops Officer
Whitwer, Eloise (Miss)	HQ	Steno-Typist
*Wiggin, Edwin D.		Chief-Admin.
Williams, John M.	HQ	Comm. Officer
Wilson, Clifford H.	HQ	Auto Mechanic
Wirta, Harvey C.	HQ	Armorer
Wolf, Fritz E.	1st	Flight Ldr
Woodward, Melvin C.	HQ	Crew Chief
Wright, Allen M.	1st	Wing Man
Wright, Peter	2nd	Flight Ldr
Wu, Lem Fong	HQ	Engineering Helper
Wyatt, Louis G.	1st	Comm.
*Wyke, William R.		Asst. Group Adjutant
Wylie, Harold G.	HQ	Clerk-Finance
*Yarbery, Glen L.		Crew Chief
Yee, Francis T.F.	HQ	Engineering Helper
Young, John P.	HQ	Clerk-Engineering

BIBLIOGRAPHY

1. Archibald, Joe, <u>Commander of the Flying Tigers: Claire Chennault</u>. Julian Messner, New York, 1966.
2. Bledsoe, Larry W., <u>The "Flying Tigers: Facts and Stats About the AVG</u>. Bledsoe's Aviation Art, Upland, CA, 1996.
3. Bond, Charles R., <u>A Flying Tiger's Diary</u>. Texas A&M University Press, College Station, 1984.
4. Caidin, Martin, <u>The Ragged, Rugged Warriors</u>. E.P. Dutton & Co., New York, 1966.
5. Chennault, Claire L., <u>Way of a Fighter</u>. James Thorvardson & Sons, Tucson, Arizona, 1949.
6. Cornelius, Wanda and Short, <u>Thayne, Ding Hao: America's Air War in China 1937-1945</u>. Pelican Publishing Company, Gretna, 1980.
7. "Fei Hu — The Story of the Flying Tigers" video script.
8. Frillmann, Paul and Peck, Graham, <u>China — The Remembered Life</u>. Houghton Mifflin, Boston, 1968.
9. Green, Peyton, <u>For God and Texas</u>. Whittlesley House, New York, 1947.
10. Kissick, Luther C., Jr., <u>Guerrilla One</u>. Sunflower University Press, Manhattan, Kansas, 1983.
11. Lopez, Donald S., <u>Into the Teeth of the Tiger</u>. Smithsonian Institution Press, Washington, 1997.
12. McClure, Glenn E., <u>Fire and Fall Back</u>. Barnes Press, San Antonio, 1975.
13. Molesworth, Carl, <u>Sharks Over China</u>. Brassey's, Washington, DC, 1994.
14. Molesworth, Carl, <u>Wing to Wing: Air Combat in China, 1943-45</u>. Orion Books, New York, 1990.
15. Rosbert, C. Joseph, <u>Flying Tiger Joe's Adventure Story Cookbook</u>. Giant Poplar Press, Franklin, NC, 1985.
16. Schultz, Duane., <u>The Maverick War: Chennault and the Flying Tigers</u>. St. Martin's Press, New York, 1987.
17. Samson, Jack. <u>Chennault</u>. Doubleday, Garden City, New York, 1987.
18. Scott, Robert L., Jr., <u>God is My Co-Pilot</u>. Buckeye Aviation Book Company, Reynoldsburg, Ohio, 1989.
19. Smith, Robert M., <u>With Chennault in China — A Flying Tiger's Diary</u>. TAB Books Inc., Blue Ridge Summit, Pennsylvania, 1984.
20. Smith, Robert T., <u>Tale of a Tiger. Tiger Originals</u>, Van Nuys, CA, 1986.
21. Time-Life Books. <u>World War II: China-Burma-India</u>. Alexandria, Virginia: Time-Life Books, 1978.
22. Whelan, Russell, <u>The Flying Tigers: The Story of the American Volunteer Group</u>. The Viking Press, New York, 1942.

SCRAPBOOK

Tex and Mazie greet Chennault and his wife Anna at an AVG reunion, mid-1950s.

At an AVG reunion, late 1950s. (L to R: Tex, Don "Rode" Rodewald, Charlie Sawyer, Ed Rector.) Rodewald, a one-time USAAF test pilot, become the only paraplegic to fly solo around the world, in a Piper Comanche in the 1980s.

Chief of the Army Air Forces, Henry "Hap" Arnold, and British Field Marshal Sir John Dill are presented with a 23rd Fighter Group insignia during a visit to Kweilin, 1944.

Tex after "checking out" in the F-15B, Hollomon AFB, New Mexico, 1982.

Tex and Mazie at Christmastime, San Antonio, 1980s.

Dancing by the bonfire at Carl Newton III's Texas ranch, 1995.

Mazie Sale Hill, 1943

Mazie Sale Hill, 1980

Tex and Ollie Crawford next to next to a replica of Tex's P-40 number 108. Crawford is the only WWII P-40 pilot still actively flying the aircraft.

Tex and Ollie Crawford, co-chairman of the American Combat Airmen Hall of Fame. Tex was the Hall of Fame's first inductee.

Painting of Tex and 23rd Fighter Group personnel next to the "Bullfrog."

Tex with Jerry Yegan next to a replica of P-40 number 108, which Tex flew to lead the Salween Gorge mission in May 1942. Yegan restored the P-40.

Don Gentile, Tex, and Dick Bong at 412th Fighter Group headquarters, Bakersfield, CA, 1945. Tex checked Gentile and Bong out in the prototype YP-59 jet aircraft.

Merian Cooper (Chennault's Chief of Staff), Chennault, and Tex, 1957.

The 229th Attack Helicopter Regiment

When the 4th Battalion, 229th Attack Helicopter Regiment was ready for re-activation in 1988, its commander, Lieutenant Colonel Gerald D. Saltness, wanted something to set it apart from other outfits. As an inspiration to his unit and a tribute to the American Volunteer Group, Jerry wanted to call his group the Flying Tigers.

LTC Saltness had his A Company commander, First Lieutenant Steve Van Allen, contact the Flying Tigers Association and ask permission to use the AVG nickname and insignia. (This was a definite departure from all others who have decided to call themselves "Flying Tigers.") The AVG considered this an honorable way to do business and an honest tribute, and agreed to the arrangement.

The activation ceremony took place on June 15, 1988 at Fort Hood, Texas, with AVG members in attendance. With their training completed, the 4th Battalion held its graduation ceremony at Fort Hood on October 5, 1988, once again with quite a few of the original Tigers on hand. Afterward, the 4th was deployed to Illesheim, Germany.

At their first dining out on October 14, 1989, in Illesheim, members of the 4th laid on a full week's entertainment and sightseeing for a large contingent of AVG members and their families.

In 1990, the 229th AHR was expanded to include a new battalion, the 2nd. In the meantime, the regiment received official permission from the Department of the Army to adopt the name and logo of the Flying Tigers.

Later that year, events in Kuwait and Iraq interrupted the activation schedule, and the 229th was deployed to Saudi Arabia during Operation DESERT SHIELD. (The 2nd Battalion would have to wait until June 1991 to hold its dining out at Fort Rucker, Alabama, and meet their AVG namesakes!)

The 229th AHR compiled a brilliant record in Operation DESERT STORM, executing its mission of deep attack and earning the Valorous Unit Award as its aviators wreaked havoc upon enemy armored columns and revetted combat vehicles. It consistently served with distinction for the next 13 years in Bosnia, Kosovo, Afghanistan, and most recently in Operation IRAQI FREEDOM. Without doubt, the 229th has significantly contributed to the U.S. government's official recognition of the vital role the original AVG played in the military effort of World War II.

The 23rd Fighter Group

On July 4, 1942, the 23rd Fighter Group was activated in Kunming, China—successor to the famous AVG "Flying Tigers" and original component of Brig Gen Claire l. Chennault's new China Air Task Force. The organization included the 74th, 75th, and 76h Fighter Squadrons, with the 16th Fighter Squadron attached. Never before had a fighter group been activated in a theater of war under combat conditions.

From July 1942 through May 1945, the 23rd Fighter Group's pilots flew 5,232 missions and 23,351 sorties—a total of 52,338 combat hours. Such figures speak for themselves in establishing the 23rd Fighter Group as a vital force in the campaigns in China during those three years.

After 12 years of inactivity, the 23rd Tactical Fighter Wing was re-activated at McConnell Air Force Base, Kansas on February 8, 1964. The 23rd inherited four operational fighter squadrons along with their F-105 D and F model aircraft. Tasked to maintain combat readiness in the event of any contingency, the 23rd distinguished itself in the Vietnam War, seeing continuous combat action in the skies over Southeast Asia and delivering outstanding performance.

The 23rd TFW continued to build upon its distinguished tradition of service and readiness in 1990-91, as it deployed to Saudi Arabia and compiled a brilliant combat record during Operation DESERT STORM flying the tank-killing A-10 "Warthog." During operation IRAQI FREEDOM, 23rd Fighter Group warfighters performed superbly in close-up, extremely dangerous combat as they supported the coalition forces; offensive through Iraq and into Baghdad.

History has clearly not heard the last of the 23rd Fighter Group, as they carry on the proud heritage of the original 23rd from wartime China to the defense of freedom anytime, anyplace.

INDEX

118th Fighter Squadron, 248
118th Tactical Reconnaissance Squadron, 245
11th Bombardment Squadron, 169, 175, 177, 179, 183
16th Fighter Squadron, 164, 174, 177, 184, 189, 192-193, 199
17th Indian Division, 135
1st Air Commando Group, 237, 253
1st Marine Division, 280
20th Pursuit Group, 48
229th Attack Helicopter Regiment, 294
23rd Fighter Group, 6, 64, 143, 164, 172, 177, 179, 181, 183-184, 189, 191-192, 194, 196-197, 199, 205, 224-225, 233, 237, 241, 243, 245, 249-250, 252-253, 256, 294, 299
308th Bombardment Group, 196, 213, 225, 242
412th Fighter Group, 10, 252, 255, 260, 273
433rd Troop Carrier Group, 279
445th Fighter Squadron, 253
4th Aviation Battalion, 294
4th of July, 1942, 177
51st Fighter Group, 174, 181, 224
5th Indian Division, 240
68th Composite Wing, 231, 245, 248, 258
68th Composite Wing Headquarters, 258
6th Fighter Command, 196
74th Fighter Squadron, 177, 196, 205, 243, 246, 248, 255
76th Fighter Squadron, 233, 237
76th Space Operations Squadron, 294
8707th Flying Training Group, 279
8th Army, 280-281
94th "Hat-in-the-Ring" Pursuit Squadron, 33

~A~

A-20 *Havok*, 204, 216
Ace of Spades, 67
Adair, C.B. "Skip", 32, 82, 85-86
Adam and Eves, 96, 105, 110-111, 122, 130, 132-134, 139, 147, 156, 169-170, 177, 204, 303
Adams, Ted, 243-244
Admiral Halsey, 250
AH-64A *Apache*, 294
Air Corps Tactical School, 33, 47, 142
Air Force Tactical Center, 202, 204
Alison, John, v, 174, 184, 186-192, 196, 198-200, 205
Allen, E.S., 24
Alsop, Joseph W., iii, 68
American Fighter Aces, 4, 293
American Lend-Lease, 121, 284, 286
American Volunteer Group, xvii, 59, 69-70, 72, 176, 250, 301
Armstrong, John, 72, 83, 86, 95
Armstrong, Raymond, 34, 82
Army Air Corps, 32, 47, 53, 62, 68-69, 89, 95, 114, 126, 133, 142-143, 145, 168, 173, 177, 183, 198, 202, 204, 253, 255
Arnold, Henry "Hap", 68, 142, 192, 202, 239, 251-253, 257, 296, 304
Assam-Bengal Railroad, 240,
Atlantic Fleet, 65-66, 73
Austin College, 25, 43, 45, 47, 50
AVG, iii, xvii-xviii, 70-83, 85-91, 95-99, 102-106, 109-115, 118-119, 121-123, 125-128, 130-132, 134-135, 137, 140-143, 145-152, 155, 157-158, 160, 164, 166-171, 174-178, 182-184, 190, 193, 200-201, 203-204, 217, 219, 224-225, 250, 252, 255-256, 264, 290, 293-294, 301

~B~

B-17 *Flying Fortress*, 204, 216
B-24 *Liberator*, 204, 213, 216, 218, 221, 224-225, 227, 236-237, 239, 242, 247
B-25 *Mitchell*, xiii, 152-153, 169, 175, 177-179, 182-183, 193, 197-199, 204-205, 216, 221, 224-225, 227-230, 235-239, 247-248, 265

B-26 *Marauder*, 204, 216
B-29 *Superfortress*, 192, 231, 239-240, 250
Bacon, Noel, 72, 86
Baisden, Chuck, 133
Bangkok, 104, 141
Barber, Rex, 220, 253
Barber, Rex T., 4
Barnum, Burrall, 196, 213
Bartelt, Percy, 60, 86, 114, 120
Bartling, Bill, 124-125
Batavia, 79-80
Baumler, Albert, 177
Beechcraft C-45 *Expeditor*, 264
Beeville, Texas, 43
Belgian Congo, 268
Bell, Paul, 224, 229
Bell P-59A *Airacomets*, 253-254
Bissell, Clayton, 142, 168
Bloemfontein, 76-80, 83, 94, 294
Boeing F4B-4, 53
Bombing Squadron Four (VB-4), 48, 64-65
Bond, Charlie, 96, 156, 170, 180, 204, 222, 264
Boushey, Homer, 253
Bradley, Jack, 256
Branch, Irving "Twig", 228
Brereton, Lewis H., 166
Bright, Gil, 53, 72, 83, 86, 96, 100, 119-120, 174, 189-190
Brisbane, 78
British Colony of Bermuda, 66
British *Spitfire*, 216
Brooks Air Force Base, 279
Bullfrog, 6, 226, 233, 239, 241, 243, 266, 296
Burma, 0, 55, 70-71, 75-76, 82-83, 88, 90, 93, 99, 101, 104, 106, 115, 118-119, 121, 126-137, 140-142, 145-155, 157, 160-161, 164, 166-169, 171, 175, 181-182, 196, 203, 205, 220, 222, 224, 237-238, 240, 250, 257, 269, 286-287
Burma Oil Company, 118-119

Burma Road, 55, 70, 106, 136, 141, 150, 152, 155, 157, 161, 167-168, 181, 196
Bush, Jr., George W., iii
Bush, Sr., George H., iii
Butsch, Leonard, 174, 180

~C~

C-119 *Flying Boxcar*, 279
C-47, 200-201, 224, 266
C-5 *Galaxy*, 279
Calcutta, 131, 166, 172
Calvary Troop A
Caniff, Milton, 64
Canton, 48, 175-176, 178-179, 193, 195, 199, 221, 233-234, 236, 247-248, 266, 284
Carey, Jack, 226, 239, 242
Carter, Dean, 174
Carter, John, 98
Central Aircraft Manufacturing Company (CAMCO), 71-73, 83, 113, 115, 141, 152
Cessna T-37 *Tweet*, 291
Chang Chi-Rang, 293
Chang Fei-Kwei, 248
Changsha, 126, 175-176, 221, 240, 243-245, 247
Charleston, South Carolina, 143
Chengtu, 192-194, 200, 220, 225-226, 239-240, 250
Chennault, Claire, xvi, xviii, xix, 25, 33, 41, 47, 67, 69, 73, 82, 205, 265, 301
Chiang Kai-Shek, 33, 41, 47-48, 54, 61, 89, 103, 114, 126, 135, 137, 142-147, 158, 161, 168, 172, 202, 265, 283-287, 293, 300
Chiengmai, 139-141, 145-146
China Air Transport, 266
China National Aviation Corporation, 109
Chindits, 205, 237
Chinese Air Force, 0, 41, 47-48, 67, 112, 126, 266
Chinese Communist Party, 283
Chinese Soviet Republic, 41, 283
Chinese-American, 228, 246

Chou En-Lai, 47, 284-286
Chow Chi-Rao, 266
Christensen, Keith, 133
Christman, Allen "Bert", xvii, 53, 64-65, 67, 69-72, 75, 78-79, 88, 90, 95-96, 104, 108, 119, 125, 125-127, 130-131, 188, 195
Chungking, 54-55, 61, 73, 115, 126, 135, 143, 155, 158, 161, 169, 176-177, 192, 196-197, 213, 220, 225, 257, 284, 287-289
Churchill, Winston, 133, 135
Class 121-C, 52, 54, 304
Coach Baker, 30, 304
Colbert, Bob, 233
Cole, Tommy, 53
Coleman, Texas, 274, 304
Collins, Callista, 261
Collins, Carr P., 259
Collins, Willie, 261
Commander Irvine, 69-72
Conant, Edwin, 97
Cook, Arthur H., 73
Cooper, Merian C., 196
Coral Sea, 77-78, 161, 171, 304
Corcoran, Tommy "The Cork", 68, 256, 266
Corps of Cadets, 44-45
Corpus Christi, 209
Corregidor, 78, 161
Cowboy Camp Meeting, 51
Croft, John, 148
Cross, Jim, 98
Culver PQ-8 *Cadet*, 218
Currie, Lauchlin, 68
Curtiss P-40 *Tomahawk*, xvii-xviii, 73, 90-91, 94, 98

~D~

Davies, John P., 285
Davis, Doreen, 303
De Bellevue, Chuck, iv
Delhi, 165-167, 171, 201, 206, 227
Department of Defense, 294
Devulakous, Joe, 269

Ding Hao, 106, 301, 304
Distinguished Flying Cross, 184, 193, 196, 201, 231, 304
Distinguished Service Cross, 231, 298
Dixon, Sam, 107
Don Maung Airdrome, 104
Doolittle, Jimmy, 153
Doolittle Raid, 142, 169
Dorn, Frank, 286
Douglas TBD-1, 57-58, 62
Douala, 268-270
Drews, T.J., 273-275
Duckworth, Dennis, 31
Durbin, Estill, 79
Dyson, James, 79

~E~

Edgerton, James, 218
Edney, Jack, 226
Eglin Field, 204, 215-216
Elias, Henry, 184, 194-195
Ellington Field, 33, 263, 267
Emmerson, John K., 285
Engle, Joe, xiv
Escadrille, Lafayette, 221

~F~

F-15 *Eagle*, 291
F-5 *Freedom Fighter*, 293
Fauth, John, 138
Fifth Air Force, 267
Fisher, Bill, 32, 223-226, 235
Fleet Problem XXI, 61
Fly, William, 209
Flying Tiger Lines, 264, 281, 292
Flying Tigers Association, 293
Flynn, John P. "Jack", 4, 256
Fogleman, Ronald, 294
Fong Hsieng-Chien, 247, 305
Ford, John, 267, 300
Formosa, 40, 201, 223, 227-232, 250, 256, 281, 289
Fort Hood, Texas, 294
Fort Sam Houston, 264
Foshee, Ben, 156

Foss, Joe, 147
Foster, Jack, 279
Fourteenth Air Force, 3, 205, 213,
 219-221, 223, 225, 227, 230, 233,
 236-238, 240, 247, 249, 251-252, 257
Fox, Harry, 98, 162
Frasier, Donald, 52
Frederick, Gertrude, 210
Frederick, Richard, 210
Frillman, Paul, 130, 135
Frost, Jr., Joseph, 30
Frye, Jack, 255

~G~

Gardner, Grandison, 204, 264
Gault, Manny, 38
General Anderson, 270
General Electric, 254, 256, 292
General Lim, 193-194
General Stratemeyer, 257
General Takahashi, 257
Gentry, Tom, 103, 200
Gia Lam Airfield, 197
Glenn, Edgar "Buzz", 238
Goddard, Robert, 256
Gorillas, 267-268, 270
Goss, Ed, 225, 282
Governor Stevenson, 259, 263
Greene, Paul J., 76
Greenlaw, Harvey, 166
Greenlaw, Olga, 166
Griffin, Joe, 220
Guadalcanal, 200
Gulf of Martaban, 81, 113, 127, 176

~H~

Haiphong, 193, 199, 221
Hair, Dick, 32, 34
Halifax, Lord, 222
Hall, Ed. Y., iv
Hamilton, Fred, 278
Hammer, Maax, 94-95, 99
Hampshire, John, 196-197, 220, 272
Hankow, 54, 175-176, 179, 182-183,
 185, 187, 199, 221, 226, 233, 236,
 238-240, 247, 257

Harrington, J.J., 98
Harris, Bill, 65, 72
Harrison, Dan, 259
Hawaii, 33, 60-61, 77-78, 305
Haynes, Caleb, xiii, 161, 175, 178, 197
Haywood, Tom, 158
Hedman, Robert "Duke", 76
Hell's Angels, 96, 104, 106, 112-115,
 118, 122, 137-138, 141, 156, 175
Hengyang, 54, 162, 168-169, 171-172,
 174-179, 182, 184-185, 187, 189-191,
 193-196, 213, 224, 226, 233, 235-236,
 238, 240, 244-245, 247-248, 251
Hennessey, John, 53
Herbst, John C. "Pappy", 217
Hermosillo, Mexico, 278
Hill, Ann Shannon, xi, 279-280
Hill, Ella, 21, 24, 28, 42
Hill, John, 21, 28, 30
Hill, Jr., David Lee, 271
Hill, Lola Sale, xi, 279
Hill, Martha, 21, 30, 32, 42, 47, 82
Hill, Mazie Lee, 260-262
Hill, Pierre Bernard, 21-22
Hill, Sam, 43, 208
Himalayas, 70, 126, 167
Hirohito, 92, 150
Hiroshima, 257
Hitler, Adolf, 66, 289
HMS *Prince of Wales*, 104
HMS *Repulse*, 104
Ho Chi Minh, 290
Hodges, Fred, 87, 123, 166-167
Hodges, Helen, 166
Hoffman, Louis "Cokey", 130
Hogue, 36-38
Holloway, Bruce, 196, 200, 205, 223,
 256, 260, 299
Hollywood, 253, 264, 267-268, 270
Hong Kong, 0, 102, 115, 176, 197-199,
 233, 235-236, 239
Honolulu, Hawaii, 77
Hoover, Robert "Bob", iv, 298
Hopkins, "Pinky", 65
Hostel Number One, 105, 132, 139, 147

Howard, Jim, xvii-xx, 86, 110, 119-120, 122, 124-125, 140
Hsueh Yueh, 226, 240, 243, 247
Hughes, John, 38
Hulbert, Arkansas, 37
Humble Oil, 280
Hump, 126, 166-167, 169, 174, 181, 194, 201-202, 213, 220, 225, 231, 237-238, 240-241, 257
Hung, Nim, 29
Hunt, Texas, 31, 34, 210, 260
Hurst, Lynn, 60

~I~

I-97, xviii, xix, 92, 112-113, 123, 130-131, 170, 178, 184, 189, 193-194
Ichi-Go, 0, 233-241, 246, 257, 287
Inchon, 280
Indochina, 70, 77, 99, 133, 139, 142, 193, 199, 221, 225-226, 238, 257, 290
Irwin "Red", 177, 188
Iwo Jima, 257

~J~

Jaegersfontein, 75
Japanese Kwantung Army, 288
Japanese Type 96 "Nell", 54
Jarman, Mike, 273
Jernstedt, Ken, 137, 143, 264
Jim Kana Club, 164-165
Johnson, Robert S., iv
Jones, Tom", 98, 108, 133, 158, 171
Jose The Javelina, 279

~K~

Kai Tak Airfield, xiii
Kan Kiang River, 195
Kane, Bill, 278
Karachi, 163-164, 166, 168, 171, 174, 201, 223
Kaveny, Ted, 183
Keeton, Robert "Buster", 53, 104, 132
Kelly Field, 25, 32
Kenney, George, 238, 267, 291

Kerrwood, Chuck, 221
Ki-21, 110, 112, 128-129
Ki-43 *Habayusa*, 112, 189, 235
Ki-44 *Shoki*, 213, 233
Ki-45 *Toryu*, 170, 197
Ki-46, 196
Ki-48, 235
King Neptune, 77
King Vidor, 253
Kipling, Rudyard, 72
Knickerbocker, General, 263
Kohima, 240, 250
Korean War, 279
Kott, Alfred, 203
Kowloon, 221, 236
Kung, H.H., 176
Kunming, 54-55, 64, 70, 88, 100-101, 103, 105-106, 108-114, 122, 126, 132, 137-138, 140-144, 152, 155-159, 161, 166-167, 169-170, 174-175, 177-178, 193-196, 200-201, 213, 217, 220-221, 224-225, 234, 237, 247, 252, 257, 266, 285
Kuomintang, 33, 283-285, 287-289
Kuper, Charlie, 276
Kuykendall, Matt, 76, 112
Kwangju, 21-22
Kweilin, 54, 162, 168-169, 175, 177, 185, 194-195, 197-199, 213, 224-227, 230, 234-238, 246-249, 251, 258, 266, 281-282
Kyedaw Airfield, 86-87, 99

~L~

LaGuardia, Fiorello, 266
Lake Buena Vista, 253
Lake Tien Chih, 105
Lampang, 140
Lampung, 139
Land of the Pintos, 278
Lashio, 55, 98, 105-106, 113, 132, 141, 148, 150-153, 169, 176, 196
Lawlor, Frank, 53, 86, 122-124, 133, 158
Layher, Bob, 86, 264
Ledo Road, 240, 257
Leibolt, Ed, 134

LeMay, Curtis, 239, 291
Liles, Bob, 225
Lin Sen, 176
Lindbergh, Charles, 217
Lingling, 54, 168-169, 174, 177, 184-185, 189-190, 192, 195, 213, 220, 235-236, 238, 245, 247-248
Loiwing, 113, 115, 138, 141-142, 145-152, 154-156, 176
Lombard, John, 195, 225
Loofbourrow, Phil, 225, 249, 271, 282, 299
Lopez, Don, 235
Lopez, Donald, iii
Los Angeles, 141, 281
Louisville, Kentucky, 23, 231
Ludden, Raymond P., 285
Lung Yun, 142

~M~

MacArthur, Douglas, 116, 161, 250, 280
Madame Chiang Kai-Shek, 48, 114, 144, 300
Magwe, 70, 134-135, 137-138, 140-141, 153
Mahony, Grant, 225
Malaria, 88, 192, 194, 198, 200, 207
Mandalay Express, 85
Mangleburg, Ken, 113
Manila, 60, 77-79, 116
Manila Bay, 78
Mao Tse-Tung, 41, 283-286, 289
March Field, 255
Marco Polo Bridge, 48
Marshall, George, 286, 288
Martin, D.K., 259
Martindale, Bruce, 35
Matthew Ridgway, 281
Maxwell Field, 33, 264
Mayor Quinn, 43
Mazie Sale Hill, Realtor, 276
McCallie School, 35
McCartney, Joey, 273
McCullough, John, 28
McDonald, Billy, 41
McGarry, William "Black Mac", 141

McMillan, George, 138
Merrill, Frank, 240
Merrill's Marauders, 241
Merritt, Ken, 113, 119
Miami, 41, 201, 221, 223
Midway, 63, 161, 171, 200
Mihalko, Alex "Mickey", 76
Miller, Quentin, 46
Mingaladon, 83, 100, 112-113, 117-119, 121-125, 127-132, 134, 138, 154
Mingaladon Airfield, xix, 100, 112-113, 117, 127,
Minor, Lee, 174, 192
Minos, 118,
Mitchell, "Mack", 143, 191
Mitsubishi A6M *Zero*, 55, 197
Mobil, 280
Mongshih, 150-151, 157, 160
Moody, Dan, 38
Morgenthau, Henry, 73
Morse, Winslow "Winnie", 218
Mosley, C.C. "Mose", 253
Moss, Robert "Moose", 96-97, 120, 122
Mott, Charlie, 60, 86, 120-121, 264
Moulmein, 126, 131, 135, 138, 143
Mount Tchsan, 235
Mountain Home, Texas, 203, 214, 260
Mow, P.T., 152
Mow Pang-Tsu, 41, 47, 62
Mrs. Berry, 30
Mrs. Gardner, 215-216
Muroc Army Air Field, 254
Muti Hotel, 212
Myitkyina, 70, 240, 247, 250

~N~

Nahmpakka, 152
Naiden, Earl, 166
Nanchang, 48, 183-184, 194-195, 221
Nanning, 237-238, 257
Nationalist Government, 284-285, 288
Naval Flight Training, 52, 204
Navy, xiii, 40-41, 43, 47, 51-52, 54-55, 57-61, 63-66, 68-73, 75-81, 93-95, 102, 104, 121, 133, 179, 197, 215-217, 227-228, 243, 250

Navy Flight Elimination Training, 47
Neale, Bob, 60, 86, 122, 127, 129-130, 132, 134, 139, 147, 155, 177-178, 180
Nellie, 214
Neumann, Gerhard, 255-256, 292
Newkirk, J.V. "Jack", xvii-xx, 95-96, 100, 108, 110, 119-120, 122-123, 125, 139-141, 145
Niels Lumholdt, 292
Nix Hospital, 39, 260, 291
Nixon, P.I., 31
Normandy, 241, 250
North Island, 57, 59-60, 62
Northrop T-38 *Talon*, 291
Northrup Aviation, 293
NSN *Canary* Trainer, 52

~O~

O'Hara, 269
O3U *Corsair*, 53
Oderkirk, Glen, 255
Ojai Valley, California, 293
Old Rodriguez Field, 275-276
Older, Chuck, 141, 264
Olds, Robin, 255
Olson, Arvid, 116, 141, 146-147, 150, 158, 160
Opalocka, Florida, 47, 55
Operation Matterhorn, 239
Orlando, Florida, 202
Oshkosh Air Show, 298
Overley, John, 60, 98

~P~

P-38 *Lightning*, 201, 216, 220-221, 225-230, 239, 252
P-39 *Airacobra*, 216
P-40B, 73, 90-91, 133
P-40E, 156-157, 179, 185, 189
P-43 *Lancer*, 164
P-47 *Thunderbolt*, 164, 204, 216
P-51 *Mustang*, 216-217, 224, 226-230, 233-234, 237-240, 244-246, 296
P-59A, 253-254, 303
P-80 *Shooting Star*, 254
Palmer, Sam, 228-229

Panda Bears, 95, 100, 105, 108-111, 115, 117-120, 122, 126, 130-132, 137-143, 155-157, 159, 169, 171, 175, 189
Paoshan, 152, 155-158, 176
Pappy, 54, 86, 97, 114, 119, 127, 146-147, 217, 246, 248, 255, 281, 295, 299
Parker, James, 253
Paull, Preston "G.I.", 177
Pawley, William, 73, 82
Paxton, George "Pappy", 54, 119, 281
PBY *Catalina*, 53-54
Pearl Harbor, xx, 101-103, 105-107, 145, 220, 286
Peiping, 33, 238
Penang Trader, 80-81, 83
Pensacola, Florida, 52
Pentagon, 202, 206, 213, 221, 249, 252, 256, 264
People's Republic of China, 283, 290
Peregrine Falcons, 189
Petach, Emma Jane "Red", 171
Petach, John, 72, 86, 96, 170, 178, 180, 188
Peterson AFB, 294
Pettit, Bob, 253
Pollywogs, 78
Poulliot, Charlie, 277-278
Pratt and Whitney, 292
Prescott, Bob, 201, 264, 281, 292
President Roosevelt, 68-69, 102, 202, 257, 286
Professor Culver, 30
Proving Ground Group, 204-205, 215, 217-218, 221
Pusan, 280

~Q~

Quick, Carl, 98, 131, 154
Quigley, Don, 225

~R~

Rabaul, 231
Rabbit Trail, 293
RAF *Hurricanes*, 122-123, 125, 138, 141
Raffles Hotel, 80, 108

Raine, R.J. "Catfish", 146
Randolph Field, 47
Rangoon, 55, 70, 75, 79-83, 85, 90, 94-95, 99-100, 103-104, 106-107, 112-115, 117-122, 126-127, 131-135, 137-138, 145, 150, 176, 185, 195, 250, 257
Rangoon, Burma, xvii, 90
Rape of Nanking, 48
Reagan, Ronald, 253
Real, Elmer, 203
Rector, Ed, 54, 64-65, 69-72, 82, 85, 89, 95-96, 103, 105, 108, 110-111, 118-119, 125, 130-132, 140-142, 146, 158-159, 171, 174, 177-178, 184, 193, 196, 200-201, 219, 221-222, 249, 291, 294, 299-300, 302
Red Dog, 96, 103, 175, 196
Red Dragons, 155-156, 160-161
Reed, Bill, 137, 143
Richards, Doc, 156
Richardson, Rolland, 224
Richardson Elmer "Rich", 217
Rickenbacker, Eddie, 202
Ricketts, Freeman, 100, 182, 264
Robbins, Jay, 256
Roberts, Lillian, 276
Rodewald, Don "Rode", 133, 217, 264, 302
Rogers, John, 38
Rommel, Erwin, 200
Rosbert, Joe, 54, 86
Rose Bowl, 251
Rossi, Dick, 264

~S~

Sale, Mazie, 107, 200, 205, 207-208, 276
Sale, Walter, 207
Salween Gorge Attack, 161
Salween River, 136, 152, 155, 157-158, 171, 241
Salween River Gorge, 136, 155, 241
Sama Bay, 237
San Antonio, Texas, 4, 24, 34
San Antonio Academy, 26, 30, 35

San Francisco, 72, 74-77, 81, 173, 253
Sandell, Sandy, 110, 122, 130-132
Sanders, Homer, 181
Saville, Gordon, 204
Schiel, Frank, 95, 146, 174, 177, 184, 193, 195-196, 200-201, 205
Scott, Robert L., iii-iv, xiii, 126, 161, 181-182, 194-195, 197, 200, 205, 253, 299, 301
Secretary of State Hull, 285
Segura, Wiltz "Flash", iv
Seoul, 280-281
Shamblin, Arnold "Red", 180
Shanghai, 40, 48, 176, 266, 284
Shark's Teeth, 98, 116, 226
Schaupp, Dawn, ix
Schaupp, Don, ix
Schaupp, Reagan, viii, ix
Shaw, John, viii
Shear, Morton, 197
Shik Shinny, 121, 308
Shilling, Erik, 95, 104, 113, 158
Shinchiku Airdrome, 227, 229
Shoemaker, Haskell, 31
Shoemaker, Pete, 31
Shoemaker, Sr., John, 39
Shojiro Iida, 126
Siang River, 175, 185, 187, 220-221, 225, 244, 247
Silver Slipper, 248
Singapore, 80-81, 83, 102, 106, 108, 133, 292
Sinjen Airfield, 192-193
Sinkiang Province, 285
Sir Archibald Wavell, 115
Skip Bombing, 236
Slocumb, Clyde, 282
Sluder, Chester, 26, 32
Smith, Bedell, 291
Smith, Robert H. "Snuffy", 134
Smith, Robert T., 76, 301
Smith, Thomas, 196
South Korea, 281, 292
Spaatz, Carl, 291
Spritzler, Ray, 220
Stallings, Lawrence, 253

Stamm, Dick, 303
Stanwyck, Barbara, 253
Stearman NS-1, 52-53
Sterling, Bill, 38
Stevenson, D.F., 141
Stilwell, Joseph W., 135
Strand Hotel, 82
Stubblefield, 182
Suichwan, 221, 224, 227-228, 230, 248
Sullivan, Agnes, 276
Sun Yat-Sen, 25, 33, 283
Swartz, Frank, 96, 138
Swede Vejtesa, 53, 68
Sykes, William, 217

~T~

T.V. Soong, 67, 99
T-28 *Trojan*, 279, 293
Taj Mahal, 165
Tarawa, 231
Taxi Accident, 199
Taylor, Robert, 253
Tennessee Middleweight Championship, 40
Tenth Air Force, 166, 174, 181, 190, 202, 205, 257
Tex Hill, iii-iv, xiii, xvii, 22-26, 28-34, 36-42, 44-48, 50-56, 58-62, 64-84, 86-90, 92-100, 102-108, 110-116, 118-126, 128-136, 138-144, 146-154, 156-162, 164-172, 174-180, 182-190, 192-200, 202-206, 208-222, 224-232, 234-242, 244-250, 252-258, 260-266, 268-272, 274-282, 284-297, 304
Texas A & M, 43, 45, 249, 301
Texas Air National Guard, 7, 263-264, 271
Texas Rangers, 38, 44, 291
Texas State Highway Department, 39
Thai Airways, 292-293
Thraves, John, 23, 42
Thraves, Patty, 39, 42
Three Men on a Flying Trapeze, 41, 47, 89
Tokyo, 75, 113, 142, 152-153

Torpedo Squadron Three, 58
Toungoo, 70, 83, 86, 94, 96-99, 101-104, 107, 113, 116, 118, 121, 132, 135, 138, 148-149, 153-154, 293
TravelAir E-4000, 32
Travis Elementary School, 30
Trinity University, 45
Tungting Lake, 175-176, 185, 199, 220-221, 224, 226, 235, 239-240, 243-244
Twentieth Air Force, 192, 239
Twining, Nathan, 291

~U~

U.S. Army, 23, 25, 97, 142, 152, 161, 265, 294
U.S. Marines, 200, 231, 257
U.S. Navy, 57, 60-61, 63, 66, 79, 94, 102, 228
USS *Brazil*, 143, 164-165
USS *Hornet*, 152
USS *Houston*, 70
USS *Lexington*, 59, 161
USS *Northampton*, 77
USS *President Pierce*, 75, 83
USS *Ranger*, 48, 63-67, 71-73, 83, 86, 130, 164, 171
USS *Salt Lake City*, 77
USS *Saratoga*, 54, 57, 59-61, 63, 65, 74, 86
USS *Yorktown*, 71-72, 161, 171

~V~

Viccelio, Henry "Butch", 298
Victoria, Texas, 200, 202, 205, 271
Viet Minh, 290
Vietnam War, iv, 290
Vincent, Casey, iii, 200, 205, 220, 226-227, 230-231, 235-236, 243, 245, 248, 264, 281-282
Vo Nguyen Giap, 290
Vought SB2U *Vindicator*, 57
Vought SBU, 53

~W~

Wagner, Earl "Hook", 79
Walker, Fred, 263
Walker, Johnny, 119
Washington, D.C., 62, 72, 200, 202, 212, 218-220, 222, 227, 250, 252, 264, 278, 298
Wayne, John, 219, 267, 273, 300
Wedemeyer, Albert C., 257, 287
Wells, "Preacher", 228
West, Bob, 276
West Point, 213
Westminster Encampment, 27
White, Teddy, 228
White, Theodore H., iii
White Cloud Airdrome, 199
Wildcats, Inc., 271, 273-275
Willauer, Whiting, 266
Williams, John "Willie", 224
Williamson, Luke, 41
Wilson, R.M., 22
Winburn Field, 32, 34
Wingate, Orde C., 205
WOAI, 29
Wright, Pete, 66, 72, 86, 96, 100, 119-120, 147-148
Wyman, Jane, 253

~Y~

Yalu River, 281
Yamamoto, Isoroku, iv, 61, 220, 253
Yeager, Charles "Chuck", iv, 298
Yellow River, 239, 242
Yochow, 187, 199, 239-240
Yunnan Province, 55, 105, 142